The Civil Rights of Students

The Civil Rights of Students

David Schimmel, J.D.
Louis Fischer, LL.B., Ph.D.
University of Massachusetts, Amherst

Harper & Row, Publishers
New York, Evanston, San Francisco, London

Sponsoring Editor: Michael E. Brown
Project Editor: William B. Monroe
Designer: June Negrycz
Production Supervisor: Will C. Jomarrón

The Civil Rights
of Students
Copyright © 1975 by **David Schimmel
and Louis Fischer**

**Library of Congress
Cataloging in Publication Data**

Schimmel, David.
    The civil rights of students.

    (Critical issues in education)
    Bibliography: p.
    College students—Legal status,
    laws, etc.—United States. I. Fischer,
    Louis, 1924-   joint author.
    II. Title
KF4243.Z9S3   344'.73'0793   74-15668
ISBN 0-06-045776-7

For Our Parents
Blanche and Bill Schimmel
and
Suzan Fischer

Contents

Editor's introduction

In a diverse, pluralistic culture the institutions, policies, and practices of education will be influenced by the major disagreements of the times. Education in America, a diverse nation searching to define its brand of pluralism, most certainly reflects the major conflicts of the culture.

The dominant tradition of our past attempted to keep the public schools above or away from the controversies of the times and attempted to transmit a common core of learnings. Those tranquil days are gone, perhaps forever. Today, consistent with John Gardner's phrase that "education is the servant of all our purposes," various interest groups attempt to influence and even control public education. Such groups represent political and economic diversities; racial, ethnic, and religious preferences; business interests, conservationists, internationalists, isolationists; proponents of women's liberation, sex education, and sensitivity training, to name but the best-known voices. In addition to these influences from the culture at large, developments more indigenous to schooling must also be considered. Among these are the various forces urging innovation, accountability, professionalism for teachers, and community control. They are also concerned with combating institutional racism and sexism, violence in the schools, and the civil rights of teachers and students.

Teachers must become informed about these issues and conflicts if they are to function as professionals. Toward this end, a beginning must be made in teacher education programs and continued into a teacher's maturing years. The titles in this series were conceived with such a goal in mind. Each volume can stand on its own, yet the several volumes are easily relatable. This arrangement maximizes flexibility for professors who may select one or more volumes, while the student's budget is also respected.

The authors were selected on the basis of their competence as well as their ability to write for an audience of nonspecialists, be they teachers, prospective teachers, or others interested in the dominant issues in our culture that influence the schools.

Louis Fischer
Amherst, Massachusetts

Biographical Note

David Schimmel (J.D., Yale University) and **Louis Fischer** (Ph.D. and L.L.B., Stanford University) are both lawyers and Professors of Education at the University of Massachusetts, Amherst. They are coauthors of *The Civil Rights of Teachers* (Harper & Row, 1973) and have published numerous articles in the areas of law and education.

Preface

A few years after I had started teaching, the principal assigned me to head the Service Squad, a group of 600 boys organized to regulate the flow of traffic and to maintain an atmosphere of civility in the high school of 6000 boys. Nothing in my teacher education courses had prepared me for this job which involved hearing and deciding each semester several hundred disciplinary cases ranging from horseplay to mayhem. What saved me from professional disaster and sustained me through many years of administrative decision making was a sense of due process derived from my study of law.

When administrators and teachers are ignorant of the dimensions of the Bill of Rights and are insensitive to the requirements of due process, the sparks generated by value confrontations fan the flames of educational disputes into judicial controversies. The same holds true when students mistake a constitutional liberty for personal license. Too many school issues are reaching the courts because too many administrators, teachers, and students know too little about the nature of civil liberties and civil rights.

Professors Schimmel and Fischer have done us all a service by writing this sober, clear, and thoughtful analysis of the rights and responsibilities of students. Educators and students who read this intriguing collection of cases should profit from the lessons of the past. With expanded legal literacy, more and more of the persistent and perplexing confrontations will be resolved within the confines of the school and within the context of due process of law.

This book should find its way into teacher education programs as well as into the hands of practicing teachers and administrators. And in the law studies movement, which is rapidly gaining recognition as a significant curricular innovation in the social studies, there is an important place for the exploration and examination of issues raised in this volume. Fortunately, we have here a textbook in the best sense of the word, one that can profitably be used by educators and students in the never-ending quest to clarify human rights within the school setting.

Isidore Starr
Professor of Education
Queens College
City University of New York

Acknowledgments

We wish to acknowledge and thank those who helped us in this effort: Penina and Mickey Glazer, Kathy Patterson, David Matz, Myra and David Sadker, Gail Sorensen, and Isidore Starr for their helpful criticism; John Adams and Eric Mondschein who reviewed the manuscript and page proofs; Allan Levine for his challenging critique and for bringing important cases to our attention; Nancy Burnette, Judy Johnson, and Nancy Rudnicki for their expert typing; and our wives, Barbara Barlin Schimmel and Barbara Bree Fischer, who supported us in this effort.

David Schimmel
Louis Fischer

Students in schools as well as out of school . . . are possessed of fundamental rights which the State must respect, just as they themselves must respect their obligations to the State.

—The U.S. Supreme Court
in *Tinker* v. *Des Moines*

Because school boards are educating the young for citizenship is reason for scrupulous protection of constitutional freedoms of the individual, if we are not to strangle the free mind at its source and teach youth to discount important principles of our government as mere platitudes.

—The U.S. Supreme Court
in *West Virginia* v. *Barnette*

The Civil Rights
of Students

Introduction

Every school system in the United States is expected to teach students to respect the Constitution and the Bill of Rights. But, many teach students to be cynical about both. This, of course, is not their intention. However, institutions, like parents, teach more by what they do than by what they say. Thus when teachers and administrators preach obedience to school rules or respect for authority while simultaneously violating the civil rights of students, they teach a powerful lesson in legal hypocrisy. There is ample evidence—from scholarly studies to the revelations of Watergate—that graduates from our public schools have learned this lesson rather well; they know many facts about our Constitution but are quite willing to curtail the rights of those with whom they disagree.[1]

An increasing number of educators and lawyers are becoming disturbed about the implications of this situation. Even before Watergate, a federal judge wrote: "One of the great concerns of our time is that our young people, disillusioned by our political process, are disengaging from political participation. It is most important that our young people become convinced that our Constitution is a living reality, not parchment preserved under glass!"[2] Because of this concern there has been a renewed effort to teach the Constitution and the Bill of Rights. New materials are being prepared, curricula are being revised, lawyers are being brought into the classroom, and trips are being taken to the local courthouse.[3] Many parents, teachers, and administrators are trying to do everything they can—everything that is except apply the Bill of Rights to students in our public schools.

There are many reasons for this. One reason is that a majority of parents, teachers, and administrators honestly do not think the Bill of Rights applies to most school situations. This is because these rights did not apply to them when they were students and because they learned almost nothing functional about this subject during their education. Even in those courses that taught about the history and principles of the Constitution, there were few texts or instructional materials that applied those principles to classroom conflicts. Today most materials continue to deal with great historical cases or other issues that seem remote from the personal experience of the average contemporary student. Thus for several related reasons, teachers, administrators, and parents are poorly prepared to apply the Bill of Rights to the public schools. They have had little education and almost no personal experience in the application of these rights to school controversies, and there is a lack of relevant educational material to assist them in the effort.* This book is intended to help meet these needs.[4]

Specifically the book is designed to help readers become more aware of student rights and how these rights can be legally asserted and protected. It should also help them become sensitive to the concerns and arguments on both sides of current civil rights controversies.[5] (Although we have chosen cases primarily concerning public schools, the constitutional principles considered here are also relevant to civil rights conflicts in the community.) In addition, the book suggests a model for teaching about the Bill of Rights in schools: Begin with cases concerning the rights of the students being taught *and* practice the Bill of Rights in formulating and applying school policy in all academic and extracurricular activities—thus simultaneously reinforcing and providing a laboratory for the lessons of the classroom.

There are many misunderstandings concerning how our educational and legal systems work. First, many who know that their

---

* We recognize that some educators consciously resist applying the Bill of Rights in their schools because they feel that "kids are immature," that "schools are for education, not protest," that "students today already have too much freedom," and so on. However, we believe that such educators are in the minority and that most do not intentionally violate the law.

rights are being abridged feel that they are unable to do anything about it. Students think they must choose between obedience and rebellion; teachers think their choice is between conforming and resigning. This book suggests other alternatives.

Second, students and teachers frequently equate the Bill of Rights with their own interests. It is then easy to use the rhetoric of constitutional rights as a cover for asserting personal interests or as an excuse for simplistic thinking. A study of civil rights cases forces the reader to go beyond this easy rhetoric and to realize that these conflicts are rarely between right and wrong, but usually involve a tough choice between competing values.

Third, teachers and students frequently feel that their rights are inherently in conflict. They believe in a "fixed-pie" theory of legal rights, that is, that there is only "a limited amount of rights," and if students get more, teachers have less. We suggest that the rights of students and teachers can be complementary rather than competitive.[6]

Although this book is aimed primarily toward teachers and students, it is also intended for administrators, parents, and others interested in the subject, and it can be used for several purposes.

To learn the law. Chapters can be read selectively to learn what courts have said about specific issues such as freedom of speech, press, religion, or association as well as personal appearance, due process, and racial or sexual discrimination.

To learn about current controversies. Through the use of court cases, the book examines a wide range of recent constitutional conflicts between students and school officials. The cases confront such issues as distributing "obscene" publications, criticizing teachers and administrators in school-sponsored newspapers, wearing provocative symbols in the classroom, organizing radical groups on campus, and refusing to salute the flag or to conform to official dress codes. Conflicts involving racist and sexist practices by schools are also included.

To learn the reasons courts give for their decisions. By borrowing generously from court opinions, we have attempted to show how judges think through their decisions from the facts of the case to their legal conclusions.

This book is intended to communciate with laymen about the law. But lawyers, like teachers and other professionals, often use a technical vocabulary of their own. This jargon or "legalese" serves as a shorthand to facilitate communication between attorneys but becomes a barrier to communication between lawyers and laymen. We have tried to minimize this problem by omitting legalese or "translating" it into English wherever possible.

The case approach. Typically the law is explained to educators and laymen through a "text" approach. Usually a text first states the statutory or case law on a subject and then gives examples of how the rules have been applied and of any exceptions that might exist. This method has the advantages of brevity and simplicity; it states the conclusions of the courts and provides answers to legal questions. The problem with the method is that it seems abstract, "legalistic," and somewhat divorced from human conflict.

Instead we generally use the "case" method. Rather than starting with the answers, this approach begins by presenting a legal controversy in an educational setting. Most of the cases are recent. All describe real and complex situations that students and school officials have been unable to resolve. After outlining the facts of the case, we pose several questions to be considered in order to confront the implications of resolving the case for or against the student. Then we summarize the opinion of the court, accompanying the judges on their journey from the facts of the case to their legal conclusions, thereby enabling the reader to better understand the reasons behind court decisions. In addition, there are summaries of the law at the end of each chapter that integrate the rulings of the diverse cases that are presented. Thus instead of totally rejecting the text method, we have attempted to incorporate some of its features into our approach.

Generally we have not chosen easy cases with obvious answers. Most illustrate a clash between alternative values and competing educational goals. Many are on the cutting edge of the law, in areas where the law is constantly changing. They raise questions about which reasonable parents, students, educators, and judges differ; and the answers are neither simple nor precise.[7]

A case approach to a legal question takes more time than a text approach, which can neatly "lay out the law." But the world of educational conflict is not a neat one, and court cases can provide readers with situations of human conflict that they can recognize and identify with. When feasible, we have selected cases that teachers and students could imagine happening in schools or to people they know.

Legal texts often begin with a description of the judicial system and the court structure. For some readers this information provides a helpful introduction. Many, however, become lost or bored with such initial descriptions because they do not yet care about juris-dictional issues or the various appellate systems; they have not yet asked the questions these descriptions answer. But as readers become involved with different types of cases, many begin to wonder about such questions as: What kind of case can I take to a federal court? Could I appeal to the Supreme Court? How can I look up a case in the library? Because different students ask these questions at different times (and some never ask them), we have put our explanations in Appendix B, How the System Works. In addition, Appendix A contains the constitutional amendments most frequently referred to in this book. The Appendixes also include two leading student rights cases, a brief bibliography, and suggestions for classroom use.

By the time this book is published, some of its cases may be outdated by more recent decisions.[8] Therefore, we note that our aims are: (1) to help students and teachers understand the legal issues in a civil rights controversy—to ask the right questions, not to teach the final answers; (2) to indicate the trend of judicial decisions, not the latest case on each issue; (3) to present representative cases in the field, not a comprehensive statement of the law; and (4) to emphasize the legal aspects of cases rather than their educational, economic, political, or sociological dimensions.

In response to increasing student demands that their rights be respected, some educators have pointed out the administrative problems and risks in trying to run a public school in accordance with the Bill of Rights. We do not minimize these problems nor do we deny that some students will abuse their rights. However, the Supreme Court has repeatedly said that the Bill of Rights applies to all students. Moreover those concerned that students "obey the law" cannot be unconcerned when school officials disobey the Constitution. And as one judge pointed out, the risk taken if a few abuse their rights "is outweighed by the greater risk run by suppressing" these freedoms among our students.[9]

NOTES

[1] See H. H. Remmers and R. D. Franklin, "Sweet Land of Liberty," *Phi Delta Kappan*, October 1962, pp. 22–27.

[2] *Shanley* v. *Northeast Independent School District*, 462 F.2d 960 (5th Cir. 1972).

[3] A number of organizations are currently developing and promoting programs of legal education for the public schools including the American Bar Association's Committee on Youth Education for Citizenship, the Constitutional Rights Foundation, and Law in a Free Society.

[4] Although there are a small but increasing number of books about the rights of public school students, we know of none that is designed for use by students and teachers in college courses and in-service training programs. For a brief bibliography of related materials, see Appendix F.

[5] We recognize that writers sometimes distinguish civil rights from civil liberties. But for most people, these distinctions have become blurred. In this book we include civil liberties within the term civil rights. As Professor Abraham wrote in his text on this subject: "Although some would object, the terms 'rights' and 'liberties' are used interchangeably in this book. They are to be distinguished from all the other rights and freedoms individuals may enjoy under law because they are especially protected . . . against violations by *governments*." Henry J. Abraham, *Freedom and the Court: Civil Rights and Liberties in the United States*, New York, Oxford University Press, 1972, p. 3.

[6] For more information on teachers' rights, see David Rubin, *The Rights of Teachers*, New York, Avon Books, 1972, or Louis Fischer and David Schimmel, *The Civil Rights of Teachers*, New York, Harper & Row, 1973.

[7] Because this book focuses on areas of conflict and change, a reader might conclude that most of the law is controversial and confusing. In fact the reverse is true. In over 90 percent of the cases that arise, almost all lawyers and judges agree on the law to be applied. Typically the facts are in dispute, but the law usually has been established through prior decisions of the legislature or the courts. This book generally deals with the other 10 percent, the atypical cases—the unresolved "hassles" that "end up in court."

[8] The legal conclusions in this book reflect most of the major cases on the subject as of June 1974.

[9] *Eisner* v. *Stamford Board of Education*, 314 F.Supp. 832, 836 (D. Conn. 1970).

1
The search for balance

It has been fashionable in recent years to speak and write on behalf of the rights of youth and to do so in strident tones. Although reasonable voices are occasionally heard urging the extension of civil rights to all, regardless of age, the loudest voices often state an extreme case. One recent work, for example, is introduced by the author as a "book about slavery—the slavery of high school and college students to their administration."[1] Another asserts that "youth are today's paternalized and oppressed group" and charges that schools, courts, and families are "three insensitive institutions" out of whose controls youth fights to break.[2]

Although overstated, such charges have a legitimate basis. The factual launching pad for these hyperboles are the many unfair practices that occur in our homes, schools, and courts in regard to children and youth. Should we be "fair" to the young? This kind of question is usually dismissed with the notion that we should be fair to everybody. Granting this basic principle, we must inquire further. Should "fair" treatment of the young mean identical treatment with adults? If not, how do we avoid charges of oppression, authoritarianism, and even slavery?

Almost all human groups treat children differently from adults, and in American society we are no exception. Ideas of fairness and justice vary from culture to culture and change over

time. In our complex, diverse nation there have always been significant disagreements over the proper upbringing of the young, including
disputes over the application of the law to those "below the legal
age of maturity." In our analysis we do not accept either of two
extreme views: neither the one that equates the differential treatment
of youth with oppression and slavery nor the one that accepts the
traditional view that "children are to be seen and not heard."
Powerful traditions support this latter view, whereas the counter-
culture tends to assert the former. We believe, however, that there
exists a large number of parents, schools, and legal principles that
rejects both of these extremes and chooses a third, albeit more
difficult, road.

This third road is more difficult because it calls for an endless
series of situational decisions. It is based on the twin principles that
there are significant differences between adults and youth *and* that
basic constitutional principles are applicable to all. These two
principles when taken together, however, are enormously difficult to
apply in daily school activities. Before we explore the various current
problems in the application of these principles, a brief historical
discussion will help to provide some perspective.

The legacy of history

The history of mistreatment of children throughout the world is
gruesome and depressing. We will not recount this history; instead,
we will limit our comments to the history of American education
and to court cases that record the formal, legal efforts to exercise
adult control over students, as well as efforts to extend constitutional
rights to them.

A key legal doctrine established early in our history and still
with us in modified form is encapsulated in the Latin phrase *in loco
parentis*, which means "in place of the parents." Legally this
doctrine empowered school officials to exercise the same control over
students at school (or even to and from school) that parents could
exercise at home. Technically this principle still left open the question
of just what powers parents have over children; however, this
generally has been interpreted as extensive, almost unlimited power,
short of obvious, gross abuse. Thus, when *in loco parentis* was
applied to the schools, it gave teachers, principals, and other administrators enormous control over students. This control extended
not only to formal studies but also to clothing, hair style, speech,
manners and morals, organizational membership, and even behavior

away from school. For example, courts in the past have upheld the authority of public school officials to expel students for the following prohibited behavior: joining a social fraternity,[3] going home for lunch,[4] contracting a venereal disease,[5] smoking off campus,[6] and violating a school rule against going to the movies on week nights.[7] Similarly courts have held that students can be expelled for speaking against school policy at a student body meeting,[8] wearing a fraternity insignia to school,[9] expressing offensive sexual views,[10] arranging for a communist speaker off campus,[11] and even for refusing to tell who wrote dirty words on the school wall.[12] Most of these cases were decided decades ago.

Changing times have brought new opportunities and problems to both students and school officials. Henry Ford and our rising standard of living, for example, brought the student-owned automobile with its attendant problems. Inexpensive methods for reproducing written material facilitated the development of the student "underground press." Added to the technological developments of recent decades were the dramatic social and political events of the 1960s. The emergence of a massive student antiwar movement was symbolized by local and national demonstrations, by peaceful protest and civil disobedience, and by strikes, marches, and teach-ins. As a result of this movement, thousands of students were willing to go to court and even to jail over issues of principle.

This confrontation with legal and political authority had widespread side effects. One of these was to challenge the way things were done in families, in churches, and in schools. Many of the cases in this book are a product of these confrontations and the new thinking they provoked. Another product of these events was the passage of the Twenty-Sixth Amendment, which lowered the voting age to 18.*

These events also led educators and judges to change their views on *in loco parentis*.[13] As a result, the doctrine has been substantially altered and restricted by state departments of education and judicial decisions. The Ohio Department of Education, for example, rejected the concept in the following statement:

> *To stand* in loco parentis, *one must assume the full duties, responsibilities and obligations of a parent toward a minor. School teachers*

* The Twenty-sixth Amendment was ratified in 1971 and provides: "The right of citizens of the United States, who are eighteen years of age or older, to vote shall not be denied or abridged by the United States or by any State on account of age."

and administrators obviously do not support the children in their care, nor do they provide most of the tangible and intangible necessities and securities that the child finds in his home. In fact, school authorities stand in loco parentis only to the degree that they may act somewhat like a parent does only some of the time for the purpose of maintaining order in the educational system. No one would saddle school authorities with the full duties of parents to care for their children until the end of minority. Thus it is misleading to term one narrow function of the school—that is, the disciplinary function—as being a function totally representative of the in loco parentis concept. In loco parentis should not, then, be the basis for defining parent-school relationship.[14]

Other states are likely to follow the example of the New York State Department of Education, which restricted the powers of school officials to those expressly granted by the legislature: "the school and all its officers and employees stand *in loco parentis* only for the purpose of educating the child. The Education Law does not give the school authority beyond that."[15]

One of the strongest statements against the principle came from a judge in a Louisiana case involving corporal punishment:

It might have been said, in days when schooling was a voluntary matter, that there was an implied delegation of such authority from the parent. Such a voluntary educational system, like a system of apprenticeship . . . has long since disappeared. Parents no longer have the power to choose either the public school or the teacher in the public school. Without such power to choose, it can hardly be said that parents intend to delegate that authority to administer corporal punishment by the mere act of sending their child to school.[15]

Although the Supreme Court has not ruled directly on the continued viability of *in loco parentis*, it has indirectly modified its application by declaring that the Constitution does not stop at the door of the public school. Thus, to the extent that civil rights have entered the schools, the principle of *in loco parentis* has been modified.[17] Even though some courts still use the Latin phrase in explaining the reasons for their decisions, the doctrine is in decline. In the future, courts are more likely to rely on the general principle that students in the public schools have constitutional rights and then proceed to apply that principle to the unique factors of each controversy.

The following chapters will present cases highlighting current legal trends and contrast these with earlier decisions. Thus the reader will come to understand the pattern of expanding student rights. Although our presentation focuses primarily on legal sources, we recognize the significant gaps between court decisions and the behavior of teachers and administrators as well as parents. Our conviction is that the more clearly everyone understands the constitutional rights of students, the more likely they will be practiced in the schools.[18]

Current controversies

The following hypothetical cases illustrate current civil rights controversies related to students. They are presented for three reasons: (1) to illustrate the types of issues that will be examined in the chapters that follow, (2) to alert and sensitize the reader to current controversies in this area, and (3) to illustrate ways in which the rights of students clash with those of other students, school officials, and members of the community.

Controversy 1. A group of students in a West Coast high school, sympathetic to the cause of migrant grape pickers, organized a rally. They proposed to have speakers appear in the school's Open Forum area; they also decided to wear Cesar Chavez hats and brown armbands. School officials agreed to permit outside speakers as long as the other side was also heard, but they forbade the wearing of the hats and armbands for fear that disruption would occur. The students claimed they had a constitutional right to wear those symbols and that they did not want their rally diluted by opposition speakers. If called in as a consultant, what suggestions would you have made to resolve the controversy?

Controversy 2. Three students at Raineer School began publishing an underground newspaper that they distributed to fellow students. The second issue contained an article entitled "High School Is Fucked," which criticized the quality of education that Raineer students were receiving. The school administration confiscated all the papers, suspended the three students, and threatened them with expulsion if they published any further issues. The students claimed that their constitutional rights were violated. Were they?

Controversy 3. Students at Old Faithful High School organized a chapter of the Students for a Democratic Society (SDS). They requested recognition by the school, along with other clubs, in order to use school facilities and recruit students. The principal refused to grant recognition and prohibited any SDS activities at school. He claimed that SDS was part of an extremist national organization and was inconsistent with the educational purpose of the high school. The students argued that his action violated their right to freedom of association under the First Amendment. Were their rights violated, or do schools have the power to exclude certain organizations?

Controversy 4. Joanna, a high school senior, would not salute the American flag. She claimed that it was against her conscience to do so since ours is not a "just country" and that she felt like a hypocrite when she participated in the pledge. When given the alternative of leaving the room during the salute, she refused to do so. Thereupon, the high school suspended her and threatened to withhold her diploma. What are the constitutional issues in this case, and how should they be resolved?

Controversy 5. Sierra High School created a dress code that provided that "boys' hair will not be over the collar, nor will it hide the ears," and that "boys will not wear bell-bottoms, dungarees, T-shirts, or sweat-shirts." The code made other provisions for both boys and girls. John F challenged the dress code, claiming it was arbitrary and violated his constitutional right of individual expression. The school officials claimed that the dress code, created cooperatively with parents and students, helped them to maintain an orderly and effective learning environment. Does John have a right to wear his hair and his clothes any way he wishes?

Controversy 6. In a large Northern industrial city, some schools have a fairly even mixture of Black and white students. Most of the schools, however, are predominantly Black or white, and some are exclusively so. A lawsuit was brought by some Black parents requesting the integration of schools so that the student population would reflect the racial composition of the city as a whole. They requested busing and other means of achieving "racial balance." The school board claimed that the population merely reflected the traditional neighborhood school policy and that they had done nothing to create segregation: "Let the city change and the schools, being color-blind, will accurately reflect these changes."

Do the schools have a duty to overcome this type of segregation? Even if officials of the state did not deliberately create segregated schooling, does the Constitution nevertheless require them to provide for racial balance in the schools?

Controversy 7. Elmwood High School has tennis, baseball, and football teams for boys but not for girls. Valerie X wants to try out for the tennis team, Cathy Y is eager to play competitive baseball, and Judy Z claims that her diving is as good as that of any of the boys on the swimming team. Each young woman wants a fair chance to try out for the school team.

Is it legitimate to segregate girls and boys in high school athletics? Do girls have a right to try out for boys' teams? Where would such a right come from? Is there a legitimate difference between sexual segregation in extracurricular activities and in academic courses (shop, typing, home economics, and others)?

Controversy 8. During a search of school lockers authorized by the vice-principal of Emerson Junior High, various illegal drugs were found. The school administration immediately suspended all students in whose lockers the drugs were discovered. The students were notified that in five days hearings would be held at which they and their parents could be present and a school official would decide on the appropriate punishment. The students objected to the search of their lockers as an "unauthorized invasion of their privacy"; they objected to the "lack of due process"; and they demanded representation by lawyers.

Do school officials have a right to search student lockers? What constitutes "due process" in school disciplinary situations? If lawyers enter such situations, isn't there a danger that our schools will become arenas of legal controversy rather than educational institutions?

The following chapters examine these and related controversies. Many similar conflicts can be found in newspapers and magazines. Although we cannot address them all, we believe that if educators understand and apply the principles we analyze, some progress will have been made toward fulfilling the ideals of our Constitution.

Traditionally our culture has overemphasized the differences between adults and the young. From this conviction arose the legal doctrine of *in loco parentis.* Some current authors overemphasize a different doctrine—that all constitutional principles are equally applicable everywhere and to everyone. It is our contention that reliance on either of these premises to the exclusion of the other leads to a variety of undesirable consequences. The search for the proper balance between them is the challenge before us.

NOTES

[1] Peter M. Sandman, *Students and the Law*, New York, Macmillan, 1971, p. 1.

[2] Bruce Wasserstein and Mark J. Green, eds., *With Justice for Some*, Boston, Beacon Press, 1970, pp. 1–2.

[3] *Smith* v. *Board of Education*, 182 Ill. App. 342 (1913).

[4] *Bishop* v. *Houston School District*, 35 S.W.2d 465 (Tex. 1931).

[5] *Kenney* v. *Gurley*, 95 So. 34 (Ala. 1923).

[6] This was a state college case; *Tanton* v. *McKenney*, 197 N.W. 510 (Mich. 1924).

[7] *Mangum* v. *Keith*, 95 S.E. 1 (Ga. 1918). Courts have also upheld the suspension of students for eating at an off-limits lunchroom, *Board of Education* v. *Luster*, 282 S.W.2d 333 (1955), and for getting drunk off campus, *Douglas* v. *Campbell*, 116 S.W. 211 (Ark. 1909).

[8] *Wooster* v. *Sunderland*, 148 Pac. 959 (Cal. 1915).

[9] *Antell* v. *Stokes*, 191 N.E. 407 (Mass. 1934).

[10] *Morris* v. *Nowotny*, 323 S.W.2d 301 (1959). In this university case, the court held that administrators had discretion to expel a student whose sexual beliefs "were advocated in a manner calculated to be offensive" to the "dignified atmosphere of University life." Id. at 312.

[11] This occured at a state college, *Zarichney* v. *State Board of Agriculture*, 338 U.S. 118 (1949).

[12] *Board of Education* v. *Helston*, 32 Ill. App. 300 (1889).

[13] Although *in loco parentis* had not been widely challenged until recent years, a Vermont court as early as 1859 noted a major flaw in the doctrine. A parent's power, wrote the court, "is little liable to abuse, for it is continually restrained by natural affection. . . . The school master has no such natural restraint. Hence, he may not safely be trusted with all a parent's authority, for he does not act from the instinct of parental affection." *Student Rights and Responsibilities: Courts Force Schools to Change*, Washington, D.C., National School Public Relations Association, 1972, p. 3.

[14] *Rights and Responsibilities: Administrative Guidelines*, Columbus, Ohio, Ohio Department of Education, Division of Urban Education, 1971.

[15] Formal Opinion of Counsel No. 91, 1 Ed. Dept. Rep. 800 (1959).

[16] *Johnson* v. *Horace Mann Mutual Insurance Company*, 241 So.2d 588 (Ct. App. La. 1970).

[17] Principles of constitutional law are violated by parents in private homes with impunity. But such principles were never intended to operate in one's home, although it might be desirable if they did.

[18] Similar concerns have led us to present and analyze the legal and educational principles related to the rights of teachers. See Louis Fischer and David Schimmel, *The Civil Rights of Teachers*, New York, Harper & Row, 1973.

2
Freedom of speech

*It can hardly be argued that either students or teachers
shed their constitutional rights to freedom of speech or
expression at the schoolhouse gate.*[1]
—*Justice Abe Fortas*
in Tinker *v.* Des Moines

*It is a myth to say that any person has a constitutional right
to say what he pleases, where he pleases, and when he
pleases.*[2]
—*Justice Hugo Black*
Dissenting in Tinker *v.* Des Moines

Introduction

During the first half of this century, the Bill of Rights rarely
assisted students who challenged the constitutionality of school
policies. Courts generally used the "reasonableness test" to judge
whether disputed school rules were constitutional. If there was
any reasonable relationship between the rule and the goals of
the school, the rule usually would be upheld. It did not matter
whether most educators (or even most judges) believed that the
rule was unwise or unnecessary. Judges felt that school boards

should have "wide discretion" and that courts should not substitute their judgment for that of school officials who were presumed to be experts in educational matters. In upholding a state educational policy that restricted student rights, the Supreme Court in 1915 held that it was up to the state to determine whether its regulations promoted discipline among its students.[3] For decades thereafter it was easy for school officials to make a "reasonable" defense of almost any challenged policy with the argument that its enforcement "promotes school discipline."[4]

In 1969 the Supreme Court handed down an historic decision that challenged many of the educational policies of the past. In *Tinker* v. *Des Moines* the Court bypassed the "reasonableness test" and ruled that students do not shed their constitutional rights to freedom of expression "at the schoolhouse gate." No other recent case has been so influential in advancing the rights of public school students.

Beginning with a brief historic perspective, this chapter focuses on the *Tinker* decision—its principles, its challenge, and the way it has been applied and interpreted in subsequent cases.

Historical Perspective

THE WOOSTER CASE: EXPULSION
FOR SUBVERSIVE SPEECH[5]

Earl Wooster was a high school student in Fresno, California, who, during a school assembly, made a speech to the student body that alleged that the auditorium and certain science rooms were unsafe because of the possibility of fire. Wooster denounced the Fresno School Board for compelling students to use these inadequate facilities. He also made some caustic comments concerning the board's management of the school and objected to its prohibition of an annual student event known as the "donkey fight," which often resulted in "cracked heads and injured bodies." During his talk Wooster argued that it was "not fair of the board of education to forbid a donkey fight, in which the boys took their own chances of being injured, and forced them to take chances of being injured in a fire trap."

This "incendiary" talk resulted in a student resolution criticizing the school board, which led the board to invite Wooster to appear and explain his actions. While attempting to justify his conduct, Wooster also acknowledged that his speech to the students "was intended as a slam" at the board. At the conclusion of the hearing the board decided that Wooster's conduct was a "breach of school discipline" and that it was "intended and calculated" to discredit the board in the eyes of the students. The board therefore demanded an apology and "a public retraction" of the "offensive remarks." Wooster refused. As a result he was expelled from high school. Since Wooster did not believe his conduct justified expulsion, he took his case to court.

Questions to Consider

1. Should students be free to publicly criticize, discredit, or humiliate school officials?
2. Can a student be punished for making an incendiary speech at a school assembly that may subvert school discipline? Or can a student say anything he wishes as long as there is no school rule that specifically prohibits his behavior?
3. If a student refuses to apologize for remarks that are intentionally offensive and insubordinate, can he be punished?

The opinion of the court

The trial court upheld Wooster's expulsion. It found that his address to the student body was delivered for the purpose of creating "a spirit of insubordination" among the students and was "subversive of the good order and discipline of the school."

Wooster appealed the decision. He argued that no school rules made his controversial speech a ground for expulsion. But the appeals court was not persuaded and quoted with approval an earlier judge who wrote that there are "certain obligations on the part of the pupil, which are inherent in any proper school system, and which constitute the common law of the school, and which may be enforced without the adoption in advance of any rules upon the subject." In this case the school board found that the conduct charged against Wooster "was intended to discredit and humiliate the board in the eyes of the students, and tended to impair the discipline of the school." The admitted purpose of Wooster's speech was to belittle the school board, and "the tenor of the address was well calculated" to produce that result and to engender in the minds of the students a feeling of disrespect for the school administration and "a secret if not open hostility to their control of the student body and management of school affairs."

Thus the appeals court ruled that Wooster's conduct "cannot be classified as anything but a species of insubordination" that "required correction" in order that "the discipline of the school might be maintained." It acknowledged that a resort to the harsh penalty of expulsion is not appropriate until milder measures have failed. However, Wooster's refusal to make the apology demanded by the board not only "accentuated his misconduct" but also "made it necessary" to resort to an order of expulsion as the "only effective means" of punishing Wooster and maintaining school discipline.

The Wooster case was decided in 1915. And none of the parties to the case even raised the possibility that Wooster's speech might be protected by the Constitution.

The Tinker Case: A Landmark Decision

In 1965 the war in Vietnam was becoming more intense. U.S. involvement in the war was escalating rapidly, and the debate over American participation was becoming vehement. There were protest marches against the war in Washington, D.C., and a wave of draft card burning incidents swept the country.

In Des Moines, Iowa, a group of Quakers who were active in the antiwar movement planned to publicize their views by wearing black armbands during the Christmas season. Their purpose was to mourn those who died in the war and to support Senator Robert Kennedy's proposal for a truce.

The principals of the Des Moines schools became aware of the plan and adopted a policy that any student wearing an armband to school would be asked to remove it. If she refused, she would be suspended until she returned without the armband.* This policy was later ratified by the school board.

Although they knew about the policy, a group of seven students insisted on wearing the armbands to school. The students were sent home and suspended until they would return without their armbands. Two high school students (John Tinker and Chris Eckhardt) and a

---

* In our culture it is conventional to use the pronoun *he* to refer to the third-person singular. Since students usually include an equal number of women and men, we purposely alternate *she* and *he* throughout the book, except where students are specifically identified. For a full discussion of this and related issues, see Nancy Frazier and Myra Sadker, *Sexism in School and Society*, New York, Harper & Row, 1973.

junior high school student (Mary Beth Tinker) did not return to school until after New Year's Day, when the planned period for wearing armbands had expired.

The students, through their fathers, brought suit in a U.S. district court against the school officials to restrain them from taking disciplinary action. The students argued that the policy of prohibiting armbands in school deprived them of their constitutional rights.

Questions to Consider

1. Should the students have been suspended for deliberately disobeying the school policy prohibiting armbands?
2. The First Amendment provides that "Congress shall make no law abridging the freedom of speech."[6] Is wearing an armband protected by this amendment?
3. If a student is entitled to freedom of speech, should this freedom be limited by school officials under certain circumstances? If so, when, and under what circumstances?
4. Should students have the same freedom of speech as adults? Should students have the same freedom of speech in school as out of school? In class as well as in the halls or in the cafeteria?

The opinion of the district court[7]

In his opinion District Court Judge Roy Stephenson outlined the legal principles applicable in this case. First, the "free speech" clause of the First Amendment protects symbolic as well as "pure" speech, and the wearing of an armband to express certain views is the type of symbolic act protected by that amendment.* Second, freedom of speech is not an absolute right and may be abridged by the state under some circumstances. Third, school officials have a responsibility to maintain a disciplined atmosphere in the classroom. Thus the question posed by this case is how to resolve a conflict between the rights of students and the need for discipline.

* Although the First Amendment restrains only Congress, courts have held that the freedoms of speech and press are among the "liberties" protected by the Fourteenth Amendment (which provides that no *state* "shall deprive any person of life, *liberty*, or property, without due process of law" [italics added]). By incorporating the First Amendment freedoms into the Fourteenth Amendment, courts have protected an individual's right of free expression against infringement by a state or state agency such as the school board.

"These officials," wrote Judge Stephenson, "not only have a right, they have an obligation to prevent anything which might be disruptive" to school discipline. Therefore, "unless the actions of the school officials in this connection are unreasonable, the courts should not interfere."

To determine whether a particular action is reasonable, the court should review the background and context of the action. In this case the students wore armbands to express their views on a subject that had become highly controversial in the nation and in the community. And school officials believed that the reactions of other students to the armbands "would be likely to disturb the disciplined atmosphere required for any classroom." Thus the court observed that "it was not unreasonable in this instance for school officials to anticipate that wearing of armbands would create some type of classroom disturbance."

Moreover the school policy infringes on the students' freedom of speech only to a limited extent. "They are still free to wear armbands off school premises." In addition Judge Stephenson noted that they are free to express their views on the Vietnam War "during any orderly discussion of that subject." While acknowledging the importance of encouraging student interest in current affairs, the court concluded that in this instance "it is the disciplined atmosphere of the classroom, not the plaintiffs' [i.e., students'] right to wear armbands on school premises, which is entitled to the protection of the law."*

The court held that "school officials must be given wide discretion and if, under the circumstances, a disturbance in school discipline is reasonably to be anticipated, actions which are reasonably calculated to prevent such a disruption must be upheld by the Court." Judge Stephenson therefore ruled that under the circumstances of this case, the action of the school district was reasonable and did not deprive the students of their constitutional rights. Because of this ruling Chris Eckhardt and the Tinkers appealed to the U.S. Supreme Court.**

* A "plaintiff" is an individual or group that initiates a legal action in court. In this case the plaintiffs were the Tinkers and Chris Eckhardt.

** Federal cases are generally tried in a U.S. district court. A losing party has the right to appeal to one of 11 U.S. circuit courts of appeals. (In the *Tinker* case the appeals court judges were evenly divided; this had the effect of affirming the district court opinion.) The party who loses the appeal may then submit a petition to the U.S. Supreme Court, asking the Court to hear his case. Because the Supreme Court receives more petitions than it can possibly consider, it generally reviews only those cases it considers especially significant. For more information on the American judicial process, see Appendix B, How the System Works.

Questions to Consider

1. Does the ruling of the district court seem fair and reasonable?
2. If you were a judge, under what circumstances would you allow school officials to restrict student speech?
3. Should freedom of speech be different for students of different ages? Should high school students, for example, have more freedom than primary school students and less freedom than college students?
4. Should evidence that the armbands caused some disruption make any difference in deciding the case?

The opinion of the U.S. Supreme Court[8]

On behalf of the majority of the Supreme Court, Justice Abe Fortas reviewed the history of the case, the decision by the district court, and the legal principles recognized by Judge Stephenson. (The full text of the Supreme Court's opinion is reprinted in Appendix C.) Unlike the opinion delivered in the lower court, Justice Fortas emphasized that First Amendment rights are available to teachers and students. "It can hardly be argued," he wrote, "that either students or teachers shed their constitutional rights to freedom of speech or expression at the schoolhouse gate." To support this assertion he cited a previous Supreme Court opinion that indicated that because school boards "are educating the young for citizenship is reason for scrupulous protection of constitutional freedoms of the individual, if we are not to strangle the free mind at its source and teach youth to discount important principles of our government as mere platitudes."[9]

On the other hand, the Court has also emphasized the need for school officials to be able to control student conduct. Thus this case presents a conflict between the rights of students and the rules of the school. To resolve this question Justice Fortas reviewed the facts of the case. He noted that there is "no evidence whatever" that the wearing of the armbands interferred "with the school's work or with the rights of other students to be secure or to be let alone." Nevertheless the district court had concluded that the action of the school authorities was reasonable because it was based upon their fear of a disturbance from the wearing of the armbands. This conclusion was rejected by the Supreme Court. "In our system," wrote Justice Fortas, "undifferentiated fear or apprehension of disturbance is not enough to overcome the right to freedom of expression."

Justice Fortas also noted that school authorities did not prohibit the wearing of all political or controversial symbols. Students in some schools wore political campaign buttons and some even wore the Iron Cross, "traditionally a symbol of Nazism." The school order prohibiting armbands did not extend to these. Singling out one particular symbol for prohibition is not constitutionally permissible, at least without evidence that the symbol caused substantial interference with school activities.

In an eloquent argument on behalf of free speech in the schools, the Court pointed out that:

> *Any departure from absolute regimentation may cause trouble. Any variation from the majority's opinion may inspire fear. Any word spoken in class, in the lunchroom, or on the campus, that deviates from the views of another person may start an argument or cause a disturbance. But our Constitution says we must take this risk; and our history says that it is this sort of hazardous freedom—this kind of openness—that is the basis of our national strength and of the independence and vigor of Americans who grow up and live in this relatively permissive, often disputatious society.*[10]

The school officials cannot prohibit a particular expression of opinion merely "to avoid the discomfort and unpleasantness that always accompany an unpopular viewpoint." Where there is no evidence that the forbidden conduct would "materially and substantially interfere" with school work, the prohibition is unconstitutional.

In a provocative and far-reaching defense of the freedom of public school students, Justice Fortas wrote:

> *In our system, state operated schools may not be enclaves of totalitarianism. School officials do not possess absolute authority over their students. Students in schools as well as out of school are possessed of fundamental rights which the State must respect, just as they themselves must respect their obligations to the State. In our system, students may not be regarded as closed-circuit recipients of only that which the State chooses to communicate. They may not be confined to the expression of those sentiments that are officially approved. In the absence of a specific showing of constitutionally valid reasons to regulate their speech, students are entitled to freedom of expression of their views . . . [and] school officials cannot suppress "expressions of feelings with which they do not wish to contend."*[11]

The Court did not limit its decision to the protection of free expression in the classroom. Instead it specifically noted that the principles of this case are "not confined to the supervised and ordained" classroom discussion. First Amendment rights extend to the cafeteria, the playing field, and the campus. There, too, students may express their opinions on controversial topics. But conduct by students, in or out of class, which "for any reason . . . materially disrupts classwork or involves substantial disorder or invasion of the rights of others is, of course, not immunized by the Constitutional guarantee of freedom of speech."

In sum, there was no evidence in this case that led school authorities to forecast substantial disruption or material interference with school activities, and none in fact occurred. The students wore their armbands to express their disapproval of the Vietnam War and their advocacy of a truce. They wanted others to adopt their views, and they provoked discussions outside of classes. But they caused no disorder or interference with school work. "Under these circumstances," concluded the Court, "our Constitution does not permit officials of the State to deny their form of expression." The opinion of the district court was therefore reversed.

A strong dissent

What are the implication of the *Tinker* case? Justice Hugo Black saw them as serious and unfortunate. He feared the decision would encourage a revolutionary era of permissiveness. Therefore, although he had been one of the Supreme Court's strongest defenders of free speech, he wrote a vigorous dissenting opinion.*

The crucial questions in the *Tinker* case, wrote Justice Black, "are whether students and teachers may use the schools at their whim as a platform for the exercise of free speech . . . and whether the courts will allocate to themselves the function of deciding how the pupils' day will be spent." Although frequently opposing government regulation of the "content" of speech, "I have never believed that any person has a right to give speeches or engage in demonstrations where he pleases and when he pleases."

As Justice Black read the record of the case, it showed that comments by some students made John Tinker self-conscious while attending school and that the armbands "took students' minds off their classwork and diverted them to thoughts about the highly emotional

* In most cases decided by the Supreme Court and other appeals courts, the judges reach unanimous agreement, but sometimes this is not possible. In such cases, a judge who does not agree with the majority may submit a dissenting opinion, which is published immediately after the opinion of the court. This is what happened in the *Tinker* case. The full text of Justice Black's dissent is reprinted in Appendix C.

subject of the Vietnam war." Even if there was no evidence on the issue of disruption, it is obvious that disputes over the wisdom of the war "have disrupted and divided this country as few other issues ever have." Students, Black argued, cannot concentrate on school work when black armbands are being "ostentatiously displayed" to call attention to the wounded and dead of the war. And it was precisely "to distract the attention of other students that some students . . . determined to sit in school with their symbolic armbands." Thus Justice Black feared that "if the time has come when pupils of state-supported schools, kindergartens, grammar schools or high schools, can defy and flout orders of school officials to keep their minds on their own school work, it is the beginning of a new revolutionary era of permissiveness in this country fostered by the judiciary."

Justice Black denied that either students or teachers take with them "into the schoolhouse gate" full constitutional rights to freedom of expression. He wrote:

> The truth is that a teacher of kindergarten, grammar school or high school pupils no more carries into a school with him a complete right to freedom of speech and expression than an anti-Catholic or anti-Semite carries with him a complete freedom of speech and religion into a Catholic church or a Jewish Synagogue. . . . It is a myth to say that any person has a constitutional right to say what he pleases, where he pleases and when he pleases.

Public school students are not sent to school at public expense "to broadcast political or any other views to educate and inform the public."

In two revealing sentences Justice Black shares his views and concerns about public education:

> The original idea of schools, which I do not believe is yet abandoned as worthless or out-of-date, was that children had not yet reached the point of experience and wisdom which enabled them to teach all of their elders. It may be that the Nation has outworn the old fashioned slogan that "children are to be seen and not heard," but one may, I hope, be permitted to harbor the thought that taxpayers send children to school on the premise that at their age they need to learn, not teach.[12]

In a final eloquent paragraph Justice Black described his perception of the current breakdown of law and discipline in American schools and his fear that decisions such as this one would encourage a dangerous trend. Since his statement articulates a concern of many parents, teachers, and administrators, we quote from it at length:

Change has been said to be truly the law of life, but sometimes the old and the tried and the true are worth holding. . . . Uncontrolled and uncontrollable liberty is an enemy to domestic peace. . . . School discipline, like parental discipline is an integral and important part of training our children to be good citizens—to be better citizens. Here a very small number of students have crisply and summarily refused to obey a school order designed to give pupils who want to learn the opportunity to do so. One does not need to be a prophet or the son of a prophet to know that after the Court's holding today some students in Iowa schools and indeed in all schools will be ready, able, and willing to defy their teachers on practically all orders. This is the more unfortunate for the schools since groups of students all over the land are already running loose, conducting break-ins, sit-ins, lie-ins, and smash-ins. Many of these student groups, as is all too familiar to all who read the newspapers and watch the television news programs, have already engaged in rioting, property seizures, and destruction. They have picketed schools to force students not to cross their picket lines and have too often violently attacked earnest but frightened students who wanted an education that the pickets did not want them to get. Students engaged in such activities are apparently confident that they know far more about how to operate public school systems than do their parents, teachers and elected school officials. . . . Turned loose with lawsuits for damages and injunctions against their teachers as they are here, it is nothing but wishful thinking to imagine that young, immature students will not soon believe it is their right to control the schools rather than the right of the States that collect the taxes to hire the teachers for the benefit of the pupils. This case, therefore, wholly without constitutional reasons in my judgment, subjects all the public schools in the country to the whims' and caprices of their loudest-mouthed, but maybe not their brightest, students. I, for one, am not fully persuaded that school pupils are wise enough, even with this Court's expert help from Washington, to run the 23,390 public school systems in our fifty states. I wish, therefore, wholly to disclaim any purpose on my part to hold that the Federal Constitution compels the teachers, parents, and elected school officials to surrender control of the American public school system to public school students. I dissent.[13]

THE AFTERMATH OF TINKER

In the years following the *Tinker* decision, no case involving the issue of freedom of student expression was argued or decided without reference to the principles and holding of this crucial opinion. The following section will illustrate the way in which *Tinker* has been applied by different courts in a variety of related situations.

This section also will illustrate two legal concepts. First, courts generally follow "precedent." This means that when a court has ruled a certain way, the same court or a lower one is obliged to rule the same way in a similar case. However, a court is not bound by precedent if it can "distinguish" the case—that is, if it can show that the case before it is significantly different, despite its apparent similarity.

The first few cases, *Guzick, Hill, Melton* and *Banks*, illustrate the way courts distinguished the situations before them from the facts of the *Tinker* case. We will then examine *Butts* v. *Dallas* and *Aquirre* v. *Tahoka* to see how, in contrast, judges used the precedent of *Tinker* to decide two cases upholding student rights.

Tinker Distinguished: Limiting Student Expression

THE GUZICK CASE: FORBIDDING ALL SYMBOLS[14]

Shaw High School in Cleveland, Ohio, had a long-standing rule forbidding the wearing of all buttons, badges, or other symbols "whereby the wearers identify themselves as supporters of a cause or bearing messages unrelated to their education."[15] The rule had its origin in the days when strong competition between fraternities disrupted the educational process at Shaw. More recently a similar problem existed when the student population became 70 percent Black and 30 percent white. Shaw officials had uniformly enforced the antibutton rule because they believed the wearing of such symbols fostered undesirable competition, magnified the differences between students, and polarized them into separate and unfriendly groups. In recent years students attempted to wear buttons expressing "inflammatory messages," such as "White Is Right," "Say It Loud, Black and Proud," and "Black Power." A fight had resulted when a white student wore a button that other students considered an insult to the memory of Dr. Martin Luther King. Whenever such controversial buttons appeared, school authorities required that they be removed.

Despite the school policy, Thomas Guzick, a junior at Shaw High School, wore a button in class that solicited participation at a Chicago demonstration against the Vietnam War.[16] The principal told Guzick to remove his button. Guzick replied that his lawyer told him that "a United States Supreme Court decision entitled him to wear the button in school" and that he would not remove it. The principal then suspended Guzick until he obeyed. Guzick, however, believed that the *Tinker* ruling applied to his case and went to court to require the principal to allow him to wear the button in school.

Questions to Consider

1. Under the circumstances of this case, was it unconstitutional for Guzick's principal to tell him to remove his button?
2. What arguments would you use in support of Guzick? What arguments could you use to defend the no-button policy of Shaw High School?
3. In what ways are the facts of *Tinker* similar to the *Guzick* case? In what ways are they different?

The opinion of the court

The trial court that heard the case dismissed Guzick's complaint and concluded that revoking the no-button rule "would inevitably result in collisions and disruptions, which would seriously subvert Shaw High School as a place of education for its students, black and white."

Guzick, however, still believed that the *Tinker* decision should apply to his situation. Therefore Guzick appealed the trial court's ruling. He argued that the wearing of the button did not and would not disrupt the work and discipline of Shaw High School. The U.S. Court of Appeals acknowledged that if the facts of this case were similar to *Tinker*, the judgment of the district judge would have to be reversed. But the majority of the judges of the appeals court believed that *Guzick* could be distinguished from *Tinker* and that the facts of this case "clearly provide such distinction."*

First, the appeals court contrasted the rule of *Tinker* with the long-standing and uniform enforcement of Shaw's no-symbol rule.

* Where the evidence is in dispute, the trial court first determines the facts of the case and then applies the appropriate law. An appeals court usually accepts the facts as determined by the trial court and focuses its attention on disputes concerning the proper legal principles to be applied to the case. For more information on this and related issues, see Appendix B, How the System Works.

School authorities in the *Tinker* case did not prohibit the wearing of all controversial symbols. The evidence showed that some students wore political campaign buttons and a few even wore a Nazi symbol. The order prohibiting armbands did not apply to these symbols but only to black armbands worn in opposition to American participation in the Vietnam War.

A second distinction concerned probable disruption. In *Tinker* the trial court found no evidence to indicate that the wearing of the armbands would cause substantial disruption. In contrast the trial court in the *Guzick* case found that "if all buttons are permitted or if any buttons are permitted, a serious discipline problem will result, racial tensions will be exacerbated, and the educational process will be significantly and substantially disrupted."

Was this a case of undifferentiated fear of disturbances likely to result from wearing buttons at Shaw? (If so, the court acknowledged that Guzick's right to freedom of expression should prevail.) On the contrary, said the court, "there is in the present case much more than an undifferentiated fear." The wearing of buttons and other symbols has caused substantial disruptive conduct at Shaw High School in the past. Furthermore "it is likely to occasion such conduct if permitted henceforth." Moreover the wearing of such symbols would serve to "exacerbate an already tense situation" and "to promote divisions and disputes, including physical violence among the students."

On behalf of the appeals court Judge O'Sullivan pointed out that any rule that attempts to permit the wearing of some buttons but not others would be virtually impossible to administer. "It would occasion *ad hoc* and inconsistent application. It would make the determination of permissible versus impermissible buttons difficult, if not impossible." And it would deprive school officials of their position of neutrality.

The court emphasized the need for proper balancing in the exercise of the guarantees of the Constitution—in this case, the need is to balance First Amendment rights with the duty of the state to protect the public school system. In arriving at this balance, Judge O'Sullivan observed:

Denying Shaw High School the right to enforce this small disciplinary rule could and most likely would, impair the rights of its students to an education and rights of its teachers to fulfill their responsibilities. . . . We must be aware in these contentious times that America's classrooms and their environs will lose their usefulness as places in which to educate our young people if pupils come to school wearing the badges of their respective disagreements and provoke confrontations with their fellows and their teachers. The buttons are claimed to be a form of free speech. Unless they have some relevance to what is being considered or taught, a school classroom is no place for the untrammeled exercise of such [a] right.[17]

Thus the court ruled that "the potentiality" of imminent rebellion among Shaw students suported the wisdom of the no-symbol rule. "Surely," concluded Judge O'Sullivan, "those charged with providing a place and atmosphere for educating young Americans should not have to fashion their disciplinary rules only after good order has been at least once demolished."[18]

THE HILL CASE: LIMITATIONS OF SYMBOLIC SPEECH[19]

The *Hill* case was similar to the *Guzick* case; it also involved students who claimed that the *Tinker* decision protected their symbolic speech and school authorities who argued that the facts of the case were different.

A group of North Carolina high school students who opposed the Vietnam War asked other students to wear black armbands to support a National Moratorium on October 15, 1969. On that day 25 to 50 students came to school with armbands. Some were black; others were red, white, and blue. A few students were noisy, disrespectful, and belligerent. Over one-third of the students of the school were children of military personnel. The principal feared substantial disruption and violence and ordered teachers not to admit any students wearing an armband to class. Most students complied with the order and removed their armbands; a few went to court.

The district court ruled that this case was distinguishable from the *Tinker* case, which did not involve disruptive action or group demonstrations. It only involved a small number of participants, and school officials had no evidence to indicate that wearing the armbands would substantially interfere with the work of the school. In the *Hill* case there were several groups of protesters with divergent views. The students had been noisy, belligerent, and disrespectful toward teachers; they also had threatened violence. Thus the situation was "explosive," the student mood was "very tense," and the order prohibiting armbands "was motivated by reasonable apprehension of disruption and violence." Under these circumstances the action of the school authorities was upheld. The court concluded the following.

*In the balancing of First Amendment rights, the duty of the State
to operate its public school system for the benefit of all its children
must be protected even if governmental regulations incidentally limit
the untrammeled exercise of speech, symbolic or otherwise, by those
who would impede the education of those who desire to learn.*[20]

THE MELTON CASE: SYMBOLIC EXPRESSION
AT A TENSE SCHOOL[21]

Rod Melton, a student at Brainerd High School in Chattanooga, Tennessee, was suspended because he refused to stop wearing a small
Confederate flag patch on one sleeve of his jacket. The principal felt
that Melton had violated the school code, which prohibited the wearing of provocative symbols on clothing; he construed "provocative
symbols" to mean those that "would cause a substantial disruption
of the student body." The principal was concerned about the tense
racial situation and disturbances that had erupted the year before.
The disruptions, which closed the school twice, resulted from controversy over the use of the Confederate flag as the school flag and the
song "Dixie" as its pep song.

Melton believed that the principal overreacted to the sleeve patch
and that his suspension violated his right to freedom of expression.
Although he knew of the disturbances the prior year, Melton argued
that the circumstances were substantially different. In the fall during
which he was suspended, the situation had become less tense, and
there had been no threats of disruption or acts of violence. The protests the previous year had been against official school symbols,
whereas the wearing of a small insignia was by a single student and
did not indicate administrative approval. Moreover the symbol in this
case was small and was worn by Melton in a quiet, peaceful manner.
Furthermore the principal conducted no inquiry to determine whether
the wearing of the insignia would lead to further trouble. Thus Melton argued that the holding of the *Tinker* case should apply and
that the wearing of this emblem "which was merely symbolic of one
of the historic facts of American life" should be protected.

On behalf of the U.S. Court of Appeals, Judge Keith wrote in the
Melton decision: "This is a troubling case; on the one hand, we are
faced with the exercise of the fundamental constitutional right to
freedom of speech, and on the other, with the oft conflicting, but
equally important, need to maintain decorum in our public schools."
The question is whether Melton's suspension violated the First and
Fourteenth Amendments under the circumstances of this case.

Unlike the *Tinker* case, in which the Supreme Court found no evidence of disruptive conduct, the record of the present case was different. According to Judge Keith, it indicated that there had been substantial disorder at Brainerd High School during the 1969–1970 school year; that this disorder "most materially disrupted the functioning of the school, so much so that the school was in fact closed on two occasions"; that much of the controversy the previous year had centered around the use of the Confederate flag as a school symbol; and that the school officials had every right to anticipate that a tense racial situation continued to exist at the time that Melton was suspended. The court concluded that under the circumstances of this case, Melton's suspension did not violate his First Amendment rights, and the school authorities were permitted "to stave off any potential danger" resulting from his conduct.

THE BANKS CASE: CAN SYMBOLIC EXPRESSION VIOLATE MINORITY RIGHTS?[22]

While somewhat different from other controversies in this section, a federal case from the midwest raises a related free speech issue and illustrates the difference between legal and educational questions. The controversy began in 1962 when students in Southside High School in Muncie, Indiana, voted to adopt symbols associated with the Old South. Accordingly the school flag resembled the flag of the Confederacy, the name of the athletic team was the "Rebels," the glee club was named the "Southern Aires," and the homecoming queen was called the "Southern Belle." Black students, who constituted 13 percent of the enrollment of Southside, felt that these symbols were offensive and inflammatory and that they discouraged Black participation in extracurricular activities. These students also felt that the symbols violated their right of free speech and were discriminatory and that they therefore should be prohibited.*

To support their case the Black students cited an Indiana Civil Rights Commission report that urged the school administration to eliminate these symbols and that noted: "It is impossible for Negro students to feel loyal to a school whose official symbols represent a system that enslaved their ancestors."

* The *Banks* case involved several other issues such as affirmative action, school site selection, and busing. Here, as in a number of other cases discussed in this book, we do not mention all the issues involved in a case unless they are relevant to the subject of the chapter in which they are included.

The school administration refused to intervene on the grounds that the Constitution does not prohibit the use of these symbols and that they were pursuing a valid educational policy of allowing students of all schools to choose their symbols democratically. Moreover school administrators indicated that they would not prohibit students of a predominantly Black school from adopting the "Black Panther" as their symbol, although it might offend white students.

Both the trial court and appeals court upheld the position of the administration. The court of appeals found no evidence that the policy on school symbols was motivated by racial discrimination. Furthermore there was nothing to indicate that Black students were denied access to any school activities or facilities because of these symbols. Finally the court failed to find "any evidence in the record that the Black students' right of free speech and expression was being abridged by use of the Confederate symbols."*

This case illustrates the difference between legal and educational issues. Both the trial court and appelate court judges felt that the student body's choice of symbols was offensive and unwise, but they did not believe the choice was unconstitutional.[23] Although the courts ruled in favor of the schools, they approved neither the symbols nor the "educational policy" which maintained them. On the contrary, the trial judge specifically recommended that school authorities "exercise their discretion to bring about the elimination of school symbols which are offensive to a racial minority." Thus, the court saw this as a matter that called for educational leadership rather than judicial intervention.

Tinker Reaffirmed:
Supporting Student Expression

THE BUTTS CASE: THE INADEQUACY
OF ADMINISTRATIVE INTUITION[24]

School authorities in Dallas, Texas, concluded that the Vietnam Moratorium of October 15, 1969, would be a day of disruption in their

* The students had also argued that the *Tinker* decision "precludes a school from compelling minority students 'to endure offensive official symbols at a tax supported institution which they are compelled to attend.'" But the appeals court held that the *Tinker* ruling protecting student symbolic speech did not apply to this case since the symbols here did not appear to restrict the Black students' right to freedom of speech.

schools. Their conclusion was based on several events: Someone published a "manifesto" calling on high school students to "boycott" their classes or to attend them "wearing black armbands of protest"; a former pupil, not connected with the Vietnam Moratorium, threatened to bomb one of the schools; and, as the day approached, disruptive sit-ins occurred in schools in a nearby community. On the morning of the moratorium a group of students massed across the street from one of the schools displaying a large banner reading "Try Peace." One student who opposed the protest snatched the banner and ran away with it, and other moratorium opponents wore white armbands.

On learning of the plan to wear black armbands, the superintendent decided that it would be disruptive. Therefore school officials requested those who wore the armbands to remove them or to leave school. Students who were sent home claimed that this administrative action was unconstitutional, especially since no substantial disruption occurred in the schools.

Although school officials did not expect the wearers of the black armbands to initiate disruption, they believed that these students would anger others not participating in the moratorium. They feared, for example, that white-armband wearers would tear the black armbands from those who wore them. Hence officials prohibited the wearing of all armbands, which they anticipated "would substantially interfere with school work."

Questions to Consider

1. What argument could be made on behalf of the Dallas school officials in support of their action?
2. How would you argue this case on behalf of the students who were sent home?
3. If officials had evidence that the wearing of black armbands would anger and disturb other students, would this be sufficient to justify their banning these armbands? Or their banning all armbands?

Judicial opinions

The trial court upheld the action of the school officials and tried to distinguish *Butts* from *Tinker*. According to Judge Taylor: "The facts here show a more aggravated situation than Justice Fortas described in the *Tinker* case." Here there was a real possibility of group demonstrations; there was "evidence of threats and counter threats";

and there was "tension and uneasiness" caused by the bomb threat. So Judge Taylor concluded that, unlike the situation in *Tinker*, the Dallas school authorities "were very concerned about disruption and had reason to anticipate problems if armbands were worn."[25]

The students took their case to the U.S. Court of Appeals, where they finally found judicial support for their position. "Whatever the black armbands may have communicated," wrote the appeals court, "the record is devoid of any evidence that it did in fact communicate to any witness an intention on plaintiff's part to engage personally in the feared disruptive action."[26]

Judge Nichols of the appeals court acknowledged that school officials were not prohibited by the First Amendment from action until disruption actually occurs. Similarly officials had a right and duty under the circumstances of this case to expect that disruption might occur on October 15. The court, however, disagreed that this "expectation" was sufficient to justify the suspension of the students' constitutional right of symbolic speech. What more was required? To justify the school's action, officials would have to determine, "based on fact, not intuition," that disruption would probably result from the exercise of the constitutional right and that not wearing the armbands "would make the expected disruption substantially less probable or less severe."

The court acknowledged that the school can restrict student language (e.g., in the case of "fighting words") and symbols (e.g., in the case of a "provocative flaunting" of Nazi "swastikas"). But in most cases, something more "than the *ex cathedra* pronouncement of the superintendent"* is required to establish that there would be disruption.

There is nothing in this record to show that school officials had developed solid information on the attitudes and intentions of the student protesters. They made no effort to bring leaders of the black- and white-armband factions together to agree on mutual respect for each other's constitutional rights. If actions such as this had been tried and failed, the court wrote, "the failure would have tended to establish that armbands of all colors should be banned." But in the *Butts* case, officials made no attempt to respond to the moratorium crisis through such democratic processes.

In conclusion the court rejected the notion that the holding of

---

* *Ex cathedra* means "authoritative"; it was originally applied to decisions of the pope from his *cathedra*, or chair.

Tinker is nullified whenever a school system is confronted with disruptive activities. "Rather we believe that the Supreme Court has declared a constitutional right which school authorities must nurture and protect, not extinguish, unless they find the circumstances allow them no practical alternative." Where there are no practical alternatives, the reasonable decisions of officials will be supported. "But there must be some inquiry, and establishment of substantial fact, to buttress the determination." Since no such facts were established in this case, the judgment of the trial court was reversed, and the superintendent was enjoined "from interferring with plaintiffs in the exercise of their First Amendment right by wearing black armbands to school to protest the Vietnam War."

THE AGUIRRE CASE: SUPPORTING EDUCATIONAL CHANGE[27]

In Tahoka, Texas, a group known as "Concerned Mexican American Parents" had become dissatisfied with certain educational policies and practices in their school system. They attempted to have these matters corrected through letters, meetings, and legal action. To support the view that these grievances were justified and that corrective action should be taken, a number of students began to wear brown armbands to school. On the next day the board of education passed a regulation prohibiting any unusual dress or wearing apparel that is "disruptive, distracting, or provocative so as to incite students of other ethnic groups."

After a number of students were suspended for refusal to remove their armbands, they sued to stop school officials from enforcing this regulation. School officials defended their action on two grounds: First, wearing of the armbands in violation of school policy "was a disruption in and of itself"; second, several incidents of "unrest and apprehension" were attributable to the wearing of the brown armbands. These included the testimony of one girl that several other girls attempted to force her to wear an armband in the gym. (But the evidence also indicated that they did not persist when she refused and that she was not harmed or frightened by the incident.) Two parents indicated that their children were afraid of "some unspecified trouble at school." (But in neither case was there evidence of force, threats, or violence.)

Based on this testimony, the trial court found school officials had not presented adequate evidence to show "that the wearing of the

armbands by plaintiffs . . . would materially and substantially interfere with the requirements of appropriate discipline or be disruptive
of normal educational functions."

The court concluded that the decision in this case should be based
on the *Tinker* ruling that the wearing of an armband to express certain views is the type of symbolic act that is protected by the First
Amendment. "The logic of such a conclusion," wrote Judge Woodward, "is obvious when the symbol, the armband, is translated back
into the expression which it symbolizes—'I support those in the community who advocate certain changes in the educational system'—
and of that expression it is asked, 'Is it within the protection of the
First Amendment?'" In answer, Judge Woodward replied, "No room
for doubt exists." The court, therefore, granted the students the "in-
junctive relief" they requested.

SUMMARY AND CONCLUSIONS

Although the Bill of Rights had always been applied to citizens in
general, courts in the past failed to apply many of its provisions to
students. The *Wooster* case illustrates how a school board, which
expelled a student for making critical statements about the school administration, was upheld by an early court. The opinion did not even
consider the application of the First Amendment to the case.

Today all courts recognize that the Bill of Rights applies to students; and it is doubtful that any court currently sitting in the United
States would support the expulsion of Wooster in a similar situation.
Individual rights, however, are not absolute. When a student's exercise of his rights comes in conflict with the rights of other students
or the obligation of the school to keep reasonable order, then judges
weigh and balance these competing interests in light of the circumstances of the particular case before arriving at their decision.

The *Tinker* case outlined the constitutional principles that are now
applied to all public schools: (1) A student's First Amendment right
of free speech is protected against infringement by a state agency
(such as the public schools) by the due process clause of the Fourteenth Amendment. (2) The wearing of an armband, button, or other
type of symbolic expression by students is protected by the free
speech clause of the First Amendment. (3) Freedom of speech is not
an absolute right and may be abridged by school officials under some
circumstances. The question posed by the cases in this chapter is:
Under what circumstances can school authorities restrict student freedom of expression?

The *Tinker* case held that restricting a student's right to freedom of expression is unconstitutional unless there is evidence to show that the forbidden conduct would "materially and substantially interfere" with school activities. "Apprehension of disturbance" on the part of school officials or their desire to avoid "the discomfort and unpleasantness that always accompany an unpopular viewpoint" is not sufficient to overcome a student's right to freedom of expression. This right extends beyond the classroom to halls, the cafeteria, and the entire school campus. On the other hand, student expression that for any reason "materially disrupts classwork or involves substantial disorder or invasion of the rights of others" is not protected by the First Amendment.

In the years following the *Tinker* decision other courts have sought to determine what rules regulating student expression were consistent with the principles of *Tinker* and under what circumstances the "substantial and material disruption" test would justify the restriction of free speech in public schools. In the process some judges tended to distinguish *Tinker* from the cases before them and limit the application of this landmark decision. In the *Guzick* case, for example, a court upheld a school rule prohibiting the wearing of all controversial buttons and badges when the wearing of such symbols had caused substantial disruption in the past and would have aggravated an already tense situation. Because of the "potentiality and imminence" of disruption, school officials were permitted to enforce disciplinary rules restricting freedom of expression before "good order" had been "demolished."

The *Hill* and *Melton* cases illustrate some of the specific circumstances in which courts have found that the restriction of student expression was justified. In the *Hill* case, a federal district court upheld the prohibition of all armbands in a tense situation where there was some evidence of student disorder and the prohibition was motivated "by reasonable apprehension of disruption and violence." In *Melton*, a federal appeals court upheld the suspension of a student who peacefully wore a Confederate flag patch in violation of a school code, since evidence indicated that the use of the Confederate flag as a school symbol had caused substantial disruption. Conversely, the *Banks* case upheld the use of controversial school symbols associated with the Confederacy where they apparently caused no disruption.

Just as the *Guzick*, *Hill*, and *Melton* cases limited the application of Tinker, other cases have reaffirmed and perhaps expanded its application. The *Butts* case, for example, indicated that an expectation of disruption by school officials is not enough to justify the suspension of students rights, unless (1) such an expectation is "based on fact, not intuition" and (2) the officials first made an honest effort to restrain those who might cause the disruption. Similarly, *Aguirre* affirmed the right of students to wear armbands in support of an ethnic community group seeking educational change where there was minimal evidence of disruption.

Will the *Tinker* holding apply to all types of school regulations? Not necessarily. Justice Fortas emphasized that *Tinker* involved "direct, primary First Amendment rights akin to 'pure speech.'" Conversely, he pointed out that the problem posed by *Tinker* "does not relate to regulation of . . . clothing, to hair style, or deportment . . . or even group demonstrations." This does not mean that the Constitution does not apply to these matters. The Court simply took no position on such issues that it considered beyond the scope of the *Tinker* case. As we will see in subsequent chapters, judges differ in the extent to which they apply the principles of *Tinker* to a variety of other controversies involving students rights.

In reviewing the cases that followed *Tinker,* it seems clear that some of Justice Black's fears have been fulfilled and others have not. The *Tinker* decision did not begin a "new revolutionary era" of judicially fostered permissiveness. On the contrary, *Guzick, Hill* and *Melton* illustrated the way in which judges have been able to limit the *Tinker* holding to the facts of that case and to allow authorities to protect schools from student expression that would lead to disorder. On the other hand, Justice Black was right in predicting that *Tinker* would lead students to demand their rights more frequently and to initiate "lawsuits for damages and injunctions" when they believed their rights had been violated. But this has not subjected "all the public schools in the country to the whims and caprices of their loudest-mouthed" students. Rather, it has led to a growing and active interest in the law on the part of students, faculty, and administrators. Unlike Justice Black, we view this as a healthy development, educationally as well as legally.

NOTES

[1] *Tinker* v. *Des Moines Independent School District,* 393 U.S. 503, 506 (1969).

[2] *Id.* at 522.

[3] *Waugh* v. *Board of Trustees,* 237 U.S. 589 (1915). In *Waugh* the Court indicated it would not annul state restrictions of student freedom "upon disputable considerations of their wisdom or necessity."

4 In 1966 federal courts were still using the "reasonableness test." For example, the trial court judge in the *Tinker* case wrote that unless the actions of the school officials in restricting student expression "are unreasonable, the courts should not interfere." *Tinker* v. *Des Moines*, 258 F.Supp. 971 (D. Iowa 1966).

5 *Wooster* v. *Sunderland*, 148 P. 959 (1915).

6 For the full text of this and other constitutional amendments especially relevant to students, see Appendix A.

7 *Tinker* v. *Des Moines*, 258 F.Supp. 971 (D. Iowa 1966).

8 *Tinker* v. *Des Moines*, 393 U.S. 503 (1969).

9 *West Virginia State Board of Education* v. *Barnette*, 319 U.S. 624, 637 (1943).

10 *Tinker* at 508–509.

11 *Id.* at 511.

12 *Id.* at 522.

13 *Id.* at 524–526.

14 *Guzick* v. *Drebas*, 431 F.2d 594 (6th Cir. 1970), cert. denied, 401 U.S. 948 (1971).

15 Symbols that supported high school athletic teams or advertised school plays were not forbidden. *Id.* at 596.

16 The button read: "April 5 Chicago, GI-Civilian, Anti-War Demonstration, Student Mobilization Committee."

17 *Guzick* at 600–601.

18 This is the text of Judge McAllister's brief dissenting opinion in the *Guzick* case:

When a few students noticed the button which appellant [Guzick] was wearing, and asked him 'what it said,' appellant's explanation resulted only in a casual reaction; and there was no indication that the wearing of the button would disrupt the work and discipline of the school.

I am of the opinion that the judgment of the district court should be reversed and the case dismissed upon the authority of Tinker v. Des Moines [Id. at 601].

19 *Hill* v. *Lewis*, 323 F.Supp. 55 (E.D.N.C. 1971).

20 *Id.* at 59. Typically courts support their opinions by quoting from the majority opinions of higher courts. In this case, however, it is interesting to note that the court also quoted from Justice Black's dissent in the *Tinker* case to the effect that children were sent to school to learn, not teach.

21 *Melton* v. *Young*, 465 F.2d 1332 (6th Cir. 1972).

22 *Banks* v. *Muncie Community Schools*, 433 F.2d 292 (7th Cir. 1970).

23 Although he did not rule in favor of the Black students, the trial court judge commented:

Tyranny by the majority is as onerous as tyranny by a select minority. The student body's choice of symbols has been shown to be personally offensive to a significant number of the students, no matter how innocuous the symbols may originally have seemed to the young, white students. An exercise in democracy which results in offense to a sizeable number

of the participants should be seriously reconsidered by the student body
[Id. at 297–298].

Similarly, the appeals court wrote that "the symbols complained of are
offensive and that good policy would dictate their removal." *Id.* at 299.

²⁴ *Butts* v. *Dallas Independent School District,* 306 F.Supp. 488 (N.D.
Tex. 1969); 436 F.2d 728 (5th Cir. 1971).

²⁵ 306 F.Supp. 488, 490 (N.D. Tex. 1969). In a paragraph that reflected
his educational concerns, Judge Taylor wrote:

The simple fact of the matter is that in order to educate a large group
of children, there must be some type of orderly process. This process may
infringe on a child's freedom of expression in varying degrees. Hopefully,
the process will teach him how to reason, assimilate ideas, and generally
think for himself. To date, the Dallas Independent School District has
been one of the most up-to-date and qualified districts in the Nation. It
has maintained an admirable degree of order in these times when other
large school systems are experiencing chaos and violence. . . . It occurs
to this Court that one obligation students have to the State is to obey
school regulations designed to promote the orderly educational process
[Id. at 491].

²⁶ 436 F.2d 728, 731 (5th Cir. 1971).

²⁷ *Aguirre* v. *Tahoka Independent School District,* 311 F.Supp. 664
(N.D. Tex. 1970).

3
Freedom of the press: the publication and distribution of student views

Tinker's *dam to school board absolutism does not leave dry the fields of school discipline. . . . It sets canals and channels through which school discipline might flow with the least possible damage to the nation's priceless topsoil of the First Amendment.*

In a recent Supreme Court opinion, Chief Justice Burger wrote: *deemed inapplicable . . . to high school students living at the threshold of voting and dying for their country.*
— Shanley v. Northeast Independent School District[1]

Introduction

In a recent Supreme Court opinion, Chief Justice Burger wrote:
  The First Amendment protects works which, taken as a whole, have serious literary, artistic, political or scientific value, regardless of whether the government or a majority of the people approve of the ideas these works represent. "The protection given speech and press was fashioned to assure unfettered interchange of ideas for the bringing about of political and social changes desired by the people."[2]

  Thus the First Amendment protects the freedom of citizens to suggest revolutionary change and to write critically about government policies and officials. Whether the criticism is balanced or biased, careful or sloppy, constructive or destructive, it cannot be prohibited.

Is a student equally free to propose radical change and to publicly criticize school officials and administrative policy? Can he publish such proposals or criticism in a school-sponsored paper? Or can faculty advisers eliminate material that attacks school policy?

What is the status of "underground" student newspapers? Can the distribution of such papers be prohibited in school? Or does a student have a constitutional right to distribute any material she wishes if she is not disruptive? These are some of the issues raised in this chapter.

The chapter is divided into three sections. After a brief examination of a 1908 case, we consider the question of "prior restraint"— whether and under what circumstances school officials can require students to submit all publications for approval prior to distribution. Second, we examine a series of cases that probe the limits of students freedom concerning underground newspapers. Can such papers be restricted by the administration if they are obscene? If they are in defiance of school rules? If they are distributed during school hours? Finally, we consider the extent to which officials can control the content, advertisements, and editorial policy in school-sponsored publications.

Historical Perspective

THE DRESSER CASE: A TRADITIONAL APPROACH TO STUDENT PUBLICATIONS[3]

Two high school students from St. Croix Falls, Wisconsin, printed a poem in the town newspaper that satirized the rules of the school. The principal believed that the poem tended to hold the "school, its discipline and its teachers to public contempt and ridicule." Therefore he told the students that they would be suspended unless they submitted a written apology "admitting that they did a wrong thing" and that they were sorry for it. The students refused and were suspended.

The father of the two students went to court and argued that the principal had no right to punish his daughters for publishing a "harmless" poem which they had written after school hours. The principal responded that it would be detrimental to the school and "subversive of proper discipline" to reinstate the students without a suitable apology.

The court held that school authorities have the power to suspend a pupil for an offense committed outside school hours that has "a direct and immediate tendency to influence the conduct of other pupils while in the schoolroom" and to impair the authority of the teachers. "Such power is essential" for the preservation of "decency, decorum and good government in the public schools."

In this case the principal considered the conduct for which the students were suspended as having a "direct and injurious effect" on school discipline. The poem they published found its way into the homes of many of their classmates, "who would be as much influenced thereby as if the writing had been printed and posted in the schoolroom, or there circulated and read." Since the judge believed that school officials are familiar with the effect such a publication would probably have, he ruled that they should be given "broad discretion" in disciplining students unless such action is clearly illegal or unreasonable. The court concluded that the principal's action was not an abuse of discretion but rather "an earnest desire" to discipline the students "for their own good as well as for the good of the school."

This case was decided by the Supreme Court of Wisconsin on May 8, 1908. The court did not consider the possibility that the First Amendment's provision concerning freedom of press might have protected the action of these students.

Administrative Approval: Constitutionality, Criteria, and Procedures

THE SHANLEY CASE: THE LIMITS OF ADMINISTRATIVE REVIEW[4]

In 1972 Mark Shanley and four high school classmates in San Antonio, Texas, were suspended for publishing and distributing an underground student newspaper entitled "Awakening." The publication discussed current controversial subjects (such as the "injustice" of current drug laws), and it offered information on birth control, venereal disease, and draft and drug counseling. In addition it expressed critical views of the school administration.

The administration believed the contents of "Awakening" to be "potentially disruptive." Moreover distribution of the paper was contrary to a school board policy that was developed to maintain "at all times a proper learning situation" in the San Antonio schools.[5] The policy provided that any student attempt "to avoid the school's established procedure for administrative approval" concerning the production and distribution of petitions or printed documents of any kind "without the specific approval of the principal" shall be cause for suspension.[6]

The facts of the *Shanley* case indicated that the suspended students had used their own resources and facilities to produce the underground paper. They distributed the paper peacefully before and after classes on a public street near the school. The distribution caused no disruption of class activities. The paper, however, was published and distributed "without the specific approval of the principal."

At a hearing before the school board, the students argued that they did not think the board policy applied to conduct outside school hours and off school grounds. The school board nevertheless affirmed the suspension. Objecting to the school board's "bootstrap transmogrification into Super-parent," the real parents of the five students took the case to court. A federal district court upheld the school board, and the parents appealed.

Questions to Consider

1. Are the First Amendment rights of students the same as those of adults? Is there a difference between freedom of press in a public school and on a public street? Should school officials be able to limit the former more strictly than city officials can limit the latter? If so, what factors might justify such differences?
2. Should school officials be able to review the content of student publications before they are distributed?
3. Under what circumstances, if any, can the distribution of a student publication be prohibited?
4. Does the Tenth Amendment, which reserves education to the states, protect school board policy from review by federal courts?*

The legal principles

On behalf of the U.S. Circuit Court of Appeals, Judge Irving Goldberg began his opinion on the *Shanley* case by reviewing the applicable law. First he took note of the principle that courts should not interfere with day-to-day operations of schools as a "platitudinous but eminently sound maxim." On the other hand, he emphasized that "this court laid to rest more than a decade ago the notion that state authorities could

---

* The Tenth Amendment provides: "The powers not delegated to the United States by the Constitution, nor prohibited by it to the States, are reserved to the States respectively, or to the people."

subject students at public-supported educational institutions to whatever conditions the state wished." Of paramount importance, wrote the judge, is "the constitutional imperative that school boards abide by constitutional precepts."

The school board argued that the Tenth Amendment reserved education solely to the states and protects its policy from interference by the federal courts. In caustic and colorful language, Judge Goldberg characterized the school board's legal position as a "judicial believe-it-or-not," a "quaint approach" to the constitutional setting of education today, and a "constitutional fossil, exhumed and respired to stalk the First Amendment once again long after its substance had been laid to rest."

Students and adults. Despite this dismissal of the board's argument, the court did not maintain that the First Amendment rights of students were always the same as those of adults. It noted, for example, that there was a significant difference between the freedom of speech of students in a public school and adults on a public street. Thus, whereas the Supreme Court protected an "inflammatory and vitriolic exhortation" before a paying adult audience, it would not protect the same speech before a high school assembly.[7] Although a school is certainly a marketplace for ideas, "it is just as certainly not a market place."

The educational process, observed Judge Goldberg, "is thwarted by the milling, mooing, and haranguing, along with the aggressiveness that often accompanies a constitutionally-protected exchange of ideas on a street corner." There is a substantive difference between schools and the street corner in weighing the competing interests of a free flow of all expression with the requirement of order and discipline. Thus courts recognize the differences "between what are reasonable restraints in the classroom and what are reasonable restraints on a street corner." This is because students and teachers cannot easily disassociate themselves from expressions directed toward them during school hours, because disciplinary problems in a crowded school setting "seriously sap the educational process," and because schools have the "vital responsibility of compressing a variety of subjects and activities into a relatively confined period of time and space."

Reviewing student materials. Given the necessity for discipline and orderly processes in high schools, the court ruled that it is not necessarily unconstitutional to require that materials destined for distribution to students be submitted to the school administration prior to distribution, as long as the requirement does not operate to stifle the content of any student publication in an unconstitutional manner and is not unreasonably onerous.

When the constitutionality of a school regulation is questioned, the burden of justifying the regulation falls on the school board. The test for curtailing student expression is whether it materially and substantially interferes with the activities of the school. The justification for allowing administrators to screen materials before they are distributed "is to prevent disruption and not to stifle expression."

In sum, the court outlined four principles applicable to student freedom of expression under the First Amendment: (1) expression by high school students can be prohibited if it "in fact" materially and substantially interferes with school activities or with the rights of students or teachers, or if the school administration can "demonstrate reasonable cause to believe" that the expression would engender such material and substantial interference; (2) expression by high school students cannot be prohibited solely because other students, teachers, administrators, or parents may disagree with its content; (3) expression by students may be "subjected to prior screening under clear and reasonable regulation"; and (4) student expression may be limited in "manner, place, or time" by reasonable and equally applied regulations.

Questions to Consider

1. Could school officials prohibit the distribution of "Awakening" if they believed it would cause disruption? What evidence would be necessary to support such a belief? Is the professional judgment of a school administrator adequate evidence?
2. Would the fact that a student newspaper dealt with topics that most students or parents considered highly controversial or disturbing justify restricting distribution?
3. Could student publications be restricted if they were critical, negative, and in basic disagreement with school policy?
4. Do you believe the San Antonio school board policy was constitutional? If not, how would you redraft it so that it would not violate the Constitution?

Can "controversy" stifle distribution?

The court next applied the legal principles to the facts of the *Shanley* case. There was no evidence that the distribution of "Awakening" caused any disturbances on or off campus. Hence there was no "disruption in fact."

The "reasonable forecast of disruption" that might result from student expression is a more difficult test to apply. However, for several reasons Judge Goldberg did not feel the test was difficult to apply in this case. First, the "Awakening" contained no remarks that could be considered obscene, libelous, or inflammatory.* Although there might be circumstances in which prior restraint is reasonable, the school board's burden of demonstrating reasonableness "becomes geometrically heavier" as its decision begins to focus on the content of materials that are not obscene, libelous, or inflammatory.[8] Second, even if the administration were genuinely concerned about several controversial topics mentioned in "Awakening," the discussion of controversial issues is no reason to restrict freedom of expression. "It should be axiomatic at this point in our nation's history," observed the court, "that in a democracy 'controversy' is, as a matter of constitutional law, never sufficient in and of itself to stifle the views of any citizen."

The "controversial" subjects in "Awakening" included a statement advocating a review of the laws regarding marijuana and a statement offering information about birth control, venereal disease, and draft and drug counseling. To the court it appeared odd that an educational institution "would boggle at controversy" to such an extent that "mere representation that students should become informed" about these widely discussed and significant issues should prompt a school to stifle the content of a student publication. Judge Goldberg observed:

Perhaps newer educational theories have become in vogue since our day, but our recollection of the learning process is that the purpose of education is to spread, not to stifle, ideas and views. Ideas must be freed from despotic dispensation by all men, be they robed as academicians or judges or citizen members of a board of education.

The school administration also expressed concern over the negative attitude of the newspaper and its criticism of the administration. In

* *Libel* is a written expression about another person that the writer knows, or should know, is not true, and that injures the person's reputation. A person who is libeled can sue for damages. What constitutes *obscenity* is considered in the *Kitchen* and *Miller* cases in the following section.

response, the court noted that "negativism" is "entirely in the eye of the beholder, and presumably the school administration's eye became fixed upon the criticism by the students." As a person to whom public criticism has been directed, the judge asserted (with "some pained assurance") that "criticism" like "controversy" is not a "bogey," at least not in a democracy. Although constructive criticism is more helpful than other sorts of critiques, the court noted that almost any effort to explain an alternative way of doing things serves to illuminate the issue being questioned. If the criticism is irrational or ill-intentioned, "then surely the American citizenry, even that of high school age, will have enough good sense to attach that much more credibility" to the actions of those unfairly criticized. In any event, aversion to criticism is not a constitutionally reasonable justification for forbidding student expression. The First Amendment's protection of speech and press is part of the Bill of Rights precisely because those regulated "should have the right and even the responsibility" of commenting upon the actions of their appointed or elected regulators.

"One of the great concerns of our time," observed the court, "is that our young people, disillusioned by our political processes, are disengaging from political participation. It is most important that our young people become convinced that our Constitution is a living reality, not parchment preserved under glass." Over thirty years ago the Supreme Court wrote that boards of education have important discretionary functions "but none that they may not perform within the limits of the Bill of Rights." Therefore "it is incredible to us that in 1972 the First Amendment was deemed inapplicable under these circumstances to high school students living at the threshold of voting and dying for their country."

No limits or standards

First, the court held that the way the school board policy was "applied" to the content of "Awakening" was unconstitutional. Next the court critically examined the wording of the policy itself. Its questionable provisions stated that:

Any attempt to avoid the school's established procedure for administrative approval of activities such as the production for distribution and/or distribution of petitions or printed documents of any kind, sort, or type without the specific approval of the principal shall be cause for suspension.[9]

The court found this policy unconstitutional, even if it could be applied in a reasonable manner, because the policy was (1) too broad and vague, (2) contained no standards to guide its application, and (3) contained no fair procedures for resolving disputes concerning its application.

The policy was "overbroad" because it established a "prior restraint" on all written expression by high school students at any time or place and for any reason.* There was no requirement in the policy that the prohibited activity (publishing or distributing any printed document without the principal's approval) have any relationship to maintaining orderly school activities. When questioned at the school board hearing regarding the scope of the policy, the assistant principal responded: "I think that any student publication should be presented to us and since this is broad, I think it is left up to the principal's good judgment." Although not derogating the good judgment of school administrators, Judge Goldberg noted that the Constitution cannot be interpreted loosely "because the motivations behind its infringement may be benign." Since the policy interfered with "protected activity wholly outside the school context," it was "overbroad and unconstitutional."

The policy was also unconstitutional because there were no standards to guide a principal in accepting or rejecting a student publication. Although the court did not doubt the good faith of administrators in attempting to enforce discipline by means of school board policy, it emphasized that "our constitutional system does not permit any school or administrator, however well intentioned, to be the unaccountable imperators of the lives of our children." In order to remedy this lack of standards, the policy in question must include guidelines stating "clear and demonstrable criteria" that administrators should use to evaluate materials submitted to them for prior clearance.

The policy was further defective because it did not state what high school activities were included in the rule. The language of the regulation regarding what was meant by "distribution" was so vague that reasonable men differed substantially as to its meaning. In fact the assistant principal conceded under questioning that one student handing *Time* magazine to another without the permission of the principal might be in violation of the policy.[10] In order to remedy such vagueness, the policy must include guidelines stating the rela-

* Authorities exercise prior restraint when they prohibit, censor, or restrict the publication of materials prior to their distribution.

tionship between the curtailment of distribution and the prevention of substantial disruption of school activities.

Finally, the policy was unconstitutional because it lacked the safeguards required for "due process."* There was no provision in the regulation for appeal from a decision by a principal prohibiting distribution nor was there an indication of how long a principal could take to make her decision. Delays in reviewing newspapers "carry the inherent danger that the exercise of speech might be chilled altogether during the period of its importance." This illustrates the many frustrating and petty ways "the constitutional ideal can be thwarted" by a school administration. Therefore any requirement for screening publications distributable to high school students under a policy purporting to prevent disruption must: (1) state clearly the means by which students are to submit proposed materials to the school administration; (2) state a brief period of time during which the administration must make its decision; (3) state a clear and reasonable method of appeal; and (4) state a brief time during which the appeal must be decided.

In conclusion, Judge Goldberg wrote:

Tinker's *dam to school board absolutism does not leave dry the fields of school discipline. . . . It sets canals and channels through which school discipline might flow with the least possible damage to the nation's priceless topsoil of the First Amendment. Perhaps it would be well if those entrusted to administer the teaching of American history and government to our students began their efforts by practicing the document on which that history and government are based. Our eighteen-year-olds can now vote, serve on juries, and be drafted; yet the board fears the awakening of their intellects without reasoned concern for its effect upon school discipline. The First Amendment cannot tolerate such intolerance. This case is therefore reversed.*[11]

Related issues

In addition to discussing criteria and procedures for administrative review of student publications, Judge Goldberg also commented on several related questions.

---

* The Fourteenth Amendment to the Constitution provides that no state shall deprive any person "of life, liberty or property without due process of law." The meaning and requirements of due process are discussed more fully in Chapter 9.

1. Does a "forecast of disruption" always justify prior restraint of student expression? For example, can a small number of students threaten disruption and thereby justify a school official prohibiting distribution of a controversial publication?

The school administration could use its discretion to regulate the time, place, and manner of distribution more strictly if the content of a student publication could lead to a disturbance by those who hold opposing views. However, students who wish "to reasonably exercise their freedom of expression should not be restrained or punishable at the threshold of their attempts at expression merely because a small, perhaps vocal or violent, group of students with differing views might or does create a disturbance."[12] Thus, in the context of the *Shanley* case, the judge emphasized that even "reasonably forecast disruption" does not always justify prior restraint of student expression.

2. What evidence is needed to constitute a reasonable forecast of disruption? Is the professional judgment or intuition of a principal or superintendent adequate?

Although the court "has great respect for the intuitive abilities of administrators," freedom of expression cannot be stiffled solely on this ground. On the contrary, Judge Goldberg emphasized that the judgment of school administrators must be "substantiated by some objective evidence" to support a reasonable forecast of disruption. Thus the court cautioned administrators against restricting student expression simply on the grounds that their professional intuition leads them to predict substantial disruption.

3. Does the *Shanley* decision mean that *any* attempt by a school to regulate the off-campus distribution of student publications would be unconstitutional?

The decision does not go that far. Although Judge Goldberg pointed out that an offense is "usually punishable only by the authority in whose jurisdiction the offense took place," he noted that the distance from the school might be a significant factor in determining the breadth of the school board's authority. The San Antonio school policy was clearly unconstitutional as it applied to the peaceful distribution of "Awakening," but the judge declined to say that a school could never regulate off-campus distribution of student publications. Rather the court suggested that the constitutionality of regulating specific off-campus activities be determined by applying the legal principles outlined in *Shanley* to the circumstances of each particular case.

Summary. The *Shanley* case indicated that the distribution of student publications cannot be prohibited simply because school officials disagree with their contents. However, the time, place, and manner of distribution can be regulated, and distribution can be prohibited if it substantially interferes with school activities. *Shanley* also held that schools can require prior review of student publications under clear and reasonable regulations. In this case the rules requiring such review were unconstitutional because they vaguely applied to all written expression ("of any kind, sort, or type"), they lacked any reasonable standard for evaluating student expression, and they lacked due process safeguards. Such safeguards include prompt, clear, and fair procedures for review and appeal.

FUJISHIMA v. BOARD OF EDUCATION: PRIOR APPROVAL PROHIBITED (OR THE CASE OF THE COSMIC FROG)[13]

In 1972 another federal court went even further than the court in the *Shanley* decision in protecting the First Amendment rights of students to publish and distribute underground newspapers. The case arose when two Illinois high school seniors, Burt Fujishima and Richard Peluso, were suspended for distributing before and between classes about 350 copies of "The Cosmic Frog," an underground student paper. They were disciplined pursuant to the following Chicago Board of Education rule: "No person shall be permitted . . . to distribute on the school premises any books, tracts, or other publications . . . unless the same shall have been approved by the General Superintendent of Schools."[14] Fujishima and Peluso challenged the constitutionality of this regulation.

The school board argued that its rule was constitutional because it does not require approval of the "contents" of a publication before it may be distributed. "Unfortunately," replied the court, "that is neither what the rule says" nor how the school board has "previously intepreted it." Because the rule requires prior approval of publications, the court held that it was "unconstitutional as a prior restraint in violation of the First Amendment." The court arrived at this conclusion by combining the Supreme Court's holdings in *Near* v. *Minnesota** and *Tinker* v. *Des Moines*. According to appeals court Judge Robert Sprecher:

* *Near* v. *Minnesota ex rel. Olson*, 283 U.S. 697 (1931). *Near* involved a Minnesota statute that allowed state authorities to bring the owner of

Tinker *held that, absent a showing of material and substantial interference with the requirements of school discipline, schools may not restrain the full First Amendment rights of their students. Near established one of those rights, freedom to distribute a publication without prior censorship.*[15]

Cannot administrators restrict the distribution of a publication if they can "forecast" that it will cause substantial disruption? Not according to Judge Sprecher.[16] On the contrary, "the *Tinker* forecast rule," wrote the judge, "is properly a formula for determining when the requirements of school discipline justify *punishment* of students for exercise of their First-Amendment rights. It is not a basis for establishing a system of censorship and licensing to *prevent* the exercise of First-Amendent rights."

This does not mean that a school board may not regulate the distribution of student publications. It may issue rules concerning the time, place, and manner of distribution and may punish students who violate those rules. It may also establish rules punishing students who publish and distribute obscene or libelous literature on school grounds. But, according to Judge Sprecher, schools may not require that publications be submitted to the administration for their approval before students may distribute them.

NOTE: As the *Shanley* and *Fujishima* cases illustrate, federal appeals courts are in conflict about whether schools may constitutionally require students to submit publications to them for review prior to distribution. And the U.S. Supreme Court has not directly ruled on this issue. Some cases like *Fujishima* hold that any requirements for prior review are unconstitutional; others, like *Shanley*,

---

a newspaper to court on charges of publishing "scandalous and defamatory matter" about public officials. According to the statute, unless the owner were able to prove that his charges were true, further publication of the paper would be prohibited. The Supreme Court ruled that the statute violated the freedom of press guaranteed by the First Amendment. The Court's opinion reviewed the rationale of the guarantee and noted that "liberty of the press, historically considered and taken up by the Constitution, has meant principally, although not exclusively, immunity from previous restraints of censorship."

What about writers and publishers that abuse this freedom and slander government officials? In answer the Court wrote: "Public officers, whose character and conduct remain open to debate and free discussion in the press, find their remedies for false accusations in actions under libel laws providing for redress and punishment, and not in proceedings to restrain the publication of newspapers and periodicals."

allow distribution to be restricted under certain circumstances.[17] In the following section, we will examine some of these circumstances.

Testing the Limits of Freedom

OBSCENITY

THE KITCHEN CASE: WHAT IS AN OBSCENE PUBLICATION FOR STUDENTS?[18]

Prior to morning classes, Paul Kitchen was standing outside an entrance to Houston's Waltrip High School selling "Space City," a controversial local newspaper that was not approved by the principal. Kitchen was a junior at Waltrip, and most of his customers were students coming to school. After he had made a number of sales, he was confronted by Gordon Cotton, the high school principal, who bought a copy of the newspaper, read a portion of the second page, and informed the student that he was violating several school board policies. But Kitchen refused to stop selling the paper. He was later suspended and responded with profanity as he left the principal's office. What provoked Cotton's action was the following letter to the editor, which was captioned "High School is Fucked":

Dear Brothers and Sisters,

What ever happened to the skools where you learned? Now you compete for grades, memorize and spit it back out on test day. It is as boring as hell, you don't talk to your friends in class or you get your ass bit. You grow your hair long because you love it and its beautiful, then you get thrown out for being a radical and not wanting to conform to the fucked rules and regulations of the so-called "great-society." Big shit! Think about your brothers and chicanos and blacks getting fucked all the time, only because they weren't born white. You write up a leaflet, pamphlet or newspaper to get your friends to get it together, and see how they are getting fucked, and you get thrown out.

The courses skools have are the same ones they have had for fifty years. They don't try to teach, they just want you to pass and get the fuck out of there. It's their jobs—they are getting paid not us. You try to get the attention of the administration and skool board by boycotts or demonstrations and you get thrown out or busted.

Like some might be trying to learn but you can't because you're busy getting hassled for the length of your hair. Big shit! Hair length or the clothes you wear don't have a fucking thing to do with learning. If you could be in a relaxed atmosphere you might could learn something. But not at skool, they're too busy telling you to "sit up straight," "don't chew gum," "you can't smoke in skool," "don't come back til you cut your hair and wear decent clothes," "don't talk or we'll bust your ass." Man it is a big fucking burn you just can't learn under those conditions.

You have read and heard the same thing before, but we have to quit fucking around and do something. Right now! I don't mean petitions and talks with the administration because they have been tried and failed. Now is the time to go to actions and not talking. Do it! Venceremos!

> Gerald (Bushman) Smith
> MacArthur High
> Houston

P.S. *Space City is the most out-a-sight paper keep putting it out. We just love you. MacArthur Sr. High is fucked.*

Mr. Cotton supended Kitchen because he used profanity in his presence. His other reasons for suspending the student were that he believed the issue of "Space City" Kitchen had sold was obscene, that it urged disobedience of school regulations, that its distribution would cause disturbance in the school, and that it had not been submitted to the principal for approval. He argued that the following school board rules supported his position:

1. A students who wishes to distribute printed materials on or near campus must submit a copy of the publication to the principal "who may take up to one school working day for the purpose of reviewing such publication before its general distribution."
2. The distribution of any publication can be prohibited if, in the opinion of the principal and the attorney for the Houston School District, it: (a) contains "obscene language" or (b) "advocates illegal action or disobedience to published rules on student conduct."
3. The distribution of materials off school premises is subject to these rules "when the manner of distribution is calculated to and in fact does result in possession by students on school premises."

Kitchen believed that the principal's action was an unconstitutional violation of his rights under the First Amendment, and he took his case to court.

Questions to Consider

1. Should Paul Kitchen have been suspended for selling "Space City"? What are the legal and educational issues raised by this case?
2. Was the letter to the editor in "Space City" obscene? What makes material obscene? Who should decide this question and how? Should there be a different standard of obscenity for adults and minors?
3. If students read and commented on "Space City" during class, would this disruption justify prohibiting the distribution of the paper near school?

The opinion of the court

In the opinion of the district court, Judge Seals considered the question of what constitutes an obscene publication and several other important free speech issues for students.

Obscenity. The opinion first reviewed the prevailing legal principles concerning the regulation of obscene material and then applied the law to the facts of the case involving Kitchen. The Supreme Court has recognized that the state sometimes has greater control over the conduct of minors than adults, even where there is an invasion of constitutional freedoms. Thus the Court indicated that a New York obscenity statute should be upheld where there was evidence to support the legislature's finding that "exposure to the condemned material is harmful to minors." But the Court required that material have some relationship to a minor's prurient interest to be considered legally obscene.

In this case the principal testified that the distribution of "Space City" violated school board policy "because it had obscene words in it and these words are obscene in our area, and on the school campus at Waltrip High School." Although Cotton may have believed that a written statement that "High School is Fucked" violated school policy prohibiting obscene language, the trial court noted that the principal failed to consider several important limitations on the obscenity test.

First, he did not consider the issue of "Space City" as a whole. Cotton testified that he had not read the paper beyond the letter to the editor, which appeared on the second page. When a federal court allowed James Joyce's *Ulysses* to be imported into the United States, it had ruled that "a publication must be considered as a whole in order to determine whether it is obscene." The Supreme Court adopted this test in 1957. And in a recent case a federal judge noted: "A publication is not obscene merely because it contains a blunt, Anglo-Saxon word. The Old Testament contains passages of sexual candor, and four-letter words are not used for the first time in the literature of the seventies."[19]

Second, Cotton failed to apply correctly another part of the obscenity test, the definition of the "common community standard" by which a word must be judged. The principal evaluated the newspaper in terms of its probable reception in the Waltrip High School area and concluded that its distribution was "unacceptable" there. However, the community whose "common standards" are at issue must be "the whole community of the Houston Independent School District" and not just the standards of the Waltrip High School community.

Third, Judge Seals ruled that the controversial letter (which was the basis for suspending Kitchen) was not in itself obscene and that "intermittent employment of 'fuck' and its ilk cannot, without more, render a publication obscene." As one expert witness on linguistics testified: "The use of 'fuck' in the declaration, 'High School is Fucked,' has no reference to sex and, in fact, denotes that high school is 'in bad shape . . . in a pretty lousy state of affairs.'" Thus the court held that the first requirement of the obscenity test, that it appeal to a prurient interest in sex, had not been satisfied.[20]

Furthermore, the judge ruled that Houston school administrators forfeited their right to object to the appearance of *fuck* in "Space City" by sanctioning the presence of various books and articles in school libraries that contained similar "vulgarisms." Such language is found in articles in *Atlantic Monthly* and *Harper's Magazine* and in such books as *A Separate Peace* by John Knowles, *The Catcher in the Rye* by J.D. Salinger, *Love Story* by Erich Segal, and *The Confessions of Nat Turner* by William Styron. The principal's justification for this double standard was the "purported educational merit" of the works that were approved by "English teachers, supervisors who know books . . . and know what is best for the students in the Houston Independent School District." On the other hand, one expert witness testified that "Space City" was "a better piece of journalism than, say, the 'Houston Chronicle,'" and therefore it too possessed educational merit. Moreover Judge Seals observed that Cotton seemed to approve the use of vulgar language when it is used "to depict the speech of a bygone era, but not when employed by a contemporary young person to describe his current dissatisfaction with the educational system." The judge indicated that he was "unable to comprehend such a distinction." Consequently he ruled that the school board failed to demonstrate a basis for discrimination between the use of vulgarity in "Space City" and its use in school-approved publications. Thus the court found that neither the letter "High School is Fucked" nor the entire issue of "Space City" in which it appeared was obscene.

In concluding this section of his opinion, Judge Seals noted a recent trend toward a "greater toleration of words that were once scrupulously avoided," and he observed:

> In a society in which the old and the traditional is daily being challenged by the new and the unprecedented, those who seek to guard against the encroachment of taboo words appear to be waging defensive warfare. The court believes that, far from signaling the moral crisis of our civilization, such a development is a healthy indicator of moral progress. In a witchhunt to expunge the momentarily embarrasing, we frequently tolerate language and name-calling that degrades the human spirit, and leaves its heritage of bitterness long after we have forgotten the reddened face and temporary loss of composure that flash our instantaneous reaction to a string of four-letter words.[21]

Disruption. Judge Seals considered as reasonable those school rules that regulated the distribution of materials "near campus" when this resulted "in possession by students on campus." This was because of the court's view that disruption was the proper criterion for restricting distribution. However, the court was quite skeptical of Cotton's attempt to demonstrate that Paul Kitchen's distribution of "Space City" resulted in significant disruption by one student who read the newspaper during class. This "negligible" evidence suggested the need to indicate the type of disruption that can justify disciplining a student distributor. To clarify this question Judge Seals wrote that if a student complies with reasonable rules as to time and place for distribution and "does so in an orderly, nondisruptive manner, then he should not suffer if other students who are lacking in self-control tend to over-react, thereby becoming a disruptive influence." The court therefore concluded that in order to sustain suspension of a student distributor, school officials must demonstrate: "(1) substantial and material interference, and (2) a good faith, but unsuccessful, attempt to discipline the disrupting student or students."

Profanity. The lawyer for the school board repeatedly emphasized Kitchen's use of profanity in the presence of the principal and others. But the court pointed out that this was not the real reason for the student's suspension, since testimony indicated that Cotton had already determined to suspend him at the time Kitchen first used profanity in his presence.[22]

Other abuses. According to Judge Seals, the possibilities of abuse in the application of the Houston School Board rules were numerous and were reflected in this case. Cotton, for example, deemed "Space City" to be "obscene" before seeking the opinion of any attorney, and the regulations did not provide any right to appeal a principal's decision that a publication was unacceptable. The court therefore found that the regulations "fail to obviate the risk" that untrained laymen will misconstrue "obscenity" and "libel" in violation of a student's First Amendment rights.[23]

In conclusion, the court quoted with approval another federal judge who wrote that "the risk taken if a few abuse their First Amendment rights of free speech and press is out-weighted by the far greater risk run by suppressing free speech and press among the young."[24]

MILLER v. CALIFORNIA:
NEW OBSCENITY STANDARDS[25]

In 1973 the U.S. Supreme Court reformulated the test for obscenity used by Judge Seals. In the *Miller* case Chief Justice Burger wrote that the first criterion for determining whether material is obscene is "whether the average person, applying contemporary community standards would find that the work, taken as a whole, appeals to the prurient interests." The second test is whether the work describes sexual conduct "in a patently offensive way," as defined by state law. The effect of these new tests is to indicate that "contemporary community standards" need not be national standards but could be those of a state or perhaps a smaller unit of government. The third test is whether the work, taken as a whole, "lacks serious literary, artistic, political or scientific value." (Here the Court rejected the old criterion that the work must be "utterly without redeeming social value" to be obscene.[26])

Might the new test allow some local governments to suppress unpopular or controversial ideas that could be potentially useful? Not according to Justice Burger, who reaffirmed an earlier opinion that stated:

> All ideas having even the slightest redeeming social importance—unorthodox ideas, controversial ideas, even ideas hateful to the prevailing climate of opinion—have full protection of the [First Amendment] guarantees. . . . But implicit in the history of the First Amendment is the rejection of obscenity as utterly without redeeming social importance.[27]

If a judge had applied the new Supreme Court test to the facts of the case involving Kitchen, would he have found that "Space City" was obscene? Probably not. Vulgar or "dirty" words still do not make a publication legally obscene. The work still must be judged "as a whole." And the community standards to be used in judging a work are those of the state (or perhaps a county or city), but not the standards of an individual school community.

DEFYING SCHOOL RULES AND AUTHORITY

THE KITCHEN CASE ON APPEAL[28]

After Judge Seals ruled in favor of Paul Kitchen, the Houston School District appealed. Because of Kitchen's defiant conduct and flagrant disregard of school regulations, the Fifth Circuit Court of Appeals dismissed his suit. The appeals court did not disagree with the position taken by Judge Seals on most of the legal issues: that the distribution of "Space City" was protected by the First Amendment, that it did not substantially disrupt school activities, and that the language of the newspaper was not constitutionally obscene. The court did not deal with these issues. It merely considered whether Kitchen's conduct in this case "outweighs his claim of First Amendment protection" and gave school officials sufficient grounds for disciplining him.

On behalf of the court Judge Thornberry pointed out that "Paul's conduct can hardly be characterized as the pristine, passive acts of protest 'akin to pure speech' involved in *Tinker*." Rather Kitchen defied Cotton's request that he stop selling the newspapers; he shouted profanity at the principal; he persisted in returning to school during his suspension period; and he "never once attempted to comply with the prior submission rule."

The judge indicated that the results of the case might have been different if Kitchen had challenged the administrative approval rule by "lawful" means. Had he submitted the newspaper to the principal prior to distribution and had it been disapproved, then he could have promptly sought relief, in the courts "without having been first suspended from school."

"Considering Paul's flagrant disregard of established school regulations, his open and repeated defiance of the principal's request, and his resort to profane epithet," the court held that school authorities could discipline him even though his actions were not substantially disruptive. Thus the appeals court did not consider whether the application of the school policy in this case was constitutional or not. Instead it simply asked whether there was "substantial evidence" to support Kitchen's suspension, and it ruled that there was.

The court hastened to point out that "by thus limiting our review in this case, we do not invite school boards to promulgate patently unconstitutional regulations" governing the distribution of student publications. Similarly the court emphasized that this decision should not encourage school authorities "to use otherwise valid regulations as a pretext" for disregarding the rights of students. "Today," concluded Judge Thornberry, "we merely recognize the right of school authorities to punish students for flagrant disregard of established school regulations; we ask only that the student seeking equitable relief from allegedly unconstitutional action by school officials come into court with clean hands."[29]

This does not mean that Judge Seals' ruling concerning the obscenity issue was wrong. Rather we believe the lower court's ruling that "Space City" was not legally obscene was correct and would have been upheld by the appeals court had it ruled on this question, even under the new Supreme Court criteria. This case, however, dramatically illustrates the dangers of ignoring and violating school rules and then objecting to them in court. Here the safer and more effective approach for Paul Kitchen might have been to try to follow the prior approval rules and then challenge them legally if their application by the principal appeared to be unconstitutional.

THE SCHWARTZ CASE[30]

A case similar to that of Kitchen occurred at New York City's Jamaica High School, where Jeffrey Schwartz, a student who had been active in student strikes, was also active in distributing the "High School Free Press," a controversial underground student paper.

After Principal Louis Schuker read Issue 4 of "Free Press," he advised Jeffrey that "under no circumstances" would he be permitted to distribute the paper in school or on school grounds because the principal found Issue 4 "contained four-letter words, filthy references, abusive and disgusting language and nihilistic propaganda."

Four days after the principal's warning, Schwartz and another student appeared on school grounds carrying 32 copies of Issue 5 of "Free Press." This issue criticized Principal Schuker, referring to him as "King Louis," "a big liar," and a person having "racist views and attitudes." The school dean asked Schwartz to surrender his copies of the newspaper. He refused and advised another student to do likewise. As a result of this action, Schwartz was suspended "for contumelious behavior." Nevertheless he returned to school in defiance of the administration's order. Schwartz and his parents believed that the suspension by the school officials was an unconstitutional restriction upon his First Amendment rights.

Judge Bartels acknowledged that the First Amendment protected the distribution of student newspapers. According to the court, however, it was not clear that Schwartz was suspended simply because he distributed an underground paper. Rather it appeared that he was punished for "flagrant and defiant disobedience of school authorities." Although his action might have included dissemination of a student newspaper, it went much further.

When cautioned not to bring copies of "Free Press" to school, Schwartz nevertheless did so; when asked to surrender the papers, he refused; and even after being suspended, he went to school in admitted defiance of an administrative order. These events confirmed "a pattern of open and flagrant defiance of school discipline." If Schwartz wished to test his right to disseminate copies of the "subterranean papers," commented Judge Bartels, "there surely was another way."[31]

In conclusion Judge Bartels stated his opposition to further expansion of educational or judicial permissiveness in cases such as these:

While there is a certain aura of sacredness attached to the First Amendment, nevertheless these First Amendment rights must be balanced against the duty and obligation of the state to educate students in an orderly and decent manner to protect the rights not of a few but of all the students in the school system. The line of reason must be drawn somewhere in this area of ever expanding permissibility. Gross disrespect and contempt for the officials of an educational institution may be justification not only for suspension but also for expulsion of a student.[32]

Thus the suspension of Jeffrey Schwartz was upheld. In the following case, however, we will see how a court in a situation that was similar to both *Schwartz* and *Kitchen* reached a different result by focusing on the unconstitutionality of the school rules rather than on the manners of the student plaintiff.

THE QUARTERMAN CASE[33]

In 1971 Charles Quarterman was a tenth grade student in North Carolina's Pine Forest High School. Without permission he distributed an underground paper that included this statement in capital letters:

. . . WE HAVE TO BE PREPARED TO FIGHT IN THE HALLS AND IN THE CLASS-ROOMS, OUT IN THE STREETS BECAUSE THE SCHOOLS BELONG TO THE PEOPLE. IF WE HAVE TO—WE'LL BURN THE BUILDINGS OF OUR SCHOOLS DOWN TO SHOW THESE PIGS THAT WE WANT AN EDUCATION THAT WON'T BRAINWASH US INTO BEING RACIST. AND THAT WE WANT AN EDUCATION THAT WILL TEACH US TO KNOW THE REAL TRUTH ABOUT THINGS WE CAN NEED TO KNOW, SO WE CAN BETTER SERVE THE PEOPLE! ! ! !

As a result of distributing the paper, Quarterman was suspended pursuant to a school rule that prohibited pupils from distributing any written material while under school jurisdiction without the permission of the school principal. Since Quarterman believed his suspension violated the First Amendment, he went to court to block the enforcement of the rule.

The appeals court acknowledged that federal courts should not intervene in the resolution of school conflicts "which do not directly and sharply implicate basic constitutional values." But the issue concerning the validity of the rule in this case, "is not a simple matter of school discipline; it is not related to any question of state law; it deals 'directly' and 'sharply' with a fundamental constitutional right under the First Amendment." This constitutional issue "is properly justiciable in the federal courts," especially since school administrative procedures provide no alternative method for resolving the controversy.

It might be argued that the newspaper distributed by Quarterman included language that was inflammatory and potentially disruptive. However, he was not disciplined because of the content of the publication, but because he had violated the school rule prohibiting distribution of printed material without permission. Therefore the appeals court did not consider the disruptive potential of the challenged publication but only the constitutional validity of the regulation under which Quarterman was suspended.

The court held that the rule in question was unconstitutional, but not because it required prior permission for the distribution of student publications. The court acknowledged that school authorities may exercise prior restraint upon publications "distributed on school premises during school hours" where they can reasonably forecast substantial disruption of school activities.[34] Rather the problem with the school regulation under which Quarterman was suspended is twofold: (1) it lacked any criteria to be followed by the principal in determining whether to grant or deny permission, and (2) it lacked any procedural safeguards in the form of an "expeditious review procedure" of the decision of the school authorities. Because the regulation included neither procedural safeguards nor guidelines for determining the right to publish or distribute, it was constitutionally defective. Therefore the court ruled that Quarterman was entitled to "declaratory judgment that, as presently framed, the regulation is invalid," and its subsequent enforcement should have been prohibited.

STUDENT CRITICISM OF SCHOOL POLICY AND PERSONNEL THE SCOVILLE CASE[35]

In the fall of 1967 the administration of Illinois' Juliet Central High School published a pamphlet entitled "Bits of Steel." The purpose of the pamphlet was to improve communications between parents and the administration. It included information concerning attendance, discipline, school committees, and student problems. Beginning with a message by the principal, it also included pieces by the freshman and senior deans.

Arthur Breen, a student at Central High, was also senior editor of an underground newspaper entitled "Grass High," published by a fellow student, Raymond Scoville. Breen was very critical of the pamphlet, and because he felt strongly about "Bits of Steel," he wrote a lengthy critique of the pamphlet, which was published as an editorial in "Grass High." The following excerpts reflect the content, style and intent of Breen's critique:

. . . The pamphlet started with a message from the principal, David Ross. This is logical because the entire pamphlet is supposed to be "The Principal's Report to Parents." In this article, Ross states why

the pamphlet was put out and the purpose it is supposed to accomplish, namely, the improvement of communication between parents and administration. He has to be kidding. Surely, he realizes that a great majority of these pamphlets are thrown away by the students, and in this case that is how it should have been. I urge all students in the future to either refuse to accept or destroy upon acceptance all propaganda that Central's administration publishes. . . .

This was followed by an article called "Did You Know?" This was supposedly to inform the parents of certain activities. Intertwined throughout it were numerous rules that the parents were to see their children obeyed. Quite ridiculous.

Next came an article on attendance. There's not much I can say about this one. It simply told the haggard parents the utterly idiotic and asinine procedure that they must go through to assure that their children will be excused for their absences. . . .

The next gem we came across was from our beloved senior dean. Our senior dean seems to feel that the only duty of a dean or parent is to be the administrator of some type of punishment. A dean should help or try to understand a student instead of merely punishing him. Our senior dean makes several interesting statements such as, "Proper attitudes must be part of our lives and the lives of our children." I believe that a person should be allowed to mold his own attitudes toward life, as long as they are not radically anti-social, without extensive interference from persons on the outside, especially those who are unqualified in such fields. Another interesting statement that he makes is "Therefore let us not cheat our children, our precious gifts from God, by neglecting to discipline them!" It is my opinion that a statement such as this is the product of a sick mind. Our senior dean because of his position of authority over a large group of young adults poses a threat to our community. Should a mind whose only thought revolves around an act of discipline be allowed to exert influence over the young minds of our community? I think not. I would urge the Board of Education to request that this dean amend his thinking or resign. The man in the dean's position must be qualified to the extent that his concern is to help the students rather than discipline or punish them. . . . .

The last thing of any interest in the pamphlet was about the despicable and disgusting detention policy at Central. I think most students feel the same way as I about this policy. Therefore I will not even go into it.

In the whole pamphlet I could see only one really bright side. We were not subjected to article written by Mr. Diekelman.

Senior Editor, Grass High[36]

The 14-page edition of "Grass High" that included this editorial also included poetry, essays, and movie reviews. It was distributed to 60 students and faculty at Central High for a price of fifteen cents. A week later Scoville and Breen were suspended. They were later expelled from day classes for a semester by the board of education because the newspaper "constitutes a disregard of and contempt for the authorities charged with the administration" of Central Campus and "encourages the disregard and disobedience of orders promulgated by the duly constituted authorities" of Central High. Although the students were permitted to attend night school, they believed their rights had been violated, and they sued.

The district court upheld the decision of the board because of allegations in the paper that "amounted to an immediate advocacy of and incitement to, disregard of school administrative procedures," especially since "Grass High" was directed to an immature audience.

The students, however, contended that their expulsion violated their First and Fourteenth Amendment freedoms, and they appealed their case.

Questions to Consider

1. Should a student newspaper be permitted to "urge all students in the future to either refuse to accept or destroy upon acceptance" information a school gives them for their parents?
2. Should a student editor be allowed to characterize a school official as having "a sick mind" and posing "a threat to our community"?
3. Could either statement justify punishment by school authorities?
4. What arguments would you use before the court of appeals on behalf of the students?
5. To what degree and under what circumstances should students be permitted to criticize school officials and school policy or urge that school policy be disregarded?

The opinion of the appeals court

In examining this case the court of appeals found that the action of the board of education infringed upon the freedom of expression of Scoville and Breen. Therefore, in order for their expulsion to be upheld, the board had the burden of showing that its action was taken upon "a reasonable forecast of a substantial disruption of school activity."

There was no evidence that the publication caused any disruption of classes, and the board of education did not claim that the publication was libelous. The board based its action on the "objectionable content" of the publication. It argued that the public interest in maintaining the school system outweighed the private interest of the students in publishing "Grass High." The district court agreed and found that the distribution of "Grass High" constituted a "direct and substantial threat to the effective operation of the high school."

However, the court of appeals questioned whether the lower court had adequate facts to support its finding. No evidence was taken, for example, to indicate the ages of the students to whom "Grass High" was sold, what impact the newspaper had on those who bought it, or whether some teachers had approved its sale, as alleged by the students.

On behalf of the appeals court Judge Kiley acknowledged that the editorial imputing a "sick mind" to the dean reflected a "disrespectful and tasteless attitude toward authority." But that alone did not justify a "forecast" of substantial disruption or interference with school policies or the rights of others. "The reference undoubtedly offended and displeased the dean," wrote the judge. But as *Tinker* pointed out, mere expression of student feelings with which school officials do not want to contend, is not enough to justify expulsion.

Nor did the published criticism of the school's disciplinary policies to 60 students and faculty justify the board's action. In fact the court noted that "prudent criticism" by high school students may be socially valuable since students possess a unique perspective on matters of school policy.

The court concluded by recognizing the need for effective school discipline but empasized that school rules must be related "to the state interest in the production of well-trained intellects with constructive critical stances, lest students' imaginations, intellects and wills be unduly stifled or chilled."[37]

Sale of periodicals. Although the Juliet school officials did not object to "Grass High" because it was being sold, can school authorities constitutionally prohibit the sale of all underground newspapers and other periodicals on school grounds? Probably not. The only federal court that has ruled directly on this question held that the flat prohibition of any sale of "distributable literature" was "overbroad and impermissible."[38]

PROHIBITING IN–SCHOOL DISTRIBUTION

THE RISEMAN CASE[39]

Edward Riseman, a junior high school student in Quincy, Massachusetts, asked school officials for permission to distribute leaflets concerning the Vietnam War on school property during class hours. The school committee denied his request. The denial was based not on the content of the material but on an existing school regulation that prohibited school facilities from being used "in any manner for advertising or promoting the interests of any community or nonschool agency or organization."

The trial court ordered the school committee not to interfere with the "orderly and not substantially disruptive distribution" of political materials "on school premises outside of school buildings." Riseman, however, appealed because he wanted to distribute his leaflets in the school, and the court order restricted distribution to "outside" areas.

A U.S. court of appeals struck down this restriction on student conduct. First, it seemed inappropriate to use a school committee rule devised to control "in-school advertising and promotional efforts of organizations" to restrict student expression on public issues. Second, as applied to First Amendment activities, the rule was unconstitutionally "vague" and "overbroad" and "does not reflect any effort to minimize the adverse effect of prior restraint." The court emphasized that school officials had the right to devise sensible rules governing the time, place, and manner of distribution of literature.[40] But the actions of the school committee and lower court went beyond that right. The appeals court could not support the school committee's denial of Riseman's request under a rule restricting advertising. Nor could it support the trial court's order, which only protected distribution "outside" school buildings. For the protection of the First Amendment does not stop "at the schoolhouse door."

CONTROVERSIAL VIEWS
IN SCHOOL–SPONSORED PAPERS

This section includes cases from New York, Alabama, and North Carolina. Two concern freedom of press in college-sponsored newspapers. Although the extent of freedom of high school and college students may not be identical, we have included the college cases because they confront important current issues of students' rights and because the principles outlined by the courts will generally apply to the publications of most public high schools.

THE ZUCKER CASE: CAN A PRINCIPAL PROHIBIT POLITICAL ADS?[41]

In 1967 a group of New York's New Rochelle High School students wanted to publish the following advertisement in the student newspaper: "The United States government is pursuing a policy in Viet Nam which is both repugnant to moral and international law and dangerous to the future of humanity. We can stop it. We must stop it." The group offered to pay the standard student rate for their advertisement. But the principal prohibited its publication. The students charged that this violated their First Amendment rights.

The principal based his action on an administrative policy that prohibits all advertising "which expresses a point of view on any subject not related to New Rochelle High School." School officials argued that the publication was not a commercial paper but an "educational device." The policy prohibiting paid political advertising had been consistently applied and was designed to prevent the paper from becoming "an organ for the dissemination of news and views unrelated to the high school." Since the war was not a school-related activity, school officials maintained that it was "not qualified . . . for advertising treatment."

The district court, however, disagreed. Judge Metzner pointed out that the paper carried a number of articles and letters on controversial political issues, including student opinions about the draft and the war, which shows that the war was considered to be a school-related subject. "This being the case," wrote the judge, "there is no logical reason to permit news stories on the subject and preclude student advertising."

The school newspaper was generally open to the free expression of student opinions in its news, editorials, and letters. Therefore the court held that it was "patently unfair" in light of the free speech doctrine to close to certain students the forum they wanted to use to present their ideas on the Vietnam War.

In conclusion Judge Metzner observed:

This lawsuit arises at a time when many in the educational community oppose the tactics of the young in securing a political voice. It would be both incongruous and dangerous for this court to hold that students who wish to express their views on matters intimately

*related to them, through traditionally accepted nondisruptive modes
of communication, may be precluded from doing so by that same
adult community.*[42]

THE DICKEY CASE: CAN CRITICISM OF
PUBLIC OFFICIALS BE PROHIBITED?[43]

In 1967 Dr. Frank Rose, the president of the University of Alabama,
came under attack by certain legislators for his refusal to censor a
controversial student publication. The publication provided background reading for a campus program entitled "A World in Revolution." It included speeches by advocates of violent revolution and
Black power as well as articles by antirevolutionaries such as the
chairman of the Joint Chiefs of Staff.

Gary Dickey, editor of Alabama's Troy State College newspaper,
prepared a thoughtful editorial criticizing the legislators for their
"harassment" of Dr. Rose. But the faculty adviser and college president ordered Dickey not to publish the editorial. Their objection was
based on a college rule prohibiting editorials in the school paper
that were critical of the governor or the legislature. The reason for
the rule was that a state institution should not criticize those who
fund it.

The faculty adviser furnished substitute material concerning
"Raising Dogs in North Carolina" to be published in lieu of Dickey's
proposed editorial. Dickey, however, decided that the substitute was
not suitable. Acting against the instructions of his adviser, he ar-
ranged to have the space that was to be occupied by the editorial left
blank (except for the title, "A Lament for Dr. Rose") and the word
censored printed diagonally across the blank space. Dickey was
expelled for his action, which was termed "willful and deliberate
insubordination."

In reviewing this case a federal judge acknowledged that rules
that are "necessary in maintaining order and discipline" should be
upheld. But he observed that the maintenance of student discipline
had nothing to do with the rule that was invoked against Dickey. In
fact the rule against criticizing the governor and legislature apparently would have been invoked no matter how reasonable the
criticism had been. Under these circumstances "the conclusion is
compelled that the invocation of such a rule against Gary Dickey
that resulted in his expulsion . . . was unreasonable."

"A state," wrote Judge Johnson, "cannot force a college student
to forfeit his constitutionally protected right of freedom of expression
as a condition to his attending a state-supported school." And the

school cannot punish Dickey for exercising this right "by cloaking his expulsion . . . in the robe of 'insubordination.' " This attempt to characterize his conduct as insubordination "does not disguise the basic fact that Dickey was expelled from Troy State College for exercising his constitutionally guarranteed right of academic and/or political expression."

There may have been no legal obligation on the part of the college to operate a school newspaper or to permit Dickey to continue as editor, but since Troy State did authorize Dickey to be editor, its officials could not expel him for his conduct in this case without violating the First Amendment of the Constitution. Hence, the court ordered that "defendant [Alabama State Board of Education] immediately reinstate Gary Clinton Dickey as a student in Troy State College" and that "costs incurred in this proceeding be . . . taxed against the defendants."

THE JOYNER CASE: IS RESTRICTING A
SEGREGATIONIST PAPER UNCONSTITUTIONAL?[44]

In a recent federal case the president of predominantly Black North Carolina Central University withdrew financial support from the official student newspaper because of its announced segregationist editorial policy. The first issue of the newspaper under this new policy made clear its opposition to the admission of more white students. For example, one article stated:

There is a rapidly growing white population on our campus. . . . We want to know why they are here? How many are here? Why more and more come every year (by the hundreds)? . . .

Black students on this campus have never made it clear to those people that we are indeed separate from them, in so many ways, and wish to remain so.

The article concluded with the words of H. Rap Brown:

"I do what I must out of the love for my people. My will is to fight. Resistance is not enough. Aggression is the order of the day." And moreover, we will take nothing from the oppressor, but only in turn get that which is ours.

Now will you tell me, whose institution is NCCU? Theirs? Or ours?[45]

The president wrote the student editor to inform him that the paper "does not meet standard journalistic criteria nor does it represent fairly the full spectrum of views on this campus." Therefore the president indicated he would withhold funds for future issues until agreement could be reached regarding publication standards. When no agreement was reached, the president "irrevocably terminated the paper's financial support." The editor believed this action abridged freedom of the press and sued to regain school support.

A federal appeals court acknowledged that a college need not establish a newspaper or may permanently discontinue publication for reasons unrelated to the First Amendment. But Judge Butzner noted that if a college has a student newspaper, "its publication cannot be suppressed because college officials dislike its editorial comment." According to the judge this principle has been extensively applied to strike down every form of censorship of student publications at state-supported institutions. In an extensively documented sentence (which summarized the holdings of more than 15 recent related cases), the court wrote:

Censorship of constitutionally protected expression cannot be imposed by suspending the editors, suppressing circulation, requiring imprimatur of controversial articles, excising repugnant material, withdrawing financial support, or asserting any other form of censorial oversight based on the institution's power of the purse.[46]

Since the student publication caused no disruption, did not reject opposing viewpoints, and did not incite anyone to harass or interfere with white students or faculty, the administration was not justified in its restriction of free expression. Although the president found the paper's editorial comment to be abhorrent, contrary to university policy, and inconsistent with constitutional guarantees of equality, the court held that the president "failed to carry the heavy burden of showing justification for the imposition of a prior restraint on expression."[47]

THE JACOBS CASE: A LIBERAL
RULING UNDER REVIEW[48]

In December 1973 a U.S. appeals court ruled in favor of a group of high school students who challenged a number of administrative policies restricting the distribution of written material by students in public schools. The court invalidated a series of specific regulations which had prohibited the distribution of (1) unsigned material, (2) articles not written by students or teachers, (3) any sale of literature at school, and (4) any distribution during class hours. The court also held that a rule prohibiting distribution of literature "likely to produce significant disruption of the normal educational process" was unconstitutionally vague and overbroad. In addition, it ruled that the occasional presence of "earthy" words in unofficial student newspapers did not render them obscene. The opinion is an unusually liberal defense of freedom of expression for students.

On June 3, 1974 the U.S. Supreme Court agreed to review this decision.[49] The Court's ruling in this case will probably not be unanimous, and the High Court may not go as far as the appeals court in protecting student freedom. Nevertheless, the Court's decision in *Jacobs* is likely to establish national standards for regulating the distribution of student publications in public schools as well as for determining what constitutes obscenity for minors.

SUMMARY AND CONCLUSIONS

Before *Tinker* administrators generally had "broad discretion" to censor school newspapers and punish students for distributing publications that "damaged school discipline" unless students could show that the school's actions were clearly unreasonable. This is no longer the law. Today expression by public school students cannot be prohibited unless it substantially and materially interferes with school activities or with the rights of others. In addition, expression by students cannot be restricted solely because teachers, administrators, parents, or other students disagree with what is being said or because the subjects discussed are unpopular or controversial. When students question the constitutionality of a restriction concerning the distribution of materials, school officials have the burden of justifying the restriction.

This does not mean that the First Amendment rights of students are always the same as adults. Because there must be order as well as free expression in the schools, authorities can impose reasonable restraints on the distribution of materials by students, such as regulating the time, place, and manner of distribution. In addition some courts hold that administrators can regulate distribution near school when this might result in substantial disruption by students on campus.

Distribution also can be restricted if school officials can demonstrate "reasonable cause to believe" that the expression would cause substantial disruption. But neither the discussion of controversial topics nor aversion to criticism is a constitutional justification for prohibiting student expression. And even a "reasonable forecast of disruption" would not always justify such a prohibition unless administrators first tried to control the potential disrupters.

Prior review. Courts differ on the question of whether school officials can constitutionally require students to submit publications to them for review prior to distribution. A few courts have held such requirements to be an unconstitutional "prior restraint." Thus *Fujishima* ruled that school officials should not be allowed to restrain student publications before their distribution. In that case the court emphasized that schools could *regulate* the distribution of publications and could *punish* students who distributed materials that were libelous, obscene, or caused substantial disruption; but administrators could not require their approval in advance or *prevent* distribution of materials.

Other courts, however, hold that school rules can require prior review of student expression. But such rules would be unconstitutional if they were overbroad and vague, had no clear standard to guide their application, or had no fair and prompt appeal procedures. Thus the review provisions in *Shanley* were not valid because they (1) vaguely applied to *all* written student expression, (2) had no standard for evaluation (but depended on the "benign intention" of school officials), and (3) lacked due process safeguards. Due process requires that any regulations for administrative screening of publications before distribution must state (1) a brief period of time for administrative review, (2) a reasonable method for appeal, and (3) the time within which the appeal must be decided.

The limits of freedom

Obscenity. Although the distribution of obscene materials is not protected, a publication is not legally obscene merely because it contains blunt, vulgar, or "dirty" words. Applying the new Supreme Court test, material for students would be considered obscene if the work (1) "appeals to the prurient interest" of minors, (2) describes sexual conduct "in a patently offensive way," *and* (3) "lacks serious literary, artistic, political, or scientific value." In applying these tests, the material must be judged "as a whole" and the "community standards" are not simply the standards of an individual school community. In addition school officials may not be able to object to certain vulgar language in student publications if the same vulgarisms are found in books and articles in the school library.

Defying school rules. When a student is disciplined for distributing materials in a manner that is "defiant" or "grossly disrespectful," then some courts may uphold his punishment without considering his claim that the rules restricting distribution were unconstitutional. Thus in the *Kitchen* case an appeals court concluded that a student's "flagrant disregard" of school regulations precluded his seeking relief (because he did not come into court with "clean hands"). Similarly in *Schwartz* a student's "gross disrespect and contempt" for school officials led the court to uphold his suspension despite his First Amendment claim.

On the other hand, when a student "lawfully" challenged an unconstitutional restriction concerning distribution of underground newspapers in *Quarterman*, the regulation was declared void even though the content of the publication was potentially disruptive. And *Scoville* upheld the right of an underground student paper to strongly criticize school administrators and their policies. Although the underground newspaper's editorial reflected a "disrespectful and tasteless attitude toward authority," the editor's punishment was ruled illegal since his criticism was protected by the First Amendment and did not result in substantial disruption.

School officials have a right to devise rules governing the time and place of distribution. They could, for example, prohibit distribution in classrooms, during and just before classes, and in narrow school corridors. But officials could not prohibit all distribution on school property, and *Riseman* even held that peaceful distribution must be allowed in school and during school hours.

School-sponsored publications. School officials naturally have some control over a publication they sponsor. They can, for example, probably determine its goals and focus, the criteria for selecting editorial staff, the level of financial support, whether it should include nonstudent writing, or whether it should accept advertising. Although the limits of administrative control over public school publications are not precise, officials clearly do not have total control over their contents. Thus *Zucker* held that students could not be prohibited from placing an antiwar advertisement in a school-sponsored newspaper that had been used as a forum for the expression of diverse student views. *Dickey* ruled that a student editor could not be prohibited from publishing responsible criticism about public officials.

And *Joyner* indicated that a state college could not terminate funding for a student newspaper merely because of its editorial policy. Although *Dickey* and *Joyner* concerned state-supported colleges, the holdings in these cases would probably apply to public secondary schools and prohibit principals from suppressing or censoring a student paper simply because they disliked its editorial content. As one federal judge wrote: "The state is not necessarily the unfettered master of all it creates. Having established a particular forum for expression, officials may not then place limitations upon the use of that forum which interfere with protected speech."[50]

Future prospects. In the *Jacobs* case, a federal appeals court broadly defended student rights to use vulgar and "earthy" language in unofficial newspapers, to publish unsigned materials, and to sell and distribute these papers on school grounds. As this book goes to press, *Jacobs* is being reviewed by the U.S. Supreme Court. Whatever the legal outcome of this case, we would agree with the federal judge who concluded that "the risk taken if a few abuse their First Amendment rights of free speech and press is outweighed by the far greater risk run by suppressing free speech and press among the young."[51]

NOTES

[1] 462 F.2d 960, 973, 978 (5th Cir. 1972).

[2] *Miller* v. *California*, 93 S.Ct. 2607 (1973).

[3] *State ex rel Dresser* v. *District Board of School District No. 1*, 116 N.W. 232 (Ct. App. Wisc. 1908).

[4] *Shanley* v. *Northeast Independent School District*, 462 F.2d 960 (5th Cir. 1972).

[5] In a preamble to the policy, the board noted that "any distraction on a school campus works against the achievement of educational objectives and against the best interests of the entire student body," and that the student government structure "provides opportunity for constructive involvement of all students in discussion and expression of opinion on appropriate topics."

[6] The school board also prohibited a student "sit-in, stand-in, walkout," or other related unauthorized activity.

[7] *Terminiello* v. *Chicago*, 337 U.S. 1 (1948).

[8] Justice Goldberg noted that the content of the underground publication in this case "could easily surface, flower-like, from its underground abode. As so-called 'underground' newspapers go, this is probably one of the most vanilla-flavored ever to reach a federal court." *Shanley* at 964.

[9] *Id.* at 964/965.

10 To further illustrate the problems with the wording of the policy in question, Judge Goldberg wrote:

If the school board here can punish students on the strength of this blunderbuss regulation for passing out any printed matter, off school grounds, outside school hours and without any disruption whatsoever, then why cannot the school board also punish any student who hands a bible to another student on a Saturday or Sunday morning, as long as it does so in good faith? We resist the temptation to answer [Id. at 977].

11 *Id.* at 978.

12 In this regard Judge Goldberg quoted with approval a strong statement by the Supreme Court explaining the importance of protecting controversial speech:

A function of free speech under our system of government is to invite dispute. It may indeed best serve its high purpose when it induces a condition of unrest, creates dissatisfaction with conditions as they are, or even stirs the people to anger. Speech is often provocative and challenging. It may strike at prejudices and preconceptions and have profound unsettling effects as it presses for acceptance of an idea. That is why freedom of speech, though not absolute . . . is nevertheless protected against censorship or punishment, unless shown likely to produce a clear and present danger of a serious substantive evil that rises far above public inconvenience, annoyance or unrest. There is no room under our Constitution for a more restrictive view [Shanley at 973 quoting Terminiello v. Chicago, 337 U.S. 1 (1948)*].*

13 *Fujishima* v. *Board of Education,* 460 F.2d 1355 (7th Cir. 1972).

14 *Id.* at 1356.

15 *Id.* at 1357.

16 Judge Sprecher listed several cases that seemed to support his position. He also acknowledged that some cases, like *Shanley*, allowed schools to require prior submission of publications if accompanied by reasonable procedural safeguards. The court, however, believed that cases such as *Shanley* erred in interpreting *Tinker* to allow prior review "as a tool of school officials in 'forecasting' substantial disruption" of school activities. The judge wrote:

Tinker in no way suggests that students may be required to announce their intentions of engaging in certain conduct beforehand so school authorities may decide whether to prohibit the conduct. Such a concept of prior restraint is even more offensive when applied to the long-protected area of publication.

17 For example, in *Riseman* v. *School Committee of Quincy,* 439 F.2d 148 (1971), the First Circuit Court of Appeals invalidated a rule against advertising on school grounds that was used to prohibit the distribution of political literature. The court said the rule was impermissible as a prior restraint, and it ruled that the school could not require advance approval of the content of student publications. The Fourth Circuit, in *Quarterman* v. *Byrd,* 453 F.2d 54 (1971), enjoined the enforcement of a rule that required prior permission from the principal before distributing any material and that lacked procedural safeguards for students. However, in *Eisner*

v. *Stamford Board of Education*, 440 F.2d 803 (1971), the Second Circuit allowed schools to require prior submission of publications if accompanied by elaborate procedural safeguards. This was similar to the position taken by the Fifth Circuit in the *Shanley* case.

In the *Fujishima* case, the Seventh Circuit joined the First and Fourth in opposing prior review of student publications and explicitly rejected the holding in *Eisner*. "We believe," wrote Judge Sprecher, "that the court erred in *Eisner* in interpreting *Tinker* to allow prior restraints of publication—long a constitutionally prohibited power," in cases where administrators could forecast that substantial disruption would result from the distribution of such publications.

18 *Sullivan* v. *Houston Independent School District*, 333 F.Supp. 1149 (S.D. Tex. 1971). The name of this case is taken from a 1969 decision involving another Houston student, Dan Sullivan, who was suspended because he distributed an underground newspaper that criticized school officials. As a result of a class action brought by Sullivan, a federal district court issued a permanent injunction prohibiting the Houston School District from unreasonably restricting the distribution of student papers. *Sullivan* v. *Houston Independent School District*, 307 F.Supp. 1328 (S.D. Tex. 1969). The case described here has the same legal title because Paul Kitchen, the student who initiated this case, asked the same federal court to hold the Houston School District in contempt for violating the 1969 permanent injunction the court had issued after the first *Sullivan* case (which is discussed in Chapter 9).

19 *United States* v. *Head*, 317 F.Supp. 1138, 1143 (E.D. La. 1970).

20 As one fifteen-year-old female student testified about the use of words like "fuck": "To young people, it's more or less accepted. I mean, it's an everyday happening. And ordinary people, they just aren't used to it, and they were raised up to believe that it was wrong." *Sullivan* at 1165.

21 *Id.* at 1167. In addition Judge Seals quoted with approval a 1965 statement printed in *Christianity and Crisis*, which observed:

For Christians the truly obscene ought not to be the slick-paper nudity, nor the vulgarities of dirty old or young literati. . . . What is obscene is that material, whether sexual or not, that has as its basic motivation and purpose the degradation, debasement and dehumanization of persons. The dirtiest word in the English language is not "fuck" or "shit" in the mouth of a tragic shaman but the word "Nigger" from the sneering lips of a Bull Connor [Ibid.].

22 On the other hand, Judge Seals warned that in the future, students should come to court "with clean hands," for the court cannot sanction "a student's defiance of every regulation he believes to be a constitutional infraction." *Id.* at 1177.

23 In addition Judge Seals noted that "prior restraint is so little favored by the United States Constitution" that school officials "assume an extremely heavy burden in attempting to justify its imposition." In this case officials did not produce proof that would justify the infringement of Paul Kitchen's right to be free of prior restraint.

24 *Id.* at 1161.

25 *Miller* v. *California*, 413 U.S. 13 (1973).

26 The problem with the old test, according to Justice Burger, is that it required the prosecution "to prove a negative, i.e., that the material was *utterly* without redeeming social value—a burden virtually impossible to discharge under our criminal standards of proof."

27 *Chaplinsky* v. *New Hampshire*, 315 U.S. 568, 571–572 (1942).

28 *Sullivan* v. *Houston Independent School District*, 475 F.2d 1071 (5th Cir. 1973). This is the same appeals court that decided the *Shanley* case examined earlier in the chapter.

29 *Id.* at 1077 The "clean hands" doctrine allows a court to deny relief to a litigant if he did not act fairly, justly, or equitably in the case.

30 *Schwartz* v. *Schuker*, 298 F.Supp. 238 (E.D. N.Y. 1969).

31 Schwartz's lawyer apparently argued that college students have been protected in similar cases. In response the court wrote that "the activities of high school students do not always fall within the same category as the conduct of college students, the former being in a much more adolescent and immature stage of life and less able to screen fact from propaganda."

32 *Id.* at 242.

33 *Quarterman* v. *Byrd*, 453 F.2d 54 (4th Cir. 1971).

34 This was similar to the *Shanley* case discussed above. *Quarterman* also pointed out that the application of the First Amendment "may properly take into consideration the age or maturity of those to whom it is addressed." Thus some publications may be protected when directed to adults but not when made available to minors. Similarly a difference may exist between publications distributed in a secondary school and those distributed in a college. Therefore a high school student's right to freedom of expression may be curtailed by regulations "reasonably designed to adjust these rights to the needs of the school environment."

35 *Scoville* v. *Board of Education of Juliet Township*, 425 F.2d 10 (7th Cir. 1970).

36 *Id.* at 16.

37 In a dissenting opinion Judge Castle wrote that the "admitted action" by Breen and Scoville in calling upon their fellow students "to flaunt the school's administrative procedures by destroying, rather than delivering to their parents," materials given to the students for that purpose justified the school's disciplinary action. Judge Castle did not believe more evidence was necessary to support the district court's decision. "In my view," he wrote, the students' "advocacy of disregard of the school's procedures carried with it an inherent threat to the effective operation of a method the school authorities had a right to utilize for the purpose of communicating with the parents of students."

38 *Jacobs* v. *Board of School Commissioners of Indianapolis*, 349 F.Supp. 605 (S.D. Ind. 1972).

39 *Riseman* v. *School Committee of Quincy*, 439 F.2d 148 (1st Cir. 1971).

[40] An earlier order of the appeals court, concerning distribution on all school grounds, including buildings, stated in part:

Students shall have the right to engage in orderly and not substantially disruptive distribution of such papers, provided that neither the distributors nor the distributees are then engaged, or supposed to be engaged, in classes, study periods, or other school duties. Nothing in this order shall prevent the principal of any school from promulgating reasonable rules setting forth in detail the times, places within that school, and manner that such matter may be distributed, provided that no advance approval shall be required of the content *of any such papers. However, the principal may require that no papers be distributed unless, at the time that the distribution commences, a copy thereof, with notice of where it is being and/or is to be distributed, be furnished him* [Italics added]. *Id.* at 149.

[41] *Zucker* v. *Panitz,* 299 F.Supp. 102 (S.D. N.Y. 1968).

[42] *Id.* at 105.

[43] *Dickey* v. *Alabama State Board of Education,* 273 F.Supp. 613 (M.D. Ala. 1967).

[44] *Joyner* v. *Whiting,* 477 F.2d 456 (4th Cir. 1973).

[45] *Id.* at 458.

[46] *Id.* at 460.

[47] The case also involved the editor's policy that no whites would serve on the staff and no advertising would be accepted from white merchants. Concerning these issues, the court upheld the president's right to prohibit racial discrimination in staffing the newspaper and accepting advertising. But the court did not agree that the appropriate remedy for the paper's discrimination was the permanent cessation of financial support. "To comply with the First Amendment," wrote Judge Butzner, "the administration's remedy must be narrowly drawn to rectify only the discrimination in staffing and advertising." *Id.* at 462–464.

[48] *Jacobs* v. *Board of School Commissioners,* 490 F.2d 601 (7th Cir. 1973).

[49] 42 *Law Week* 3666 (1974).

[50] *Trujillo* v. *Love,* 322 F.Supp. 1266, 1270 (D. Colo. 1971). The case involved the suspension of a student editor and faculty review of "controversial" writing in a college newspaper. Because the policy regarding faculty review was unclear, the court held that it abridged the editor's freedom of expression and that her suspension was unconstitutional.

[51] *Eisner* v. *Stamford Board of Education,* 314 F.Supp. 832, 836 (D. Conn. 1970).

4
Freedom of association

The right of Americans freely to associate with whomever they choose is universally recognized in a democratic society.
—Robinson v. Sacramento School District[1]

While the last thing we would wish to do is to interfere with the right of freedom of association or the civil rights of the students involved, we must maintain an orderly system of administration of our public schools.
—Passel v. Fort Worth School District[2]

When they ask for change, they, the students, speak in the tradition of Jefferson and Madison and the First Amendment.
    The First Amendment does not authorize violence. But it does authorize advocacy, group activities, and espousel of change.
—Healy v. James[3]

Introduction

"Among the rights protected by the First Amendment," wrote Supreme Court Justice Lewis Powell, "is the right of individuals to associate to further their personal beliefs." Although freedom of association is not explicitly set out in the First Amendment, the Supreme Court has long held the right to be "implicit in the freedoms of speech, assembly, and petition."[4]

What behavior is protected by this right? Courts have held that freedom of association allows Americans the right to organize all types of social and political groups if their purposes are legal. It also protects citizens who wish to organize for the purpose of promoting unpopular and undemocratic causes. Thus courts have protected the right of the American Nazi party to hold meetings and demonstrations and to recruit new members. Similarly the Constitution protects adults who wish to organize and promote the goals of the Ku Klux Klan, the Communist party, or the Black Panther party, as well as sexist and racist social organizations.

Do students attending public schools have similar rights? Should students be able to organize fraternal or secret clubs that promote undemocratic practices? Should they be able to form radical political organizations that promote a revolutionary philosophy and discuss illegal behavior? Are such groups entitled to official recognition by school authorities? Should they be allowed to use school facilities? Do student groups have a right to demonstrate on school grounds? Can administrators prohibit membership in out-of-school organizations that influence in-school behavior? Can officials prohibit students from inviting controversial speakers to school? These are some of the questions confronted by the cases presented in this chapter.

Fraternities, Sororities, and Secret Clubs

HISTORICAL PERSPECTIVE: CAN SECRET SOCIETIES BE PROHIBITED?[5]

In 1909 the California legislature declared it unlawful for any elementary or secondary school student "to join or become a member of any secret fraternity, sorority or club" formed from among students attending public schools. After the adoption of this act, Doris Bradford, a student at San Francisco's Girls High School, joined a "secret, oathbound Greek letter sorority" known as Omega Nu. As a result Doris was suspended. She took her case to court, arguing that the law was unfair in allowing fraternities and sororities at public colleges but prohibiting them among precollege students.

Questions to Consider

1. Should school boards be able to prohibit secret student organizations? What are the reasons for upholding or prohibiting such regulations?

2. Should schools be able to regulate any off-campus student organizations? Under what circumstances would such rules be reasonable?
3. Should a school's power to regulate student organizations depend
on the age of the students? Should different standards be applied
to high school (or elementary) students than to college students?
4. Should schools be able to prohibit "undemocratic" organizations?
Could honor societies, leadership fraternities, or charity clubs be
prohibited?

The opinion of the court

In the *Bradford* case the legislation prohibiting secret societies was
upheld. Explaining the California appeals court's decision, Judge Ker-
rigan reviewed the history of Greek letter societies before 1912 and
wrote:

> *In time many educators came to believe that whatever good might
> be claimed for college fraternities was not shared by secret fraternities
> organized among boys and girls attending the preparatory schools
> whose characters are yet unformed. It has been said of such societies
> that they tend to engender an undemocratic spirit of caste, to pro-
> mote cliques, and to foster a contempt for school authority. Doubtless
> these organizations have many redeeming features. . . . Nevertheless,
> in order to curb what is said to be their evil effects in secondary
> schools, rules and regulations have recently been adopted by boards
> of education in many of the cities of the country . . . and courts have
> uniformly held valid reasonable rules adapted by school authorities
> to prevent the establishment and development of those secret so-
> cieties.*[6]

History repeated

After the *Bradford* decision the Omega Nus reorganized themselves
into a club called K.Ts, and another high school sorority, Alpha
Sigma, became the Manana Club. Other Greek letter organizations
followed the same pattern. During the following decades these "new"
clubs abandoned their secret handshakes, Greek letter names, and
much of the "ritualistic nonsense which had been part of their pro-
genitors."[7] However, many educators believed that there was no real
difference between them and the original fraternities and sororities
that had been their parent organizations. Therefore in 1959 the Cal-

ifornia legislature enacted a revised antifraternity law, and various school districts adopted rules designed to implement the new statute.

On the basis of this law the Sacramento Board of Education resolved that it was "detrimental and inimical to the best interests of the public school" and to the "government, discipline, and morale of the pupils" for any student to belong to any fraternity, sorority, or nonschool club that perpetuates its membership by the decision of its own members. The board determined that such organizations "engender an undemocratic spirit in the pupils." The regulation, however, was not intended to prohibit membership in nationally known movements "organized for citizenship training," such as the YMCA, the Girl Scouts, or youth groups sponsored by recognized churches and service clubs.

THE CASE OF THE MANANA CLUB: ARE UNDEMOCRATIC CLUBS UNCONSTITUTIONAL?[8]

When the Sacramento Board of Education began to enforce its rule against the Manana Club, one of its members, Judy Robinson, went to court to have the rule declared unconstitutional. She argued that the club was not a secret society and submitted to the court a copy of the club's constitution and bylaws, which described its objectives as being "literature, charity and democracy." The trial court agreed with Robinson's position. However, a California appeals court "looked beyond" the club's stated objectives, found that it had very different purposes, and upheld the rules of the school board.

In regard to Robinson's contention that only secret organizations were prohibited, the appeals court wrote that when the legislature referred to "secret" fraternities, sororities and clubs, it spoke generally of those social organizations that (1) derive their membership principally from the public schools, (2) use a selection process designed to create a membership composed of the "socially elite," and (3) try to maintain class segregation and distinction by "self-perpetuation, rushing, pledging," and admitting a "select few" from the total student body. Those were the practices that the legislature considered harmful and that it sought to stamp out. "And those were the practices," wrote Judge Pierce, "which these clubs, the offspring of the fraternities and sororities, have carefully nurtured and perpetuated over the years."

The practices and rules of the Manana Club belied its stated democratic objectives. Only 20 girls throughout the entire Sacramento school system could be "rushed" each semester, each candidate had to be sponsored by three members, and new members were chosen through a secret process by an admissions committee that investigated each candidate.

Despite these factors Judy Robinson contended that the school board rule violated the First Amendment, which guaranteed her freedom of association. The court acknowledged that the right of Americans "freely to associate with whomever they choose is universally recognized as fundamental in a democratic society." However, the court pointed out that like all rights this one does not function "in a social or political vacuum, which means that under some circumstances it is legitimate for government to regulate in order to protect other rights." Judge Pierce further noted that the right of a state to forbid student membership in secret societies in public institutions "is now well-established in American constitutional law."

The court further pointed out that statutes in over 20 states outlawed high school fraternities and organizations such as the Manana Club;[9] that numerous cases over the past fifty years had upheld such legislation against attack on the ground of unconstitutionality;[10] and that only a 1922 Missouri case had held that such prohibitions by a school board went beyond its authority.[11]

The court acknowledged that adults have the right to join together socially, that this includes the right to form clubs ("secret or nonsecret") and the right to be "as snobish as they choose." Moreover any attempt to interfere with that right by the legislature would be "arbitrary, unreasonable, and therefore in violation of the First Amendment." But the court emphasized that the constitutional right of free assembly as applied to adults (or even college students) was not involved in this case. Here we are not dealing with adults "but with adolescents in their formative years."

The court also acknowledged that high school fraternities, sororities, and clubs undoubtedly accomplish some good—"mostly to those who belong to them, giving them a sense of security, a feeling of being wanted." But the school board had said that the harm these societies do outweighs the good. School boards are professional in the field; the courts are laymen. "Under these circumstances," wrote Judge Pierce, "we cannot superimpose our judgment over theirs."

Here the school board was not dealing with activities that occurred only within the home. It was dealing "under express statutory mandate" with activities that reached into the school and that were believed "to interfere with the educational process." Thus Judge Pierce concluded that the activities of these prohibited organizations were designed "not to foster democracy (as the Manana Constitution preaches) but to frustrate democracy (as the Manana Club by its admitted activities practices)."

THE PASSEL CASE: PROHIBITING
MEMBERSHIP IN CHARITY CLUBS

A recent freedom of association case that spent several years winding its way through the Texas courts was finally decided in 1970.[12] It involved a 1966 Fort Worth school board regulation requiring the parents of all students entering high school to certify that their son or daughter was not and would not become a member of any fraternity, sorority, or secret society. The rule was authorized by state legislation similar to the California statute in the *Robinson* case. Students who failed to submit the form were not enrolled in school.

Janie Passel belonged to a "charity club" that was prohibited by the board policy since it admitted new members from the student body of the public schools based on the decision of the old members and did not allow students to join by their own free choice. The club held meetings and social functions off school premises. Passel contended that the statute and regulation as applied to her club was an unconstitutional interference with her freedom of association.

The Texas Court of Civil Appeals disagreed. It indicated that similar cases in the past had held that a board of education "may forbid fraternities, sororities or other secret organizations such as the charitable clubs here involved." The purpose of the regulation was not to hamper any educational organization that had standards "by which any student can qualify on the same basis as other students." But in the case of the charity clubs, it was admitted that "the basis for membership is by the secret ballot of the clubs themselves rather than upon rules under which any student could qualify."

The court acknowledged that the argument that "causes us the most concern" was that the statute involved constituted an invasion of the right of parental control over their children. "Certainly," wrote Judge Langdon, "neither the school system or the church or any other organization however well motivated should or could replace parents in the rearing of a child." Nevertheless the court ruled that requiring parents to sign the school board form did not constitute such an invasion of parental control as to render the regulation constitutionally invalid. The court concluded:

> *We believe that our duly constituted independent school districts with appropriate guidance from the legislature should run our public school system. While the last thing we would wish to do is to inter-*

fere with the right of freedom of association or the civil rights of the students involved, we must maintain an orderly system of administration of our public schools.[13]

For these reasons the Court of Civil Appeals declined to hold the statute unconstitutional.

A dissenting view

Janie Passel next appealed to the Texas Supreme Court. Despite her persistence the state high court also failed to hold that the Texas law violated her civil rights.[14] Justice Smith, however, strongly disagreed. In a dissenting opinion, he emphasized that the nature of the organization to which Janie Passel belonged was a "charity" club whose purpose was to "promote friendship" among its members. The dissent pointed out that no club meetings were to be conducted during school hours or on school property. The objective of the club (and others that belonged to a council of charity clubs) was "to contribute to local charitable institutions through proceeds from various non-professional entertainments and to promote loyalty, congeniality, lofty ideals and character among high school students, girls and boys." There was "no hint in the evidence" that the charity clubs were charged with subversive or any other improper activity, except in the selection of members contrary to the rule of the school district. On the other hand, the evidence showed that certain clubs had raised as much as $4,000 for such organizations as the Mental Health Association and the Fort Worth Children's Hospital.[15]

The dissent pointed out that the legislature had only authorized school boards to regulate organizations "in" the public school system. Justice Smith therefore argued that since these charity clubs were not in the schools, they could not be regulated by school boards. (On the other hand, if the statute had been intended to apply to clubs that were outside the schools, then it was unconstitutional.) Moreover, there is nothing in the evidence to authorize the school board to suspend the members of these clubs and "deprive them of the protection in their right of freedom of association" guaranteed by the First and Fourteenth Amendments to the Constitution. "In my opinion," wrote the justice, "the statute is unconstitutional not only because of deprivation of freedom of association, but also because of discrimination in favor of those clubs or organizations specifically exempted," such as Boy Scouts, Hi-Y, De Molay, and similar educational organizations.

Justice Smith acknowledged that some behavior attributed to club members might have been distracting and subject to regulation. But he concluded: "I cannot conceive of any justification for a requirement that these clubs be disbanded or that the children be suspended from the school of their choice."

This dissent would seem to be in accord with the principles of *Tinker* and a trend of decisions expanding student rights. However, no reported cases have yet overturned fifty years of judicial opinion upholding state legislation prohibiting fraternities, sororities, and secret societies among public school students.

The Right to Organize and Use School Facilities

THE HEALY CASE: CAN RADICAL GROUPS BE DENIED RECOGNITION?[16]

Introduction. In 1969 a climate of unrest prevailed on many campuses in this country. There had been widespread civil disobedience at some colleges, accompanied by the seizure of buildings, vandalism, and arson. During that time local chapters of SDS (Students for a Democratic Society) had engaged in disruption and violence on some of those campuses. During the 1968–69 academic year, 850 demonstrations were reported, resulting in over 4000 arrests, 125 students injured, and more than 60 arson incidents.[17] The causes and results of the demonstrations were complex. Some observers, however, believed that "one of the prime consequences of such activities was the denial of the lawful exercise of First Amendment rights to the majority of students by the few."[18] It was in this climate of unrest that a group of students attending Central Connecticut State College (CCSC) began to organize a local chapter of SDS in September 1969.

The Supreme Court case of *Healy* v. *James* was a result of these SDS efforts. Although college cases are not always applicable to high school students, we have included this one because: there is no recent Supreme Court case on this topic involving high school students; the principles laid down by the Court in *Healy* have been applied to public school situations; and this is one of the few recent cases on the civil rights of students handed down by the Burger Court.

Facts of the case. Following publication of a notice in the college newspaper of a meeting to organize a local SDS chapter, the students voted to request the administration to grant the chapter official recognition. They filed their request with the Student Affairs Committee pursuant to established procedures. The request specified three purposes for the proposed organization: (1) it would provide "a forum of discussion and self-education for students developing an analysis of American society and institutions"; (2) since "ideas without parallel in deeds are empty," it would serve as "an agency for integrating thought with action so as to bring about constructive changes in the university, in American life and the world"; (3) "because of the responsibilty of all peoples for the welfare of others, SDS would provide a coordinating body for relating the problems of leftist students and other groups."

The Student Affairs Committee was satisfied with the statement of purposes, but was concerned over the possible relationship between the local group and the national SDS. Representatives of the proposed group, however, stated they would not affiliate "with any national organization." One of the organizers explained that the national SDS was divided into several "factional groups," that the national-local relationship was a loose one, and that the local organization accepted certain but not all of the national organization's aims and philosophies. By a vote of 6 to 2 the committee approved the application and recommended that the college president, Dr. James, grant the organization official recognition.

The president, however, rejected the recommendation. These are some of his reasons:

1. The statement of purpose to form a local chapter of SDS "carries full and unmistakable adherence to at least some of the major tenets of the national organization."
2. The aims and philosophy of SDS, "which includes disruption and violence," are contrary to the college policy that states: "Students do not have the right to invade the privacy of others, to damage the property of others, to disrupt the regular and essential operation of the college, or to interfere with the rights of others."
3. If the proposed group intends to follow this established college policy, they have not clarified why they wish to become a local chapter of an organization that openly repudiates such a policy.
4. Freedom of speech, the right to establish a forum for the exchange of ideas, and the right to organize public demonstrations and protests in an orderly manner are all "freedoms on which we stand." But to approve any local organization that joins another organization that "openly repudiates those principles" threatens the freedoms of both students and faculty.

The president concluded that approval should not be granted to the proposed SDS chapter or any other group that "openly repudiates" the college's dedication to academic freedom.

Effect of nonrecognition. Denial of recognition posed serious problems for the organization. Its members were not allowed to place announcements in the student newspaper; they were precluded from using campus bulletin boards; and nonrecognition barred them from using campus facilities for holding meetings. Shortly after the official rejection, for example, they called a meeting in the Student Center to discuss further action. However, the meeting was disbanded by two of the college's deans on the president's order, since nonrecognized groups were not entitled to use such facilities. As a result of these events, they filed suit in a U.S. district court on the grounds that the denial of recognition violated their First Amendment rights of expression and association.

The district court dismissed the suit on two grounds: (1) the students had failed to prove that they could function free from the national organization, and (2) the college's refusal to approve an organization (whose conduct it found "likely to cause violent acts of disruption") did not violate the students' constitutional rights. The district court's decision was approved by a divided U.S. court of appeals, and the students appealed to the U.S. Supreme Court.

Questions to Consider

1. If you were the president of the college, would you have approved the local SDS chapter? Under what circumstances, if any, would you disapprove of a student organization? Would nonrecognition of a student group violate any constitutional rights?
2. Can a school administration deny recognition to a local group because of its affiliation with a national organization that has caused campus violence? Because the proposed group refuses to affirm its willingness to adhere to school rules?
3. Can nonrecognition be based on a proposed organization's philosophy that is in basic conflict with the goals of the school? On an administration's honest fear that the student organization would be a disruptive influence on campus?

Legal principles

At the outset of its opinion the Supreme Court outlined the constitutional principles applicable to the case. Justice Powell pointed out that public colleges "are not enclaves immune from the sweep of the First Amendment." At the same time, these rights must always be applied "in light of the special characteristics of the environment in the particular case." Despite the recognized need for order in the schools, Justice Powell noted that "the precedents of this Court leave no room for the view that . . . First Amendment protections should apply with less force on college campuses than in the community at large." On the contrary, as the Court has repeatedly emphasized, "the vigilant protection of constitutional freedoms is nowhere more vital than in the community of American schools."[19] And among the rights protected by the Constitution is the right of individuals to associate to further their personal beliefs.

Is nonrecognition a constitutional question? Although the lower courts had acknowledged the principles outlined by Justice Powell, they held that President James's denial of official recognition "cannot be legitimately magnified and distorted" into an unconstitutional interference with the rights of the students. Furthermore they did not believe his action substantially deterred the "individual advocacy" of a student's personal beliefs. The circuit court pointed out that the SDS students could still meet as a group and distribute materials off campus and meet together informally on campus as individuals. According to this view, all that was denied was the "administrative seal of official college respectability." The Supreme Court, however, disagreed.

"There can be no doubt," wrote Justice Powell, "that denial of official recognition, without justification, to college organizations" abridges their constitutional right of association. Although President James may have taken no direct action to limit the students' right to associate freely, the Constitution's protection is not confined to direct interference with fundamental rights. "Freedoms such as these," wrote the Court, "are protected not only against heavy-handed frontal attack, but also from being stifled by more subtle governmental interference."

If an organization is to remain a viable entity in a school community, it must possess the means of meeting and communicating with students on campus. In this case nonrecognition denied the students the use of campus facilities, bulletin boards, and the school newspaper. Since this clearly limited the organization's "ability to participate in the intellectual give and take of campus debate and to pursue its purposes," nonrecognition could not be viewed as "insubstantial." Thus the Court held that this was an issue involving the students' constitutional rights and was not merely a matter of college formalities.

Burden of proof. According to the Supreme Court the lower courts also erred in assuming that the students had the burden of proving that they were entitled to recognition by the college and that President James's rejection could rest on the students' failure to convince the administration that their organization was unaffiliated with the national SDS. In this case the students should not have had the "burden of proof." Once they filed an application in conformity with the college requirements, the burden should have been on the administration to justify its decision of rejection. "It is to be remembered," wrote Justice Powell, that the effect of the college's refusal of recognition "was a form of prior restraint" denying to the students' organization a wide range of "associational activities." Although a school has a legitimate interest in acting to prevent disruption, a "heavy burden" rests on the college to demonstrate the appropriateness of that action.

Critique of the president's decision

Two fundamental errors required the Supreme Court to reverse the lower court rulings. The errors were discounting the First Amendment implications of nonrecognition and misplacing the burden of proof. In addition to ruling on these questions Justice Powell wrote a detailed analysis of President James's decision, examining four possible justifications for the action and considering whether any of them were constitutionally adequate to support the decision.

The relationship with national SDS. Because some SDS chapters had been associated with disruptive and violent campus activity, President James apparently considered that an affiliation between the students and national SDS was sufficient justification for denying recognition. The Supreme Court, however, "has consistently disapproved governmental action . . . denying rights and privileges solely because of a citizen's association with an unpopular organization." In numerous cases it has been established that "guilt by association" alone is an impermissible basis upon which to deny First Amendment rights. To restrict such rights the government has the burden of establishing not only "a knowing affiliation with an organization possessing unlawful aims" but also "a specific intent to further those illegal aims."

SDS is a loosely structured organization with various factions that promote diverse social and political views, only some of which call for unlawful action. Not only did the students in this case proclaim their independence from national SDS, but they also indicated that they shared only some of its goals. Therefore the Court concluded that this relationship was not an adequate ground for denial of recognition.

The philosophy of SDS. President James had characterized the local SDS group as adhering to "some of the major tenets of the national organization," including a philosophy of violence and disruption. He wrote that he was unwilling to "sanction an organization that openly advocates the destruction of the very ideals and freedoms upon which the academic life is founded."

The Court, however, ruled that "the mere disagreement of the President with the group's philosophy affords no reason to deny it recognition." As repugnant as these views might be to a college president, the mere expression of them would not justify the denial of First Amendment rights. Whether the students did or did not advocate "a philosophy of destruction" is immaterial. A public college "may not restrict speech or association simply because it finds the views expressed by any group abhorrent." To support this point, the Court quoted a 1961 opinion by Justice Black: "I do not believe that it can be too often repeated that the freedoms of speech, press and assembly guaranteed by the First Amendment must be accorded to the ideas we hate, or sooner or later they will be denied to the ideas we cherish."[20]

A disruptive influence. A third reason for President James's decision was his conclusion that the local SDS group was likely to be a "disruptive influence" at the college. If this conclusion was based on the organization's activities rather than its philosophy, and if it was factually supported by the evidence, there might have been a basis for nonrecognition. As the Court pointed out, "associational activities" need not be tolerated where they "infringe reasonable campus rules, interrupt classes, or substantially interfere with the opportunity of other students to obtain an education."

Justice Powell emphasized the importance of distinguishing between speech and action, between the permissible discussion of *any* question (including violence and disruption) and impermissible advocacy "directed to inciting or producing imminent lawless action." Thus if there had been adequate evidence to support the conclusion that the proposed SDS chapter posed "a substantial threat of material disruption," the president's decision could have been affirmed.

In this case, however, there was no substantial evidence to indicate that these students acting together would constitute a disruptive force on campus. Therefore "insofar as non-recognition flowed from such fears, it constituted little more than the sort of 'undifferentiated fear or apprehension of disturbance which is not enough to overcome the right to freedom of expression.'"

Refusal to follow school rules. At the Student Affairs Committee hearing, representatives of the proposed SDS group had stated that they did not know whether they might respond to "issues of violence" as had SDS chapters on other campuses or whether they might ever "envision interrupting a class." If these remarks were read as announcing the students' "unwillingness to be bound by reasonable school rules governing conduct," it suggested to Justice Powell a fourth reason for nonrecognition. Although students may advocate amending or even doing away with any or all campus regulations, they may not ignore such rules.

In schools, as in the general community, individuals must respect reasonable regulations concerning the time, place, and manner in which groups may conduct their activities. As the Court indicated, a school administration may require that a group seeking official recognition "affirm in advance its willingness to adhere to reasonable campus law." Such a requirement "does not impose an impermissible condition on the students' association rights." It would not infringe their freedom to speak out, assemble, or petition for changes in school rules.

In this case it was unclear whether the college had such a rule and if so whether the proposed group intended to comply with it. Assuming the existence of a rule such as this, the Court emphasized that "the benefits of participation in the internal life of the college community may be denied to any group that reserves the right to violate any valid campus rules with which they disagree."

Conclusion. In sum the Court held that nonrecognition by the college deprived the students of their constitutional rights and that the college had the burden of proving that nonrecognition was justified. Furthermore, in discussing the possible grounds for the president's action, it outlined the criteria and principles to be applied by schools and courts in other cases similar to this. In conclusion Justice Powell observed:

The wide latitude accorded by the Constitution to the freedoms of expression and association is not without its costs in terms of the risk to the maintenance of civility and an ordered society. Indeed, this latitude often has resulted, on the campus and elsewhere, in the infringement of the rights of others. Though we deplore the tendency of some to abuse the very constitutional principles they invoke, and although the infringement of rights of others certainly should not be tolerated, we reaffirm this Court's dedication to the principles of the Bill of Rights upon which our vigorous and free society is founded.[21]

Concurring critique

In an unusual concurring opinion, Justice William O. Douglas presented a personal analysis of the current confrontation between students and faculty and a strong defense of student demands for change:

Many inside and out of faculty circles realize that one of the main problems of faculty members is their own re-education or re-orientation. Some have narrow specialities that are hardly relevant to modern times. History has passed others by, leaving them interesting relics of a by-gone day. More often than not they represent those who withered under the pressures of McCarthyism or other forces of conformity and represent but a timid replica of those who once brought distinction to the ideal of academic freedom.

The confrontation between them and the oncoming students has often been upsetting. The problem is not of choosing sides. Students —who by reason of the Twenty-sixth Amendment become eligible to vote when 18 years of age—are adults who are members of the college or university community. Their interests and concerns are often quite different from those of the faculty. They often have values, views, and ideologies that are at war with the ones which the college has traditionally espoused or indoctrinated. When they ask for change, they, the students, speak in the tradition of Jefferson and Madison and the First Amendment.

The First Amendment does not authorize violence. But it does authorize advocacy, group activities, and espousel of change.

The present case is miniscule in the events of the 60's and 70's. But the fact that it has to come here for ultimate resolution, indicates the sickness of our academic world, measured by First Amendment standards. Students as well as faculty are entitled to credentials in

their search for truth. If we are to become an integrated, adult so-
ciety, rather than a stubborn status quo opposed to change, students
and faculties should have communal interests in which each age
learns from the other. Without ferment of one kind or another, a
college or university (like a federal agency or other human institu-
tion) becomes a useless appendage to a society which traditionally
has reflected the spirit of rebellion.[22]

The Right to Protest and Demonstrate

THE GEBERT CASE: ARE SIT-INS PROTECTED?[23]

On December 14 and 15, 1970, 36 students who attended Pennsylvania's Abington High School participated in sit-in demonstrations
during and after school. On the second day of the sit-in the students
were cleared from the high school pursuant to a court injunction. The
same day they were suspended for participating in the demonstrations that the administration characterized as "an activity disruptive
to the normal operation of the school."

Evidence gathered by the court indicated that: (1) the students
attempted to conduct their sit-in "with respect" for orderly school
operations; (2) the demonstrations attracted a crowd that congregated in the hallways; (3) school officials could not attend to their
normal duties because they had to keep close watch on the sit-in;
and (4) some of the demonstrators did not attend classes, were noisy
in the halls, and forced the rescheduling of a few classes.

The students claimed that the sit-in was an activity that should
be protected under the First Amendment and that the action of the
school administrators in suspending them was unconstitutional.
Therefore, the suspended students took their case to court.

Questions to Consider

1. Was this sit-in protected by the First Amendment? Was the suspension of these students a violation of their constitutional rights?
2. Should sit-ins or other demonstrations be permitted in school? If
   so, when and under what circumstances?
3. What should justify the prohibition of a demonstration? The response of curious or angry students? A substantial disruption in
   the duties of school officials? Missing classes by demonstrators?
   Noise in the hallways? The need to reschedule classes?

4. Should the intention of the demonstrators to be peaceful and non-disruptive be a significant factor in determining whether or not to punish them?

The opinion of the court

The trial court turned to the *Tinker* case to find the relevant guiding principles. There the Supreme Court had defined the following limits of First Amendment activity:

> *A student may express his opinions even on controversial subjects, if he does so without materially and substantially interfering with the requirements of appropriate discipline. . . . But conduct by the student, in class or out of it, which for any reason—whether it stems from time, place or type of behavior—materially disrupts classwork or involves substantial disorder or invasion of the rights of others is, of course, not immunized by the constitutional guarantee of freedom of speech.*[24]

In the *Gebert* case the evidence indicated that the sit-in interfered with the normal operation of the school. The question before the court was whether the interference was so "material and substantial" as to justify the suspension of the student demonstrators.

In deciding this issue, should school officials consider the disruptive reaction of the nonparticipating students? Not according to Judge Joseph Lord. In cases such as this, courts and administrators should only consider "the conduct of the demonstrators and not the reaction of the audience." Therefore, the fact that the demonstrations attracted a crowd that congregated in the hallways "cannot be a basis for punishing the demonstrators' exercise of their First Amendment rights."

Was the fact that school officials could not attend to their normal duties an adequate basis for suspending the students? No, this fact was not a sufficient basis for determining that the sit-in materially disrupted the school program. Judge Lord wrote:

> *If the test of material interference depends alone on what others do in response to the demonstrators' activity, then all forms of constitutionally-protected expression could be barred from the schools by a showing that administrators could not attend to their scheduled duties on any grounds related to the conduct engaged in by the students.*

Therefore the court emphasized the importance of distinguishing between "evidence that administrators left scheduled duties in order to keep an eye on potentially disruptive conditions in the schools from evidence that disruptive activity by demonstrators actually occurred."

Did the conduct of the sit-in participants themselves substantially interfere with appropriate school discipline? The court found that it did. "Appropriate discipline," wrote the judge, "certainly requires students to attend their scheduled classes and to refrain from preventing other students from attending classes in their scheduled location." The court recognized that the students involved in the sit-in did not intend to be disruptive, but the evidence indicated that student demonstrators did not attend classes, forced some classes to be relocated, and moved noisily through the halls. Based on such facts, the court found that the demonstrations did substantially disrupt the educational program, and, therefore, the action of the school officials in terminating the sit-in by suspending the students did not violate First Amendment rights.

In sum the *Gebert* case held that a student sit-in was not illegal merely because it was in school, because other students gathered to watch, or because school administrators could not attend to their regular duties. In deciding when a demonstration materially interfered with school activities, Judge Lord wrote: "The courts can only consider the conduct of the demonstrators and not the reaction of the audience." The court, however, found that these demonstrators did substantially interfere with school activities because they were noisy, missed scheduled classes, and required others to be relocated.

THE SWORD CASE: PROHIBITING
IN-SCHOOL DEMONSTRATIONS[25]

Although Judge Lord ruled against the students who brought the *Gebert* case to his court, his opinion indicated a flexible attitude concerning student demonstrations. However, as *Sword* v. *Fox* illustrates, other judges have not been as liberal or as flexible in their approach.

The *Sword* case involved the rules of a public college in Virginia that categorically prohibited all student demonstrations inside any school building. Pursuant to these rules, a group of students were disciplined for taking part in a sit-in demonstration in the administration building. The students challenged the regulation as an unconstitutional restraint on their freedom of speech and assembly. A federal appeals court said that the basic question posed by the case was whether a public college that permitted demonstrations elsewhere on campus may deny students the right to demonstrate in classrooms or administrative buildings.

In upholding the regulation the court pointed out that the rule did not restrict "the *right* to protest but the *place* of protest." Although the court acknowledged that "a flat ban on campus demonstrations would be manifestly invalid," it emphasized that students do not have an "unlimited right to demonstrate." Hence schools may place "reasonable, non-discriminatory" restrictions on demonstrations "to protect safety and property" and "maintain normal operations." The court held that this regulation was reasonable since it was not used to deny students the right to protest; it only denied the right to protest in college buildings "where order and study" are expected. "It can scarcely be argued," wrote the court, "that demonstrations in a classroom or administration building during the day would not create a disruption in the education activity of the institution." Demonstrations in such buildings at night could also be banned since they offer "too many opportunities for vandalism, and, in some instances, lawlessness." In sum the court held that the regulation prohibiting demonstrations in school buildings was a valid exercise of the school's authority to enforce reasonable rules and was not an unconstitutional limitation on the students' First Amendment rights.[26]

THE GRAYNED CASE: REGULATING DEMONSTRATIONS NEAR SCHOOL[27]

This Supreme Court case involved Richard Grayned, a high school student who participated in a demonstration in support of minority student grievances on a public sidewalk about 100 feet from a school building. He was convicted of violating a city "anti-noise" ordinance that prohibited any demonstrations on or near school grounds that disturbed classes. Grayned argued that the restriction was unconstitutional.

In upholding the ordinance Justice Thurgood Marshall noted that the constitutionality of a restriction may depend upon what is being regulated and where. "Although a silent vigil may not unduly interfere with a public library, making a speech in the reading room almost certainly would." That same speech, however, would be perfectly appropriate in a park. "The crucial question," wrote the Court, "is whether the manner of expression is basically incompatable with the normal activity of a particular place at a particular time."

Just as *Tinker* made clear that "school property may not be declared off-limits for expressive activity by students, we think it clear that the public sidewalk adjacent to school grounds may not be declared off-limits for expressive activity by members of the public." But in each case protected expression may be prohibited if it "materially disrupts classwork."

The Court recognized that public schools are often the focus of significant grievances and that picketing or handbilling near a school "can effectively publicize those grievances" to pedestrians, teachers, administrators, and students "without interfering with normal school activities." On the other hand, "schools could hardly tolerate boisterous demonstrators who make studying impossible, block entrances, or incite children to leave the schoolhouse." The Court concluded that the antinoise ordinance went no further than *Tinker* said a city may go to prevent interference with its schools.

Controversial Speakers

THE VAIL CASE: CAN SCHOOL OFFICIALS
PROHIBIT CONTROVERSIAL SPEAKERS?[28]

Prior to the March 1972 New Hampshire presidential primary, a number of candidates spoke at Portsmouth High School, including George McGovern, Edmund Muskie, and Paul McCloskey. Shortly thereafter two students attempted to secure permission for Andrew Pulley, vice-presidential candidate of the Socialist Workers party, to speak in school. School policy provided that "candidates seeking political office who are bona fide candidates are given equal time." In this case the superintendent denied the student request on the grounds that Pulley was not a bona fide candidate since he was not 35 years old and therefore was ineligible to serve as vice-president. But the students argued that the school policy and its application violated the First Amendment.

Questions to Consider

1. Should Andrew Pulley have been allowed to speak?
2. Should candidates generally be given an opportunity to present their views to public school students? Should all candidates for every office be given this opportunity? Or can school officials limit speeches to "major candidates" for certain offices?
3. Can schools flatly prohibit all candidates from appearing?

The opinion of the court

The district court noted that this type of case involves the balancing of the rights of students protected by the First Amendment with the responsibilities of school officials to regulate public speaking on school property. Since the election had passed by the time this case was decided, Judge Bownes did not order that Pulley be given an opportunity to address the students at Portsmouth High School. He did, however, clarify some of the constitutional principles to be applied by school officials in future controversies involving outside speakers.

First, the school had argued that the students had no right to sue since Andrew Pulley was not a party to the suit. Judge Bownes rejected this argument. Instead he emphasized that freedom of speech "encompasses the right to receive information and ideas." Since the First Amendment includes the right to hear, its protection extends to listeners as well as speakers. Thus the students of Portsmouth High as well as Andrew Pulley could appropriately take a case such as this to court.

Second, the judge indicated that the school might have the authority to bar "all outside speakers." But he felt this would be an unwise policy since "the interchange of ideas and beliefs that is fostered by providing a forum for outside speakers is healthy and beneficial to the entire educational process."

Third, when a school chooses to provide a forum for outside speakers, as Portsmouth High School had, it must do so in a manner consistent with constitutional principles. According to Judge Bownes, this means that:

1. Access to the podium must be permitted without discrimination.
2. The school may not control the influence of a public forum by censoring the ideas, the proponents, or the audience.
3. The right of the student to hear a speaker cannot be left to the discretion of school authorities "on a pick and choose basis."
4. Freedom of speech and assembly requires that "outside speakers be fairly selected and that equal time be given to opposing views."

Although these four principles give some indication of the limits of administrative discretion, the following Mississippi case goes much further in detailing what is and is not proper in the regulations of invited speakers. Although the case involves public institutions of higher education, the reasoning of the court is also relevant to elementary and secondary schools.

STACY v. WILLIAMS: JUDICIAL GUIDELINES
FOR OUTSIDE SPEAKERS[29]

During the 1968 presidential campaign, student members of the University of Mississippi Young Democrats were denied permission to invite Charles Evers to campus to speak on behalf of the Humphrey-Muskie ticket. The denial was based on regulations of the Board of Trustees of Mississippi's Institutions of Higher Learning. The students believed some of the regulations were unconstitutional and went to court to challenge the following:

No speaker shall be invited or permitted to speak on any campus . . . without first having been investigated and approved by the head of the institution involved. . . .

No person may be permitted to speak . . . who has announced as a political candidate for public office.

No person shall be permitted to use the facilities of the state institutions of higher learning whose presence will constitute a clear and present danger of inciting a riot.

No person shall be invited or permitted to speak . . . who advocates the violent overthrow of the government.

Any person feeling aggrieved at any adverse ruling . . . may file an appeal within five days [to the Board of Trustees] for a hearing at their next succeeding regular Board meeting.[30]

Questions to Consider

1. Which, if any, of these rules do you believe to be unconstitutional?
2. Is it unconstitutional for school officials to investigate invited speakers? Can administrative approval be required? Under what circumstances can officials legally disapprove speakers?
3. Can schools bar outsiders whose "presence" would constitute a danger of riot? If the vast majority of both students and faculty voice strong opposition to a proposed speaker, does this justify administrative disapproval?
4. Can speakers who advocate the violent overthrow of the government be prohibited?
5. Do students have a right of appeal if administrators disapprove of a proposed speaker? Does a procedure that provides for appeal at the "next regular Board meeting" protect student rights?

The opinion of the court

In a long and careful opinion a U.S. district court analyzed each of the above regulations challenged by the students, indicated why several were unconstitutional, and then issued new guidelines for outside speakers.

The prohibition of nonapproved speakers. Judge Keady noted that some notification and approval requirements are constitutional in order to avoid scheduling conflicts, provide adequate security, and allow authorities to rule on proposed speakers in accordance with careful standards. This, however, does not mean that the head of a public educational institution possesses "unbridled discretion" in approving or determining who may speak. Furthermore there must be a fair review procedure that allows students to challenge administrative decisions and requires a ruling within a reasonable time. The trustee regulations failed to include such procedures. They also failed to provide that requests for speakers might be initiated by students. "The university," wrote Judge Keady, "may not give its administration the power to invite outside speakers and at the same time withhold the opportunity from student groups to make similar invitations."

The prohibition of speakers who are candidates for public office. This regulation involved the right of the campus community to hear and participate in discussions of public policy. The court noted that "any classification which bans political speeches is arbitrary and unreasonable" and that a major purpose of the First Amendment was to protect the free discussion of candidates, governmental operations, and related political questions. Concerning this regulation, the judge concluded that so long as the campus remained open to other outside speakers, "it is patently clear that invited political candidates and their standard bearers . . . may not, consistently either with the First Amendment rights of the students or with the Equal Protection Clause of the Fourteenth Amendment, be barred except upon the clear and present danger criterion."

Prohibition of persons whose presence will constitute a danger of disruption. The constitutional difficulty with this provision is that it allows a person to be barred from campus because his mere "presence" creates a danger. The court noted that this regulation reflected a misconception of the "clear and present danger" doctrine.

"For it is fundamental," wrote Judge Keady, "that one may not be barred from speaking merely because his presence alone provokes riotous conduct among the audience." A person cannot be restrained from speaking and his audience cannot be prevented from hearing him unless the feared riot is likely to be caused by what the speaker himself says or does. In circumstances where the presence of an invited speaker might cause disruption, "attendant law enforcement officers must quell the mob, not the speaker." That a speaker may hold views disliked by a majority of the campus community is not a permissible basis for the denial of the students' right to hear him.

Prohibition of speakers who advocate the violent overthrow of the government. This regulation is defective in that it bars one who "advocates" violent overthrow of the government without differentiating between "the mere abstract teaching of the moral propriety for a resort to force and violence and preparing a group for violent action." The distinction is that those to whom the advocacy is addressed must be urged to *do* something rather than merely to *believe* in something. And there must be more than "advocacy to action"; there must also be "a reasonable apprehension of imminent danger."

Provision for appeal at next regular board meeting. Since aggrieved persons must be afforded prompt review of an adverse decision, which should be conducted prior to the proposed speaking engagement, they may not be required to await the next regularly scheduled board meeting. "For fundamental constitutional liberties," wrote the court, "may well be lost or substantially diluted by such delay." Hence a prompt, fair, and efficient review is necessary to satisfy the students' right to due process.

A judicial code for outside speakers

Since the Board of Trustees failed to develop constitutional rules concerning the regulation of guest speakers, the court took the unusual step of issuing its own regulations. This judicial code emphasized that the freedoms of speech and assembly guaranteed by the Constitution provide an opportunity for students at all institutions of higher education in the state to hear outside speakers. This meant that "free discussion of subjects of either controversial or non-controversial nature shall not be curtailed." However, as "there is no absolute right to assemble or to make or hear a speech at any time or place regardless of the circumstances," the judicial code included the following limitations concerning the invitation of outside speakers:

1. Requests to invite speakers will be considered only when made by a recognized student organization.
2. No invitation shall be issued by an organization without prior written concurrence by the head of the institution or his designee. Any request not acted upon within four days shall be deemed granted.
3. A request may be denied only if the institution determines that "the proposed speech will constitute a clear and present danger to the institution's orderly operation by the speaker's advocacy" of such actions as the violent overthrow of the government; the willful destruction or seizure of the institution's buildings; the forcible interference with classes or other educational functions; the physical harm, intimidation, or invasion of the rights of faculty, students, or administrators; or other violent campus disorders.
4. When an organization's request for an outside speaker is denied, it may appeal and obtain a hearing within two days before a Campus Review Committee composed of three faculty members appointed by the Board of Trustees plus the president and secretary of the student body.
5. When the request for an outsider speaker is granted, the administration may require that the meeting be chaired by a faculty member or administrator and that a statement be made that the views presented are not necessarily those of the institution.

Comment

What are the implications of the *Stacy* decision for public schools? The judicial code in this case was developed for institutions of higher education, but it nevertheless illustrates the way schools can protect themselves against disruptive speakers and at the same time protect the rights of student organizations. Although schools may not be required to have any regulations concerning invited speakers, the case emphasized that any regulations that are developed must be constitutional.

The *Tinker* case indicated that the constitutional principles concerning freedom of expression that apply in communities or on college campuses also apply in public schools. Does this mean that courts would guarantee the same freedom to students in high schools as to college students? Not necessarily. The answer would depend on the circumstances of each case; and several courts have pointed out that many of the circumstances of high school are different from those at most universities.[31] Because of these differences—such as age, maturity, facilities, teacher qualifications, and compulsory attendance laws—public school officials might be allowed to regulate invited speakers more closely.

In *Stacy* Judge Keady used the "clear and present danger" test to determine when an institution of higher education might turn down a proposed speaker. This famous judicial standard has been used for over 50 years to test the limits of permissible speech in the adult community.[32] In *Tinker* Justice Fortas translated this formula into the "substantial and material disruption" test that is now generally used by courts for determining the limits of permissible expression in public schools and can be expected to be applied in cases involving outside speakers as well.

SUMMARY AND CONCLUSIONS

Although the right to freedom of association is not explicitly set forth in the Constitution, courts have held the right to be implicit in the First Amendment freedoms of speech, assembly and petition. As this chapter has illustrated, the freedom encompasses a wide range of issues and is related to cases cited in earlier chapters, such as Chapter 2, Freedom of Speech. As in the case of other student rights, the law in this area is changing and is sometimes subject to variations in accordance with state statutes. The chapter has been organized around four topics:

Fraternities, sororities, and secret clubs

The right of a state to forbid public school students from joining secret societies became well established in American constitutional law during the first half of this century. As the *Robinson* case pointed out, statutes in over twenty states outlawed high school fraternities, sororities, and similar organizations that chose their members in an undemocratic manner. Numerous antifraternity cases over the past 50 years have upheld such legislation against charges of unconstitutionality. And many parents and school officials continue to believe that such groups interfere with the educational process and "with the morale of high school student bodies." Although courts acknowledged that adults had the right to join secret and undemocratic organizations, they declined to grant these rights to public school students. Instead they "deferred to the judgment" of legislatures and school boards in these cases. Furthermore, they distinguished adults from high school students, whom they characterized as "adolescents in their formative years." As recently as 1970 the Supreme Court of Texas reaffirmed this approach in the *Passel* case.

To some lawyers cases such as *Robinson* and *Passel* seem inconsistent with the principles and spirit of the *Tinker* decision. In fact we suspect that future courts may rule that students have a constitutional right to join any out-of-school organization that they wish, so long as the organization does not substantially interfere with the operation of the school. But until courts begin to rule this way, students should be aware of the possible risks involved in organizing or joining a high school fraternity, sorority, or secret society, especially in those states that have legislation prohibiting such organizations.

The right to organize and use school facilities

The *Healy* case established that denial of official recognition to student organizations without justification abridges their constitutional right of association.[33] Therefore if administrators deny recognition to a student organization, they bear a "heavy burden" to demonstrate the appropriateness of their action.

A relationship between a local student group and an unpopular national organization is not an adequate basis to deny recognition. In *Healy* the Supreme Court rejected this type of "guilt by association." Furthermore school officials may not deny recognition because they disagree with the philosophy of a student group.

On the other hand, a school may issue reasonable regulations concerning the time, place, and manner in which student groups may conduct their activities. Hence officials may deny recognition to groups that announce their unwillingness to be bound by such rules. Furthermore, schools need not tolerate student organizations that pose "a substantial threat of material disruption" or that "interfere with the opportunity of other students to obtain an education." Such action, however, must be based on substantial evidence, not merely on administrative fear or apprehension of disturbance.

The right to protest and demonstrate

The *Tinker* case indicated that a student demonstration that "materially disrupts classwork or involves substantial disorder or invasion of the rights of others" is not protected by the Constitution.

The *Gebert* case held that a demonstration is not illegal merely because it is in school, because other students gathered to watch, or because school administrators could not attend to their regular duties. Furthermore, in determining whether there was substantial interference with school activities, the court indicated that it would "only consider the conduct of the demonstrators and not the reaction of the audience." However, when protestors are noisy, when they miss scheduled classes, or require classes to be relocated, such behavior would constitute evidence of substantial interference with school activities.

The *Sword* case held that schools that permitted student demonstrations on campus could prohibit them "inside" any building. This was based on the theory that the prohibition did not restrict "the *right* to protest" but only "the *place* of protest." The court acknowledged that schools cannot prohibit all student demonstrations but may subject them to reasonable, nondiscriminatory restrictions in order to maintain normal school operations and to protect safety and property.

Although the principles of *Tinker* apply to all student demonstrations, they are not always applied in the same way. Thus the *Gebert* case illustrates a flexible, liberal attitude concerning student protests, whereas the *Sword* opinion shows a more conservative, more likely approach. Despite these differences, the law concerning student demonstrations can be summarized as follows:

1. Generally courts can be expected to acknowledge the First Amendment right of students to "peaceably assemble"; and most judges probably would hold the categorical prohibition of *all* student demonstrations on school grounds unconstitutional.
2. Most courts will probably not protect student demonstrations *inside* school buildings, especially during school hours. Judges are likely to find that such protests substantially interfere with school activities.
3. A protest *outside* the school building is more likely to be protected than one inside. However, outside demonstrations might not be protected during school hours, especially if protestors are illegally absent from classes or disrupt the classes of others.

Controversial speakers

Whether controversial speakers invited by student groups can appear before public school audiences involves the balancing of the responsibilities of officials to regulate public speaking on school property with the First Amendment rights of students. Despite these rights, administrators apparently have authority to bar all outside speakers from school.[34] Thus conflicts arise primarily when school authorities permit some outside speakers but not others.

The *Vail* case indicated that when public school officials choose to provide a forum for outside speakers, they must give equal time to opposing views and may not discriminate among proposed speakers or censor their ideas.

Stacy held that student groups can be required to notify and seek approval of school officials before inviting an outside speaker. This does not mean that administrators possess "unbridled discretion" in determining who may speak. Nor does it mean that students have an absolute right to hear a speech at any time or place regardless of the circumstances. It does mean, however, that if the school is open to other outside speakers, officials cannot ban all candidates for public office or prohibit views which the majority of the students or teachers find disagreeable. Furthermore, if an organization's request for an outside speaker is denied, there must be a fair and prompt review procedure that allows students to challenge the administration's decision. An administration's denial of a request would be upheld if there is evidence that the proposed speech would constitute "a clear and present danger" to the school's orderly operation.

Stacy also ruled that on a public college campus, a speaker cannot be barred because his mere "presence" constitutes a clear and present danger. (He can be barred only if the feared danger is likely to be caused by what the speaker himself says or does.) Furthermore a college speaker cannot be barred for merely advocating the violent overthrow of the government unless there is also "a reasonable apprehension of imminent danger." Whether courts would also apply these two rules to the high school situation where students are considered to be more immature, where conditions are more crowded, and where attendance is compulsory is uncertain since there is no reported case on this point. The opinions of *Stacy* and *Vail*, however, would seem to indicate that courts are tending to expand the rights of student groups to invite controversial speakers in public schools where outside speakers are permitted.

In the *Robinson* case Judge Pierce observed that the right of

Americans "freely to associate with whomever they choose is universally recognized as fundamental in a democratic society." In the same opinion he concluded that the right did not apply to high school students in their formative years. This conclusion, we suggest, is both outmoded and unwise. Legally it illustrates the way many judges approached student cases in the years before *Tinker* applied the Constitution to the schools. Educationally it is unwise because those schools that fail to recognize the right of their students "freely to associate" are probably doing a poor job in teaching their students to respect such rights when they become adults.

NOTES

[1] *Robinson* v. *Sacramento City Unified School District*, 53 Cal. Rptr. 781, 788 (1966).

[2] *Passel* v. *Fort Worth Independent School District*, 429 S.W.2d 917, 925 (Ct. App. Tex. 1968).

[3] *Healy* v. *James*, 408 U.S. 169, 198 (1972).

[4] *Id.* at 182.

[5] *Bradford* v. *Board of Education*, 121 P. 929 (Ct. App. Cal. 1912).

[6] *Id.* at 931.

[7] The quotations in this section are from *Robinson* v. *Sacramento City Unified School District*, 53 Cal. Rptr. 781 (Ct. App. Cal. 1966).

[8] *Ibid.*

[9] Judge Pierce noted that the following states have legislation similar to the California statute: "Arkansas, Colorado, Florida, Illinois, Indiana, Iowa, Kansas, Louisiana, Maine, Massachusetts (optional with local boards), Michigan, Minnesota, Mississippi, Montana, Nebraska, New Jersey, Ohio, Oklahoma, Oregon, Pennsylvania, Rhode Island, Texas (limited), Vermont, Virginia, and Washington." *Id.* at 788.

[10] In his opinion Judge Pierce explained the rationale for eight of these cases, including a 1915 decision by the U.S. Supreme Court that upheld a prohibition against Greek letter societies in all Mississippi educational institutions against an attack based on due process and equal protection arguments. *Waugh* v. *Board of Trustees*, 237 U.S. 589 (1915).

[11] This was the case of *Wright* v. *Board of Education*, 246 S.W. 43 (Ct. App. Mo. 1922), which held that a St. Louis school board regulation forbidding membership of high school students in secret organizations was not authorized by the legislature and that no rule should be adopted that attempted to control the conduct of pupils out of school hours after they have reached their homes, except such conduct that would clearly interfere with school discipline.

[12] *Passel* v. *Fort Worth Independent School District*, 429 S.W.2d 917 (1968); 440 S.W.2d 61 (1969); 453 S.W.2d 888 (1970). This was a long and difficult case that illustrates why citizens sometimes feel frustrated

by the procedural and jurisdictional complexities of the law. It began in a Texas district court and was appealed to the state Court of Civil Appeals in 1968. Both courts ruled in favor of the school board. Passel next appealed to the Texas Supreme Court which reversed (in 1969) for jurisdictional and procedural reasons, and declined to rule on whether the state antifraternity statute was unconstitutional. The case then returned to the district court which again ruled in favor of the school board. This decision was finally affirmed by the Court of Civil Appeals in 1970.

[13] 429 S.W.2d 917, 925 (1968).

[14] 440 S.W.2d 61 (1969).

[15] The dissent minimized the evidence of two athletic coaches who testified that club members had caused problems in the past. One testified that five or six years earlier some pledging activities had been carried on in the school lunchrooms. Another said that the clubs destroyed school spirit and team unity, but under questioning he admitted that there is "not one scintilla of evidence" that these clubs conduct their meetings or other activities on school grounds.

[16] *Healy* v. *James,* 408 U.S. 169 (1972).

[17] The increase in campus disturbances during this period was indicated by Jerris Leonard, assistant U.S. attorney general who wrote: "In the first half of the 1967–68 academic year, 71 demonstrations were reported on 62 campuses across the nation. In the second half of that same year, 221 demonstrations took place on 101 campuses." In 1969–70 these incidents had increased dramatically: "1,785 demonstrations were reported on campuses across the United States, causing some 462 injuries and eight deaths; 7,200 arrests were made, 246 arson incidents or attempts, and 14 bombings." To the Second Circuit Court of Appeals there was "a nationwide campus atmosphere of ticking timebombs" during this period. *Healy* v. *James*, 445 F.2d 1122, 1131–1132 (2nd Cir. 1971).

[18] *Healy*, 408 U.S. 169, 172 (1972).

[19] *Shelton* v. *Tucker*, 364 U.S. 479, 487 (1960).

[20] *Communist Party* v. *Subversive Activities Control Board*, 367 U.S. 1, 137 (1961).

[21] *Healy* at 195.

[22] *Id.* at 197–198.

[23] *Gebert* v. *Hoffman*, 336 F.Supp. 694 (E.D. Pa. 1972).

[24] *Id.* at 696. The Supreme Court has held that even outside the school environment, "where speech is mixed with conduct, as in the case of a sit-in, the state may reasonably regulate the time, place and manner of such activity in order to prevent serious interference with the normal usage of the facility or area in which the demonstration is to take place." *Ibid.*

[25] *Sword* v. *Fox*, 446 F.2d 1091 (4th Cir. 1971).

[26] In addition to having authority to regulate the place of demonstrations, school officials appear to be able to prohibit totally demonstrations that take the form of class boycotts or walkouts. Thus the Fifth Circuit

Court of Appeals held that a group of Black students could be disciplined for walking out of school to conduct a demonstration protesting school policies. In rejecting the claim that such conduct was permissible unless prohibited by a valid regulation, the court said: "No student needs a regulation to be told he is expected and required to attend classes." Hence disciplinary action "with regard to a mass refusal to attend classes" was upheld. *Dunn* v. *Tyler Independent School District*, 460 F.2d 137, 142 (5th Cir. 1972).

[27] *Grayned* v. *City of Rockford*, 408 U.S. 104 (1972).

[28] *Vail* v. *Board of Education of Portsmouth*, 354 F.Supp. 592 (D. N.H. 1973).

[29] *Stacy* v. *Williams*, 306 F.Supp. 963 (N.D. Miss. 1969).

[30] *Id.* at 974–978.

[31] For example, in a 1971 case Judge Wyzanski explained why it was more reasonable for secondary schools than colleges to limit academic freedom. He noted that in secondary schools:

Some teachers and most students have limited intellectual and emotional maturity. . . . While secondary schools are not rigid disciplinary institutions, neither are they open forums in which mature adults, already habituated to social restraints, exchange ideas on a level of parity. Moreover, it cannot be accepted as a premise that the student is voluntarily in the classroom and willing to be exposed to a teaching method which, though reasonable, is not approved by the school authorities [Mailloux v. Kiley, 323 F.Supp. 1387, 1392 (D. Mass. 1971)].

[32] In *Schenck* v. *United States*, 249 U.S. 47, 52 (1919), Justice Holmes wrote that the question in every case is whether the words used under the circumstances "create a clear and present danger that will bring about the substantive evils that Congress has a right to prevent." This opinion also includes his frequently quoted comment: "The most stringent protection of free speech would not protect a man falsely shouting fire in a theatre and causing a panic."

[33] Similarly a federal appeals court held that a high school policy that denied recognition to student clubs that expressed a "partisan" point of view was inconsistent with student First Amendment rights. *Garvin* v. *Rosenau*, 455 F.2d 233 (6th Cir. 1972).

[34] But we suspect that few educators today will prohibit *all* outsiders from coming to speak at their schools.

5
Freedom of religion and conscience

*If there is any fixed star in our constitutional constellation,
it is that no official, high or petty, can prescribe what shall
be orthodox in politics, nationalism, religion, or other
matters of opinion or force citizens to confess by word or
act their faith therein. If there are any circumstances which
permit an exception, they do not now occur to us.*

—Justice Jackson in
West Virginia v. Barnette[1]

Freedom of Religion

THE GOBITIS CASE:
COMPULSORY FLAG SALUTE

In thousands of schools children stand each morning and, with
hands on their chests, recite: "I pledge allegiance to the flag of
the United States of America and to the Republic for which it
stands; one nation, under God, indivisible, with liberty and
justice for all." This is a relatively simple, routine type of
patriotic exercise, less than what is expected of public school
children in most countries of the world.

In 1940 in Minersville, Pennsylvania, Lillian Gobitis, age 12,
and her ten-year-old brother William were expelled from school

because they refused to salute the flag as part of the daily opening ceremonies. Participation was mandatory for both teachers and students, as prescribed by the local board of education. Having been denied tax-supported education, the Gobitis parents enrolled the children in private schools. In order to avoid the financial costs of private education, the father went to court seeking an injunction to eliminate the requirement of participation in the flag salute as a condition for his children's attendance at the Minersville school.[2] He argued that compulsory flag salute in the schools violated the freedom of religion provisions of the First Amendment.

To support its case for expulsion, the board of education presented the following arguments.[3]

1. The expulsion of the children did not violate any constitutional rights, because their refusal to salute the flag was not founded on a religious belief.
2. The act of saluting the flag is not, by any stretch of the imagination, a "form of worship." The salute has no more religious implication than the study of history or civics or any other act that might make a pupil more patriotic as well as teach him "loyalty to the State and National Government."
3. The act of saluting the flag is only one of many ways in which a citizen may evidence his respect for the government. Every citizen stands at attention and men remove their hats when the national anthem is played; yet such action cannot be called a religious ceremony. The same respect is shown the American flag when it passes in a parade; yet that is not a religious rite.
4. The act of saluting the flag does not prevent a pupil, no matter what his religious belief may be, from acknowledging the spiritual sovereignty of Almighty God by rendering to God the things that are God's.

On behalf of the Gobitis children it was argued that the flag salute requirement violated their freedom of religion because they were Jehovah's Witnesses and relied on the following verses from chapter 20 of Exodus: "Thou shalt have no other gods before me. Thou shalt not make unto thee any graven image, or any likeness of anything that is in heaven above, or that is in the earth beneath, or that is in the water under the earth; Thou shalt not bow down thyself to them, nor serve them." The following points were made by Gobitis.

1. Although many people believe that saluting the flag has nothing to do with religion, the Supreme Court has repeatedly held that the individual alone is privileged to determine what he shall or shall not believe. The law therefore does not attempt to settle differences of creeds and confessions or to say that any point or doctrine is too absurd to be believed.
2. The saluting of the flag of any earthly government by a person who has promised to do the will of God is a form of religion and constitutes idolatry.
3. Shall man be free to exercise his conscientious belief in God and his obedience to God's law or shall he be compelled to obey the law of the State, which he believes is in direct conflict with the law of Almighty God?

Questions to Consider:

1. Does saluting the flag violate religious freedom?
2. Does saluting the flag engender patriotism and national unity?
3. Which of the arguments do you find more convincing, those for the school board or those for the Gobitis children?

The opinion of the court

The U.S. district court and the circuit court of appeals both decided in favor of the Gobitis children, but the Supreme Court reversed the rulings. In explaining the opinion of the Court, Justice Frankfurter recognized the grave responsibility of the Court when it has to reconcile a conflict between religious liberty and state authority. He noted the centuries of strife over religion that led our founding fathers to include a guarantee of religious freedom in the Bill of Rights. Thus Justice Frankfurter wrote that the First Amendment:

sought to guard against repetition of those bitter religious struggles by prohibiting the establishment of a state religion and by securing to every sect the free exercise of its faith. So pervasive is the acceptance of this precious right that its scope is brought into question, as here, only when the conscience of individuals collides with the felt necessities of society.[4]

No right, however, is absolute, not even the right to practice one's religious beliefs. Any liberty when carried to an extreme is likely to deny some other right. As Justice Frankfurter phrased it: "Our present task, then, as so often is the case with courts, is to reconcile two rights in order to prevent either from destroying the other. But, because in safe-guarding conscience we are dealing with interests so subtle and dear, every possible leeway should be given to the claims of religious faith."[5]

Cases before the court generally involve a central issue, and in this case the issue was whether legislatures and local school boards may determine the appropriate means to develop certain common, basic attitudes on the part of schoolchildren.

The Court asserted that the goals of patriotism and loyalty were clearly legitimate. It is proper for a state, through its schools, to attempt to develop "a common feeling for a common country"; consequently the disagreement, as the Court saw it, centered on the legitimacy of the means selected to attain this end. In discussing the question of the appropriateness of the means (compulsory flag salute), the Court exhibited restraint from entering what it considered to be the educator's arena:

The wisdom of training children in patriotic impulses by those compulsions which necessarily pervade so much of the educational process is not for our independent judgment. . . . The courtroom is not the arena for debating issues of educational policy. It is not our province to choose among competing considerations in the subtle process of securing effective loyalty to the traditional ideals of democracy, while respecting at the same time individual idiosyncracies among a people so diversified in racial origins and religious allegiances. So to hold would in effect make us the school board for the country. That authority has not been given to this Court, nor should we assume it.[6]

In the final paragraphs of the opinion, the Court acknowledged the need for an ordered society symbolized by the flag but attempted to balance this with strong protection of freedom of religion.

The preciousness of the family relation, the authority and independence which give dignity to parenthood, indeed the enjoyment of all freedom, presuppose the kind of ordered society which is summarized by our flag. A society which is dedicated to the preservation of these ultimate values of civilization may in self-protection utilize the educational process for inculcating those almost unconscious feelings which bind men together in a comprehending loyalty, whatever may be their lesser differences and difficulties. That is to say, the process may be utilized so long as men's right to believe as they please, to win others to their way of belief, and their right to assemble in their chosen places of worship for the devotional ceremonies of their faith, are all fully respected.[7]

Then the Court called attention to the role of the legislature in altering or eliminating "foolish legislation."

Judicial review, itself a limitation on popular government, is a fundamental part of our constitutional scheme. But to the legislature no less than to courts is committed the guardianship of deeply-cherished liberties. Where all the effective means of inducing political changes are left free from interference, education in the abandonment of foolish legislation is itself a training in liberty. To fight out the wise use of legislative authority in the forum of public opinion and before legislative assemblies rather than to transfer such a contest to the judicial arena, serves to vindicate the self-confidence of a free people.[8]

A dissent

Eight of the Supreme Court justices upheld the compulsory flag salute, but the ninth, Justice Stone, wrote a powerful dissenting opinion. He recognized the right of governments to ensure their survival, even if in so doing they must suppress religious practices dangerous to morals, public safety, health, and good order. However, he saw no such dangers involved in the refusal of two children to participate in a school ceremony contrary to their religious convictions. In his words:

The Constitution may well elicit expressions of loyalty to it and to the government which it created, but it does not command such expressions or otherwise give any indication that compulsory expressions of loyalty play any such part in our scheme of government as to override the constitutional protection of freedom of speech and religion. And while such expressions of loyalty, when voluntarily given, may promote national unity, it is quite another matter to say that their compulsory expression by children in violation of their own and their parent's religious convictions can be regarded as playing so important a part in our national unity as to leave school boards free to exact it despite the constitutional guarantee of freedom of religion.[9]

The Supreme Court, then, in an eight to one decision, upheld the Minersville Board of Education in its requirement that students, as a condition of school attendance, must salute the flag.

THE BARNETTE CASE: GOBITIS OVERRULED

After the Court upheld the mandatory flag salute, the West Virginia legislature passed a law requiring its schools to teach civics, history, and the Constitution "for the purpose of teaching, fostering and perpetuating the ideals, principles and spirit of Americanism, and increasing the knowledge of the organization and machinery of the government." The West Virginia Board of Education followed such legislation with various regulations including a compulsory flag salute. The regulations ordered the following:

Failure to conform is "insubordination" dealt with by expulsion. Readmission is denied by statute until compliance. Meanwhile the expelled child is "unlawfully absent" and may be proceeded against as a delinquent. His parents or guardians are liable to prosecution, and if convicted are subject to fines not exceeding $50 and jail term not exceeding thirty days.

This led to the case of *Barnette v. West Virginia.*[10]

In *Barnette* children of Jehovah's Witnesses refused to comply with the law, although they did offer to give the following pledge in place of the official one:

I have pledged my unqualified allegiance and devotion to Jehovah, the Almighty God, and to His Kingdom, for which Jesus commands all Christians to pray. I respect the flag of the United States and acknowledge it as a symbol of freedom and justice to all. I pledge allegiance and obedience to all the laws of the United States that are consistent with God's laws, as set forth in the Bible.[11]

Since only three years intervened between the *Gobitis* ruling and the *Barnette* case, we would expect the Court to follow precedent. *Barnette,* however, overruled *Gobitis* and protected the religious freedom not to salute the flag. The Court split six to three in favor of the children who were Jehovah's Witnesses. There had been some changes in the membership of the Court after the *Gobitis* decision, and some of the judges changed their minds in the interim, pursuant to extensive and careful deliberations. The three dissenting judges would have reaffirmed *Gobitis,* including Justice Frankfurter, who wrote a long and scholarly dissent.

While respecting the states' desire to build national unity and their use of schools toward that end, the Court struck down compulsion in the expression of sentiment or belief as illegitimate. In the words of the Court,

the state may *"require teaching by instruction and study of all in our history and in the structure and organization of our government, including the guarantees of our civil liberty, which tend to inspire patriotism and love of country." Here, however, we are dealing with a compulsion of students to declare a belief. They are not merely made acquainted with the flag salute so that they may be informed as to what it is or even what it means. The issue here is whether this slow and easily neglected route to arouse loyalties constitutionally may be short-cut by substituting a compulsory salute and slogan.*[12]

Speaking to this issue, Justice Jackson wrote this often quoted paragraph:

If there is any fixed star in our constitutional constellation, it is that no official, high or petty, can prescribe what shall be orthodox in politics, nationalism, religion, or other matters of opinion or force citizens to confess by word or act their faith therein. If there are any circumstances which permit an exception, they do not now occur to us.

He then applied these principles to the *Barnette* case.

We think the action of the local authorities in compelling the flag salute and pledge transcends constitutional limitations on their power and invades the sphere of intellect and spirit which it is the purpose of the First Amendment to our Constitution to reserve from all official control.[13]

Justice Jackson also disagreed with the notion that the remedy to wrong legislation is through new legislation or through the political process.

The very purpose of a Bill of Rights was to withdraw certain subjects from the vicissitudes of political controversy, to place them beyond the reach of majorities and officials and to establish them as legal principles to be applied by the courts. One's right to life, liberty, and property, to free speech, a free press, freedom of worship and assembly, and other fundamental rights may not be submitted to vote; they depend on the outcome of no elections.[14]

Justice Jackson made it clear that First Amendment freedoms are *preferred* freedoms. Whereas some rights can be restricted if the government has a legitimate end and chooses reasonable means, preferred rights receive more protection. If a right is a preferred, or a *fundamental*, one, then the state must show a *compelling* need before such a right can be restricted.* Applying this to the controversy surrounding the compulsory flag salute, the state has a legitimate purpose in seeking to gain social unity and patriotism. Saluting the flag is one reasonable means to attempt to accomplish this end. However, religious freedom is a preferred right. Consequently it cannot be restricted unless the state can show a compelling need for the flag salute requirement. Thus in the *Barnette* case, in which rights were in conflict, the state could not show sufficiently powerful interest to override a fundamental right of private citizens.

Justice Frankfurter's dissent explained his views concerning the constitutional protection of religious freedom:

* For example, in order to cut down on pollution and congestion our right to commute to work or school daily by car can be restricted by the government through reasonable means, such as issuing stickers that permit us to drive only on Mondays and Wednesdays, thus forcing us to use public transportation or car pools. The end (reducing pollution and congestion) is legitimate and the means (restricting the use of private cars) is reasonable. By contrast, the government may not prevent an individual from making speeches in public parks even if the government proclaimed the goal of creating parks as quiet, peaceful places for people to enjoy. Although the goal is legitimate and the means reasonable, the preferred, or fundamental, right of free speech receives a higher degree of protection. The state must show a compelling need before the right to free speech can be restricted.

Its essence is freedom from conformity to religious dogma, not freedom from conformity to law because of religious dogma. . . . Otherwise each individual could set up his own censor against obedience to laws conscientiously deemed for the public good by those whose business it is to make laws. . . .

The essence of the religious freedom guaranteed by our Constitution is therefore this: no religion shall either receive the state's support or incur its hostility. Religion is outside the sphere of political government. This does not mean that all matters on which religious organizations or beliefs may pronounce are outside the sphere of government. Were this so, instead of the separation of church and state, there would be the subordination of the state on any matter deemed within the sovereignty of the religious conscience. Much that is the concern of temporal authority affects the spiritual interests of men. But it is not enough to strike down a non-discriminatory law that it may hurt or offend some dissident view. It would be too easy to cite numerous prohibitions and injunctions to which laws run counter if the variant interpretations of the Bible were made the tests of obedience to law. The validity of secular laws cannot be measured by their conformity to religious doctrines. It is only in a theocratic state that ecclesiastical doctrines measure legal right or wrong.[15]

A close reading of the case indicates that the dissent used the "reasonableness" test to uphold the school board regulation, whereas the majority applied the "compelling interest" test. Thus the current law is that in public elementary and secondary schools, school boards or legislatures may not require participation in saluting the flag for students who have religious objections to such practices.

THE SCHEMPP AND MURRAY CASES:
MUST STUDENTS PRAY OR READ THE BIBLE?

Pennsylvania passed a law in 1959 requiring that "at least ten verses from the Holy Bible shall be read, without comment, at the opening of each public school on each day. Any child shall be excused from such Bible reading, or attending such Bible reading, upon the written request of his parents or guardian."[16] Roger, Donna, and Ellory Schempp were Unitarians from Germantown, Philadelphia, who attended the Abington Senior High School. There, as in many other high schools throughout the state, opening exercises were conducted each morning, pursuant to the statute. Ten verses from the Holy Bible were broadcast over the intercommunications system to all homerooms, where the students stood and repeated them in unison. Students could absent themselves from the classroom if they wished; or they could remain and not participate. After the Bible reading came the salute to the flag and school announcements.

The district court ruled that the Pennsylvania statute violated the First and Fourteenth Amendments and ordered the schools to discontinue the practice it required. The school district, together with the attorney general of Pennsylvania, appealed to the Supreme Court.

Questions to Consider

1. Do you find the practice described desirable or objectionable? On what theory do you base your opinion?
2. What section of the Constitution is relevant to the situation?
3. Is there anything coercive in the situation described?
4. Can a small minority prevent a practice the majority sees as desirable? Should it be able to do so?

A companion case

In the meantime another controversy involving similar issues was working its way up the court hierarchy. This controversy was based on a 1905 rule of the Board of School Commissioners of Baltimore, Maryland, which provided for the "reading without comment, of a chapter in the Holy Bible and/or the use of the Lord's Prayer."

William J. Murray, III, and his mother, Mrs. Madalyn Murray, were professed atheists who objected to this rule and asked for its cancellation. At their insistence the rule was amended to permit children to be excused from the exercise on their parents' request. The Murrays, not satisfied with permission to be excused, went to court to rescind the entire rule. As serious atheists they claimed that the rule violated their rights.

In that it threatens their religious liberty by placing a premium on belief as against non-belief and subjects their freedom of conscience to the rule of the majority; it pronounces belief in God as the source of all moral and spiritual values, equating these values with religious values, and thereby renders sinister, alien and suspect the beliefs and ideals of your Petitioners, promoting doubt and question of their morality, good citizenship and good faith.

The Maryland courts found in favor of the school practices and against the request of the Murrays, who then appealed to the Supreme Court. As in other instances in which the legal issues are substantially the same, the Court ruled on the *Schempp* and *Murray* cases in one opinion.* In a landmark decision the Court declared that Bible reading and prayers in the schools were unconstitutional. It did so only after a careful review of previous cases and after making clear that the Court has consistently through the years taken a position of neutrality toward religion, and "while protecting all, it prefers none, and it disparages none."

In probing the intent and meaning of the principle of separation of church and state, Justice Clark, a devout Catholic, wrote:

> The First Amendment's purpose was not to strike merely at the official establishment of a single sect, creed or religion, outlawing only a formal relation such as had prevailed in England and some of the colonies. Necessarily it was to uproot all such relationships. But the object was broader than separating the church and state in this narrow sense. It was to create a complete and permanent separation of the spheres of religious activity and civil authority by comprehensively forbidding every form of public aid or support for religion.[17]

After examining the sequence of previous cases that interpreted the religious freedoms of the First Amendment, the Court concluded that in the *Schempp* and *Murray* cases the

> exercises are prescribed as part of the curricular activities of students who are required by law to attend school. They are held in the school buildings under the supervision and with the participation of teachers employed in those schools . . . such as opening exercises in a religious ceremony. Given that finding, the exercises and the law requiring them are in violation of the establishment clause.[18]

The Court rejected the argument that since students may absent themselves from the exercises, no coercion is involved and therefore Bible reading and prayers are legitimate.[19]

Schempp, in an eight to one decision, reviewed with painstaking scholarship the legal history of the church-state relationship in America. It firmly prohibited religious exercises, Bible reading, and prayers

---

* For this reason the citation for the *Murray* case is the same as in *Abington v. Schempp*, 374 U.S. 203 (1963).

in the public schools, both compulsory and voluntary. The Court also made it clear that hostility toward religion is also unconstitutional and that nothing in the law prohibits studying religion, comparative religion, or the history of religion.

Freedom of Conscience

THE SPENCE CASE:
ROTC AND RELIGIOUS FREEDOM[20]

In 1972 John Spence, Jr., was a student at Central High School in Memphis, Tennessee, where, according to state law, every student was required to take one year of either physical education or ROTC training. Since no physical education was offered for male students at Central High School, although facilities were available nearby, ROTC was the only alternative.

Retired army officers taught ROTC using materials developed by the U.S. Army. Once a week the students wore military uniforms, studied military drill and tactics, and worked with firearms. Spence refused to attend the ROTC classes on the grounds that he was a conscientious objector, stating:

> By reason of religious training and belief, I am conscientiously opposed to participation in war in any form and am opposed to being subjected to combat training for the purpose of being prepared to enter war. As stated above, my convictions are based upon religious training and belief which is in turn based upon a power or being or upon a faith to which all else is subordinate and upon which all else is ultimately dependent. This sincere and meaningful belief occupies in my life a place parallel to that filled by the Supreme Being, God.

Spence's request was denied and, because he refused to attend ROTC classes, he was not awarded his diploma, although he had fulfilled all other requirements.

Questions to Consider

1. Is the ROTC requirement a reasonable condition attached to high school attendance? Should the requirement be waived on the grounds of conscientious objection?
2. Should all requirements be subject to such objections? If so, would this nullify the laws requiring compulsory schooling?

3. Is there a distinction between high school ROTC training as a substitute for physical education and serving in the armed forces?

The opinion of the court

In an earlier case the Supreme Court held that a state college or university can require ROTC training as a condition of attendance.[21] The arguments in behalf of Central High School relied heavily on this case, in which the Court said:

Instruction in military science is not instruction in the practice or tenets of religion. Neither directly nor indirectly is government establishing a state religion when it insists upon such training. Instruction in military science, unaccompanied here by any pledge of military service, is not an interference by the state with the free exercise of religion when the liberties of the Constitution are read in the light of a century and a half of history during the days of peace and war.[22]

Judge Clark, formerly of the Supreme Court*, however, distinguished the case of Spence, a high school student, from the earlier *Hamilton* case on the grounds that high school attendance was not a matter of choice. The *Hamilton* case had ruled that if a state university requires ROTC as a condition of attendance, a student who voluntarily attends the university cannot insist on being excused from the prescribed course. The court found crucial the distinction between voluntary and compulsory attendance. In upholding Spence's right to be excused from ROTC, Justice Clark recognized that the sincere beliefs of a conscientious objector must receive the same constitutional protection as traditional religious beliefs. Without a compelling state interest, such beliefs cannot be violated.

As the trial judge aptly observed, the ROTC course requirement forced John to choose between following his religious beliefs and forfeiting his diploma, on the one hand, and abandoning his religious beliefs and receiving his diploma on the other hand. The State may not put its citizens to such a Hobson's choice consistent with the Constitution without showing a compelling state interest . . . within the State's constitutional power to regulate.[23]

Judge Miller, dissenting in the *Spence* case, found the distinction between compulsory and voluntary attendance "to be unpersuasive"

* After Mr. Clark resigned from the High Court when his son became U.S. Attorney General, he served on other federal courts by assignment.

and would have followed the *Hamilton* ruling. He saw serious dangers if the majority doctrine were broadly applied:

> *The conscientious objector, if his liberties were to be thus extended, might refuse to contribute taxes in furtherance of any other end condemned by his conscience as irreligious or immoral. The right of private judgment has never yet been so exalted above the powers and the compulsion of the agencies of government. One who is a martyr to a principle—which may turn out in the end to be a delusion or an error—does not prove by his martyrdom that he has kept within the law.*[24]

Judge Miller in his dissent made it clear that *he* would extend the protection of the First Amendment only to groups whose religious views and convictions have been firmly established over long periods of time. This would exclude the "mere subjective evaluation" of conscientious objectors.*

It is clear, however, that the courts extend the protection of the First Amendment not only to established religions but to newer ones as well. Furthermore the amendment applies to sincere conscientious objectors whether they are religious or not. In each case, however, the particular issues must be considered, since even First Amendment rights are not absolute. The particular rights in conflict must be examined and the relative importance of the state interests and those of the individuals considered. Since freedom of and from religion are among the preferred rights of our Constitution, governments must show a compelling state interest before their actions will be upheld over the rights of individuals.**

THE BANKS CASE: PLEDGE OF ALLEGIANCE AND FREEDOM OF CONSCIENCE[25]

Andrew Banks, a senior at Florida's Coral Gables High School, refused to stand during the Pledge of Allegiance. He claimed that the

* More recently, however, it has been questioned whether a compulsory ROTC requirement would be upheld even at the college level in state institutions. See, for example, *Anderson* v. *Laird*, 466 F.2d 283 (2nd Cir. 1972), which strikes down compulsory chapel attendance at the U.S. service academies. The opinion (in note 80 on page 295) raises questions about the continued validity of the *Hamilton* holding.

** Such a compelling state interest, for example, upheld the requirement of polio immunization for all school children over the religious objections of some.

school board regulations requiring him to stand during the salute to the flag violated his constitutional right of free speech and expression.

The board policy stated that "students who for religious or other deep personal conviction, do not participate in the salute and pledge of allegiance to the flag will stand quietly." The school officials denied that Banks's refusal to stand was an exercise of his constitutional right to free speech and expression. They also claimed that a compelling governmental purpose required students to stand during the pledge. When Banks was suspended from school for his refusal he went to court to challenge the policy.

Questions to Consider

1. May student objection to saluting the flag be based on freedom of conscience, or must it be based on freedom of religion?
2. Is it reasonable to require students who do not wish to salute the flag to stand quietly?
3. Is standing at a flag salute a form of speech or expression? Is refusing to stand a form of expression?

The opinion of the court

The District Court of Florida relied on the *Barnette* and *Tinker* cases in reaching its decision. It noted an interesting distinction between the two cases, indicating that the tenor of *Barnette* was negative whereas that of *Tinker* was positive. *Barnette* was negative in that it prohibited the state from compelling individuals to act in a manner that would violate their convictions in "politics, nationalism, religion, or other matters of opinion." By contrast, Tinker positively asserted that students carry their constitutional rights into the schools.

The conduct of Andrew Banks was scrutinized by the court in light of the "material disruption test" proclaimed in *Tinker*. Evidence showed that Banks caused no disturbance by refusing to stand, that he did not attempt to influence other students, and that he was not conspicuous in his behavior. His testimony showed that his refusal to stand was based on his own Unitarian beliefs as well as being a "simple protest against black repression in the United States."

The court recognized that "standing is an integral portion of the pledge ceremony and is no less a gesture of acceptance and respect than is the salute or the utterance of the words of allegiance." It went on to recognize Banks's right to express his opinion by refusing to stand and participate in the Pledge of Allegiance as a right protected by the First Amendment.

A related case

Results similar to those in the *Banks* case were reached on somewhat different facts in a New York case during 1969. School officials insisted that students who refused to participate in the Pledge of Allegiance should stand quietly or leave the room.[26] Three students involved in the lawsuit objected to the pledge because they did not believe that the words "with liberty and justice for all" were true in America today. One of them, an atheist, also objected to the phrase "under God." They refused to leave the room and wait in the hall during the ceremony "because they considered exclusion from the room to be a punishment for their exercise of constitutional rights."

The reasoning of the New York court was substantially the same as in the *Banks* case. The court upheld the right of the students not to participate in the flag salute for reasons of conscience. Their right to remain quietly in the room was also protected.

When school officials pointed out that others had joined the protesting students in sitting out the pledge, the court noted that "the First Amendment protects successful dissent as well as ineffective protests."

Religious Objections to School Attendance

A growing minority of critics of education have begun to argue that the changes needed in our system are so great that they cannot take place within the present framework of compulsory education. Some call for an end to required education and urge free choice by parents and students. Such critics see the *Yoder* case, which involved a legal exemption from compulsory education for a group of Amish children, as a first step in that direction.

Others—those who favor community control and alternative schools—also see the *Yoder* case as supporting their position. In this vein the editors of *Of Education and Human Community* wrote that the Supreme Court's *Yoder* decision "indicates strong support for community control of schools where the values and life styles of a community are threatened by the rules and regulations of the larger community."[27]

Is the *Yoder* case the first step toward "a deschooled society"? Does it challenge our traditional acceptance of compulsory education? Will it lead other groups to follow the Amish example and request exemptions from state educational statutes? These are the questions raised by the landmark case of *Yoder* v. *Wisconsin*.

THE YODER CASE: WHO HAS A RIGHT NOT TO GO TO SCHOOL?[28]

Jonas Yoder, Adin Yutzy, and Wallace Miller were sincere and committed members of the Amish community in Green County, Wisconsin. Because they believed that high school attendance was contrary to the Amish religion—namely, that it would endanger their own salvation and that of their children—they decided not to send their fourteen and fifteen-year-old children to school after they had graduated from the eighth grade. In so doing they violated Wisconsin's compulsory school attendance law (which requires attendance until age sixteen). As a result the parents were charged, tried, and convicted of violating the law and fined five dollars each by the local county court. The Amish parents believed that the compulsory attendance law abridged their rights under the First and Fourteenth Amendments, and they appealed their conviction.

In support of their position the parents presented expert witnesses on religion and education who testified about the tenets of the Amish religion and the impact that high school attendance could have on the Amish communities. The Amish, for example, deemphasize material success, reject the competitive spirit, and believe that salvation requires life in a church community separate from worldly influence. They object to high schools because the values they teach conflict with the Amish way of life. The high schools tend to emphasize intellectual and scientific accomplishments, self-distinction, competitiveness, worldly success, and social life with other students. In contrast, Amish society emphasizes informal learning-through-doing, a life of "goodness" rather than a life of intellect, wisdom rather than technical knowledge, community welfare rather than competition, and separation rather than integration with contemporary society.

The Amish argued that high school education is contrary to their beliefs, not only because of its emphasis on competition in classwork and sports and its pressures of peer group conformity but also because it physically and emotionally removes Amish children from their community during formative adolescent years, a time when they need to acquire the attitudes and skills to carry on the roles of Amish farmers or housewives. These roles can best be learned through example in the Amish community rather than in non-Amish schools that tend to develop values that "alienate man from God."

One expert witness testified that "compulsory high school attendance could not only result in great psychological harm to Amish children because of the conflicts it would produce" but could "ultimately result in the destruction" of the Amish church community. Another educational expert described the Amish system of learning-through-doing the skills relevant to their adult roles in the Amish community as "ideal" and "perhaps superior to ordinary high school education."

The Amish do not object to elementary education because they believe their children must know the three Rs in order to read the Bible, to be good farmers and citizens, and to deal with non-Amish people when necessary. They accept such basic education because it does not "significantly expose their children to worldly values or interfere with their development in the Amish community."

Questions to Consider

1. Do you agree that compulsory high school attendance would endanger the religious values of Amish children? Would it endanger the values of youngsters of other religions?
2. Should Amish children be exempt from high school attendance? Are there others who should also be exempt?
3. What criteria should be used to determine who should and should not be required to attend school? Who should make this decision —the student, the parents, the school board, or the courts?

The opinion of the court

After reviewing the evidence the Supreme Court turned to the constitutional principles and substantive issues in the *Yoder* case. First the Court noted that "there is no doubt" that a state has power "to impose reasonable regulations for the control and duration of basic education." On the other hand, the state's interest in universal compulsory education is not absolute; when it impinges on other fundamental rights, such as those protected by the First Amendment freedom of religion clause, then the rights in conflict must be balanced by the court. Thus in order for Wisconsin to compel school attendance against a claim that such attendance interferes with the practice of the Amish religion, the state must show either that it does not significantly deny the free exercise of religious belief by its requirement or that its interest in compulsory education is "of sufficient magnitude to override the interest claiming protection" under the freedom of religion clause.

Based on the unchallenged testimony of experts in education and religious history and strong evidence of a sustained faith pervading the Amish way of life, the Court concluded that compulsory secondary schooling "would gravely endanger if not destroy" the free exercise of Amish religious beliefs. The Court reached this decision because it found such schooling exposes Amish children "to worldly influences in terms of attitudes, goals, and values" contrary to their beliefs and interferes with the religious development of the Amish child and "his integration into the way of life of the Amish faith community at the crucial adolescent state of development." The Wisconsin compulsory attendance law undermines the Amish religion by requiring the Amish to "either abandon belief and be assimilated into society at large, or be forced to migrate to some other and more tolerant region." Thus the law carries with it "precisely the kind of objective danger to the free exercise of religion which the First Amendment was designed to prevent."

Wisconsin claimed that even if the compulsory education law did conflict with Amish religious practice the state's interest in such a law is paramount. The state argued the law should be upheld for two reasons: education prepares individuals to be self-reliant members of society, and it is necessary to prepare citizens to participate effectively and intelligently in our open political system. Moreover Wisconsin attacked the Amish position as one "fostering 'ignorance' from which the child must be protected by the State." In addition Wisconsin claimed that without additional schooling, Amish children who wished to leave their religious community would be ill equipped for life.

The Court was not persuaded by these arguments. On the contrary, the evidence in this case, wrote Justice Burger, "is persuasively to the effect that an additional one or two years of formal high school for Amish children in place of their long established program of informal vocational education" would do little to serve compelling state interests. He further noted: "Whatever their idiosyncrasies as seen by the majority, this record strongly shows that the Amish community has been a highly successful social unit within our society even if apart from the conventional 'mainstream.'" The Amish are "productive law-abiding members of society"; they provide for their own dependents and accept no public welfare. According to the Court:

> The Amish alternative to formal secondary school education has enabled them to function effectively in their day-to-day life under self-imposed limitations on relations with the world, and to survive and prosper in contemporary society as a separate, sharply identifiable and highly self-sufficient community for more than 200 years in this country. In itself, this is strong evidence that they are capable of fulfilling the social and political responsibilities of citizenship without compelled attendance beyond the eighth grade at the price of jeopardizing their free exercise of religious belief. . . . There can be no assumption that today's majority is "right" and the Amish and others like them are "wrong." A way of life that is odd or even erratic but interferes with no rights or interests of others is not to be condemned because it is different.[29]

Wisconsin also argued that if the Court exempted Amish children from compulsory attendance, it would fail to recognize the individual Amish child's right to a secondary education. Such an exemption would take no account of a possible conflict between the wishes of parents and children and "might allow some parents to act contrary to the best interests of their children by foreclosing their opportunity to make an intelligent choice between the Amish way of life and that of the outside world."

In response Justice Burger observed that the same argument could apply to all students in church schools and that there is no evidence "that non-Amish parents generally consult with children up to ages 14-16 if they are placed in a church school of the parents' faith." Furthermore, if the state is empowered to "save" a child from his Amish parents by requiring an additional two years of a formal high school, the state will in effect influence the religious future of the child. Therefore this case involves "the fundamental interest of parents, as contrasted with that of the State, to guide the religious future and education of their children." In addition the Court noted that this primary role of parents in the upbringing of their children "is now established beyond debate as an enduring American tradition."

This does not mean the power of the parent may not be subject to limitation if it appears that parental decisions will jeopardize the health or safety of the child, or have a potential for significant burdens for society. But the evidence in this case indicated that accommodating the religious objections of the Amish by foregoing one or two additional years of compulsory education for Amish children would not impair the physical or mental health of the children or result in their inability to be responsible citizens.

In sum Justice Burger wrote that the Amish in this case have "convincingly demonstrated": (1) the sincerity of their religious beliefs, (2) the interrelationship of their belief and their way of life, (3) the vital role that belief and daily conduct play in the continued survival of the Amish religious communities, (4) "the hazards presented by the State's enforcement of a statute generally valid as to others," and (5) "the adequacy of their alternative mode of continuing informal, vocational education." In light of this evidence and "weighing the minimal difference between what the State would require and what the Amish already accept," Wisconsin was unable to show "how its admittedly strong interest in compulsory education would be adversely affected by granting an exemption to the Amish." For these reasons the Court held that the First and Fourteenth Amendments "prevent the State from compelling respondents [Jonas Yoder, Adin Yutzy, and Wallace Miller] to cause their children to attend formal high school to age 16."

A dissenting opinion

In a lone dissent Justice Douglas disagreed with the Court's opinion, which considered only the interests of the Amish parents on the one hand and the state of Wisconsin on the other. Instead Justice Douglas argued that:

> No analysis of religious liberty claims can take place in a vacuum. If the parents in this case are allowed a religious exemption, the inevitable effect is to impose the parents' notion of religious duty upon their children. Where the child is mature enough to express potentially conflicting desires, it would be an invasion of the child's rights to permit such an imposition without canvassing his views. . . . And if an Amish child desires to attend high school and is mature enough to have that desire respected, the State may well be able to override the parents' religiously motivated objections.[30]

There was no evidence that the 14- and 15-year-old children in the *Yoder* case testified concerning their educational views. But, in the opinion of Justice Douglas, a child of this age should have the right to be heard on the matter of education. "He may want to be a pianist or an astronaut or an ocean geographer." To do so, observed Douglas, "he will have to break with the Amish tradition."

It is the future of the student not the parent that is "imperiled" by the decision not to attend high school. If a parent keeps his child out of high school, the child will be "barred from entry" into today's "new and amazing world of diversity." The child may rebel or prefer the course of his parents, but this should be decided by the student "if we are to give full meaning to what we have said about the Bill of Rights and of the right of students to be masters of their own destiny."

Viewing the Amish religious tradition as less positive than did the majority, Justice Douglas concluded that if the student "is harnessed to the Amish way of life by those in authority over him or if his education is truncated, his entire life may be stunted and deformed."

The implications of Yoder

Could the Court's decision in this case lead people to attempt to escape the reach of compulsory education by organizing into a community and calling themselves a religious group? Could it lead sensitive humanists who reject material values or radical educators who oppose state-regulated education to seek exemptions for their children? Not according to the Court. For such groups, despite the sincerity of their beliefs, would not be able to use the religion clauses of the First Amendment to support their case. As Justice Burger wrote:

> A way of life, however virtuous and admirable, may not be interposed as a barrier to reasonable state regulation of education if it is based on purely secular considerations. . . . Thus, if the Amish asserted their claims because of their subjective evaluation and rejection of the contemporary secular values accepted by the majority, much as Thoreau rejected the social values of his time and isolated himself at Walden Pond, their claim would not rest on a religious basis.[31]

To further ensure that the Court's opinion would not be interpreted too broadly, Justice Burger returned to this question a second time in the opinion when he indicated that the decision in this case was a narrow exemption that applied only to a special religious group and was not an attack on the Wisconsin program of compulsory education. Furthermore, he wrote: "It cannot be over-emphasized that we are not dealing with a way of life and mode of education by a group claiming to have recently discovered some 'progressive' or more enlighted [sic] process for rearing children for modern life."

Despite these disclaimers by Justice Burger, the Supreme Court in this case allowed a group of parents to defy a state's compulsory education law. Whether other groups will find other arguments to support similar challenges, only time and future litigation will tell.

Related cases and issues

Other issues relate to the religious freedom of students, some of which have led to court cases and community controversies.

Church school at home? Early in 1973, in Duval County, Florida, two children were adjudged to be "in need of supervision as persistent truants from school." The parents of the children appealed this school board decision to the District Court of Appeals of Florida.[32]

The facts showed that the children were not attending public schools because of their parents' religious belief that "race mixing as practiced in public schools was sinful." Instead, they were taught in their home "school," called the Ida M. Craig Christian Day School, where their mother was the only teacher. She was not certified to teach and did not meet the state-prescribed regulations for private tutors. Furthermore the Covenant Church of Jesus Christ, under whose aegis the "school" operated, was not a regularly established church in Florida. The principal tenet of this church is that of racial segregation. Its members believe "that blacks and Orientals were conceived through the copulation of Eve and Satan, who was disguised as the serpent in the Garden of Eden, and it is therefore sinful and evil to associate with people of those races."

The compulsory school attendance law of Florida could be satisfied by attending: (1) a public school; (2) a parochial or denominational school; (3) a private school supported by tuition, endowments, or gifts; or (4) an at-home school with private tutors who meet the qualifications specified by the state board of education. But the court ruled that the home teaching arrangements in this case did not satisfy the Florida law and that, clearly, the Ida M. Craig Christian Day School "is neither a parochial nor denominational school within the generally accepted meaning of those terms."

The right to attend private schools. The *Yoder* case and the Florida case are interesting recent controversies related to the issue of who has the right not to attend public schools. Such controversies are best viewed against the backdrop of an important historical decision. The Supreme Court ruled as early as 1925 in *Pierce* v. *Society of Sisters of the Holy Name*[33] that it was unconstitutional for the state of Oregon to require all children to attend *public* schools for the first eight grades. Although the court upheld the right of the state to require school attendance, such attendance could be satisfied in private schools, both parochial and secular, as well as in public schools.

Religion and folk dancing. The physical education programs of many schools include folk dancing and at times even social dancing. Vigorous folk and square dancing is often part of the daily schedule of elementary schools and is justified in two ways: It is claimed that it has value as an integral part of physical exercise that is healthy for growing young bodies and that properly timed physical exercise will enable children to concentrate better on the academic tasks of the schools.

What action should a school take if certain children believe that dancing of any kind, violates their religious convictions? If such an objection is respected, could it not also be raised against science instruction, the learning of history, foreign languages, or any other segment of the curriculum? What does compulsory schooling mean if any part of it can be vitiated by claiming it to be repugnant to one's religious beliefs?

A California case centered on religious objections to social and folk dancing that were part of the school's physical education program.[34] In the *Hardwick* case the court upheld the objection and exempted the student from the requirement of dancing. The court reached its decision on two grounds: that freedom of religion must be protected against abridgement by school officials and that the schools could not interfere with the rights of parents to control the upbringing of their children, as long as the views of the parents were not "offensive to the moral well-being of the children or inconsistent with the best interests of society."

Other courts have reached similar conclusions in cases involving religious objections to school-required dancing. When courts apply the balancing test, they conclude that protecting religious freedom outweighs the social interests entailed in the dance segment of a physical education program. It is quite probable that the benefits gained from dancing can be reached in ways that do not violate the students' religious convictions.

The limits of religious objections to curricular content have not yet been completely established. Perhaps the *Yoder* case provides the most useful basis for predicting future judicial behavior.

Skullcaps in the school. A conflict that never reached the courts occurred in Fall River, Massachusetts, in 1971.[35] A twelve-year-old junior high school student in that city was sent home by the principal because he insisted on wearing a *yarmulke,* a skullcap worn by orthodox Jewish men. The principal, also a Jew, contended that anyone entering a public building such as a school should remove his hat. The student, on the other hand, claimed that his religious beliefs required him to wear his skullcap and that his action was therefore protected by the First Amendment.

Many school-related legal controversies do not reach the courts. They are resolved by accepting the legal opinion of the city attorney, the city corporation counsel, the attorney general, or other legal source that acts in an impartial advisory capacity. Schools constantly rely on such advice.

In the controversy at hand, the city corporation counsel ruled that the school authorities acted illegally in suspending the youth because he was wearing the skullcap. His religious freedom was protected and prevailed over whatever minor annoyances his wearing a skullcap might have occasioned.

It is interesting to speculate just what other grooming or clothing practices would or would not be so protected. Does a teacher have the right to wear a skullcap? What would be the reaction if followers of Hare Krishna insisted on attending school in peach-colored flowing robes with heads shaved except for pigtails? Would the *Tinker* test be appropriate in these situations?

Black armbands on the football team. In 1972 several Black members of the University of Wyoming football team planned to wear black armbands during a game against Brigham Young University. They wanted to protest what they believed to be racist views of the Mormon Church, which supports Brigham Young University. The athletes claimed that the First Amendment protected their right to free expression and that wearing the armbands is protected by symbolic speech.

The Wyoming coach, backed by the board of trustees of the university, forbade the wearing of the armbands. In the dispute that ensued, the football players were dismissed from the team. The coach and the university officials claimed that the First Amendment required complete neutrality on religious matters on the part of state institutions. They claimed that the display of black armbands by a state university team would be an expression of opposition to certain religious beliefs and therefore a violation of the principle of neutrality.

This situation presented conflicting claims under the First Amendment. Both sides claimed the protection of the amendment—one for free expression, the other for religious freedom. Furthermore, both claimed the *Tinker* case to support their position.

How would you rule in this conflict? Why? Does *Tinker* apply, and for which party to the conflict?

The U.S. Court of Appeals for the Tenth Circuit ruled in favor of religious neutrality.[36] It carefully considered the facts of the case as well as the *Tinker* principles. It also emphasized earlier Supreme Court pronouncements on religious freedom that "the government is neutral, and while protecting all, it prefers none, and it *disparages* none." The court explained that the decision of the trustees prevented a hostile expression by members of the university team, and thus "it was in furtherance of the policy of religious neutrality by the State."

This case illustrates two major principles. First, it clearly shows a conflict between two powerful constitutional freedoms, those of speech and religion. This conflict calls for an incompatible resolution of a dilemma. Both rights cannot be protected; thus a difficult balancing test must be attempted by the court to reach a resolution not between a right and a wrong but between competing constitutional rights. The second principle illustrated is that the courts tend to give strong protection to religious freedom. One way that this is expressed is through the principle of official neutrality, whereby agents of the government, including schools, may not favor or disfavor religious beliefs and expressions. The armband case should also remind us that although the constitutional principles seem to be clear and bold in the abstract, they become less clear and more difficult to apply in the complex affairs of education.

SUMMARY AND CONCLUSIONS

Conflicts over the proper relationship between church and state seem to be perennial. They were among the most important reasons for the migration of people to the United States, yet the conflicts continued here. Just as most cultural conflicts find expression in our schools, differing interpretations of the proper relationship between religion and public education have led to bitter disagreements and lawsuits.* From among these conflicts, those selected for analysis in this chapter were ones that centrally involved the rights of students. The issues in these cases arose out of compulsory flag salute in the schools, Bible reading and prayers, and religious objections to ROTC and compulsory schooling.

Although the issue of what the policy in relation to such conflicts should be is not closed, authoritative court cases have ruled as follows:

1. The Supreme Court held that the requirement that students participate in a compulsory flag salute may be an infringement of their religious beliefs.
2. Courts have also upheld the right of students not to salute the flag if they object to such a practice as a matter of conscience. School requirements that students stand during the pledge have been rejected by courts since standing is "a gesture of respect and acceptance." Refusal to stand in such a situation is protected by the First Amendment. Furthermore, students who refuse to participate in the flag salute or to stand during it may not be removed from the classroom, for that would constitute punishment for the exercise of a constitutional right.
3. The practices of Bible reading or prayers in the public schools violate the establishment clause of the First Amendment and therefore are unconstitutional, whether students must participate in such exercises or are excused from them. The activities themselves are unconstitutional when carried on in a public school.
4. A student who attends school pursuant to a compulsory attendance law may not be required to participate in ROTC if he objects to it as a matter of conscience or religion. A 1934 case held that a state college or university may require ROTC participation as a condition of attendance, since students choose to go to college and are not forced by law to do so. Whether this distinction would be applied by the courts today is an open question.
5. The Supreme Court ruled that Amish children do not have to

---

* These controversial issues involve significant policy matters. Students not acquainted with the issues might read some of the many available books or pamphlets. See, for example, Lawrence Byrnes, *Religion and Public Education*, New York, Harper & Row, 1975, and *Religion in the Public Schools*, Washington, D.C., American Association of School Administrators, 1964.

attend public high schools because the curriculum would conflict with their religious beliefs and way of life. This decision, which seems to challenge state-required high school attendance, was carefully limited by the Court and is not likely to be applied to religious groups of more recent origin. The Court emphasized the unique characteristics of the Amish, including their close-knit communal living for over three hundred years.

It is clear from the analysis of relevant cases that a student's religious rights under the First Amendment are among the preferred rights of our Constitution, and a public school may restrict them only by showing that a compelling state interest must take precedence over the individual's right. This is a significant change from earlier practices whereby the religious rights of the individual student could be curtailed if the schools had reasonable grounds to do so. The current legal test thus favors the civil rights of students.

NOTES

[1] 319 U.S. 624 (1943).

[2] *Minersville* v. *Gobitis*, 310 U.S. 586 (1940). Note: The phrase "*under God*" was not in the pledge when this case arose, having been added by an act of Congress in 1954.

[3] These arguments are paraphrased from the case. *Id.* at 587–588.

[4] *Id.* at 593. The Court also noted that "the affirmative pursuit of one's convictions about the ultimate mystery of the universe and man's relation to it is placed beyond the reach of law. Government may not interfere with organized or individual expression of belief or disbelief. Propagation of belief—or even disbelief—in the supernatural is protected, whether in church or chapel, mosque or synagogue, tabernacle or meeting house. Likewise the Constitution assures generous immunity to the individual from imposition of penalties for offending, in the course of his own religious activities, the religious views of others, be they a minority or those who are dominant in government."

[5] *Id.* at 593–594.

[6] *Id.* at 598.

[7] *Id.* at 600.

[8] *Id.* at 600.

[9] *Id.* at 605.

[10] 319 U.S. 624, 629 (1943).

[11] *Id.* at 628.

[12] *Id.* at 631.

[13] *Id.* at 642.

[14] *Id.* at 638.

[15] *Id.* at 653, 654.

[16] *Abington School District* v. *Schempp*, 374 U.S. 203, 205 (1963).

[17] *Id.* at 31–32.

[18] *Id.* at 223.

[19] For authority it simply referred to a case it had adjudicated the year before, *Engle* v. *Vitale*, 370 U.S. 420 (1962).

[20] *Spence* v. *Bailey*, 465 F.2d 797 (6th Cir. 1972).

[21] *Hamilton* v. *Regents*, 293 U.S. 245 (1934).

[22] *Id.* at 265–266.

[23] *Spence* at 800.

[24] *Id.* at 801.

[25] *Banks* v. *Board of Public Instruction of Dade County*, 314 F.Supp. 285 (S.D. Fla. 1970).

[26] *Frain* v. *Baron*, 307 F.Supp. 27 (E.D. N.Y. 1969).

[27] James Bowman *et al.*, eds., *Of Education and Human Community*, Lincoln, University of Nebraska Press, 1973, p. 106.

[28] *Wisconsin* v. *Yoder*, 92 S. Ct. 1526 (1972).

[29] *Id.* at 1537–1538.

[30] *Id.* at 1546.

[31] *Id.* at 1533.

[32] *F. and F.* v. *Duval County*, 273 So.2d 15 (Fla. 1973).

[33] 268 U.S. 510 (1925).

[34] *Hardwick* v. *Board of School Trustees*, 54 Cal. App. 696, 205 P. 49 (1921).

[35] Reported in the "Daily Collegian," University of Massachusetts, February 9, 1971.

[36] *Williams* v. *Eaton*, 468 F.2d 1079 (10th Cir. 1972).

6
Personal appearance

I t comes as a surprise that in a country where the states are restrained by an Equal Protection Clause, a person can be denied education in a public school because of the length of his hair.

—Justice William O. Douglas
in Ferrell v. Dallas Independent School District[1]

Courts have other and more important functions to perform than that of hearing the complaints of disaffected pupils of the public schools against rules and regulations promulgated by the school boards.

—Pugsley v. Sellmeyer[2]

Introduction

Should students have the freedom to choose their dress and hair style? Should there be any limits on that freedom? Should the Constitution protect student grooming and clothing just as it protected Mary Tinker's right to wear her armband? Or is the conflict over personal appearance a less significant issue? Should schools be able to establish dress codes? If so, what criteria should be used to judge whether such codes are constitutional?

The judicial response to these seemingly mundane questions has been quite remarkable: First, the questions have led not only to an extraordinary volume of litigation but also to a large collection of lengthy and lively court opinions. Second, the issues have provoked an unprecedented degree of disagreement—between courts as well as between judges on the same court. Despite the substantial differences among the conflicting judicial rulings on these issues, the Supreme Court has declined to perform its usual role of resolving such differences in constitutional interpretation.

Because the number of controversies has been so great (especially concerning the constitutionality of hair regulations), in this chapter only a fraction of the recent decisions will be examined.[3] After looking at a 1923 case on cosmetics, we will examine closely the majority and minority opinions in *Karr* v. *Schmidt*. This 1972 case on the regulation of boys' hair split the Fifth Circuit Court of Appeals and illustrates the detail and determination with which each side supports its view. We will then briefly consider how the other federal appeals courts are divided on this issue. The chapter will conclude with an examination of several cases concerning the regulation of student clothing.

Grooming

THE PUGSLEY CASE:
AN HISTORICAL PERSPECTIVE

On the opening day of school in Clay County, Arkansas, in 1921 Principal Hicks read several rules that had been adopted by the school board. He announced that their observance would be required of all students. One of the rules stated: "The wearing of transparent hosiery, low-necked dresses or any style of clothing tending toward immodesty in dress, or the use of face paint or cosmetics, is prohibited."

Pearl Pugsley broke this rule by using talcum powder on her face. Her teacher told her to wash it off and not to return with it again. A day or two later she returned with powder on her face and was denied admission to school until she obeyed the rule. Pearl refused and asked a local Arkansas court to set the rule aside. The court dismissed her case, and Pearl appealed. In a split decision the Supreme Court of Arkansas ruled in favor of the school board for several reasons:

First, although the authority of school boards is not without limit, they have "a wide range of discretion" in matters of school policy and administration. Since school management involves many details, it is important that courts not interfere with board regulations made in good faith unless they are illegal or clearly unreasonable.

Second, the question in this case "is not whether we approve this rule as one we would have made" nor "whether it was essential to the maintenance of discipline." On the contrary, "we must uphold the rule" unless we find that the board "clearly abused their discretion" and that the rule is not reasonably calculated to promote discipline.

Third, courts have "more important functions to perform than that of hearing the complaints of disaffected pupils" against school board regulations. Although the reasonableness of such rules is a judicial question, it should be kept in mind that board members are usually elected each year and that they are in close touch with the affairs and conditions of their school districts. Therefore courts should hesitate to substitute their judgment for that of school boards, which are responsible for prescribing rules governing the public schools.

Fourth, "respect for constituted authority and obedience thereto" is an essential lesson to qualify students for the duties of citizenship, and the schoolroom is an appropriate place to teach that lesson.

Fifth, a rule might be improper if it involved oppression or humiliation, or if it required extensive time or money. But the rule in question does not appear unreasonable in any of these respects and imposes no affirmative obligation. Similarly the use of the powder might be permitted if it "possessed any medicinal properties." But in this case it was used only as a cosmetic.

For these reasons the court was unwilling to say that the rule might not be desirable in aiding school discipline. "We will not annul a rule of this kind," wrote the court, unless there is "a valid reason"; whereas to uphold it, "we are not required to find a valid reason for its promulgation."

NOTE: When Pearl Pugsley was suspended she was 17 years old. In a dissenting opinion Judge Hart wrote: "I think that a rule forbidding a girl pupil of her age from putting talcum powder on her face is so far unreasonable" that the court should say that the board abused its discretion in making it. The dissent concluded: "Useless laws diminish the authority of necessary ones," and the tone of the majority opinion "exemplifies the wisdom of this old proverb."

Whether grooming regulations are useless rules that diminish student respect for all rules is a question that is very much alive today and is reflected in the current controversies that follow.

THE KARR CASE: A DECISION
THAT DIVIDED THE COURT[4]

In 1970 a Committee on Student Grooming and Dress composed of
a student, parent, and administrator from each of the El Paso, Texas,
high schools proposed a code that was adopted by the school board.
The code included the following statements and provisions:

> In order to help ensure proper acceptable behavior on the part of
> the students, it becomes necessary to establish certain guidelines to
> aid parents and students in selecting the proper attire for the school
> year. . . . The role of the school is one of guidance for pupils in an
> effort for total education and the development of proper attitudes.

> Student dress will be considered acceptable if it does not violate
> any of the three following principles:

> 1. Clothing worn is not to be suggestive or indecent.
> 2. Clothing and general appearance is not to be the type that would
>   cause a disturbance or interfere with the instructional program.
> 3. Clothing and general appearance is to be such as not to constitute
>   a health or safety hazard.

> Guidelines for dress and grooming . . . : [Boys] Hair may be blocked,
> but is not to hang over the ears or the top of the collar of a standard
> dress shirt and must not obstruct vision. . . .

> No child shall be admitted to school or shall be allowed to con-
> tinue in school who fails to conform to the proper standards of
> dress.[5]

On August 12, 1970, Chelsey Karr, a 16-year-old student attempted to enroll at Coronado High School in El Paso for his junior
year. He was not enrolled because he was in violation of the school
board regulation limiting the length of boys' hair. After several
conferences with school officials proved futile, Karr took his case to
court.

Questions to Consider

1. Does the El Paso grooming code seem reasonable? Do the three
   principles seem fair? Or does a student have a constitutional right
   to wear his hair as he pleases?
2. Do you think long hair is a form of symbolic speech? If so, what
   message does it convey? If it does not communicate that message,

is long hair still entitled to protection? How is long hair similar
to and different from Tinker's armband?
3. Do the El Paso school regulations violate the Fourteenth Amendment?*
4. Should public school students be able to sue school administrators
to protect against *any* infringement of their freedom? Or should
courts be expected to protect only those liberties that are important and socially useful?
5. Should a school have to prove that a rule is reasonable to have it
upheld? Or should a student be required to prove it is unreasonable to have it declared unconstitutional?

The opinion of the trial court

After a four-day trial a U.S. district court concluded that the denial
of a public education to Karr on the basis of the El Paso regulations
violated the due process and equal protection guarantees of the
federal Constitution. The court ruled that "one's choice of hair style
is constitutionally protected" and that the burden was on school
authorities to demonstrate that long hair disrupted the educational
process.

The court heard evidence from both sides. Fifteen witnesses
testified for the school board, including students, teachers, and administrators, who stated that students with long hair caused disruption in the classroom, disciplinary problems, and safety problems.
Karr called seventeen witnesses on his behalf, who testified that they
did not believe long hair caused disciplinary problems. (Some, however, acknowledged that they had seen fights between "long- and
short-haired" students.) Two college teachers also testified that "hair
regulations may alienate students from school authorities" and may
"adversely affect the parent-child relationship."

The court rejected the justifications offered by the school authorities in defense of their rule. The contention that long hair could be
prohibited because it is difficult to keep clean was invalid because
the length of hair is unrelated to the "habits of personal hygiene
one develops through parental training." The preponderance of evidence indicated that long hair "does not create a safety hazard in

* Two relevant provisions of the Fourteenth Amendment provide that
no state shall "deprive any person of life, liberty, or property, without
due process of law; nor deny to any person within its jurisdiction the
equal protection of the laws."

science laboratories." Concerning fights that had occurred between long- and short-haired students, the court suggested that the school authorities "teach tolerance" rather than ban long hair. Having found no reasonable relationship between the hair regulation and legitimate school objectives, the court ruled that the regulation was unconstitutional. The trial court concluded that the enforcement of the haircut rule "causes far more disruption of the classroom instructional process than the hair it seeks to prohibit." The El Paso School Board disagreed and appealed the decision.

The opinion of the appeals court

The *Karr* case, wrote the appeals court, presents this question: "Is there a constitutionally-protected right to wear one's hair in a public high school in the length and style that suits the wearer?" The appeals court acknowledged that a number of judges have held that there is such a right. Some have relied on the First and Fourteenth Amendments; a few have based this right on the Eighth, Ninth, and Tenth Amendments. However, a majority of the judges on the U.S. Court of Appeals for the Fifth Circuit did not agree. On behalf of the court Judge Morgan considered and rejected each of the following theories.

The First Amendment. This is the most frequently asserted basis for the right to wear long hair. It is argued that long hair is a form of symbolic speech by which the wearer conveys his individuality or rejection of conventional values, and it should be protected under the principles of the *Tinker* case.

The problem with this approach, wrote Judge Morgan, is that "it is doubtful that the wearing of long hair has sufficient communicative content to entitle it to the protection of the First Amendment." The court acknowledged that for some the wearing of long hair "is intended to convey a discrete message to the world." But for many the wearing of long hair is simply a matter of personal taste or the result of peer-group influence. Chesley Karr, for example, brought this suit not because his hair conveys a message but "because I like my hair long." Should First Amendment protection extend to those students who intend to convey a message in wearing long hair but not to others? The court felt that such a rule would be unworkable and that constitutional protection should not depend on the subjective intent of the student in wearing long hair.

Moreover the court believed that the *Tinker* decision supported its

view. When the Supreme Court distinguished the prohibition of armbands from grooming regulations, it observed: "The problem posed
by the [Tinker] case does not relate to regulation of the length of
skirts or the type of clothing, to hair style or deportment . . . [It]
involves direct, primary First Amendment rights akin to 'pure
speech.' " Judge Morgan believed this statement was intended "to
delimit the outer reach" of the Supreme Court holding and to indicate that "the right to style one's hair as one pleases in the public
schools does not inherit the protection of the First Amendment."

The Fourteenth Amendment. Some courts have held that the right
to wear hair at any length is part of the individual "liberty" protected by the due process clause of the Fourteenth Amendment.
However, Judge Morgan pointed out that individual liberties may be
"ranked in a spectrum of importance." At one end of the spectrum
are the "great liberties" such as speech and religion that are specifically guaranteed in the Bill of Rights. Of equal importance are
liberties such as the right of marital privacy and the right to travel
to a foreign country that are so fundamental that "even in the
absence of a positive command from the Constitution, they may be
restricted only for compelling state interests." At the other end of
the spectrum are the "lesser liberties" that may be curtailed by the
state if the restrictions are reasonably related to proper state activities. Thus the question posed by this case is not whether hair regulations may restrict a student's liberty but where that liberty should
be ranked on the spectrum of importance. Is it so significant that
courts should recognize it as a "fundamental" constitutional right?
The court concluded it should not.

One reason for this conclusion is that the interference with liberty
is a "temporary and relatively inconsequential one." The regulation
in question still leaves students a "wide range of personal choice in
their dress and grooming." Second, there are "strong policy considerations in favor of giving local school boards the widest possible
latitude in the management of school affairs." School administrators,
observed Judge Morgan, "must daily make innumerable decisions
which restrict student liberty." These range from regulations restricting student parking to a variety of rules regulating student eating
and movement during the school day. Each of these rules could also
be attacked as a restriction on student liberty. Does it follow that
school officials should be called into court and required to demonstrate that these restrictions serve "compelling" state interests and

that no "alternatives less restrictive of liberty" are available? Not in cases such as these where "fundamental" rights are not involved. Admittedly the courts should intervene to ensure the right to an equal education and to protect other basic student rights. But in the "grey areas" where "fundamental rights are not implicated," the courts should not tell local school authorities how to run their schools.

Equal protection. The trial court had held that the denial of public education to Karr on the basis of the length of his hair was an "arbitrary classification" that violated the equal protection clause of the Constitution because it discriminated among male students based solely on hair length.

The appeals court, however, found this theory "without merit." Since the classification is not based on a "suspect" criterion such as race (which would require a "rigorous standard of equal protection scrutiny"), the regulation would be invalid only if a court could perceive that it had no rational basis. Furthermore state regulations that do not affect fundamental freedoms are subject to a much less rigorous standard of judicial review than when fundamental rights are at stake. In cases such as this, the question is simply "whether the regulation is reasonably intended to accomplish a constitutionally permissible state objective." Moreover the burden is not upon the school board to establish the rationality of its restriction, but upon the challenger to show that the restriction is "wholly arbitrary."

Based on the record of this case, the court found:

> The school authorities seek only to accomplish legitimate objectives in promulgating the hair regulation here in question. The record nowhere suggests that their goals are other than the elimination of classroom distraction, the avoidance of violence between long and short-haired students, and the elimination of potential health hazards resulting from long hair in the science labs. On a record such as this, we hold that it was clear error to conclude that the school board regulation failed to meet the minimum test of rationality that was properly applicable.[6]

Confusion and burden. The appeals court was disturbed that different district courts in the circuit have, "on strikingly similar records, reached wholly dissimilar results." Most district judges concluded that grooming regulations are reasonable, whereas some struck them down as "arbitrary." But the validity of these regulations, wrote Judge Morgan, "should not turn on the individual views of the district judges" concerning their "reasonableness."*

What seemed to disturb the court even more was "the burden which has been placed on the federal courts by suits of this nature." This case, for example, required four full days of testimony in the district court. It went to the circuit court with a printed appendix exceeding 300 pages. "Within this circuit alone, there have been numerous other cases" in which students made similar arguments and school boards offered the same justifications. And in each case district courts have been required to hold a "full evidentiary hearing on the issue."

Because of this burden and because these cases do not raise issues of "fundamental" liberty, Judge Morgan announced that henceforth such regulations would be presumed valid. Thus where a student lawsuit "merely alleges the constitutional invalidity" of a high school grooming regulation, district courts would dismiss the case "for failure to state a claim for which relief can be granted."

The court emphasized that its decision did not indicate indifference to the personal rights of Chesley Karr and other young people. Rather it reflected the "inescapable fact" that neither the Constitution nor the federal judiciary "were conceived to be keepers of the national conscience in every matter great and small."[7]

A dissenting view

The opinion of the court was not unanimous. On the contrary, Judge Wisdom, joined by several of his "Brethren," wrote a long, strong, and sometimes eloquent minority opinion. The dissent contains an unusual quantity of social commentary combined with cutting criticism of the majority opinion. It begins with this observation: "Hair styles change. A high school boy if he chooses should be able to wear his hair as Yul Brynner does or as Joe Namath does without fear of being deprived of an education by a majority of school board members who grew up at a time the crew-cut was fashionable."[8]

The majority opinion holds that it is "but a trifling interference with a young person's freedom" to deny him the right to wear his hair as he pleases. "Individual rights," notes Judge Wisdom, "never seem important to those who tolerate their infringement." Thus the

* For information on the relationship between district and circuit courts and a description of the federal court system, see Appendix B, How the System Works.

majority ruled that hair length is not a "fundamental right," and "with a few pecks of the typewriter advises the district courts of this circuit that they no longer need distract themselves with lawsuits of the gossamer stuff of this one." Judge Wisdom vigorously dissented for a number of reasons.

First, in determining whether this particular liberty is "fundamental" or not, "the majority and I part company." The majority establishes a spectrum of values along which individual liberties can be ranked. It then places a student's right to determine his hair length among the "lesser liberties" because this interference with liberty is "temporary and relatively inconsequential." For many students, however, hair regulations "will restrict their personal appearance for four or even six years." That is hardly a minimum restriction even if our Constitution can be construed to overlook "small infringements" of constitutionally guaranteed interests. "And I do not think it can," wrote Judge Wisdom.

More important, the range of student choice "is substantially reduced" by today's decision. Speculating on the possible dangers to freedom implicit in the majority ruling, the dissent stated:

> The Court has given the public high schools in this circuit a green light to ban jeans, T-shirts, sandals, wide ties, maxi-skirts, "distractingly" colorful garb of all kinds—in short the chosen attire of many of our young people. Indeed as I read the Court's opinion, it precludes constitutional examination of a public high school requirement of a daily uniform dress.[9]

Second, the majority fears that a parade of school officials will be hauled into court to justify the restrictions they impose on their students. "It is true," notes the dissent, "that the Court's decision aborts the development of potentially far-reaching litigation over the rights of students, but these considerations do not explain the Court's belittling characterization of a young person's right to present himself to the world as he pleases so long as he causes no one any harm." Although Judge Wisdom acknowledged and regretted the overcrowded court dockets, he argued that even "the prospect of exacerbating that condition is no reason to blink at a violation of a liberty which obviously means a great deal to many young people."

To a minority of the court, the right to wear one's hair as one pleases is a "fundamental" right protected by the due process clause. In explaining its rationale, the dissent also presented a strong defense for individual freedom and diversity.

*Like other elements of costume, hair is a symbol of elegance, of
efficiency, of affinity and association, of non-conformity and rejection
of traditional values. A person shorn of the freedom to vary the
length and style of his hair is forced against his will to hold himself
out symbolically as a person holding ideas contrary, perhaps, to ideas
he holds most dear. Forced dress, including forced hair style,
humiliates the unwilling complier, forces him to submerge his individuality in the "undistracting" mass, and in general, smacks of
the exaltation of organization over member, unit over component,
and state over individual. I always thought this country does not
condone such repression.*[10]

Thus, to the minority, hair length regulations "impinge upon the
'fundamental' diversity, freedom and expressiveness of our society,
no small portion of which is comprised of students in our public
schools."

Third, the dissent disagreed with the majority concerning the
equal protection issue. The trial court found that the hair regulation
created two classes of citizens: those males who are denied a public
education because of their hair length and those who receive that
education. The lower court concluded that such a classification established by the hair regulation "has no reasonable relationship to its
professed purposes or to the educational process as a whole," and
therefore violated the equal protection clause of the Constitution.
Judge Wisdom agreed with the trial court and believed that the
analysis of the majority that led them to reject the lower court's
conclusion was "just dead wrong."

The problem with the analysis of the majority is that it upholds
the hair regulation simply because it is "reasonably intended" to
accomplish a legitimate educational objective. This means that the
majority accepts a test for rationality that looks exclusively to the
"intentions" of those who issued the regulations. "But the goals of
the school authorities," wrote the dissent, "have nothing at all to do
with the resolution of this case."

The failure of a regulation to achieve constitutionally permissible
objectives "surely cannot be cured by the good intentions of those
who enact it." Thus the majority has not addressed the central
question in this case: whether denying an education to a young man
"because he has long hair does in fact—not in hope, aspiration or
theory—bear a fair and substantial relation to the objectives of the
regulation." The district court concluded that "weeding out long-
haired young men bore no reasonable relationship" to the stated
educational objectives. In fact the lower court found nothing to

justify the regulation but "undifferentiated and unrealized fears and speculations." Moreover the evidence suggests the regulation is not only unreasonable but also "does more harm than good."

Finally, the dissent asked: How could the majority of the circuit court uphold a regulation that bears no reasonable relationship to a legitimate educational objective?

By sugaring over with talk of "good intentions" the total failure of this regulation to carry those intentions into effect. I dissent from this novel and unexplained method of writing the Equal Protection clause out of our Constitution even if it threatens to impose on this court the task of bringing to fruition the full spectrum of rights which high school students enjoy with all other Americans.

I ask: What is the important state interest that permits a public school board to deny an education to a boy whose hair is acceptably long to his parents but too long to suit a majority of the School Board of El Paso, Texas?

I submit that under the First and Fourteenth Amendments, if a student wishes to show his disestablishmentarianism by wearing long hair, antidisestablishmentarians on public school boards have no constitutional authority to prevent it.[11]

Related cases: a diversity of judicial opinion

Just as the judges of the Fifth Circuit were divided over the grooming issue in the *Karr* case, so the various federal appeals courts are also sharply divided among themselves. The Supreme Court has on several occasions refused to review this constitutional question. And as one federal judge complained: "What little guidance we have from the Court in this area is conflicting."[12]

By the end of 1973 four circuit courts had taken positions upholding the right of local school boards to regulate hair length, while four other circuits had held such regulations unconstitutional. The rationales used by the courts have varied, but the intensity and eloquence of the opinions are unparalled. Perhaps no other issue in the field of student rights has been the subject of so much judicial attention and disagreement.

In *Karr* we examined in detail the conflicting arguments of one circuit court on the question. In the following section we will briefly consider the opinions of the other circuit courts. We review these opinions for several reasons. First, the cases will indicate the prevailing legal opinion on grooming regulations in most states. (The circuit court that decided each case will be indicated.) A map at the end of this chapter will enable most readers to determine what the law is where they live, unless they are in one of the few states where a federal circuit court has not yet ruled on the issue.* Second, the cases illustrate the diversity of judicial reasoning that is found on both sides of the hair length controversy. Third, the cases provide a feeling for some of the liveliest legal language that can be found in the *Federal Reporter*. This should challenge the popular concept of judicial writing as dull, colorless, and dispassionate.

Upholding School Regulations

FREEMAN v. FLAKE:
A PROBLEM FOR THE STATES[13]

In *Freeman* v. *Flake* the Tenth Circuit reviewed three combined appeals in similar cases from Utah, New Mexico, and Colorado. In each case students claimed that school regulations that restricted the length of their hair were unconstitutional. In unanimously rejecting these claims, the court made the following points:

Regulation of hair styles of male students in state public schools is becoming a matter of major concern to federal courts if one is to judge by the ever-increasing litigation on the subject or by the days of court time expended, and the lengthy briefs presented, in the cases now before us. We are convinced that the United States Constitution and statutes do not impose on the federal courts the duty and responsibility of supervising the length of a student's hair. The problem, if it exists, is one for the states and should be handled through state procedures.

No apparent consensus exists among the lawyers for the students as to what constitutional provision affords the protection sought. . . . The uncertainty of position complicates, rather than clarifies, the

* There are two other qualifications concerning the map. In a few states where U.S. circuit courts have not considered hair length cases, state courts or federal district courts may have ruled on the issue. Furthermore, where circuit courts have refused to invalidate hair regulations because they held this to be a state and not a federal question, it is possible that state courts may declare the regulations invalid.

issue. . . . The hodgepodge reference to many provisions of the Bill of Rights and the Fourteenth Amendment shows uncertainty as to the existence of any federally-protected right.

Recognition of the principle that neither students nor teachers shed their constitutional rights to freedom of speech or expression at the schoolhouse gate, does not mean that the First Amendment contains an express command that the hair style of a male student in the public school lies within the protected area.[14]

KING v. SADDLEBACK: DOES TINKER APPLY TO HAIR?[15]

The California Education Code delegates to each school district the power "to adopt a Code of Pupil Discipline and, as a part thereof, a 'Good Grooming Policy' to insure personal cleanliness and neatness of dress." Pursuant to this authority, one school district approved a set of personal appearance regulations that included this provision: "A boy's hair shall not fall below the eyes in front and shall not cover the ears, and it shall not extend below the collar in back." This policy was adopted by vote of 22 to 2 by a student-parent-teacher committee that included seven students. Robert Olff, a 15-year-old San Jose high school student, violated these regulations, was refused enrollment, and took his case to court. Since there was no evidence that Olff's hair led to any disruption, he argued that the *Tinker* ruling should apply to his case. The Ninth Circuit Court of Appeals disagreed.

Judge Trask acknowledged that the wearing of black armbands by the students was a First Amendment right, but he did not believe the California hair regulations conflicted with freedom of speech. By wearing his hair long, Robert Olff was not purporting to say anything. In fact he "flatly stated that his hair style was not a badge or symbol of any group." Hence Olff's wearing of long hair was an activity akin to "conduct," and "the attachment of the label 'symbolic speech' does not make it symbolic speech in the absence of circumstances showing it to have been so intended." Thus the court ruled that the *Tinker* decision did not control this case.

Judge Trask also rejected Olff's argument based on "the right to be let alone" or "the right of privacy" implicit in the Fifth Amendment. "The conduct to be regulated here," wrote the court, "is not conduct found in the privacy of the home but in public educational institutions where individual liberties cannot be left completely uncontrolled to clash with similarly asserted liberties of several thousand others."

Concerning Olff's argument that the hair regulations violated the equal protection clause of the Constitution, the court said there was no evidence of unequal protection "other than the assertion that boys were treated differently than girls; i.e., girls could have long hair and boys could not." The court did not consider this difference in treatment "as creating any substantial constitutional question."[16]

Since the court concluded that the case did not involve "a clear violation of a constitutional right," the burden was on the student to prove the invalidity of the hair regulations. This Olff did not do. The school district, however, presented 11 affidavits from high school teachers and administrators based on their professional experience indicating that "extreme hair lengths of male students interferes with the educational process." Olff emphasized that his long hair caused no disruption. But this absence of disruption, wrote the court, "does not establish that long-haired males cannot be a distracting influence which would interfere with the educative process the same as any extreme in appearance, dress or deportment."

Judge Trask emphasized that "this is not a question of preference for or against certain male hair styles or the length to which persons desire to wear their hair. This court could not care less." It is a question of the right of school authorities to develop a dress code in accord with their responsibility to educate. The court concluded:

> We are satisfied that the school authorities have acted with consideration for the rights and feeling of their students and have enacted their codes . . . in the best interests of the educational process. A court might disagree with their professional judgement, but it should not take over the operation of their schools.

JACKSON v. DERRIER: A PROBLEM WITH THE PURPLE HAZE[17]

Michael Jackson and Barry Barnes were members of a combo band known as "The Purple Haze" and grew their hair far longer than permitted by the rules at Nashville's Donelson High School. Evidence indicated that they were a "distracting influence" in several classes and were constantly looking in mirrors, combing and rearranging their hair. One teacher testified that "hardly a day would go by" that she would not have to interrupt her teaching and say: "Put your combs away. This is not a beauty parlor. This is a school classroom."

Based on this evidence, the Sixth Circuit Court of Appeals found that the "deliberate flouting" of school regulations by Jackson and Barnes "created problems of school discipline." The court also found that the students "pursued their course of personal grooming for the purpose of enhancing the popularity of the musical group in which they performed." Neither student testified that his hair style was intended as an expression of any idea or point of view. Hence the court concluded that "the growing of hair for purely commercial purposes is not protected by the First Amendment's guarantee of freedom of speech."

Grooming as a Constitutional Right

RICHARDS v. THURSTON: EMBRACING FREEDOMS GREAT AND SMALL[18]

Bob Richards, a 17-year-old senior from Marlboro, Massachusetts, was suspended for refusing to comply with a school policy against "unusually long hair." In holding the school policy unconstitutional, the First Circuit Court of Appeals commented that the case involved "a very fundamental dispute" over the extent to which the Constitution protects certain "uniquely personal aspects of one's life." The court found that Richards' hair was protected by the due process clause of the Fourteenth Amendment, which "establishes a sphere of personal liberty for every individual" subject to restriction only if the exercise of that liberty interferes with the rights of others.

The governance of hair length and style, wrote Judge Coffin, may not be so fundamental as some substantive rights already found implicit in the "liberty" that is assured to citizens by the due process clause.[19] "Yet 'liberty' seems to us an incomplete protection if it encompasses only the right to do momentous acts, leaving the state free to interfere with those personal aspects of our lives which have no direct bearing on the ability of others to enjoy their liberty." A narrower view of liberty in a free society might allow a state to require "a conventional coiffure of all its citizens, a governmental power not unknown in European history." For these reasons, the court ruled that "within the commodious concept of liberty, embracing freedoms great and small, is the right to wear one's hair as he wishes."

When can the state restrict a person's liberty? The answer depends on the nature of the liberty and the context in which it is asserted. Judge Coffin noted, for example, that "the right to appear *au naturel* at home is relinquished when one sets foot on a public sidewalk." Similarly the nature of public school education required limitations on one's personal liberty in order for learning to take place. The court, however, saw "no inherent reason why decency, decorum or good conduct requires a boy to wear his hair short." Certainly "eccentric hair styling" is no longer a reliable signal of "perverse behavior." Thus the court concluded:

> We do not believe that mere unattractiveness in the eyes of some parents, teachers or students, short of uncleanliness, can justify the proscription. Nor, finally, does such compelled conformity to conventional standards of appearance seem a justifiable part of the educational process.[20]

BISHOP v. COLAW: WHERE A BROMIDE IS IN ORDER[21]

The St. Charles, Missouri, school administration suspended Stephen Bishop because his hair style violated the school dress code. School officials believed that long hair caused disruption. Several administrators asserted that male students with long hair "tended to be rowdy, created a sanitation problem in the swimming pool, caused a safety problem in certain shop classes, and tended to make poorer grades than those with shorter hair." The principal even indicated that if boys were allowed to wear long hair so as to look like girls, it might create problems with the continuing operation of the school "because of confusion over appropriate dressing room and restroom facilities."

The Eighth Circuit Court of Appeals rejected these arguments. On behalf of the court, Judge Bright wrote that Stephen possessed "a constitutionally protected right to govern his personal appearance while attending public high school." The judge noted that there is some disagreement as to the nature and source of this right. Some have referred to it as "fundamental" or "substantial," others as "basic," and still others as simply a "right." However, Judge Bright emphasized that the apparent differences in approach are more semantic than real. "The common theme underlying decisions striking down hairstyle regulations is that the Constitution guarantees rights other than those specifically enumerated, and that the right to govern one's personal appearance is one of those guaranteed rights."

The court pointed out that this right is not newly discovered. It has been recognized since 1891, when Justice Gray wrote: "No right is held more sacred, or is more carefully guarded, by the common law, than the right of every individual to the possession and control of his own person, free from all restraint or interference of others, unless by clear and unquestionable authority of law."[22] Moreover Judge Bright observed: "It is apparent that the opinion testimony of the school teachers and administrators, which lacks any empirical foundation, likely reflects a personal distaste of longer hair styles, which distaste is shared by many in the older generation." Furthermore the acceptance of the dress code by the majority of students and parents does not justify the infringement of Bishop's liberty to govern his personal appearance. "Toleration of individual differences," wrote the court, "is basic to our democracy, whether those differences be in religion, politics, or life style."

In concurring opinions, two other judges added these wide-ranging judicial observations:

The connection between long hair and the immemorial problems of misdirected student activism and negativism, whether in behavior or in learning, is difficult to see. No evidence has been presented that hair is the cause, as distinguished from a possible peripheral consequence, of undesirable traits, or that the school boards, Delilah-like, can lop off these characteristics with the locks.[23]

I cannot help but observe that the city employee who collects my rubbish has shoulder-length hair. So do a number of our nationally famous Boston Bruins. Barrel tossing and puck chasing are honorable pursuits, not to be associated with effeteness on the one hand, or aimlessness or indolence on the other. If these activities be thought not of high intellectual calibre, I turn to the recent successful candidates for Rhodes Scholarships from my neighboring institution. A number of these, according to their photographs, wear hair that outdoes even the hockey players.[24]

To say that the problem is best left to local authorities demeans the intrinsic constitutional issue involved. Such a rationale could sustain any school prohibition of the recognized constitutional rights of students.[25]

The gamut of rationalizations for justifying this restriction fails in light of reasoned analysis. When school authorities complain variously that such hair styles are inspired by a communist conspiracy, that they make boys look like girls, that they promote confusion as to the use of restrooms, and that they destroy the students' moral

*fiber, then it is little wonder even moderate students complain of
"getting up-tight." In final analysis, I am satisfied a comprehensive
school restriction on male student hair styles accomplishes little more
than to project the prejudices and personal distastes of certain adults
in authority on to the impressionable young student.*[26]

*It is bromidic to say that times change, but perhaps this is a case
where a bromide is in order.*[27]

MASSIE v. HENRY: IN THE STYLE
OF THE FOUNDING FATHERS[28]

The student body president of North Carolina's Tuscola High School
requested that guidelines be established for student grooming following an incident in which a student with long hair was called a "hip-
pie" and a fight ensued. As a result of his request, grooming guidelines were adopted by the school. Joe Massie and a classmate were
suspended for their "deliberate refusal" to conform to the guidelines.
Evidence indicated that the length of their hair "evoked considerable
jest, disgust and amusement," making it difficult to preserve classroom order.

Since the students wore long hair simply because of personal preference, it was not entitled to protection as a form of symbolic
speech. Therefore the court in this case considered their right to wear
their hair as they wished as "an aspect of the right to be secure in
one's person" guaranteed by the Due Process clause.

Judge Winter included these rare observations in his opinion:

*Whether the right of a male to wear long hair and to have long
or fulsome side burns is a constitutionally protected right is a question which has given birth to a rash of recent litigation resulting in
conflicting adjudication. . . . Unquestionably the issue is current because there is abroad a trend for the male to dress himself more
extravagantly both in the nature, cut and color of his clothing and
the quantity and mode of his facial and tonsorial adornment. . . .*

*With respect to hair, this is no more than a harkening back to
the fashion of earlier years. For example, many of the founding
fathers, as well as General Grant and General Lee, wore their hair
(either real or false) in a style comparable to that adopted by the
[student] plaintiffs. Although there exists no depiction of Jesus Christ,
either reputedly or historically accurate, he has always been shown
with hair at least the length of that of plaintiffs. If the validity and*

enforcement of the regulation in issue is sustained, it follows that none of these persons would have been permitted to attend Tuscola Senior High School.[29]

Was the evidence that the plaintiffs' long hair had a disruptive effect sufficient to restrict their rights? The Fourth Circuit Court of Appeals ruled that it was not. Judge Winter noted that the administration made little effort to convey to students the "salutary teaching" that "there is little merit in conformity for the sake of conformity" and that one may exercise a personal right any way he chooses "so long as he does not run afoul of considerations of safety, cleanliness, and decency." The court concluded that "faculty leadership in promoting and enforcing an attitude of tolerance rather than one of suppression or derision would obviate the relatively minor disruptions which have occurred."

CREWS v. CLONCS: A DENIAL
OF EQUAL PROTECTION[30]

Eugene Cloncs, principal of Indiana's North Central High School, did not admit Tyler Crews to class because he violated the school grooming regulations. Cloncs defended his action with two arguments. Since Crews's hair distracted other students, the principal considered it disruptive. Second, he argued that it posed a health and safety problem.

To what extent can disruptive conduct of others in response to Crews's long hair be used to justify his expulsion from school? In response to this question, the Seventh Circuit Court of Appeals observed that "it is absurd to punish a person because his neighbors have no self-control and cannot refrain from violence."[31] A similar principle, wrote Chief Judge Swygert, "operates to protect long-haired students unless school officials have actively tried and failed to silence those persons actually engaged in disruptive conduct." Since there was no evidence that school officials tried to punish the students who caused the "relatively insubstantial disruption," the principal failed to justify his action against Crews under his first theory.[32]

The principal's second argument was that short hair was required for health and safety reasons. Testimony indicated the various problems that long hair could cause in the gym, the swimming pool, and the laboratory. The court rejected this theory because health and safety objectives could be achieved through narrow rules directed specifically at the problems created by long hair—for example, by requiring swimming caps in pools and hair nets around machinery or Bunsen burners. Moreover, although girls engage in similar activities, only boys had been required to cut their hair to attend classes, and school officials offered no reasons why health and safety objectives were not equally applicable to girls. The court concluded that the school board's action "constitutes a denial of equal protection to male students" and therefore violated the Fourteenth Amendment of the Constitution.

ARNOLD v. CARPENTER: IS A STUDENT-APPROVED CODE CONSTITUTIONAL?[33]

In this final grooming controversy, which occured in Syracuse, Indiana, the Seventh Circuit Court of Appeals went even further in protecting a nonconforming student than it had in the *Crews* case. The controversy was based on the Wawasee High School's 1970–1971 dress code that had been carefully and democratically prepared by a committee of students, teachers, and administrators. The student members were elected by the students, and the code was adopted by a vote of 75 percent of the student body. Furthermore the code included a "consent provision" that authorized noncompliance if, at the beginning of the semester, a parent appeared before the principal and gave written consent for the exception of his child. In addition all parents were given written notice of the adoption of the code and the consent provision before the beginning of the 1970 school year. Nevertheless when school opened Greg Carpenter chose to violate the code's "long hair provision," and his parents did not request an exception. Carpenter therefore was disciplined as the code provided. He and his father sued to prohibit enforcement of the hair provision.

Questions to Consider

1. Should a grooming code be upheld if elected students participate in its formulation and if it is democratically approved by a student majority?
2. Even if you believe that no code should be enforced upon students against the wishes of their parents, does a code that allows for exceptions based on parental request seem reasonable?

The opinion of the court

In prior cases this appeals court had held that the right to wear one's hair at any length is "an ingredient of personal freedom" protected by the Constitution.[34] In this case, however, the school board argued that previous decisions upholding the right of students to wear long hair did not control "because of the 'unique' democratic formulation of the dress code by Wawasee High School." The board claimed that the adoption of the code by the democratic process justified enforcing it. But Judge Kiley noted that a school code cannot restrict a student's rights unless the restriction has a reasonable relation to a proper school purpose, such as avoiding substantial disruption. Since no such purpose had been shown, the court held that "mere student participation in adoption of the code" did not justify the limitation imposed on Greg Carpenter's constitutional right to wear long hair.

The school board, nevertheless, claimed that the "consent provision" saved the hair regulations from "fatal constitutional infirmity" since it "places responsibility for non-compliance with the parent where it belongs." In response the court acknowledged that had Carpenter's father given written consent there would have been no conflict between the operation of the code and the parents' wishes. "However," the court wrote, "the mere failure of the parents to sign the consent form should not be used by the school as a basis for denying Greg the constitutional right to determine his own hair length." Moreover, his appearance at school with long hair was an indication that his parents were agreeable to it. "Not all fathers," observed Judge Kiley, "prefer to have their student sons conform unquestionably to the decision of the majority, or look upon dissent as meriting punishment."

In 1963 the Supreme Court held that a provision excusing students from religious exercises in a public school did not save a statute that violated First Amendment provisions concerning religious liberty. Similarly the appeals court ruled that the "consent clause" in the high school dress code "does not cure the fatal constitutional infirmity in the hair provision." A school board cannot require a parent's written consent in order for a student to exercise his legal rights. For these reasons the court declared that the hair length provision of the dress code was "null and void" and that the consent provision improperly attempted to "chill" or discourage Greg's exercise of his right to wear his hair at any length he wished.

A dissenting opinion

In a lively dissent Judge Stevens sprinkled his opinion with the following sociological and philosophic comments.

The fact that absurd arguments have been advanced to support certain dress codes, or the fact that the older generation has over-

*reacted in its response to the younger generation's desire to do its own
thing, should not obscure the fact that society does have a legitimate
interest in both the continuity and mutability of its mores.*[35]

*Since the child has no enforceable right to remain unshorn or un-
washed without parental consent, I find nothing offensive in a dress
code which merely requires conformity unless excused by a child's
parents.*[36]

The right which Greg and his parents seek to vindicate in this
case does not "warrant invasion" in an area in which other parents,
in partnership with the teachers and a majority of the students,
have agreed that a measure of conformity to tradition is desirable.
"Just as the majority must learn to tolerate the non-conformist, so
must he learn to tolerate transient customs of his elders."

The only thing that would be accomplished by invalidating this
dress code would be to make it possible for Carpenter both to wear
his own hair long and to enable more of his peers to do likewise,
"thus enabling him to be more of a conformist." Hence, the decision
in this case does nothing to protect any significant interest in non-
conformity. Indeed if the slight inconvenience to his father "of evi-
dencing his consent in person has a 'chilling effect' on that interest,
our would-be non-conformist might as well get a haircut."[37]

In sum Judge Stevens opposed the majority for these reasons: (1)
There was no danger that Greg would be arbitrarily denied an education or irreparably injured in this case. (Students who violated the
dress code were prohibited from participating in certain classroom
activities; they were not suspended.) (2) If courts intervene in educational conflicts that do not endanger basic constitutional values,
"the quality of our work, and the respect which it commands in the
community, must inevitably decrease as our workload increases." (3)
The decision of the court "nourishes the pernicious seed of intolerance by encouraging confrontation rather than accommodation."
Judge Stevens concluded his dissent with these words: "I would not
force Gregory to fast on Saturday when he visits Rome, but I would
teach him not to sneer at Romans who do."

BLACK v. DOUGLAS: THE SUPREME COURT
AND THE GROOMING CONTROVERSY

When federal circuit courts differ in their interpretation of the Constitution, the Supreme Court usually reviews the question, renders

a decision, and thus establishes a uniform "law of the land." Despite the sharp differences of opinion among federal courts concerning grooming regulations, the Supreme Court has consistently declined to review circuit court decisions on the issue. Why? The following opinions give us an insight into the probable answer.

To distribute the powers of government: the opinion of Justice Black

In 1971 Justice Black reviewed a motion arising out of *Karr* v. *Schmidt*.* The district court had enjoined the enforcement of the El Paso grooming code, and the appeals court had reversed that injunction. Chesley Karr then presented to Justice Black (as the Supreme Court Justice assigned to the Court of Appeals for the Fifth Circuit) an "Emergency Motion" to suspend the action of the circuit court pending appeal to the Supreme Court. In denying this motion, Justice Black wrote:

> *The motion in this case is presented to me in a record of more than 50 pages . . . The words used throughout the record such as "Emergency Motion" and "harassment" and "irreparable dangers" are calculated to leave the impression that this case over the length of hair has created or is about to create a great national "crisis." I confess my inability to understand how anyone would thus classify this hair length case. The only thing about it that borders on the serious to me is the idea that anyone should think the Federal Constitution imposes on the United States courts the burden of supervising the length of hair that public school students should wear. The records of the federal courts, including ours, show a heavy burden of litigation in connection with cases of great importance—the kind of litigation our courts must be able to handle if they are to perform their responsibility to society. Moreover, our Constitution has sought to distribute the powers of government in this nation between the United States and the States. Surely the federal judiciary can perform no greater service to the nation than to leave the states unhampered in the performance of their purely local affairs. Surely few policies can be thought of that states are more capable of deciding*

* A motion is a request for a ruling or order that is made to a court or judge.

than the length of the hair of school boys. There can, of course, be honest differences of opinion as to whether any government, state or federal, should as a matter of public policy regulate the length of haircuts, but it would be difficult to prove by reason, logic, or common sense the federal judiciary is more competent to deal with hair length than are the local school authorities and state legislatures of all our 50 states.[38]

Permitting idiosyncrasies to flourish: Justice Douglas dissenting

In an earlier Texas case, the Fifth Circuit had upheld a grooming code regulating student hair length, and the student had petitioned the Supreme Court to review the decision. The court denied the petition, with Justice Douglas writing this lone dissent:

It comes as a surprise that in a country where the states are restrained by an Equal Protection Clause, a person can be denied education in a public school because of the length of his hair. I suppose that a nation bent on turning out robots might insist that every male have a crew cut and every female wear pigtails. But the ideas of "life, liberty, and the pursuit of happiness," expressed in the Declaration of Independence, later found specific definition in the Constitution itself, including, of course, freedom of expression and a wide zone of privacy. I had supposed those guarantees permitted idiosyncrasies to flourish, especially when they concern the image of one's personality and his philosophy toward government and his fellow men.

Municipalities furnish many services to their inhabitants, and I had supposed that it would be an invidious discrimination to withhold fire protection, police protection, garbage collection . . . [or an education] merely because a person was an offbeat nonconformist when it came to hairdo and dress as well as diet, race, religion or his views on Vietnam.[39]

Justice Douglas concluded that he would "grant the petition in this Texas case" and schedule it for argument. Despite a variety of petitions to the Supreme Court from conflicting circuit court cases,[40] it appears that only Justice Douglas has been willing to grant such petitions, hear the arguments, and establish a national policy on the issue.

Clothing

JONES v. DAY: CAN SCHOOL UNIFORMS BE REQUIRED? AN HISTORICAL PERSPECTIVE[41]

In 1920 a Mississippi public agricultural high school established a policy that all students must wear a khaki uniform while in school and "when visiting public places within five miles of the school, even on Saturdays and Sundays." One of the students and his father objected. They denied that the school had authority to prescribe student dress "at all times and at all places," and they took their case to court.

The Supreme Court of Mississippi began its opinion by noting that the school had day students as well as students who lived in dormitories. Since the boarding students were under the care of school authorities during the entire term, the authorities had the right to require such students to wear a uniform not only while at school but also in public places. Therefore the uniform requirement was not so unreasonable that courts should interfere with it, especially "when the testimony shows that it aids in the discipline of the school." But if the purpose of the regulation was to say what students should wear at home, "that would be unreasonable." Thus the regulation could not apply to day students while under the control of their parents—that is, from the time they return home in the afternoon until they start for school the next day.

The court held: (1) the school could require all students to wear uniforms at school and while traveling between school and home; (2) it could require boarding students to wear uniforms after school hours and on weekends; and (3) it could not require day students to wear uniforms after school hours or on weekends while under the authority of their parents. In sum when students were under the custody of the school, uniforms could be required; when under parental control, their parents' wishes governed. No question was raised concerning the rights of the students.

BANNISTER v. PARADIS: DO BOYS HAVE A RIGHT TO WEAR JEANS?[42]

Twelve-year-old Kevin Bannister was a sixth grade student in Pittsfield, New Hampshire, who liked to wear blue jeans to school. But on April 27, 1970, the Pittsfield School Board unanimously passed an elaborate dress code that included this provision: "Dungarees will not be allowed."[43] Although Kevin and his parents knew of this provision, he nevertheless wore jeans to school on at least two occasions. Bannister was sent home for violating the code. Because he and his parents believed the dungarees prohibition was unconstitutional, they went to court.

The findings. At the outset the trial court had an interesting problem determining exactly what was prohibited by the no-dungarees rule. The principal defined *dungarees* as "working clothes made of a coarse cotton blue fabric"; the chairman of the school board defined them as "a denim fabric pant used for work," with color of no significance; and the dictionary gave a third definition.[44] But Judge Bownes side-stepped the definitional argument by ruling that for the purpose of this case "blue jeans and dungarees are synonymous" and that Bannister "deliberately violated the school dress code . . . by wearing blue jeans to school." In any event there was no evidence that the wearing of dungarees of any color had ever caused any disturbance at the school.

The testimony. The principal of Bannister's school, Mr. Paradis, testified that discipline is essential to the educational process and that proper dress is part of a good educational climate. It was his opinion that if students wear work or play clothes to school "it leads to a relaxed attitude, and such an attitude detracts from discipline and a proper educational climate." Paradis further stated that students with patches on their clothes or with dirty clothes of any type "should be sent home." Although the dress code said nothing about clothing being clean or neat, the principal stated: "I apply the dress code as I see it." Similarly the chairman of the school board testified that "the relaxed atmosphere induced by wearing work or play clothes to school does not fit into the atmosphere of discipline and learning."

Questions to Consider

1. Does a student have a right to wear dungarees to school? What would be the constitutional basis for such a right?
2. Does a boy have the right to wear any kind of clothing he wishes? Does a girl have the same right? If so, should there be any limit to these rights?
3. Should student rights concerning hair and clothing be treated in

the same way by the schools? By the courts? Are there any reasons for treating them differently?

The ruling of the court

The first issue the court addressed was whether the prohibition against wearing dungarees was a deprivation of any constitutional right. At the time of this 1970 controversy, the court was unable to find any other reported cases brought under the 1964 Civil Rights Act where clothing was the issue.[45] Judge Bownes noted:

Students and school boards "seem to have become entangled in the hirsute aspect of school dress codes to the exclusion of almost everything else. . . . . This dearth of cases relative to wearing apparel in the Civil Rights field may be an indication that neither pupils nor school boards look on clothes with the same emotion and fervor with which they regard the length of a young man's hair or it may indicate, as the Court believed it does, that most school boards are no longer concerned with what a student wears to school as long as it is clean and covers adequately those parts of the body that, by tradition, are usually kept from public view.

Judge Bownes did not believe that the wearing of blue jeans could be protected under the "right of privacy"; nor did he believe it constituted the kind of expression that is protected by the First Amendment. In fact the court was "tempted to dispose of the matter" on the grounds that there was no deprivation of any constitutional right, except for the precedent of *Richards* v. *Thurston,* a decision of the First Circuit Court of Appeals, which includes New Hampshire.

The language and reasoning of the *Richards* case convinced Judge Bownes that a person's freedom to wear the clothes of his own choosing was a constitutional right protected by the Fourteenth Amendment. "Surely," wrote the judge, "the commodious concept of liberty" invoked in the *Richards* case, "embracing freedoms great and small" was large enough "to include within its embrace the right to wear clean blue jeans to school, unless there is an outweighing state interest justifying their exclusion."

Was there such a state interest that would justify the regulation against wearing dungarees? To answer this question, the court considered: (1) the nature of the liberty, (2) the context in which it was asserted, and (3) the extent to which the intrusion on the liberty served the public interest.

Judge Bownes acknowledged that "on the scale of values of constitutional liberties," the right to wear jeans to school "is not very high." However, no evidence was presented to show that the wearing of dungarees inhibited the educational process. Although the judge was "mindful of the testimony" of the principal and school board chairman, he confessed considerable difficulty accepting the proposition that wearing work or play clothes "is subversive of the educational process because students tend to become lax and indifferent."

Does this mean that students can wear anything they wish to school? Not according to Judge Bownes. In fact the judge noted that a school "can, and must, for its own preservation exclude persons who are unsanitary, obscenely, or scantily clad." Good hygiene and the health of others may require that dirty clothing be prohibited, "whether they be dress clothes or dungarees." Nor did the court see anything unconstitutional in a school prohibiting scantily clad students "because it is obvious that the lack of proper covering, particularly with female students, might tend to distract other pupils and be disruptive of the educational process and school discipline." While thus recognizing the school's power to adopt "reasonable restrictions on dress," the court concluded with this observation:

> The standards of appearance and dress of last year are not those of today nor will they be those of tomorrow. Regulation of conduct by school authorities must bear a reasonable basis to the ordinary conduct of the school curriculum or to carrying out the responsibility of the school.[46]

Since Judge Bownes did not believe that the dungaree prohibition was reasonably related to the school's responsibility or curriculum, he ruled that the board had not justified its intrusion on Bannister's personal liberty, "small as that intrusion may be," and that the prohibition was therefore "unconstitutional and invalid."

SCOTT v. HICKSVILLE BOARD OF EDUCATION: CAN GIRLS BE PROHIBITED FROM WEARING SLACKS?[47]

By a majority vote the students and parents of a New York school district approved a detailed dress code for secondary schools. The code included a prohibition against "girls wearing slacks" except when "permitted by the principal between December 1 and March 31 on petition by the student council when warranted by cold or inclement weather." On two days in October a tenth grade student, Lorri Scott, wore slacks to school. Pursuant to the new code, she was "placed in detention and thereby missed her classes." Lorri believed the enforcement of the no-slacks rule unlawfully interfered with her right to an education. She therefore went to the local state court to ask that the rule be annulled.

Questions to Consider

1. Is the code's general prohibition against "girls wearing slacks" reasonable? If not, could a dress code that prohibited specific kinds of slacks be upheld?
2. What criteria should be used to distinguish reasonable from unreasonable clothing regulations?
3. If you were a high school principal, what clothing regulations would you establish in your school? Would they be different for boys and girls? If so, would such differences be constitutional under the equal protection clause?

The opinion of the court

To determine whether a school board has the power to proscribe the wearing of slacks by female students, Judge Meyer first turned to the New York State Education Law. He noted that this law gives school boards the power to establish "regulations concerning the order and discipline of the schools," but he found nothing that "deals explicitly with dress." Nevertheless he concluded that school boards have "implied power to regulate dress for reasons of safety, in addition to the express power to do so for reasons of order and discipline." Thus a board has broad discretion concerning what safety, order, and discipline require, but it has no authority to enforce a regulation "which bears no reasonable relation" to these factors. Although the court commended the board for submitting the proposed dress code to referendum, Judge Meyer noted that "such a referendum cannot supply authority that does not otherwise exist."

Does the prohibition of girls wearing slacks fall within the board's authority? "The simple facts that it applies only to female students and makes no differentiation as to the kind of slacks mandates a negative answer." For those facts, observed Judge Meyer, "make evident that what is being enforced is style or taste and not safety, order, or discipline."

Are there clothing regulations that might be within the school's authority to enforce? Although courts generally restrict their rulings to the facts of the case before them, Judge Meyer was unusually expansive in his effort to illustrate the type of clothing prohibitions that might be upheld. In the interest of "safety," for example, a school board can "probably be justified" in prohibiting "the wearing of bell-bottomed slacks by students, male or female, who ride bikes to school." In the interest of "discipline," a regulation against slacks that are "so skintight and, therefore, revealing as to provoke or distract students of the opposite sex" might be valid. And in the interest of "order," a rule against slacks "to the bottoms of which small bells have been attached" would be upheld. Such regulations would be valid because they clearly relate to the school board's "authorized concerns"; the flat prohibition against all slacks is invalid "precisely because it does not."

The school board argued that regulations that differentiated the type of slacks prohibited would be too difficult to administer and might lead to greater controversy because of the individual judgments involved. To that argument the court gave two answers. First, the difficulty of staying within the limits of its authority does not alter those limits. The legislature might extend them, but the school board cannot "lift itself by its bootstraps over them." Second, other provisions in the board's own dress code showed just the kind of proper discrimination in regard to "facial adornment" and "ornamentation" that it argued is impossible in the case of slacks. Thus the code prohibited facial adornment that provoked "so widespread or constant attention as would interfere with teaching and learning" and ornamentation that would make "distracting noises, espouse violence, be obscene . . . or call for an illegal act."

In sum the court annulled the "flat prohibition of girls wearing slacks" and held that a board's regulation of dress was valid only to the extent necessary "to protect the safety of the wearer, male or female, or to control disturbance or distraction which interferes with the education of other students."

DUNHAM v. PULSIFER AND WESTLEY v. ROSSI: GROOMING v. CLOTHING

Just as courts differ on whether a student has a right to wear his hair as he pleases, so they differ about clothing regulations. Can we expect a court to rule the same way in clothing cases as in hair controversies? Yes and no. Those courts that do not protect a student's choice of hair style will probably not protect his choice of clothing. But courts that do protect hair style may (or may not) protect student freedom in matters of dress. The *Bannister* case was illustrative of a court that believed that the constitutional liberty that guarded a student's right to wear hair as he wished similarly protected his right to wear the clothing of his choice. Other courts, however, have distinguished hair from clothing and indicated that restrictions on hair style are more serious invasions of individual freedom than are clothing regulations. The *Dunham* and *Westley* cases illustrate the reasoning behind this distinction.

Dunham involved a Vermont high school grooming code for athletes. In this 1970 case a federal district court held that the code that restricted the hair length of male athletes was unconstitutional. Although the judge ruled that the freedom "to determine one's own hair style" and "personal appearance" is protected by the Constitution, he also noted that "the cut of one's hair style is more fundamental to personal appearance than the type of clothing he wears. Garments can be changed at will whereas hair, once it is cut, has to remain constant for substantial periods of time."[48]

Similarly in the *Westley* case a U.S. district court in Minnesota struck down a public high school rule requiring boys to have "neat conventional male haircuts."[49] In his opinion Judge Neville questioned whether the length of a boy's hair today is as distracting as "girls scantily clad, for instance" so as to justify the conventional haircut rule. Furthermore, he emphasized that the rule had an effect beyond class hours. "Were a school to prohibit a boy attending school with no shirt," wrote the judge, he could take off his shirt as he leaves the school grounds and "go bare waisted in life at home." But a hair regulation "invades private life beyond the school jurisdiction."

Thus some courts distinguish clothing from hair style on the following grounds: (1) hair style is more fundamental to personal appearance, (2) restrictions concerning hair have a long-term effect, and (3) hair styles today usually do not involve issues of morality and distraction as do some clothing styles. For these reasons some courts that recognize choice of hair style as a constitutional right do not protect choice of clothing style, whereas others give school boards much wider discretion to regulate clothing in the interests of health, safety, order, or discipline.

SUMMARY AND CONCLUSIONS

In 1925 the *Pugsley* case upheld a high school regulation that prohibited the wearing of any cosmetics. In its opinion the Askansas Supreme Court ruled that the local school board had a "wide range of discretion" in matters of school policy, and board regulations concerning student appearance should not be questioned by the courts unless they were illegal or clearly unreasonable. Although few federal or state courts today would support the suspension of a 17-year-old girl for using talcum on her face, the arguments of the Arkansas court are still alive in the current controversy concerning the regulation of student appearance. (A sample of recent public school dress and grooming codes appears in Appendix E.)

Hair

Eight out of the eleven U.S. circuit courts of appeals have ruled on the constitutional right of students to choose the length of their hair. As the map at the end of this chapter indicates, of the circuits that have so ruled, the division is four to four. The Supreme Court has repeatedly declined to rule on the issue. As we have seen, the arguments used to support each side (and attack the other) are varied and vigorous.

Constitutional arguments

Upholding student rights. Some of the reasons advanced by the circuit courts to support a student's right to wear his hair as he wishes follow.

In *Richards* the First Circuit ruled that a student's hair style was part of the personal "liberty" assured to every citizen by the due process clause of the Fourteenth Amendment. In *Bishop* the Eighth Circuit identified the right as the "freedom to govern one's personal appearance" that is retained by individual citizens under the Ninth Amendment.* In *Massie* the Fourth Circuit considered the right to choose one's hair style as "an aspect of the right to be secure in one's person" guaranteed by the due process clause and also protected by the equal protection clause. And in *Arnold* and *Crews* the Seventh Circuit identified the right as either within the First Amend-

---

* The Ninth Amendment reads: "The enumeration in the Constitution, of certain rights, shall not be construed to deny or disparage others retained by the people." As Justice Arthur Goldberg has pointed out, the amendment was specifically designed "to quiet expressed fears that a bill of specifically enumerated rights could not be sufficiently broad to cover all essential rights and that the specific mention of certain rights would be interpreted as a denial that others were protected." *Griswold* v. *Connecticut*, 381 U.S. 479 (1965).

ment freedom of expression or as an "ingredient of personal freedom" constitutionally retained by the people.

Upholding school rules. In contrast, the Fifth, Sixth, Ninth, and Tenth Circuits have upheld school regulations limiting the length and style of hair. Although their approaches have differed, the most prevalent view among these courts is that the "long hair" problem is "too insubstantial" to warrant federal court consideration.

In *Karr* the Fifth Circuit held that hair regulations did not violate the First Amendment (long hair does not have "sufficient communicative content"); the Fourteenth Amendment (it is one of the "lesser liberties" and not a "fundamental" right); or the equal protection clause (grooming regulations seek to accomplish "legitimate objectives.") In *Freeman* the Tenth Circuit doubted that any constitutional right was involved. In *King* the Ninth Circuit noted that student grooming is not like a right to privacy or personal liberty at home; it is behavior in a public educational institution where individual liberties cannot be left uncontrolled. And in *Jackson* the Sixth Circuit ruled that the regulation of grooming has "a real and reasonable connection" with the maintenance of school discipline.

Other arguments

In addition to the legal arguments, each side bolsters its position with a variety of philosophic, educational, and administrative reasons. Judges protecting student rights have offered arguments such as those that follow.

Hair regulations bear no reasonable relation to a legitimate educational objective; they restrict fundamental freedoms of diversity and expression; they teach conformity for its own sake; they force students to submerge their individuality; and they are not necessary for health or safety. Their enforcement accomplishes little more than "to project the prejudices and personal distastes of certain adults in authority" and causes more disruption in schools than does the presence of long-haired students. If such students cause others to be disruptive, it would be better for officials to teach disrupters an attitude of tolerance rather than to suppress diversity and teach conformity. It is dangerous to simply say that the problem is best left to local authorities; such a rationale could support any school prohibition of student rights. Moreover if most high school grooming codes were upheld, then many of America's greatest leaders would not have been permitted to attend these schools.

Those judges upholding school regulations offer several arguments. They claim that reasonable grooming codes do not violate student rights. The purpose of these codes is to eliminate distracting extremes in hair style, to avoid possible conflicts, and to eliminate potential health and safety hazards. Even if some codes do restrict student freedom, their effect is temporary and "relatively inconsequential," and they still leave students "a wide range of personal choice in their dress and grooming." Local boards should have wide latitude in the management of school affairs, and school officials should have authority to develop dress codes in accordance with their responsibility, without having to be called into court to justify such regulations. Although courts might disagree with the judgment of professional educators, they should not interfere with their work. Moreover the Constitution does not give the federal courts the job of "supervising the length of hair that public school students should wear." Finally, all school regulations restricting student liberty cannot be litigated in the courts, for the judicial process is administratively unable to deal with the infringement of every minor right.

Clothing

Courts are divided on whether students have a constitutional right to wear the clothing of their choice to school. Most courts hold that they do not. These include all courts that support the right of schools to regulate hair length. Each of the legal arguments used to reject the right of students to wear long hair has been used to reject the claim of students to wear unconventional clothing. In addition some courts that protect the right of students to wear their hair as they choose reject the students' claim to wear the clothing of their choice. Such courts justify this distinction on the grounds that restriction on hair style is a more serious invasion of individual freedom: Clothing can be easily changed after school hours; but if haircuts are required, the effect is more lasting. Unlike hair length, certain types of clothing are generally acknowledged to be distracting if not immoral.

Some courts, however, protect clothing as well as hair style. *Bannister*, for example, ruled that a prohibition against wearing dungarees deprived students of their constitutional rights. Although clothing may not be the kind of expression protected by the First Amendment, it does fall within the Fourteenth Amendment's "commodious concept of liberty," which protects "freedoms great and small." *Bannister* held that schools can exclude persons who are "unsanitary, obscenely, or scantily clad." But dress regulations must be reasonably related to the school's responsibility or its curriculum, and the prohibition against wearing dungarees was related to neither. Hence, the prohibition was an unjustified intrusion on student liberty, "small as that instrusion may be." Similarly *Scott* held that a flat prohibition against female students wearing slacks was unreasonable. School regulations prohibiting certain kinds of dress in order to protect the safety of the wearer and to control disturbances or distraction might be valid, but a rule that applied only to females and applied to all slacks was clearly enforcing "style or taste, and not safety, order, or discipline."

By the end of the 1970s some readers may find it difficult to understand why so many students, parents, school officials, and judges were so concerned with issues such as hair length during the past decade. By then this raging controversy of the late 1960s may seem distant and trivial. But the question, of course, is larger than "the length of a school boy's hair." It involves such fundamental legal and educational issues as: When and for what reasons can school officials restrict student freedom? Should nonconformity be prohibited or guarded in our public schools? Should the courts protect personal preferences or just "fundamental" freedoms? As this chapter has indicated, these issues are still being confronted by our schools and our courts.

In the coming years hair length may no longer be the symbol that triggers this larger debate. But the underlying issues will be with us as long as our democracy continues to struggle with the problems of freedom and conformity in the public schools.

NOTES

[1] 393 U.S. 856 (1968).

[2] 250 S.W. 538 (Ark. 1923).

[3] School officials have apparently been making and enforcing grooming codes against nonconforming students for hundreds of years. In 1560, for example, the Cambridge University in England "fined a student six shillings and eight pence for breaking a school rule that 'no scholler doe weare any long lockes of Hayre uppon his heade, but that he be polled, notted, or rounded after the accustomed manner of the gravest Schollers of the Universitie.'" Peter M. Sandman, *Students and the Law*, New York, Macmillan, 1971, p. 14.

Controversy over hair length has been taking place on this continent at least since 1649 when the magistrates of Portsmouth issued the following regulation: "For as much as the wearing of long hair, after the manner of ruffians and barbarous Indians, has begun to invade New England, we, the magistrates, do declare and manifest our dislike and detestation against the wearing of such long hair, as against a thing uncivil and unmanly, whereby men do deform themselves and do corrupt good manners." Dale Gaddy, *Rights and Freedoms of Public School Students: Directions from the 1960's*, Topeka, Kansas, National Organization on Legal Problems in Education, 1971. p 25.

[4] *Karr* v. *Schmidt*, 460 F.2d 609 (5th Cir. 1972).

[5] *Id.* at 610–611.

[6] *Id.* at 617.

[7] In conclusion, Judge Morgan wrote:

The regulations which impinge on our daily affairs are legion. Many of them are more intrusive and tenuous than the one involved here. The federal judiciary has urgent tasks to perform, and to be able to perform them, we must recognize the physical impossibility that less than a thousand of us could ever enjoin a uniform concept of equal protection or due process on every American in every facet of his daily life [Id. at 618].

[8] *Id.* at 619.

[9] *Id.* at 620.

[10] *Id.* at 621.

[11] *Id.* at 623–624.

[12] *Bishop* v. *Colaw*, 450 F.2d 1069, 1071 (8th Cir. 1971).

[13] *Freeman* v. *Flake*, 448 F.2d 258 (10th Cir. 1971).

[14] *Id.* at 261.

[15] *King* v. *Saddleback*, 445 F.2d 932 (9th Cir. 1971). This decision involved two cases: *King* v. *Saddleback Junior College District* and *Olff* v. *East Side Union High School District*. Since they were both appeals from district court decisions concerning dress codes that limited the hair length of male students, they were argued and decided at the same time.

[16] For an additional discussion of the kinds of school policies that might violate the equal protection clause, see Chapters 7 and 8.

[17] *Jackson* v. *Derrier*, 424 F.2d 213 (6th Cir. 1970), cert. denied, 400 U.S. 850 (1970).

[18] *Richards* v. *Thurston*, 424 F.2d 1281 (1st Cir. 1970).

[19] Other "liberties" that the Supreme Court has found implicit in the Due Process clause include the right of parents to send their children to private schools and the right of citizens to travel to a foreign country.

[20] *Id.* at 1286.

[21] *Bishop* v. *Colaw*, 450 F.2d 1069 (8th Cir. 1971).

[22] *Union Pacific Railway Company* v. *Botsford*, 141 U.S. 250 (1891).

[23] *Bishop* at 1077.

[24] *Id.* at 1077–1078. This quotation was from the concurring opinion of Judge Bailey Aldrich of the First Circuit Court of Appeals who lives in Boston and was "sitting by designation" in this Eighth Circuit case.

[25] *Id.* at 1078.

[26] *Ibid.*

27 *Ibid.*

28 *Massie* v. *Henry,* 455 F.2d 779 (4th Cir. 1972).

29 *Id.* at 780.

30 *Crews* v. *Cloncs,* 432 F.2d 1259 (7th Cir. 1970).

31 Judge Swygert noted: "History contains many examples of regimes which have attacked and silenced their opponents by requiring conformity of hairstyle or dress." Thus in 1644, the Ching dynasty sought to consolidate its power by compelling the male population "to shave the front of the head, and to wear the hair in a queue." The new rulers also required a change in dress. The opposition to such measures was so intense that many chose to die "rather than adopt the marks of servitude." Another example was the "official prohibition of beards during the reign of Peter the Great." *Crews,* at 1264.

32 Furthermore Judge Swygert pointed out that even if school officials have tried and failed to control the disruptive students, "emergency action against the long-haired student may be justified only by exceptional circumstances."

33 *Arnold* v. *Carpenter,* 459 F.2d 939 (7th Cir. 1972).

34 After reviewing several decisions which had concluded that the "long hair" problem was not substantial enough to warrant judicial intervention, Judge Kiley observed:

It is understandable why some judges find students' "long hair" claims constitutionally insubstantial. Measured against today's great constitutional issues (capital punishment, abortion, school segregation), the question of whether a student may or may not have constitutional protection in selection of his hair dress appears de minimus. Perhaps even judges who sustain the right are nagged with impatience and doubt when faced with student claims. But we look across a gap of a generation or two, from the Olympian heights of what we consider the great issues. For the high school student claimant, however, the right to wear long hair is an issue vital to him . . . and there appears to be no reason why the values of freedom are less precious in a younger generation than in an older [Id. at 941–942].

35 Furthermore Judge Stevens noted: "It does not take the wisdom of Solomon to recognize that dress codes which have been judicially condemned were doomed to fall in due course in any event. Judicial participation in the process of changing mores can affect the rate of change, but we certainly do not decide whether or not the change will occur."

36 "I cannot understand," wrote Judge Stevens, "why we should intervene in this case to save a child's parent from walking over to the principal's office" where the only legal relief his son may obtain "is available for the asking."

37 *Id.* at 944–946.

38 *Karr* v. *Schmidt,* 401 U.S. 1201 (1971).

39 *Ferrell* v. *Dallas,* 393 U.S. 856 (1968).

40 For example, the Supreme Court declined to review both *Breen* v. *Kahl* 419 F.2d 1034 (7th Cir. 1969), cert. denied 398 U.S. 937 (1970), which

recognized grooming as a constitutional right, and *Jackson* v. *Dorrier* cert. denied 400 U.S. 850 (1970) which did not recognize such a right. For more information on Supreme Court review, see Appendix B, How the System Works.

[41] *Jones* v. *Day,* 89 So. 906 (Miss. 1921).

[42] *Bannister* v. *Paradis,* 316 F.Supp. 185 (D. N.H. 1970).

[43] The full text of the Proposed Pittsfield Dress Code is included in Appendix E.

[44] *Webster's Third International Dictionary* unsurprisingly defines *dungarees* as "heavy cotton work clothes usually made of blue dungaree." *Bannister* at 186.

[45] Section 1983 of the 1964 Civil Rights Act provides that "Every person who, under color of any statute of any state subjects any citizen to the deprivation of any rights . . . secured by the Constitution and laws, shall be liable to the party injured in an action at law." Judge Bownes found that the enforcement of the Pittsfield dress code was clearly an action by the state of New Hampshire, *Id.* at 187.

[46] From *Westley* v. *Rossi,* 305 F.Supp. 706, 714 (D. Minn. 1969), as quoted in *Bannister* at 189.

[47] *Scott* v. *Board of Education, Hicksville,* 305 N.Y.S. 2d 601 (1969).

[48] *Dunham* v. *Pulsifer,* 312 F.Supp. 411, 419 (D. Vt. 1970).

[49] *Westley* v. *Rossi,* 305 F.Supp. 706 (D. Minn. 1969).

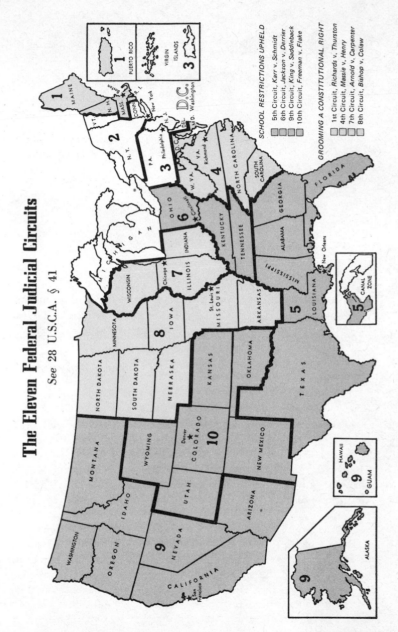

The Eleven Federal Judicial Circuits

See 28 U.S.C.A. § 41

SCHOOL RESTRICTIONS UPHELD

5th Circuit, *Karr v. Schmidt*
6th Circuit, *Jackson v. Dorrier*
9th Circuit, *King v. Saddleback*
10th Circuit, *Freeman v. Flake*

GROOMING A CONSTITUTIONAL RIGHT

1st Circuit, *Richards v. Thurston*
4th Circuit, *Massie v. Henry*
7th Circuit, *Arnold v. Carpenter*
8th Circuit, *Bishop v. Colaw*

SOURCE: Courtesy of West Publishing Company, St. Paul, Minnesota.

7

Racial and ethnic segregation

Racial hatred is an adult rather than a childhood disease.
                                    —Johnson v. San Francisco Unified[1]

The only school desegregation plan that meets constitutional standards is one that works.
                                    —U.S. v. Jefferson[2]

Introduction

Our schools have always reflected the racism found in the larger culture. In the nineteenth century, racial discrimination in the schools was often official policy, reflected in separate schools for different races. For many decades these schools were not only separate but unequal; the schooling provided for minorities—Blacks, Mexican-Americans, and Indians—was clearly inferior.

The twentieth century ushered in the "Separate but Equal" doctrine which, in turn, was challenged by the many legal and political attacks on racist practices. This chapter examines racism as it has affected the civil rights of students. The leading cases are presented so that the reader may come to understand the legal principles related to racially separate schools, the racial aspects of school staffing, "freedom of choice" plans, busing, and related issues.

Chinese schools for Chinese-American children?

San Francisco is a city of immigrants as well as a cosmopoliton city and is composed of many ethnic and racial groups. Most of its inhabitants are of European, African, and Asian ancestry, and they often live and work in ethnic or racial enclaves. The distribution of these groups was due in part to free choice and in part to racial, ethnic, and economic discrimination. The city's schools, particularly the neighborhood elementary schools, tend to reflect the population composition of the surrounding areas that they serve. For example, in an area populated by Chinese-Americans, three elementary schools "are filled predominantly with children of Chinese ancestry—in one 456 out of 482, in another 230 out of 289, and in a third, 1,074 out of 1,111."[3]

The San Francisco Unified School District created a plan for the overall desegregation of its schools. The plan included, among its many features, a reassignment of pupils of Chinese ancestry to certain elementary schools away from their neighborhoods in order to "reduce racial imbalance." Busing was to be one of the means used to eliminate segregation. In addition to children of Chinese ancestry, children of other ancestries were to take part in the reassignment plan; these included children of Japanese, Filipino, African, and Spanish ancestry, as well as of various European ethnic backgrounds.

Chinese-American parents objected to the reassignment plans on behalf of their children. In the *Lee* case they requested the school district and the courts to continue the pattern of neighborhood schools that allows children of Chinese ancestry to attend school together. The parents urged that there are important cultural values that cannot be preserved and passed on to future generations if the children are dispersed throughout the city. In addition to the Chinese cultural heritage, the very survival of their language might be in jeopardy if their children could not remain together.

Questions to Consider

1. Does a subculture have a right to perpetuate itself?
2. Should the majority culture force a subculture to accept integration and thus probable assimilation?
3. Do parents have the right to educate their children in a neighborhood school?
4. What parts of the Constitution relate to these issues?

The problem of the Chinese children and parents, briefly stated above, makes it clear that racial and ethnic segregation is not just a problem affecting Blacks and whites. Furthermore, it emphasizes the often overlooked fact that minorities do not always wish to integrate with majorities, and it suggests that rather than having solved our problems of racial and ethnic integration, we can expect a variety of new situations calling for novel applications of the Fourteenth Amendment to school-related issues.

The constitutional provision most directly relevant to questions of racial segregation and integration is the following portion of the Fourteenth Amendment: "No State shall . . . deny to any person within its jurisdiction the equal protection of the laws."

The application of the equal protection clause of this amendment to school situations has a substantial history involving hundreds of court cases. For the purposes of this discussion it will be sufficient to examine the landmark decisions of *Brown I, Brown II*, and *Swann* and to mention *Plessy* v. *Ferguson* briefly in order to provide historical perspective. After that we will return for a brief look at the issues raised by the Chinese parents in San Francisco.

THE PLESSY CASE: SEPARATE CAN BE EQUAL

In 1890 Louisiana passed a law that in part required

> *that all railway companies carrying passengers in their coaches in this state shall provide equal but separate accommodations for the white and colored races, by providing two or more passenger coaches for each passenger train, or by dividing the passenger coaches by a partition so as to secure separate accommodations. . . . No person or persons shall be permitted to occupy any coaches other than the ones assigned to them, on account of the race they belong to.*[4]

The statute provided for enforcement of the separation of the races by train officials and specified a fine of twenty-five dollars or imprisonment for no more than twenty days for violators.

Mr. Plessy was assigned by the railroad officers to a coach "for the use of the race to which he belonged, but he insisted upon going into a coach used by the race to which he did not belong." He was forcibly ejected from the coach for white passengers and imprisoned for the violation. His petition asserted that "petitioner was seven-eighths Caucasian and one-eighth African blood." He challenged the constitutionality of the law on various grounds, including the claim that it violated the Fourteenth Amendment.

Although the *Plessy* case did not directly involve the civil rights of students or teachers, it announced a principle that was used in school-related cases to support laws, policies, and practices of racial segregation. The *Plessy* v. *Ferguson* case broadly legitimized the "separate but equal" doctrine.

The Supreme Court applied the test of reasonableness to the legislation and concluded that the Louisiana legislature must have broad discretion to decide what was reasonable "with reference to the established usages, customs, and traditions of the people, and with a view to the promotion of their comfort, and the preservation of the public peace and order." Applying this standard, the Court concluded that the law was not unreasonable.

Does separation of the races imply a superior-inferior relationship? Not in the eyes of the *Plessy* Court in 1896: "We consider the underlying fallacy of the plaintiff's argument to consist in the assumption that the enforced separation of the two races stamps the colored race with a badge of inferiority. If this be so, it is not by reason of anything found in the act, but solely because the colored race chooses to put that construction upon it." The Supreme Court, with only Justice Harlan dissenting, upheld the constitutionality of the Louisiana law, and the case became authority for the principle that "separate but equal" is constitutionally permissible.

The interim years

Separate schools for white, Black, Indian, Mexican, and other ethnic children had existed in many parts of the country for years before the *Plessy* case. In fact the Court in that decision referred to acts of Congress "requiring separate schools for colored children in the District of Columbia." Although logically it was arguable that separate schools can be equal, in fact, they were usually not equal. In the years following *Plessy* various court challenges resulted not in the reversal of the *Plessy* doctrine but in the requirement that schools become more equal. These attempts focused on improving physical facilities and providing better books and instructional materials, as well as upgrading the teaching staff of Black and other minority schools.

In the meantime the separate but equal doctrine was being successfully challenged in the courts as it applied to colleges and graduate schools. We will not pursue that line of legal development here, but these cases are alluded to lest the reader infer that the Supreme Court abruptly changed its mind from *Plessy* v. *Ferguson* to *Brown* v. *Board of Education*, the next case to be discussed. During the fifty-eight years separating the two cases significant developments occurred, which make it clear to knowledgeable observers that the *Brown* case is an evolutionary development rather than an abrupt change.

BROWN I

Kansas enacted a law in 1949, which permitted, but did not require, cities with a population of more than 15,000 to maintain separate schools for Negro and white students. Under the authority of this state law the Topeka Board of Education chose to establish segregated elementary schools.

Oliver Brown, a student, and others filed a class suit* challenging the constitutionality of segregated schools, claiming that such an arrangement, when conducted by officials pursuant to law, violated the equal protection clause of the Fourteenth Amendment. The district court found "that segregation in public education has a detrimental effect upon Negro children," but it upheld the arrangement since white and Negro schools "were substantially equal with respect to buildings, transportation, curricula, and educational qualifications of teachers."[5] Brown appealed to the Supreme Court, where his case was heard along with similar cases from South Carolina, Virginia, and Delaware.

School districts and state officials who urged the legitimacy of segregated schooling presented two basic arguments. First, when the Fourteenth Amendment was adopted in 1868 it was not intended to apply to public education; second, the Court should be bound by the separate but equal principle established in the case of *Plessy* v. *Ferguson* in 1896 and followed as precedent in several cases thereafter.

Questions to Consider

1. Did the authors of the Fourteenth Amendment intend it to apply to public education?

* A class suit is a lawsuit brought by one or more individuals on behalf of a group of people who fall into the same general class or category, for example, a class of consumers, women, tenants, and so on.

2. Can schools be "separate but equal"? How would you determine if two or more schools were equal?
3. Should the Court be bound by the precedent of *Plessy* v. *Ferguson*? When should the Court follow precedent and when not?

The opinion of the court

Chief Justice Earl Warren delivered the unanimous opinion of the Court. He explained that the case must be decided in light of the facts and conditions of contemporary American life and not those of 1868 when the Fourteenth Amendment was adopted. Only by considering the significance of public education in the middle of the twentieth century could it be determined whether segregated schooling deprived children of equal protection of the laws.

In reaching its decision the Court considered the history of public education in America. It noted that the quality of the schools varied by locality and by region and that the South, for various reasons, was slower than the North in its provision for public schools. It also recognized "the low status of Negro education in all sections of the country, both before and immediately after the [Civil] War." The Court quoted Professor Ellwood Cubberley to the effect that "compulsory school attendance laws were not generally adopted until after the ratification of the Fourteenth Amendment, and it was not until 1918 that such laws were in force in all the States."[6]

The Court, after exhaustive consideration of the circumstances surrounding the adoption of the amendment, became convinced that historical considerations by themselves were inconclusive. There was no clear and convincing evidence as to what, if anything, was originally intended for public education by the authors of the Fourteenth Amendment. Furthermore no case prior to this one had raised the direct question of the constitutionality of segregated schooling.

In moving toward its decision, the Court, in an often quoted paragraph, emphasized the centrality of schools in modern life:

Today, education is perhaps the most important function of state and local governments. Compulsory school attendance laws and the great expenditures for education both demonstrate our recognition of the importance of education to our democratic society. It is required in the performance of our most basic public responsibilities, even service in the armed forces. It is the very foundation of good citizenship. Today it is a principal instrument in awakening the child to cultural values, in preparing him for later professional training, and

*in helping him to adjust normally to his environment. In these days,
it is doubtful that any child may reasonably be expected to succeed
in life if he is denied the opportunity of an education. Such an
opportunity, where the state has undertaken to provide it, is a right
which must be made available to all on equal terms.*[7]

Justice Warren then concluded that segregation of public school
children solely on the basis of race deprives minority group children
of equal educational opportunity even though the "tangible factors
may be equal."[*]

Why did the Court reject *Plessy* v. *Ferguson?* First, it pointed out
that the *Plessy* case involved transportation and not public education.
Second, courts do not follow precedents blindly; changing circumstances as well as new knowledge may reasonably lead to new
conclusions. This latter factor—namely, a more advanced state of
social and psychological knowledge of schooling—had significant
influence on the Court. It quoted with approval an earlier Kansas
case:

*Segragation of white and colored children in public schools has a
detrimental effect upon the colored children. The impact is greater
when it has the sanction of the law; for the policy of separating
the races is usually interpreted as denoting the inferiority of the
Negro group. A sense of inferiority affects the motivation of the child
to learn. Segregation with the sanction of law, therefore, has a
tendency to (retard) the educational and mental development of
Negro children and to deprive them of some of the benefits they
would receive in a racial(ly) integrated school system.*[8]

The Court also relied on the writing of various psychologists,
including Dr. Kenneth B. Clark, who analyzed and established the
devastating effects of discrimination and prejudice on the personality
development of children. Thus, in part as a result of advances in
the social sciences, the Court rejected the precedent of *Plessy* v.
Ferguson. "We conclude that in the field of public education the

[*] In these days of intense efforts to place education on a scientific
basis, it is significant to note that the Court considered the intangible,
nonmeasurable qualities of schooling as most important. It quoted with
approval an earlier case concerning segregated law school education and
emphasized the significance of "those qualities which are incapable of
objective measurement but which make for greatness in a law school."
Id. at 493.

doctrine of 'separate but equal' has no place. Separate educational facilities are inherently unequal."

The Court, realizing the complexities of desegregating the schools in light of the "great variety of local conditions," requested all parties involved or wishing to be involved to return at a later date and submit arguments for implementation of the *Brown* decision. Thus *Brown* I, within a year, led to *Brown* II.

BROWN II

The first *Brown* case declared the fundamental principle that racial discrimination in public education is unconstitutional. In *Brown* II the Court said: "All provisions of federal, state, or local laws requiring or permitting such discrimination must yield to this principle."[9]

Because segregated and discriminatory schooling existed in so many places and under such varied conditions, the Court requested arguments on the question of relief. In other words, what kind of a legal order should it issue to remedy the widespread, massive discrimination?

Questions to Consider

1. What order would you have issued if you had the authority of the Supreme Court?
2. What factors and conflicting interests would you consider before issuing the order?

The opinion of the court

Chief Justice Warren again delivered the unanimous opinion of the Court. He noted that already some steps had been taken toward desegregation as a result of *Brown* I. He also emphasized that local school authorities had the primary responsibility for clarifying, assessing, and solving local educational problems. The local courts, however, must consider whether or not the actions of school authorities constitute "good faith implementation of governing constitutional principles."

Justice Warren recommended that principles of equity and fairness should guide the courts. School districts should consider the interests of minority children in opening the schools as soon as practicable on a nondiscriminatory basis and make a "prompt and reasonable start toward full compliance." "Once such a start has been made, the courts may find that additional time is necessary to carry out the ruling in an effective manner."

The local courts retained jurisdiction over such cases, and the burden of proof was to be on the defendant school district to show that it was proceeding reasonably and in good faith toward "compliance at the earliest practicable date." In its last paragraph the opinion used the now famous phrase "with all deliberate speed" as a general guideline to be used by local school districts in the elimination of unconstitutional racial segregation.

"With All Deliberate Speed"

What were the reactions to the desegregation decisions of Brown I and II? How did school districts and states respond to the call to eliminate racial discrimination with all deliberate speed?

The initial attention focused on the South, where segregation was openly practiced and supported by law. Separate schools existed for Blacks and whites, the so-called dual school systems. The North maintained more subtle forms of segregation, often not officially stated or sanctioned. Therefore it was widely believed that the desegregation decisions would apply only to the South. One New Jersey newspaper announced the court ruling with this headline: "It Doesn't Affect Us."

THE GRIFFIN CASE: THE CLOSING OF SCHOOLS

In the South, although some school officials urged compliance, resistance was the more typical initial reaction. Such resistance took many forms: governors standing in schoolhouse doors, legislatures passing new laws as delaying tactics, local school boards simply ignoring the decision. One of the most publicized cases arose in Prince Edward County, Virginia, where the supervisors chose to levy no school taxes so that the schools did not reopen in the fall of 1959 when "confronted with a court decree which requires the admission of white and colored children to all the schools of the county without regard to race or color."[10]

The supervisors of Prince Edward County took this action after the General Assembly of Virginia (the state legislature) tried various means of frustrating the intent of the Brown decision. When these various efforts were found to violate the Virginia constitution, the "General Assembly abandoned 'massive resistance' to desegregation and turned instead to what was called a 'freedom of choice' plan."

This plan repealed "Virginia's compulsory attendance laws and instead made school attendance a matter of local option." We can more readily understand the effectiveness of the resistance to integration when we realize that the initial litigation to desegregate the schools of Prince Edward County began in 1951 and the opinion in this case was handed down in 1964!

In this case, *Griffin* v. *Prince Edward County*, the Supreme Court struck down the efforts of state and school officials to avoid or delay school desegregation. The Court carefully considered the reasons for the closing of the schools and found them to be racist and therefore unconstitutional. In its own words:

> But the record in the present case could not be clearer that Prince Edward's public schools were closed and private schools operated in their place with state and county assistance, for one reason and one reason only: to ensure, through measures taken by the county and the state, that white and colored children in Prince Edward County would not, under any circumstances, go to the same school. Whatever nonracial grounds might support a state's allowing a county to abandon public schools, the grounds of race and opposition to de-segregate do not qualify as constitutional.[11]

The facts in this case showed that the children of Prince Edward County were treated differently from those in other counties in the state. "Prince Edward children must go to a private school or none at all; all other Virginia children can go to public schools." The result of this is that if children in Prince Edward County go to school, they must go to racially segregated ones, which, "although designated as private, are beneficiaries of county and state support." The Court found that such an arrangement violated the equal protection clause of the Fourteenth Amendment. Furthermore, indicating its lack of sympathy with the variety of delaying tactics, it noted that "the time for mere 'deliberate speed' has run out, and that phrase can no longer justify denying these Prince Edward school children their constitutional rights to an education equal to that afforded by the public schools in the other parts of Virginia."

"Freedom of Choice"

The phrase "freedom-of-choice" had a broad appeal. It caught on rapidly in the various state legislatures and local school district of-fices as everyone searched for a palatable way to satisfy the law.

Some wanted to use it to abide by the law, whereas others saw in the phrase a new and powerful subterfuge. Some of these issues surfaced in the *Green* case.

THE GREEN CASE

New Kent County is a rural area in eastern Virginia with a population of about 4500, half of whom are black. Since there was no residential segregation in the county, persons of both races resided throughout. "The school system has only two schools, the all white New Kent School on the east side of the county and the all black George W. Watkins school on the West side."[12] Of the 1300 students, 750 were black and 550 were white. Twenty-one school buses traveled overlapping routes throughout the county to transport students, 11 serving the Watkins school and 10 serving the New Kent school.

The segregated schools were initially established and maintained under a 1902 Virginia law that mandated racial segregation in public education. After the *Brown* decisions a State Pupil Placement Board was established under which children were automatically assigned to schools they had previously attended, unless upon their application the board reassigned them to a different school. No student asked for reassignment under this law to a school other than that of his own race. However, while the *Green* case was pending, the School Board of New Kent County adopted a new "freedom-of-choice" plan, in order to be eligible for federal financial aid.

Under the freedom-of-choice plan, first and eighth grade students had to choose a school to attend whereas all other students each year might choose between New Kent and Watkins schools. Students who did not choose were assigned to the school previously attended. The school district argued that such a plan completely satisfied the Fourteenth Amendment since every student, regardless of race, might "freely" choose which school to attend. Charles C. Green and other students argued that the board had not yet satisfied the nondiscriminatory intent of the Fourteenth Amendment, as interpreted in the *Brown* decisions.

Questions to Consider

1. Does freedom-of-choice satisfy the equal protection clause of the Fourteenth Amendment?
2. When is choice really free? Since we all have a history that influences us, are our choices ever really free?
3. Does the Fourteenth Amendment make integration compulsory?

The opinion of the court

Justice Brennan, in delivering the opinion of the Court, expressed serious concern about the long delays in desegregating the schools of New Kent County. He noted that the freedom-of-choice plan was first offered eleven years after *Brown* I and ten years after *Brown* II. "This deliberate perpetuation of the unconstitutional dual system can only have compounded the harm of such a system." Consequently it is not sufficient that the district merely make available some choices to students and their parents. "Moreover, a plan that at this late date fails to provide meaningful assurance of prompt and effective disestablishment of a dual system is also intolerable."

Does this decision mean that the "freedom-of-action" plan was illegitimate? Not necessarily, said Justice Brennan. "All we decide today is that in desegregating a dual school system a plan utilizing 'freedom-of-choice' is not an end in itself." Then he incorporated some of the words of Judge Sobeloff of the district court:

"Freedom-of-choice" is not a sacred talisman; it is only a means to a constitutionally required end—the abolition of the system of segregation and its effects. If the means prove effective, it is acceptable, but if it fails to undo segregation, other means must be used to achieve this end.* The school officials have the continuing duty to take whatever action may be necessary to create a "unitary, non-racial system."[13]

In applying the test of effectiveness to this case, Justice Brennan concluded:

The New Kent School Board "freedom-of-choice" plan cannot be accepted as a sufficient step to "effective transition" to a unitary system. In three years of operation, not a single white child has chosen to attend Watkins School and although 115 Negro children enrolled in New Kent School in 1967 (up from 35 in 1965 and 111 in 1966) 85 percent of all the Negro children in the system still attend the all-Negro Watkins School.[14]

The Court concluded that the dual system had not been dismantled. The Court, having declared the arrangement unconstitutional, or-

---

* An earlier, lower court case, *U.S.* v. *Jefferson*, 372 F.2d 836 (1966), pronounced a simple, pragmatic test: "The only school desegregation plan that meets constitutional standards is one that works."

dered the school board of New Kent County to formulate a new plan that would desegregate the schools. The case was then returned to the district court "for further proceedings consistent with this opinion."

Busing

As the years passed, hundreds of desegregation suits were filed as the nation underwent massive readjustments to remedy the unconstitutional arrangements spawned by decades of segregated schooling. First local, then regional, and finally national political figures expressed themselves for and against school desegregation, and busing as a method to combat it, until busing became the most controversial symbol of the struggle.

THE SWANN CASE[15]

The Charlotte-Mecklenburg (North Carolina) school system enrolled over 84,000 students in 107 schools during the 1968–69 school year. Approximately 24,000 of the students were Black, about 14,000 of whom attended 21 schools that were at least 99 percent Black. This pupil distribution resulted from a desegregation plan put into effect by the district court in 1965. Pursuant to the *Green* case discussed above, James E. Swann, a student, and others requested that the school board create a plan that would work more realistically toward removing state-imposed segregation. When the school board's new plans were found to be unsatisfactory by the district court, the court appointed an expert to submit a desegregation plan. When the expert and the board each submitted a desegregation plan, the district court adopted some elements of each.

The controversial aspects of the plan developed by the expert were described by the district court as follows:

The plan does as much by rezoning school attendance lines as can reasonably be accomplished. However, unlike the board plan, it does not stop there. It goes further and desegregates all the rest of the elementary schools by the techniques of grouping two or three outlying schools with one black inner city school; by transporting black students from grades one through four to the outlying white schools; and by transporting white students from the fifth and sixth grades from the outlying white schools to the inner city black school.

Under the . . . plan, nine inner-city Negro schools were grouped in this manner with 24 suburban white schools.[16]

The court of appeals affirmed part of the district court's order, but it overruled the district court's plans related to pairing and grouping of elementary schools as placing unreasonable burdens on students and on the board.

The Supreme Court, with Chief Justice Burger writing the opinion, saw four central issues in the *Swann* case:

1. To what extent may racial balance or racial quotas be used to correct a previously segregated system?
2. Must one-race schools, whether all-black or all-white, be eliminated as a necessary part of desegregation?
3. Are there any limits on the rearrangement of school district or attendance zones?
4. Are there any limits on the use of buses or other transportation to correct segregated schooling?

Questions to Consider

1. What would be your response to the four issues posed above, in light of the facts of the *Swann* case and applying the legal principles derived from *Brown* I and II and *Green*?
2. Would your answers differ if the issues arose in a community without a long history of racial segregation in the schools?

The opinion of the court

The following summaries represent the Supreme Court's position on each of the major issues of the *Swann* case.

On racial balance. Justice Burger relied heavily on the principles of the *Brown* cases and their progeny in his analysis of the facts and applicable law. He emphasized that the application of a "particular degree of racial balance or mixing" would be disapproved. "The constitutional command to desegregate schools does not mean that every school in every community must always reflect the racial composition of the school system as a whole."

He noted that in the *Swann* case the district court had made use of mathematical ratios as starting points in formulating a remedy and not as fixed requirements. A limited use of ratios was within the discretion of the district court in an effort to correct past constitutional violations.

One-race schools. The Court recognized the widespread phenomenon that in large cities with racial or ethnic ghettos neighborhood schools are often one-race schools. These schools, according to Justice Burger, must be closely scrutinized to determine "that school assignments are not part of state-enforced segregation."

The existence of a small number of one-race or virtually one-race schools was not in itself illegal segregation. However, the legal presumptions were against districts that had one-race schools, and this put the burden on the school authorities to show that such school assignments were genuinely nondiscriminatory. When plans were presented to change the dual system to a unitary one, the schools had to satisfy the courts that their racial composition was not the result of present or past discriminatory action.

Altering of attendance zones. In this issue the Court again relied on the more intimate knowledge of local conditions by the district court. A wide variety of arrangements, including "pairing," "clustering," or "regrouping" of schools might be necessary interim measures to remedy a heretofore segregated school system. At times the results were very awkward and resembled extreme forms of gerrymandering. The Court, speaking through a "conservative" Chief Justice, made this statement about such an arrangement:

All things being equal, with no history of discrimination, it might well be desirable to assign pupils to schools nearest their homes. But all things are not equal in a system that has been deliberately constructed and maintained to enforce racial segregation. The remedy for such segregation may be administratively awkward, inconvenient, and even bizarre in some situations and may impose burdens on some; but all awkwardness and inconvenience cannot be avoided in the interim period when remedial adjustments are being made to eliminate the dual school systems.[17]

The Supreme Court established no fixed guidelines in this area except to indicate that the objective was to dismantle dual school systems. Thus a "racially neutral" plan would be inadequate. Beyond that, the district courts, which were closest to the schools, could consider such local variables as highways, traffic patterns, and travel time. "Conditions in different localities will vary so widely that no rigid rules can be laid down to govern all situations."

Busing. Justice Burger expressed a similar need for substantial reliance on the lower courts in the matter of pupil transportation. But he maintained the following.

*Bus transportation has been an integral part of the public educa-
tion for years, and was perhaps the single most important factor in
the transition from the one-room schoolhouse to the consolidated
school. Eighteen million of the Nation's public school children, approximately 39%, were transported to their schools by bus in 1969–
1970 in all parts of the country.[18]*

Therefore, after considering the facts of the *Swann* case, the Court
approved the proposed busing plan. It noted that the average time
spent on the bus would be less under the new plan then the one
previously in operation. Bus transportation was found to be a normal
and accepted tool to further the development of a unitary school
system.

Does that mean that there can be no objection to the busing of
school children to achieve desegregation? Not at all. Justice Burger
indicated that valid objections may be raised when "the time or
distance of travel is so great as to either risk the health of the
children or significantly impinge on the educational process. It
hardly needs stating that the limits on time of travel will vary
with many factors, but probably with none more than the age
of the students."

With the foregoing responses to the key issues, the Supreme
Court upheld the initial action of the district court. The principles
set forth in the *Swann* case have become very important in the process of desegregating the city schools of the South and the North
alike. Thus, in the case involving the Chinese subculture of San
Francisco, to which we now turn, the court relied heavily on *Swann*.

THE JOHNSON AND LEE CASES:
A CITY OF IMMIGRANTS

San Francisco is a city of immigrants, and in 1971, in the *Johnson*
case, which involved *all* of San Francisco, the district court ordered
the city to put into effect one of two plans that would eliminate
segregation.[19] Thereafter the Chinese parents brought suit in the *Lee*
case and expressed their disagreement with the overall decision of
the federal court in its effort to achieve racial and ethnic balance
in the schools of the city.

In the *Johnson* case it had been argued by the defendant school
district that earlier decisions of the Supreme Court on behalf of
desegregation did not apply to San Francisco for the following reasons.

1. Decisions forbidding segregation applied only to those states "which at an earlier time, had dual school systems" (i.e., schools that had separate schools for black and white students).
2. San Francisco's school actions were not unconstitutional because district officials merely drew attendance lines year after year, and there were no rules or regulations segregating racial or ethnic groups.
3. Since the city's population "is more diverse than in other communities, racial segregation in the elementary schools ought to be permitted."

The district court, however, was not favorably impressed by any of these arguments. In rejecting the first, the court admitted that historically it may well have been the case that desegregation orders applied primarily to the dual school systems of the South. That was no longer the case; for "it is shocking, indeed, it is nonsensical, to assume that such practices are forbidden to school authorities in Florida or North Carolina, for example, but are permitted to school authorities in California. Neither the United States Supreme Court nor any other court has drawn a Mason-Dixon line for constitutional enforcement."[20]

In rejecting the second argument of the defendant, the court clarified some confusion about *de facto* and *de jure* segregation.* It made it plain that any action, rule, or regulation "by school authorities which creates or continues or heightens racial segregation of school children is *de jure*." If a school board draws attendance lines that provide for reasonable racial balance, and if solely by virtue of population mobility the racial balance of the school becomes lopsided, that segregation is *de facto*. However, if the school officials were aware of the population shift and drew attendance lines year after year, "knowing that the lines maintain or heighten racial imbalance, the resulting segregation is *de jure*."[21]

In the *Johnson* case no evidence was presented to show that the San Francisco school authorities had ever changed any attendance boundaries for the purpose of eliminating racial imbalance. The court also made it clear, however, that evil or criminal intent was irrelevant to *de jure* segregation. Board members may act in all innocence,

---

* *De jure* segregation means segregation by some official action, and it is unconstitutional. *De facto* segregation means segregation through social developments without any official action involved. *De facto* segregation has not been declared unconstitutional. *De jure* means "under color of law," and *de facto* means "as a matter of fact."

yet if their official action "creates or continues or increases substantial racial imbalance in the schools," the action is *de jure*.

Finally, the court rejected the suggestion that racial segregation in the elementary schools of the city should be permitted because the population of San Francisco was more diverse than in other communities. After noting that "the law allows no such latitude," Judge Weigel expressed the view that the multiplicity of races made desegregation all the more important. He further indicated that the "evils of racism and ethnic intolerance are not limited to blacks and whites." His comments about the significance of the elementary years are generally shared by educators: "Opposition to desegregation in the elementary schools is particularly ill-advised. It works to prevent the kind of exchange in formative years which can best innoculate against racial hatred. Racial hatred is an adult rather than a childhood disease."[22]

Judge Weigel concluded that *de jure* segregation had been practiced in San Francisco and ordered the school officials to select one of the two alternative plans to achieve a more reasonable racial balance in the elementary schools of the city. Both plans included a certain amount of busing of children as a necessary means to achieve desegregration. He emphasized that no race or ethnic group should be favored in the schools, that high-quality education should be emphasized for all, and that bilingual classes teaching cultural awareness were not to be restricted.

The extent of the court's concerns were stated in its detailed orders to the school district:

The District is directed and ordered:

"A. To carry out, effective at the start of the next term of the schools on September 8, 1971, desegregration of the student bodies of each and all of the schools as provided for by the Horseshoe Plan or by the Freedom Plan.*

B. To carry out, diligently and promptly, all other provisions of the Horseshoe Plan or the Freedom Plan provided, however, that if any provision is in conflict with any provision of this Final Judgment and Decree, the latter shall control.

C. To make bona fide, continuing and reasonable efforts, during the next five years, to eliminate segregation in each and every school.

D. To establish and carry out, diligently and promptly, practices for

---

* "Horseshoe Plan" and "Freedom Plan" were the names of the two plans submitted as alternative ways of achieving racial and ethnic balance.

the *hiring* of certificated and classified personnel which will effectively eliminate segregation in the respective staffs, overall, and in each school.

E. To establish and carry out, diligently and promptly, practices for the *assignment* of certificated and classified personnel in a manner which will effectively eliminate segregation in the respective staffs, overall, and in each school.

F. To establish and carry out, diligently and promptly, practices for the assignment of certificated and classified personnel, which will effectively promote *equalization of competence* in all schools.

G. To exercise, at all times, the highest degree of care for the safety and security of all school children at all times during their school attendance and transportation.

H. To provide, to the fullest extent feasible, racial and ethnic balance among students to be bused.

I. To inform all parents in writing, as soon as reasonably possible before the start of the school term this fall (1) of their children's school assignments and (2) of the details regarding bus transportation including, but not limited to, an outline of the safety measures which the District will utilize and of the procedures for enabling parents promptly to reach children in case of emergency.

J. To file with the Court within sixty (60) days after the end of each school year, until the Court may otherwise order, a report showing in reasonable detail all actions taken to comply with this Judgment and Decree. [Italics added]."[23]

In addition to the foregoing order, the court issued an injunction permanently restraining the school district from encouraging or supporting segregation in any form in its schools, whether among students, teachers, or other employees.

Self-segregation in Chinatown

It was Judge Weigel's order in the *Johnson* case that precipitated the objections of Chinese-American parents discussed earlier (the *Lee* case). In most desegregation cases racial or ethnic minorities seek to eliminate segregation. In the *Lee* case, however, Americans of Chinese ancestry requested the federal appeals court to nullify the order issued in the *Johnson* case.

However, in *Lee*, the appeals court upheld the *Johnson* case as it applied to Chinese-American school children. It noted that until 1947 California had provided for the establishment of separate schools for children of Chinese ancestry. This type of *de jure* segregation was declared unconstitutional in the 1954 *Brown* case. The *Johnson* case properly ordered the various remedies to overcome the effects of earlier segregationist policies. The court noted that the *Brown* decision "was not written for Blacks alone." Earlier cases were cited to document the fact that the equal protection clause of the Fourteenth Amendment applied to all racial minorities and that among its first beneficiaries were the Chinese people of San Francisco.

The court recognized the interests and concerns of the Chinese parents. It upheld the desegregation plan, however, and noted that the plan made possible bilingual classes as well as courses that taught the "cultural background and heritages of various racial and ethnic groups."

Thus, if we view this controversy as one that involved the interests of the Chinese parents on one hand and those of the entire school district on the other, the courts ruled in favor of the larger district while trying to respect and protect some of the concerns of the parents. Both the *Lee* and the *Johnson* cases relied heavily on the previous decisions of the Supreme Court, particularly the landmark cases of *Brown* and *Swann*.

SUMMARY AND CONCLUSIONS

The history of racial and ethnic segregation in the United States is a long and complex one. Without dealing with all its intricacies in this chapter, we highlighted the key historical cases and indicated what the current law seems to be.

The *Plessy* case, although not directly related to education, was historically accepted as authority for the principle that racially separate but equal education was constitutional. *Plessy* was overruled by *Brown* I in 1954, perhaps one of the most important Supreme Court cases related to education. In its now famous opinion the Warren Court ruled that "in the field of public education the doctrine of 'separate but equal' has no place. Separate educational facilities are inherently unequal," and therefore they violate the Fourteenth Amendment.

Within less than a year, *Brown* I was followed by *Brown* II, which set forth the general principles to guide the implementation of the desegregation decision. Because segregated and discriminatory schooling existed in so many communities under such varied conditions, the Court recognized that primary responsibility for desegregation must rest with local school boards. Local courts, of course, would consider whether or not the school authorities had acted in good faith and in a manner consistent with constitutional principles. Compliance was urged "at the earliest practicable date" and school boards were to proceed "with all deliberate speed."

The intentions of the Court were carried out in some communities, but most cities and towns resisted in various forms, ranging from the closing of schools to "freedom of choice" plans. Literally hundreds of lawsuits had to be brought to overcome the noncompliance.

In the *Griffin* case the Court struck down the closing of schools in Prince Edward County, Virginia. It ruled that such action was illegitimate when it was racially motivated. The "freedom-of-choice" plan suffered a similar fate in the *Green* case, where the Court urged the creation of unitary, nonracial school systems to replace earlier segregated ones. A lower court flatly stated that "the only school desegregation plan that meets constitutional standards is one that works."

In the *Swann* case the Burger Court established four key points: (1) In considering "racial balance" the courts may use mathematical ratios as starting points in formulating remedies but not as fixed quota requirements. (2) One-race schools are not necessarily unconstitutional. School districts will be closely scrutinized to determine whether the one-race schools are part of a plan to segregate children. The presumption is against the existence of such schools; therefore the burden of proof is on the school officials to show that such school assignments are genuinely nondiscriminatory. (3) The altering of attendance zones is a legitimate means to desegregate heretofore segregated school districts. This may include "pairing," "clustering," or "regrouping" of schools to eliminate dual school systems. (4) Busing can be a valid means to integrate the schools. Busing can also be objectionable when the time or distance of travel is so great as to be detrimental to the student's health or education.

There are school districts, however, where racial balance in the schools cannot be achieved by busing. This is true in some of our large cities, like Detroit, where blacks constitute a large majority of the population. Cross-district busing, or metropolitan area desegregation (i.e., combining cities and suburbs) has been suggested as a way to achieve a desirable racial balance in such situations. But in 1974 the Supreme Court in a 5-to-4 decision rejected this proposed solution and ruled that Detroit does not have to look beyond its school district boundaries in its efforts to satisfy the Fourteenth Amendment.[24]

The *Johnson* case involved a Northern city, San Francisco. The district court ruled that segregation in a racially and ethnically diverse Northern city is as unconstitutional as anywhere else. It held that if the school board creates or continues to draw attendance lines that increase racial imbalance, its action will violate the equal protection clause of the Fourteenth Amendment. The *Johnson* case also provided an example of a court specifically detailing a plan of actions the schools must take to comply with the spirit of *Brown* I and II.

The *Lee* case, in which some Chinese-American parents objected to the court-ordered desegregation, derived from *Johnson*. The case was significant because it showed that desegregation was not only a "black and white" issue but affected Orientals, Chicanos, Indians, and others as well. Furthermore it was an example of minority parents who did not want integrated schooling. Although the Court upheld desegregation in this case, it respected some of the wishes of the Chinese parents and supported bilingual classes as well as courses that taught about the "cultural background and heritages of various racial and ethnic groups."

Hundreds of other decisions could be cited in support of the principles set forth in this chapter. Many other cases are currently under litigation—in Boston, Dallas, and Denver; in Ohio, Michigan, Mississippi, Texas, and California; in the North and in the South. The specific factual conditions call for various situational remedies, but they all must be consistent with the powerful principles enunciated in *Brown* v. *Board of Education of Topeka.**

NOTES

[1] 339 F.Supp. 1315 (N.D. Cal. 1971).

[2] 372 F.2d 836 (9th Cir. 1966).

[3] *Guey Heung Lee et al.* v. *David Johnson et al.* 404 U.S. 1215 (1971).

[4] *Plessy* v. *Ferguson*, 163 U.S. 537 (1896).

[5] *Brown* v. *Board of Education of Topeka*, 347 U.S. 483, 484 (1954).

[6] *Id.* at 489.

[7] *Id.* at 493.

[8] *Id.* at 494.

[9] *Brown* v. *Board of Education of Topeka, Kansas*, 349 U.S. 294, 298 (1955), commonly referred to as *Brown II*.

[10] *Griffin* v. *County School Board of Prince Edward Co.*, 377 U.S. 218, 222 (1964).

[11] *Id.* at 231.

* The related question of economic discrimination is briefly explored in the Frontier Issues section of Chapter 10. (See p. 280.)

[12] *Green* v. *County School Board of New Kent Co., Va.,* 391 U.S. 430 (1968).

[13] *Id.* at 440.

[14] *Id.* at 441.

[15] *Swann* v. *Charlotte-Mecklenburg Board of Education,* 402 U.S. 1 (1971).

[16] *Id.* at 9–10.

[17] *Id.* at 28.

[18] *Id.* at 29.

[19] *Johnson* v. *San Francisco Unified School District,* 339 F.Supp. 1315 (N.D. Cal. 1971).

[20] *Id.* at 1318.

[21] The distinction between *de jure* and *de facto* segregation has come under increased legal attacks and judicial scrutiny in recent years. Social scientists have now joined this attack. In fact, a well-known sociologist from Harvard University flatly states: "*De jure* segregation is the harsh fact of American society; so-called *de facto* segregation is simply a myth." See Thomas F. Pettigrew, "The Case for the Racial Integration of the Schools," an address delivered at the 1973 Cubberley Conference, Stanford University. (Mimeographed.)

[22] *Id.* at 1320.

[23] *Id.* at 1324.

[24] *Milliken* v. *Bradley et al.,* 42 Law Week 5249 (1974). The dissenting justices argued that since the state has responsibility to provide desegregated education, school district boundaries should not be sacrosanct obstacles in the way to achieving this goal.

8

Sex discrimination in education

The pedestal upon which women have been placed has all too often, upon closer inspection, been revealed as a cage.
—*California Supreme Court*[1]

The Fourteenth Amendment does not create a fictitious equality where there is a real difference.
—*Justice Oliver Wendell Holmes*[2]

Introduction

Historically our schools, like the rest of our culture, have treated girls differently from boys in many respects. Whether or not the different treatment was discriminatory was a question seldom raised. In recent years it has been established that sex discrimination is widely practiced in our culture and in the schools. Educators' awareness of such discrimination has been heightened, and various policies and practices are being examined to eliminate sexism. Disagreements have arisen, however, concerning efforts to create nonsexist schools, and some of these disagreements have resulted in lawsuits. In this chapter cases related to alleged sexist practices in the schools are examined—practices in athletic activities, in admissions, and in curricula, as well as in school policies concerning student marriage, pregnancy, and parenthood.

Equality in School Sports

THE BRENDEN CASE

In 1972 the Northeastern Lawn Tennis Association ranked Peggy Brenden the number one 18-year-old woman tennis player in her area. Since there was very little interest in tennis among the girls of her school, Brenden, a senior at Minnesota's St. Cloud Technical High School, expressed a desire to play on the boys' team. The team had a coach and a schedule of interscholastic matches, neither of which was available for girls. Peggy was informed by the school that she could not participate on the boys' team because of the following rule of the Minnesota State High School League:

Girls shall be prohibited from participating in the boys' interscholastic athletic program either as a member of the boys' team or a member of the girls' team playing the boys' team.

The girls' team shall not accept male members.[3]

The League Handbook, which contains this rule, has an equivalent regulation for boys. All 485 public schools in the state of Minnesota are members of the League.

Peggy Brenden claimed that her civil rights, specifically her right to due process and equal protection, had been violated. She sought an injunction against the enforcement of any rule that would prevent her from participating in interscholastic athletic events.

The school district contended that the rule was a reasonable one and that its objective was to achieve fair and equitable competition among school athletes. They argued that because there are significant differences in physiology and growth patterns between boys and girls, sex is a reasonable basis of classification in athletic competition.

Questions to Consider

1. Are there significant differences between the sexes that would relate to competitive athletics? What are they? Are these natural or cultural differences?
2. What differences, if any, justify separating boys and girls for purposes of interscholastic competition?
3. What would happen to girls' sports if all teams were open equally to boys and girls?
4. Would you differentiate between contact and noncontact sports?

A companion case

The *Brenden* case was joined by that of Tony St. Pierre, a 17-year-old female student at Eisenhower High School, Hopkins, Minnesota. She wanted to compete on the boys' cross-country running and cross-country skiing teams. She too was excellent in these sports and her reasons for wanting to join the boys' team were the same as Peggy Brenden's. Since the legal issues and principles involved were the same, the two cases were decided together by the federal district court in Minnesota.

The opinion of the court

Was the classification arbitrary and thus a violation of the girls' constitutional rights? The district court used the governing principles set forth by the Supreme Court: "A classification must be reasonable, not arbitrary, and must rest upon some ground of difference having a fair and substantial relation to the object of the legislation, so that all persons similarly circumstanced shall be treated alike."[4] Is it then reasonable to differentiate between boys and girls for purposes of interscholastic athletic competition?

The court acknowledged that there are substantial physiological differences between boys and girls:

As testified to by defendants' expert witnesses, men are taller than women, stronger than women by reason of a greater muscle mass; have larger hearts than women and a deeper breathing capacity, enabling them to utilize oxygen more efficiently than women, run faster, based upon the construction of the pelvic area, which, when women reach puberty, widens, causing the femur to bend outward, rendering the female incapable of running as efficiently as a male. These physiological differences may, on the average, prevent the great majority of women from competing on an equal level with the great majority of males. The differences may form a basis for defining class competition on the basis of sex, for the purpose of encouraging girls to compete in their own class and not in a class consisting of boys involved in interscholastic athletic competition.[5]

Should these general differences prevent Brenden and St. Pierre from playing on the boys' teams? The court was not bound by statistical abstractions but looked at the particular individuals at hand and challenged the application of the rules in these instances.

It must be emphasized in this case, however, that these physiological differences, insofar as they render the great majority of females unable to compete as effectively as males, have little relevance to Tony St. Pierre and Peggy Brenden. Because of their level of achievement in competitive sports, Tony and Peggy have overcome these physiological disabilities. There has been no evidence that either Peggy Brenden or Tony St. Pierre, or any other girls, would be in any way damaged from competition in boys' interscholastic athletics, nor is there any credible evidence that the boys would be damaged.[6]

The school district had also argued that separate competitive programs in interscholastic athletics was desirable and a ruling in favor of the girls would hamper such a development. In rejecting this argument, Justice Lord noted: "There is a vague and undocumented fear on the part of the defendants that the goal of achieving equitable competition will perhaps be hampered. Peggy Brenden and Tony St. Pierre should not be sacrificed upon this altar."

The district court, although ruling in favor of Tony and Peggy, distinguished between the general rule separating girls' and boys' athletics and the application of such a rule to Brenden and St. Pierre. This court's opinion is quite typical of the judicial desire to avoid sweeping decisions and to stay close to the facts at hand.

This court is not deciding whether the League rules providing that there shall be no participation by girls in boys' interscholastic athletic events is unconstitutional or constitutional. Given the narrow factual situation with which the court is confronted, it is unnecessary and it would be inappropriate to make a determination as to whether the rule would be unconstitutional on its face or in all its applications.[7]

In other words, the court decided only the constitutionality of the application of the League rule to two young women of high skill and achievement as related to the three sports in two high school districts. Judge Lord emphasized these factors to point up the narrowness of the decision.

In sum, the court noted that the two girls had been prevented from participating in interscholastic athletics "on the basis of the fact of sex and sex alone." There were no alternative competitive programs provided for them by the schools. Thus, because the rules as applied to them* were unreasonable and discriminatory, the court

* Although the rules themselves were not necessarily unconstitutional, their application in these instances was.

declared Brenden and St. Pierre eligible to compete on the boys' teams. It further enjoined the Minnesota State High School League from imposing any sanctions on the two schools on whose teams the girls would compete.

THE BUCHA CASE:
SEXUALLY SEGREGATED SWIMMING[8]

In 1972 Sandra Lynn Bucha was a student in Hinsdale Center Township High School in Illinois. She and another girl were excluded from participating on the boys' swimming team. They filed a class action suit to eliminate or modify the rules of the Illinois High School Association, which regulates interscholastic sports for approximately 790 Illinois high schools.

They challenged the bylaws of the association, which placed limitations on girls' athletic events and not on those in which boys participated. For example, "a prohibition on organized cheering, a one dollar limitation on the value of awards, and a prohibition on overnight trips in conjunction with girls' contests." Although there was an organized athletic program for girls at the high school, the plaintiffs claimed that girls' contests were more like intramural, "multi-sport activities which are devoid of the concentration and competitive emphasis that is characteristic of boys' extracurricular sports." They also challenged the rule against competition between members of the opposite sex.

Questions to Consider

1. Were the rules of the Illinois High School Association reasonable?
2. Should boys and girls compete against each other? Would most girls and boys be helped by such competition?
3. Should different rules apply to the athletic events of girls than to those of boys?

The opinion of the court

Were plaintiffs denied equal protection? Judge Austin of the federal court replied in the negative. According to the judge, the "relevant inquiry here is whether the challenged classification is rational." The *Bucha* court then used the same Supreme Court principles as did the *Brenden* court,[9] but based on the facts of this case, it came to a different conclusion.

To determine whether there was a denial of equal protection, a two-step process was used by the court. The first step identified the purposes or objectives of the school activity, and the second asked whether the classification bore any reasonable relationship to any of those purposes.* Applying the two-step test to the girls' challenge of the rules of interscholastic competition, what were the results?

Are there legitimate purposes or objectives for interscholastic sports? The court replied in the affirmative; such participation, in its opinion as well as in the opinion of educators, will benefit students both physically and mentally. No one in this case challenged this proposition. The plaintiffs' challenge was aimed at the separation of the sexes and at the different rules applied to the programs of the boys and the girls. The key question was whether or not it was rational to separate girls and boys and to provide different regulations for their contests.

The court quoted with approval an old dictum of Justice Holmes from 1912: "the Fourteenth Amendment does not [create] a fictitious equality where there is a real difference." It then proceeded to note that "at the pinnacle of all sporting contests, the Olympic games, the men's times in each event are consistently better than the women's." In the case at hand it was also "shown that the times of the two boy swimmers sent to the state championship contest from Hinsdale were better than those ever recorded by either of the named plaintiffs." Expert testimony also pointed up significant physical and psychological differences between male and female athletes.

The court further considered the opinion of women's coaches that "unrestricted athletic competition between the sexes would consistently lead to male domination of interscholastic sports and actually result in a decrease in female participation in such events." These reasons led the court to conclude that the rules and regulations had a rational basis and that therefore the classification was reasonable and did not violate the equal protection clause of the Fourteenth Amendment.

The court noted that a *bona fide* athletic program existed for the girls as well as the boys, even though some of the regulations governing them differed. Exercising judicial restraint, Judge Austin observed that the issue of what is the best program is for the experts in education and coaching to decide and not for judges. His task was to judge not what is best but whether or not the arrangement

---

* The court rejected the "compelling state interest test," saying that sex is not an inherently suspect category, such as race. Later Supreme Court cases, however, have held sex to be an inherently suspect category.

was constitutionally permissible. Here, as elsewhere, there may be a difference between what is wise educational policy and what the law permits. To put it another way, there are many educational practices that are unwise or possibly foolish and damaging to students, even though they are constitutional. Judge Austin made it clear that it is up to educators and legislators to change such situations and that the courts should limit themselves to legal matters.

Although the emphases are different in the *Brenden* and *Bucha* cases, the two are not inconsistent. It is easy to distinguish between them, for in the *Bucha* case there was a program provided for girls as well as boys, whereas there were no such equivalent programs provided in the *Brenden* case. Thus the discriminatory practice was clear in *Brenden*.*

THE REED CASE: IS GOLF
A RIGHT OR A PRIVILEGE?[10]

In 1972 a case was filed in the U.S. district court of Nebraska by Debbie Reed, who wanted to be on the school golf team. However, Nebraska's Norfolk High School only had a boys' team, which competed in interscholastic golf meets and tournaments. There was no girls' team at all, and the Nebraska School Association bylaws forbade boys and girls from competing against each other or from being members of the same team.

When Reed sought an injuction that would enable her to play on the boys' team, various arguments were raised against her. It was alleged, for example, that she had no *right* to play golf on the team, that golf, unlike education, is a *privilege* rather than a right.

The court rejected this argument. Justice Urborn explained that even if golf is not educational, the privilege/right distinction is not viable. "The issue is not whether Debbie Reed has a 'right' to play golf; the issue is whether she can be treated differently from boys in an activity provided by the state. Her right is the right to be treated the same as boys unless there is a rational basis for her being treated differently." When the school authorities argued that Debbie was free to play golf even if she were not on the team, the court was again unimpressed by the weight of such an argument. It recognized that just like the male golf players, "Debbie Reed seeks the value of local and regional competition, an opportunity to en-

---

* The *Bucha* case seems to conclude that there is discrimination only if girls have *no* program whatever. This holding is not consistent with current law.

hance her reputation, and instruction afforded by the coaching staff. Though the defendants argue that she is free to play golf even though she is not a member of the school team, the values she seeks cannot be lightly set aside."

Moreover Judge Urborn emphasized the requirement of equal access to educational benefits for males and females. He wrote: "The state affords interschool competition and instruction at some expense and effort, surely for the reason that it and the defendant think that the program is of benefit to the participants. If the program is valuable for boys, is it of no value to girls?" The injunction requested by Reed was granted.

Summary and related issues

Increasingly the schools are reexamining their practices in the area of athletics. Sexist policies are scrutinized and often altered without lawsuits. New York, for example, through a ruling of the state commissioner of education, provided for equal participation in non-contact sports; New Jersey ruled similarly in cases where there is no separate interscholastic competition for girls. Michigan went further in providing, by law, the opportunity for girls to participate in non-contact sports with boys, even if the schools had all-girl teams.

Other states and districts are currently studying this question to develop fair, nondiscriminatory policies and regulations that will enhance athletic participation by an increasing number of students, whether male or female. Ideologically based solutions do not necessarily optimize such opportunities, even though on paper they seem to provide full equality. Educators must be mindful of relevant educational as well as constitutional principles.

It is generally known that schools and communities value athletic activities for boys more than for girls. Evidence for this abounds in comparing budget allocations as well as interscholastic athletic schedules. Although discriminatory practices are still quite common, the legal trend is against them. In many communities they persist simply because no one has challenged them. Lawsuits are expensive as well as embarrassing for many people. Families prefer to avoid the notoriety and even harassment that accompanies suing the local schools. However, where suits are brought, the courts are likely to give close scrutiny to allegations of unequal treatment in school-related athletic activities.

The trend of legal decision is clear: If team competition is available for boys, it should also be available for girls. In noncontact sports, if there are no teams for girls, they may compete for positions on the boys' team. If there are teams for both, courts respect the separation of the sexes for athletic activities, where there are reasonable grounds for such separation. As a result, state legislatures or local district policies are increasingly providing more equal treatment of girls and boys in school-related athletic programs.

Sexist Policies in the Curriculum

Until recently, many schools denied boys and girls equal access to certain courses.[11] The most obvious examples came from sexist restrictions on courses in metal-working, wood-working, auto shop, cooking, and sewing.

These practices represent such obvious examples of discrimination that policies and rules creating and enforcing them are rapidly crumbling. In some states, such as Massachusetts and New York, specific laws have been passed by the state legislatures prohibiting the exclusion of a student from any course of instruction by reason of that student's sex. In other states, lawsuits are challenging such denial of equal protection. For example, two suits in California were settled out of court when school authorities agreed to desegregate wood shop[12] and auto shop[13] courses.

When girls are denied equal access to the curriculum by policy or school rule, the law will assist them. There are other types of sexist practices that are more difficult to combat. These are the ingrained customs, values, and attitudes that operate in any social system, including the schools. The informal practices of schools as well as the attitudes of counselors, teachers, parents, and even of other students often deny equal access to the curriculum. These, of course, can only be changed by the difficult processes involved in changing peoples' attitudes, dispositions, and stereotypes. This is an educational and not a legal problem, although court pronouncements also have an educating influence.

Unequal Treatment in Admissions

Admission to public schools below the college level has generally not presented a problem. The obvious exception has been the racial discrimination discussed earlier. At least one case of discriminatory admissions, however, arose in Massachusetts, the birthplace of public education in America.

THE BOSTON LATIN SCHOOLS

In 1970 a group of girls took a competitive examination in Boston, Massachusetts, trying to gain entrance into Boston Latin School.[14] Boston Latin, part of the Boston public school system, has two separate schools: Girls Latin School and Boys Latin School. During the 1970 entrance period, in order to be admitted to Girls Latin, a girl had to score 133 or above out of a possible 200 points on the examination. To be admitted to Boys Latin during the same period, a score of 120 or above was required on the same examination. Janice Bray and others filed suit, alleging discrimination against them on the basis of sex.

In order to understand the situation more fully, it should be noted that "the Boys Latin building has a seating capacity for approximately 3,000 students and the Girls Latin building has a seating capacity for approximately 1500 students." The Boston School Department, in order to determine the cut-off points on the examination scores, first determined how many vacancies there would be in each building. In this way they arrived at the score of 120 for boys and 133 for girls for the school year beginning in September 1970.

Questions to Consider

1. Was the method used by the Boston School Department to determine cut-off scores reasonable and fair?
2. If you do not think the method was fair, what method would you use?
3. Is building capacity a reasonable basis to determine admission policy?
4. What part of the Constitution is relevant to this issue?

The opinion of the court

Judge Caffrey of the U.S. district court struck down the admissions process used by the Boston school authorities. Since the facts were agreed upon by all parties, he readily concluded "that the use of separate and different standards to evaluate the examination results to determine the admissibility of boys and girls to the Boston Latin Schools constitutes a violation of the Equal Protection Clause of the Fourteenth Amendment, the plain effect of which is to prohibit disparities before the law."

Judge Caffrey's analysis indicated that if boys and girls had been admitted on an equal basis, a cut-off point of 127 would have been used on the examination for all students. Thus if building capacities were to be used to determine total numbers for admission, the schools must use the same cut-off scores for boys and girls in order to satisfy the constitutional requirement of equal treatment.*

Marriage, Pregnancy, Parenthood, and the Schools

It is often said than an unstated goal of our schools is the prolonging of childhood and adolescence. Since it is generally believed that marriage or parenthood immediately transforms people into adults, many feel that in order to prolong adolescence, schools ought to discourage their students from marrying or from becoming pregnant. As we know, however, school success in these endeavors has been less than complete.

Through the years three lines of reasoning were offered by parents and school authorities as justification for school rules related to marriage, pregnancy, or parenthood. Broadly stated these were: (1) sexual relations by teenagers are immoral; (2) the presence of pregnant girls or married students in the schools disrupts educational activities; and (3) pregnant girls and married students should be excluded from the schools for their own physical and psychological well-being.

Questions to Consider

1. Do you believe it is immoral to be unmarried and pregnant?
2. Should pregnant, unwed girls be excluded from regular classes? Should they be in special classes or special schools?
3. Does the presence of pregnant girls or married students disrupt

---

* *Kirstein* v. *Rector and Visitors of University of Virginia,* 309 F.Supp. 184 (E.D. Va. 1970), an earlier case at the college level, reached similar results. A district court held in Virginia that a state university could not exclude women since its special programs were not available in another Virginia school on an equal basis. The fact that the job market might favor males over females is not a legally valid reason to deny admission to females or to impose an unfavorable quota on them. It is common knowledge that professional schools have perpetuated such practices for many years with the support of the rest of society. These practices are being challenged and reexamined in light of current interpretations of the Fourteenth Amendment, and the trend is for courts to strike them down.

schooling? Do they contribute more than other students to "sex talk" in schools?

4. Do you believe that the embarrassment pregnant girls are likely to suffer in school will do psychological harm to them?

5. Is there any basis for treating expectant mothers and fathers differently in the schools?

THE COOPER CASE: MARRIAGE AND SCHOOLING

An appeals court in Texas had before it the case of a 16-year-old girl seeking readmission to the public school. She had withdrawn from school at the age of 15 and married. After bearing a child, she filed for divorce and also wanted to return to school. A district rule forbade her admission in the following words:

A pupil who marries can no longer be considered a youth. By the very act of getting married, he or she becomes an adult and assumes the responsibility of adulthood. As a married student he or she shall not serve as an officer of the student body or any class or organization. A married student shall not represent the school in an inter-school contest or activity and shall not participate in school activities other than regular classes. If a married pupil wants to start her family, she must withdraw from public school. Such a pupil will, however, be encouraged to continue her education in the local adult education program and correspondence courses.[15]

When the evidence also showed that Kathy Cooper could not be admitted to the adult education program until she was 21 years old, the Texas court ordered her readmission to high school. It did so by directly relying on a state law that makes public education in Texas available to all persons between the ages of 6 and 21, provided they and their parents or guardians reside in the district. Therefore, the rule quoted above was declared illegal.

THE KISSICK CASE: MARRIAGE
AND SCHOOL FOOTBALL

Jerry Kissick, Jr., was a letterman on the 1958 football team of Garland Public School, Texas. In March 1959, at the age of 16, he married a 15-year-old girl. After his marriage, Kissick received notice barring him from further participation in school athletic activities pursuant to the following school policy: "Married students or previously married students may be barred from participating in athletics or other exhibitions, and not be permitted to hold class offices or other positions of honor. Academic honors such as Valedictorian and Salutatorian are excepted."[16]

Kissick had planned to play football during his remaining years of high school and had anticipated earning an athletic scholarship for college. He therefore filed suit to restrain enforcement of the policy on the grounds that it was unreasonable and discriminatory and that it violated the due process and equal protection clauses of the Fourteenth Amendment.

The school officials claimed that the policy was reasonable and well supported by evidence. They argued that it was calculated to discourage "teen-age" marriages, which tend to lead to dropping out of school. Furthermore they contended that Kissick did not have a right to play football, whereas his right to pursue his academic program was unimpaired.

Questions to Consider

1. Do you consider the school policy to be reasonable?
2. Should early marriages be discouraged?
3. Is nonparticipation in school athletics a reasonable way to discourage early marriages?
4. Is there a right to get married? Where in the Constitution is such a right guaranteed?

The opinion of the court

The school district and its Parent-Teachers Association argued on behalf of the school policy. They presented the following evidence:

1. That an extensive study of "teen-age" marriages in their community showed ill effects of married students participating in extracurricular activities with unmarried students.
2. That there had been "an alarming increase in juvenile marriages at Garland School."
3. That parents favored the school policy nine to one.
4. That of a total of 64 married students during the previous year 24 had dropped out of school.
5. That of those married students who remained in school, at least 50 percent experienced a drop in grades of 10 points or more.
6. That a professional psychologist testified in favor of the school policy.

The court of civil appeals of Dallas, Texas, ruled in favor of the school district. In its reasoning it reflected the historical views of restrictions related to extracurricular activities, restrictions that are still found in some school districts.*

The court in effect ruled that extracurricular activities such as football are distinguishable from the essential programs of the school. Although Jerry Kissick, Jr., certainly had a right to attend school, the Dallas court held that it was not unreasonable to bar him from playing football. The court concluded:

> Boards of Education, rather than Courts, are charged with the important and difficult duty of operating the public schools. So, it is not a question of whether this or that individual judge or court considers a given regulation adopted by the Board as expedient. The Court's duty, regardless of its personal views, is to uphold the Board's regulation unless it is generally viewed as being arbitrary and unreasonable. Any other policy would result in confusion detrimental to the progress and efficiency of our public school system.[17]

THE DAVIS CASE

Albert Davis was a senior in Ohio's Fremont Ross High School. He became 18 years old on January 15, 1972, and seven days later he married a 16-year-old girl who was at the time pregnant with his child. He was an honor student and an excellent baseball player who was a member of the varsity for at least two years. Major league scouts were interested in him, and several colleges were willing to grant him an athletic scholarship.

When Davis married, he was aware of the following school rule:

A. Married pupils are permitted to attend school.

B. Married pupils are not permitted to participate in school sponsored extracurricular activities including the Junior-Senior Prom.[18]

After his marriage he was informed "that the rule would be enforced against him, and his name was not placed on the eligible list

---

* The court's opinion included some discussion of Texas law related to marriages of minors. Although most states have similar laws, our discussion reflects only the relevance of the civil rights provisions of the U.S. Constitution, as interpreted by the Dallas court.

for baseball when the list was prepared and filed." Davis went to court to enjoin the school from enforcing the rule. He claimed that he had a constitutional right to get married and that the school rule deprived him of an important part of the school program because of his marriage and had thereby interfered with his civil liberties.

As in the *Kissick* case, the school authorities argued: (1) that the rule was intended to discourage early marriages because students who married usually dropped out of school and (2) that after the adoption of the rule, fewer dropped out, and of those who did, a larger number continued their education through home instruction.

A different result

The U.S. district court in Ohio cited the generally accepted fact that "the right to get married is traditionally a strictly local matter, which each state may regulate as it sees fit." Ohio by law specifies the legal age for marriage; and Albert Davis had acted within it. In various cases the Ohio courts recognized a state policy against "child marriages" whose minor participants are "more to be pitied than scorned." This attitude was a reflection of an understanding that the failure of teenage marriages is appallingly high. Furthermore, the drop-out rate of married high school students is also very high, with almost 67 percent of the married girls dropping out in Ohio.

In spite of this, Justice Young recognized that Davis was legally married. Furthermore, evidence showed that the district policy was not successful in discouraging students from getting married. Thus, if the intent of the rule was to deter students from earlier marriage, why punish a student in a case in which the deterrent had not succeeded?

Since Davis' punishment consisted of exclusion from the school baseball team, the question was raised whether extracurricular activities were part of the school program. The court answered affirmatively.[19] Acknowledging the importance of various extracurricular activities, Judge Young specifically recognized the significance to Davis of playing on the baseball team. Any school rule that deprived the student of an important school activity would be carefully scrutinized by the courts. The court invoked the *Tinker* case to see whether the school rule was necessary to maintain appropriate discipline or whether it was but part of an "enclave of totalitarianism." Having found that Davis was legally married and that his marriage did not materially or substantially interfere with school discipline, the court ruled in his favor.

THE ORDWAY CASE:
UNMARRIED PREGNANT STUDENTS[20]

Fay Ordway was an 18-year-old pregnant unmarried senior at the North Middlesex Regional High School, Townsend, Massachusetts. On January 28, 1971, she informed Mr. Hargraves, the principal, that she was pregnant and expected her child in June, 1971. The principal informed her that she would have to stop attending classes as of February 12, when the school closed for a vacation. His action was based on a policy that provided: "Whenever an unmarried girl enrolled in North Middlesex Regional High School shall be known to be pregnant, her membership in the school shall be immediately terminated."

Pursuant to this policy, the principal wrote a letter to Ordway informing her that she may continue her studies on her own, use all school facilities after school hours and have access to school services, senior activities, games and dances, and free tutoring. Her name would continue on the school roster until graduation in June 1971, but she could not be in regular attendance. Ordway, however, wanted to continue attending school with the other students, and she took her case to court.

Questions to Consider

1. Should Ordway be allowed to continue attending classes?
2. How would you justify the school policy? Do you know people who would support it?
3. Were the provisions offered Ordway in the principal's letter reasonable?

The opinion of the court

Judge Caffrey delivered the opinion of the U.S. district court. First, he summarized evidence presented by physicians and psychiatrists to the effect that there were no health reasons to exclude Ordway from attending classes. With the exception of "violent calisthenics," she could participate in all normal school activities; in fact, exclusion was likely to "cause plaintiff mental anguish which will affect the course of her pregnancy." According to psychiatric testimony, "young girls in plaintiff's position who are required to absent themselves from school become depressed, and the depression of the mother has an adverse effect on the child, who is frequently born depressed and lethargic."

Social workers also recommended giving students like Ordway the choice of either remaining in class or receiving private instruction after school hours. Fay, whose grades ranged from C pluses to an A, expressed a strong desire to attend regular classes.

Hargraves could not state any educational reasons for Ordway's exclusion, and there were no school disruptions related to her pregnancy. His only rationale for the school policy was the apparent desire on the part of the school committee "not to appear to condone conduct on the part of unmarried students of a nature to cause pregnancy."

Since the school included both junior and senior high school students, there seemed to be a concern that the 12 to 14 age group "might be led to believe that the school authorities were condoning premarital relations if they were to allow girl students in plaintiff's situation to remain in school." This concern, the court pointed out, was inconsistent with the provisions contained in the principal's letter to Ordway.

Considering all the testimony, the court ordered the readmission of Ordway to regular classes. In sum, Judge Caffery found no health reasons to exclude her, no valid educational purpose to be served by her exclusion, and no likelihood that her presence would lead to disruption or interference with school activities or pose any kind of threat to others. (The *Tinker* test.) Since the court considered public education to be "a basic personal right or liberty" the burden of proof would be on the schools to justify limiting or denying it to a student. Mere pregnancy is not a sufficient reason for such a denial or limitation.*

Summary and comment

Early marriages have been discouraged in our culture, at least since the advent of industrialization. The schools, as significant institutions of social control, have been used by society to help deter "child marriages." One means widely used by schools has been the policy and practice of excluding married students from school. Another has been the denial to such students of the "privilege" of participating in extracurricular activities.

Although some of these policies are still in effect, their legal legitimacy is doubtful. Since 1929 the reported cases have con-

---

* Since the *Ordway* case involved an unmarried pregnant girl, the reasons should apply with even more force to married pregnant students.

sistently supported the right of married students to attend public schools.[21] Courts have supported this right on the basis of the equal protection clause of the Fourteenth Amendment or simply by reference to state laws requiring or permitting school attendance between certain ages, as in the *Cooper* case in Texas. Public policy is better served by teenagers continuing their schooling, whether married or not.*

Participation in extracurricular activities by married students had a more complex legal history. Although school rules denying such a "privilege" have often been upheld by the courts, the trend is clearly otherwise. The "right versus privilege" doctrine has been thoroughly discredited and is no longer viable. Even if extracurricular activities were a privilege, a state agency such as a school must not attach arbitrary or discriminatory conditions to participation in the privilege. Thus, increasingly, marriage *per se* cannot be used to bar membership on an athletic team or participation in school clubs, social functions, or student government, although some courts will probably uphold such a restriction when applied to students who marry *below* the legal age specified by their state.

Many school districts have policies that exclude pregnant students from regular classes and extracurricular activities. These rules are usually justified on moral grounds when the pregnant student is unmarried and on grounds of "contagion" in the case of married girls. Interestingly enough, neither the unwed fathers nor the married fathers are excluded from school under most of these policies. Even the courts that assure the girls' right to continue school seldom speak about the fathers, wed or unwed.

Most pregnant girls who are denied the right to participate in school programs simply drop out of school. Some continue in "home classes" or tutorials. Neither of these arrangements is considered by knowledgeable educators to be on a par with the regular schools. In fact, girls who interrupt their schooling during pregnancy seldom return. On the other hand, those who are given a chance to continue their education during pregnancy are twice as likely to graduate as those denied such an opportunity.[22]

---

* We realize that this is a value assertion, current critics notwithstanding. The courts as well as scholarly articles take this position. See, for example, Brian E. Berwick and Carol Oppenheimer, "Marriage, Pregnancy, and the Right to Go to School," *Texas Law Review*, 50 (1972), 1196–1228.

Strong reasons support the right of pregnant girls, married or not, to continue schooling. Not only are their personal and occupational lives likely to be affected by dropping out, but also the lives of their children. Since their ability to support their children will be influenced by their school attendance, they need all the education society is capable of providing.

Are pregnancy exclusion policies racist? Surveys indicate that such policies fall heaviest on members of minority groups—black, Chicano, and others. These girls account for a disproportionate number of pregnancies, which correlate with poverty and unequal access to birth control information, contraceptives, and legal abortions.[23]

As noted above, most instances of exclusion for pregnancy do not reach the courts. When they do, however, the current trend is to protect the right to attend classes and participate in other school activities. Such court holdings are generally based on the equal protection clause of the Fourteenth Amendment, on state laws providing schooling between certain ages, and even on the reasoning of the *Tinker* case. Applying the principles of *Tinker*, one could argue that before a pregnant student may be excluded, the school authorities would have to show that her presence caused a "substantial and material disruption" of the educational process.

Thus the trend of judicial opinion clearly protects the right to continue schooling despite pregnancy. This development supports individual rights as well as the public policy of having a better educated electorate.

Other Aspects of Equal Protection

Traditional attitudes toward male-female differences linger in our culture and inevitably affect the schools. New expressions of sexist attitudes appear from time to time, and they may or may not reach the courts, depending upon how aware people are of their rights and how vigorously they protect them.

As indicated in Chapter 9, schools may not legally prevent pregnant students from participating in graduation exercises. All the more reason why they may not exclude married students from such participation.

A related question arises concerning the right of pregnant or married students not to attend school. Schools in general have not attempted to enforce compulsory attendance laws against such students. Most schools specifically allow them to drop out though they are within the ages of compulsory schooling. In the rare instances in which schools wanted to enforce compulsory attendance against such students, the courts ruled in favor of the students.[24]

Two legal scholars propose the following policy, which, we believe, is consistent with the cases in this chapter. Although their specific reference is to the state of Texas, there is no reason why the proposal should not apply with equal logic to other states.

Pregnant and/or married students within the compulsory school age retain their entitlement to a free public education. The Texas Education Code requires school districts to admit them to a full school program of regular classes and activities. The compulsory attendance law continues to apply to them unless they can prove exemption under state statutes.

(a) Punitive action against pregnant students violates state law and the United States Constitution. It is also unwise, because it causes girls to hide their pregnancies from school authorities, who are often the only adults in a position to ensure that they get appropriate medical care. Therefore, it is the policy of the State Board of Education that the public schools shall not make or enforce rules that mandatorily transfer pregnant girls out of regular classes or to different schools, or that otherwise punish them.

(b) It is both inconsistent with state law and unconstitutional for schools to punish students for marrying. It is the policy of the State Board of Education that the public schools shall not make or enforce rules that bar married students from attendance or participation in extracurricular activities, that restrict their eligibility for academic or other honors, or that otherwise punish them.[25]

SUMMARY AND CONCLUSIONS

Various school policies and practices have been scrutinized in recent years under the charge of sexism. Phrased in terms of constitutional law, the claim has been made that these policies and practices violated the equal protection clause of the Fourteenth Amendment. Another line of attack has claimed that such policies were arbitrary and unreasonable and therefore they violated the due process clause of the same amendment. The school policies and practices referred to can be analyzed under the following headings: (1) equality in school sports, (2) equality in admissions and in the curriculum, and (3) restrictions on married and pregnant students.

Equality in sports

Although schools still provide more athletic activities for boys than for girls, some progress is being made toward equity. Lawsuits in recent years have required that schools make available individual and team competitive sports for girls as well as for boys. Schools do not have to provide interscholastic athletics for any student. If they have them, however, sex must not be the basis for exclusion or inclusion.

In noncontact sports, such as golf, tennis or swimming, if there are no teams for girls, they may compete for positions on the boys' teams. If there are teams for both, courts will respect the separation of boys and girls for athletic activities, since there are reasonable grounds for such separation. In the face of court rulings, together with increased awareness by the public of sexist policies, legislatures and local school boards are gradually bringing about more equal treatment of girls and boys in school-related athletic programs.

Admissions and curriculum

Historically there have been relatively few practices of sexual discrimination in admission to public elementary and high schools. The case involving the Boston Latin Schools was found to be one such discriminatory practice, and the court ordered an end to the unequal treatment. In effect the court ruled that if standardized tests are used for admission into a public high school, the same cut-off scores must be used for boys and girls.

Although sexist policies related to the curriculum were more commonly found, these too are rapidly disappearing. Many of these policies applied to courses in wood shop, metal shop, auto shop, cooking, sewing and home economics. Most school districts are changing such discriminatory policies voluntarily or under local political pressures. Some have changed in the face of lawsuits. Sexual discrimination in the curriculum is unconstitutional, but informal practices often perpetuate long-held beliefs. Thus girls are all too often counselled not to enroll in physics or algebra, and similar practices discourage boys from taking dance, sewing, and, at times, even Latin.

Marriage, pregnancy, and parenthood

Many school districts have policies related to married students, pregnant girls, or students who are parents. Some of these rules exclude them from school altogether, whereas others only deny participation in student government, athletics, and other extracurricular activities. These policies are aimed at discouraging "teen-age" marriages and pregnancies, since adults tend to believe that early marriage leads to dropping out of school or to poor school performance.

The law is clear that students have a right to continue schooling even if they marry. State laws that make attendance compulsory usually do so between specified age limits. Within those limits, students have a right to attend school even if they violate adult values against early marriages. The same rule holds true for pregnant girls, married or not.

The law is not as clear or uniform concerning participation in extracurricular activities by married students. School policies that exclude them from athletic teams have been upheld in some states as exemplified by the *Kissick* case in Texas. Other court decisions are consistent with the *Davis* case from Ohio and rule such policies arbitrary and discriminatory. Perhaps the key distinction between these different holdings is that some courts consider extracurricular activities to be less important than the regular school program and therefore grant the school boards greater discretion in their regulation. Other courts, such as the one in the *Davis* case, hold that extracurricular activities can be very important and might make a significant impact on the life of a student. In our opinion, this will become the dominant judicial view. This view is also shared by many schools which now refer to such activities as cocurricular rather than extracurricular Thus courts are increasingly extending the right of participation in these activities to married and pregnant students, and to those students with children.

The U.S. Department of Health, Education and Welfare, independent of the courts, has proposed regulations for ending sexual discrimination in education. While the proposed regulations do not go beyond what some courts have already decided, they would apply broadly to all schools, public and private, that receive Federal aid.[26]

NOTES

[1] *Sail'er Inn, Inc.* v. *Kirby*, 485 P.2d 529 (Cal. 1971).
[2] *Quong Wing* v. *Kirkendall*, 223 U.S. 59, 63 (1912).

[3] *Brenden* v. *Independent School District* 742, 342 F.Supp. 1224 (D. Minn. 1972). This case has been affirmed in the Court of Appeals 477 F.2d 1292 (8th Cir. 1973).

[4] *Reed* v. *Reed*, 404 U.S. 71 (1971).

[5] *Brenden* at 1233.

[6] *Ibid.*

[7] *Id.* at 1231–1232.

[8] *Bucha* v. *Illinois High School Association*, 351 F.Supp. 69 (N.D. Ill. 1972).

[9] See *Reed* v. *Reed*, 404 U.S. 71 (1971).

[10] *Reed* v. *Nebraska School Activities Association*, 341 F.Supp. 258 (D. Neb. 1972).

[11] See, for example, Nancy Frazier and Myra Sadker, *Sexism In School and Society*, New York, Harper & Row, 1973.

[12] *Seward* v. *Clayton Valley High School District*, Civ. Action No. 134173 (Contra Costa Sup. Ct.).

[13] *Della Casa* v. *South San Francisco Unified School District*, Civ. Action No. 171–673 (San Mateo Sup. Ct.).

[14] *Bray* v. *Lee*, 377 F.Supp. 934 (D. Mass. 1972).

[15] *Alvin Independent School District* v. *Cooper*, 404 S.W.2d 76 (Tex. 1966).

[16] *Kissick* v. *Garland Independent School District*, 330 S.W.2d 708 (Tex. 1959).

[17] *Id.* at 712.

[18] *Davis* v. *Meek*, 344 F.Supp. 298 (N.D. Ohio 1972).

[19] For authority, the court cited the Supreme Court in *Brown* v. *Board of Education of Topeka, Kansas*, 349 U.S. 294 (1955).

[20] *Ordway* v. *Hargraves*, 323 F.Supp. 1155 (D. Mass. 1971).

[21] *McLeod* v. *Mississippi*, 122 So. 737 (1929).

[22] See Marion Howard, "Pregnant School Age Girls," *Journal of School Health*, *41*, no. 361 (1971), 361–362.

[23] Berwick and Oppenheimer, *op. cit.*, 1214, f.n. 92.

[24] See, for example, *In re Goodwin*, 39 So.2d 731 (1949); and *In re Rogers*, 234 N.Y.S.2d 172 (1962).

[25] Berwick and Oppenheimer, *op. cit.*, 1228.

[26] Reported in *The New York Times*, June 19, 1974, pp. 1, 32.

9
Due process of law

Due Process of law is the primary and indispensable foundation of freedom. . . . Procedure is to law what "scientific method" is to science.

Under our Constitution, the condition of being a boy does not justify a kangaroo court.

— Justice Abe Fortas in In Re Gault[1]

Introduction

The phrase "due process of law" appears in most of the chapters in this book as well as many of the cases we discuss. Although its application to the rights of students is relatively recent, a wide variety of school policies and practices come under its purview. In fact, all school policies and practices must satisfy the constitutional requirement of due process. For example, if a student is charged with disrupting the school by making inflammatory speeches or by distributing obscene pamphlets in classrooms, fair procedures (due process) must be used to prove the allegations. In this chapter we discuss some key cases that clarify the nature of fair procedures in student-related conflicts. Do students have a right to a hearing and to have lawyers represent them? Are there different requirements for fair procedures in serious offenses and in minor ones?

Are school rules sufficiently clear and specific to provide workable standards for student conduct? Or are they vague and overly broad? All these concerns fall under due process. In the last part of the chapter, we examine cases related to school discipline, locker searches, and access to school records.

Fair Procedures

If one takes seriously the principle of *in loco parentis*, discussion of due process in the schools seems somewhat odd.* For if teachers and administrators act in place of the parents while the child is at school, should we not expect the behavior of educators to be similar to that we find in homes? The concept of *in loco parentis* suggests that disciplinary matters in school are approached with a "guidance" attitude, with care and informality, and not with a legalistic or technical set of mind. In contrast, due process suggests a variety of formal, legalistic procedures that we are not likely to find in homes as parents and children negotiate the daily problems of life.

How many parents have formal hearings, with notice and an impartial judge, before they take Suzy's television privileges away for watching forbidden programs? How many parents grant Johnny a right to counsel before he is spanked for destroying Josi's favorite finger painting? If we do not expect due process in the home, and if we consider schools to be extensions of the home, why should we expect due process in the schools?

Reasoning similar to the above has led to the idea that children and youth *are* different from adults and should be treated differently when they do something adults consider wrong. High motives and enlightened impulses have led to a unique treatment of juveniles that was hoped would be fair and equitable. "The basic right of a juvenile is not to liberty but to custody. He has a right to have someone take care of him, and if his parents do not afford him this custodial privilege, the law must do so."[2]

The ideals embodied in the above quotation, however, have not worked in practice. In the field of juvenile justice, recent court opinions urge that some elements of due process must be accorded to children and youth as well as to adults. "Juvenile Court history has

* *In loco parentis* means "in the place of a parent."

again demonstrated that unbridled discretion, however benevolently motivated, is frequently a poor substitute for principle and procedure."[3] In a leading case involving juvenile courts, the Supreme Court made the following statement on behalf of due process:

Failure to observe the fundamental requirements of due process has resulted in instances, which might have been avoided, of unfairness to individuals and inadequate or inaccurate findings of fact and unfortunate prescriptions of remedy. Due process of law is the primary and indispensable foundation of individual freedom. It is the basic essential term in the social compact which defines the right of individuals and delimits the powers which the state may exercise."[4]

The *Gault* case, from which this quote was taken, involved a 15-year-old boy accused of using lewd words in an anonymous telephone call to a woman. Does it make sense to use the Court's words from a delinquency proceeding and apply it to the daily life of the school? When children get into a fight on the playground during recess, must due process be used in resolving the conflict? If a 16-year-old is suspected of cheating on a test by two student monitors or a teacher's aide, does due process require a hearing? When and how should the requirements of fair procedures be applied to school matters?

THE TIBBS CASE[5]

In Franklin, New Jersey, on October 7, 1970, two sisters were walking home after classes from high school, when they were assaulted by a group of students, mostly girls. They were struck with a stick, pushed to the ground and kicked, and some of their possessions were taken or scattered about. Both had minor injuries, and one had her glasses broken.

They ran back to the school guidance office, crying. Although they could not or would not identify the attackers, some other student witnesses identified about ten of the students involved in the attack, Tanya Tibbs among them. Tibbs claimed that she saw the attack but did not participate. All ten students identified as the alleged attackers were suspended until an informal hearing was held, and the suspension was lifted from five. The other five were given further hearings and then expelled by the board of education.

Tibbs's parents were notified on October 27 that the board of education would meet on November 2 for a full hearing to consider the recommendation of the principal and superintendent that their daughter be expelled from school. They were told that they could be represented by an attorney, that the administrators would testify and could be cross-examined, that unsigned written statements of student witnesses would be presented (but that the students would not be there), and that Tibbs could present testimony or statements by witnesses on her behalf.

The hearing was postponed to November 9 at Tibbs's attorney's request. Her lawyer was informed that written statements by student witnesses would not be signed or identified. The administrators explained that the reason for the unsigned statement was that the witnesses feared retaliation if their identities were revealed. The principal testified that "he had received a telephone call from the mother of one of the accused students threatening the life of one of the prospective student witnesses." The situation was seriously aggravated by a history of racial conflict in the schools, and this was considered by the board in its acceptance of unsigned and unidentified statements by student witnesses.

The board found several students guilty, Tanya Tibbs among them. Thereafter, considering her prior poor disciplinary record, she was expelled from school. Her attorney "objected throughout the hearing to the failure to identify and produce and subject to cross-examination any of the accusing witnesses whose statements were read." On appeal to the commissioner of education, it was decided that the action of the local board satisfied due process and "that [the commissioner] was satisfied by the testimony of the principal 'that school officials had sufficient cause for concern regarding the safety of potential witnesses' so as to justify not releasing the students' names or permitting their cross-examination."[6]

Questions to Consider

1. Do you think Tibbs was accorded due process? Were the school procedures fair and reasonable? Were there other ways to get the truth and also protect those who feared retaliation if they testified?
2. Should she or her attorney have had a right to face and cross-examine witnesses against her?
3. If you were a witness in such a racially tense situation, would you volunteer to testify?
4. Would your testimony be influenced by threats or anonymous phone calls attempting to intimidate you?

5. At what age would it be appropriate to have witnesses appear for cross-examination?
6. What procedures are required by due process? Would you require such procedures for *all* school-related offenses?

The opinion of the court

The New Jersey trial court ruled that Tanya Tibbs was not given sufficient due process. The opinion noted that earlier cases generally did not extend due process to school disciplinary cases, not even serious ones. However, with the increasing importance of formal schooling, "when the sanction applied for misconduct was expulsion or suspension of severe duration, especially in college-level cases, the decisions began to speak in terms of hearing requirements of due process."

In the case at hand, the decision for expulsion "constitutes deprivation of a most drastic and potentially irreparable kind. In that setting compromise with punctilious procedural fairness becomes unacceptable." The court recognized differences in the severity of punishment for various kinds of school disciplinary infractions. It stated that for the treatment of school problems in general, formal "due process" is not required. Teachers and administrators must live with those daily problems, and they are best suited to take care of them. However, if the alleged violation is serious enough to bring about long periods of suspension or expulsion, the law requires that school officials follow more careful procedures. High among these procedures is the right to confront and cross-examine witnesses, whenever the decision turns on questions of fact.

Cross-examination of school children witnesses in proceedings like these should, however, be carefully controlled by the hearing officer or body, limited to the material essentials of the direct testimony, and not be unduly protracted. Such a proceeding is decidedly not in the nature of a criminal trial nor to be encrusted with all the ordinary procedural and evidential concommitants of such a trial.[7]

Concerning the fears of student witnesses the court noted: "The school community must be content to deal with threats or intimidation of the kind allegedly encountered by invoking the jurisdiction of the law enforcement authorities who must be presumed equal to their responsibilities."

Related Cases

THE DIXON CASE

The most significant decision in the due process area of students' rights is *Dixon v. Alabama State Board of Education.*[8] In this case a number of students were expelled from college for participating in a lunch counter sit-in and civil rights demonstration. When they were expelled without notice, hearing, or an opportunity to defend themselves, they went to court.

The *Dixon* decision, applying a "balancing test," set forth minimal requirements for due process concerning notice and hearing. Since *Dixon* is relied upon quite heavily by other courts, we quote it at length:

For the guidance of the parties in the event of further proceedings, we state our views on the nature of the notice and hearing required by due process prior to expulsion from a state college or university. They should, we think, comply with the following standards. The notice should contain a statement of the specific charges and grounds which, if proven, would justify expulsion under the regulations of the Board of Education. The nature of the hearing should vary depending upon the circumstances of the particular case. The case before us requires something more than an informal interview with an administrative authority of the college. By its nature, a charge of misconduct, as opposed to a failure to meet the scholastic standards of the college, depends upon a collection of the facts concerning the charged misconduct, easily colored by the point of view of the witnesses. In such circumstances, a hearing which gives the Board or the administrative authorities of the college an opportunity to hear both sides in considerable detail is best suited to protect the rights of all involved. This is not to imply that a full-dress judicial hearing, with the right to cross-examine witnesses, is required. Such a hearing with the attending publicity and disturbance of college activities, might be detrimental to the college's educational atmosphere and impractical to carry out. Nevertheless, the rudiments of an adversary proceeding may be preserved without encroaching upon the interests of the college. In the instant case, the student should be given the names of the witnesses against him and an oral or written report on the facts to which each witness testifies. He should also be given the opportunity to present to the Board, or at least to *an administrative official of the college, his own defense against the charges and to produce either oral testimony or written affidavits of witnesses in his behalf. If the hearing is not before the Board directly, the results and findings of the hearing should be presented in a report open to the student's inspection. If these rudimentary elements of fair play are followed in a case of misconduct of this particular type, we feel that the requirements of due process of law will have been fulfilled* [italics added].[9]

Does the *Dixon* case apply to high school? It probably does. Although the U.S. Supreme Court has never ruled directly on the due process right of public school students, it has cited *Dixon* with approval on several occasions.* In addition, several other courts, both federal and state, have relied on *Dixon* and extended due process rights to high school students.

Thus the general rule is that in serious disciplinary matters students have a right to due process. But what does due process entail? Even the *Dixon* case indicated that a "full-dress judicial hearing" is not necessary in all situations. The following complete standards have been *suggested* by Robert Ackerly for infractions that could result in serious penalties, such as an expulsion or long-term suspension:

1. *Notice of hearing, including*
   a. *the time and place*
   b. *a statement of the alleged infraction(s)*
   c. *a declaration of the student's right to legal counsel*
   d. *a description of the procedures to be followed in the hearing*
2. *Conduct a hearing, including*
   a. *advisement of student's right to remain silent*
   b. *the presentation of evidence and witnesses against the student*
   c. *cross-examination of the accusatory evidence*
   d. *the presentation of witnesses on behalf of the student*
   e. *the recording (either by tape or in writing) of the proceedings*
3. *Finding(s) of hearing, including*
   a. *recommendation(s) for disciplinary action, if any*
   b. *reporting of findings to appropriate school authorities (e.g., the Board of Education) and to the student*
4. *Prompt application of disciplinary measure(s), if any, including the right to appeal.*[10]

* See, for example, *Tinker* at 506, f.n. 2.

These suggestions are a model for serious disciplinary cases, but they are rarely adopted in their entirety by courts or school authorities.

THE LOPEZ CASE: ARE SUSPENDED
STUDENTS ENTITLED TO DUE PROCESS?[11]

During the 1970–1971 school year, Dwight Lopez and a number of other students were suspended from various schools in Columbus, Ohio. Although the students were dismissed for less than ten days, they claimed that they were entitled to an adequate hearing and other due process safeguards. Courts have generally recognized that a student has the right to notice and a hearing prior to expulsion, but it has not been clear whether a student is entitled to such rights prior to a relatively short suspension.

In this case a federal district court wrote: "If education is a protected liberty when expulsion is involved, then it remains a liberty when suspension occurs. . . . The difference between expulsion and suspension becomes important only when the Court confronts the question of what process is due to protect the Fourteenth Amendment liberty." Judge Kinneary noted that "the nature of the due process protection of the right of education is dependent on the severity of the sanction." When the sanction is a short suspension, more informal procedures may be adopted by school authorities. In such cases if school administrators follow procedures which result in a fair determination of the facts after notice and an opportunity to respond to charges of misconduct, then no matter how informal the procedures, the student has been accorded the minimum requirements of due process.

For the guidance of school authorities, the court held that "minimum procedural fairness" requires the following:

1. *Immediate removal of a student whose conduct disrupts the academic atmosphere of the school, endangers fellow students, teachers or school officials, or damages property.*
2. *Immediate written notice to the student and parents of the reason(s) for the removal from school and the proposed suspension should be given within 24 hours.*
3. *Not later than 72 hours after the actual removal of the student from school, the student and his parents must be given an op-*

*portunity to be present at a hearing before a school administrator who will determine if a suspension should be imposed**

This decision by Judge Kinneary went further than most courts have gone to guarantee due process in cases of suspension for less than ten days. In February 1974, the *Lopez* case was accepted for review by the U.S. Supreme Court.[12] Whether or not the High Court supports Judge Kinneary in requiring schools to insure due process safeguards for suspension as well as expulsion, they are safeguards that thoughtful administrators should voluntarily consider implementing.

THE GOLDWYN CASE: THE RIGHT TO COUNSEL?

Marsha Goldwyn was a senior at Flushing High School in New York. At the beginning of the New York State Regents Examination, yellow scrap paper was distributed with the test papers. During the examination the proctor saw Goldwyn referring to "a piece of scrap paper containing notes on both sides." The paper was confiscated, and after the examination Marsha was taken to the principal's office. According to the acting principal's affidavit:

Since it seemed impossible for Marsha to have written the notes as she said in a half hour at the beginning of the examination, I challenged her, not to duplicate this feat but just to copy over the notes as fast as she could on the same kind of 6 x 9 paper. In twenty minutes she had not succeeded in copying one-quarter of her notes. . . . I questioned Marsha again and she finally admitted to the cheating, whereupon I tore up her original statement and gave it back to her asking her for a written statement of her new story. This she gave me. All through this Marsha was in a highly excited, emotional state and in tears.[13]

---

* The court also stated that such a hearing ("which is not a judicial proceeding") must provide at a minimum: "(a) Statements in support of the charge(s) against the student upon which the hearing is conducted. (b) Statements by the student and others in defense of the charge(s) and/or in mitigation or explanation of his conduct. (c) The administrator is not required to permit the presence of counsel or follow any prescribed judicial rules in conducting the hearing. (d) The administrator should, within 24 hours, advise the student and his parents by letter of his decision and the reasons therefor."

The next day Goldwyn recanted her confession. However, shortly thereafter, Regents Examination privileges were withdrawn from Goldwyn for a year; after this, if her behavior were exemplary, "consideration will be given to the recommendation of the principal that these privileges be restored."

Marsha Goldwyn's parents retained a lawyer, who complained to the board of education that serious punishment was imposed on Marsha without "even a semblance of a hearing." Following this the assistant superintendent suggested a conference that the lawyer could attend, but only as an observer. A lawsuit was brought challenging the procedures that denied Goldwyn the right to be represented by her lawyer.

Questions to Consider

1. Should students have a right to be represented by lawyers in conflicts involving school matters?
2. Can the schools function efficiently if all conflicts with students merit full procedural safeguards?
3. What kinds of conflicts should require more complete procedures and what kinds less?
4. Should we distinguish elementary and secondary schools from colleges in regard to procedural safeguards?

The opinion of the court

The court in part relied on the reasoning of the U.S. Supreme Court in the *Gault* decision,[14] in which procedural due process was required for a 15-year-old youth charged with delinquency before a juvenile court. In that case the high court ruled that the state may not act arbitrarily and without regard to the individual rights of a child.

In the *Goldwyn* case the school officials argued that theirs was but an administrative proceeding, not a criminal matter or a delinquency hearing; thus the same rules should not apply. The New York court disagreed. It saw no reason why fair treatment should not be afforded a student in an administrative hearing when "serious and stringent sanctions may be imposed." Clearly the punishment in this case was significant. Serious consequences flow from the denial of a right to take the Regents Examination in the state of New York. The withholding of a high school diploma would affect employment opportunities as well as one's chance for scholarships and college entrance. In view of such severe consequences, the court ruled that the board of education had deprived Marsha of her right to a hearing "to ascertain the truth of the charges at which she might defend herself with the assistance of counsel."

The court explicitly recognized the difference between the Regents Examination and tests of lesser importance that are conducted almost daily in the schools. It expressed no opinion on what appropriate procedures are for dealing with students suspected of cheating on routine tests. For such situations the *Goldwyn* case would be a weak precedent.

THE MADERA CASE: A GUIDANCE CONFERENCE[15]

Should a student be entitled to due process at a guidance conference? Does he have a right to be represented by counsel at such conferences? Not according to the *Madera* case from New York. This decision held that guidance conferences are not judicial or serious disciplinary proceedings. Rather, they are interviews or conferences that include school officials and the student's parents. They are administrative and not punitive. Thus a federal court ruled that due process does not require that a lawyer be present to protect the interests of the student at such conferences. In the words of the court: "Law and order in the classroom should be the responsibility of our respective educational systems. The courts should not usurp this function and turn disciplinary problems, involving supervision, into criminal adversary proceedings—which they definitely are not."

In sum, courts have indicated that the right to counsel does not apply to all school proceedings. It applies to those involving disciplinary matters with possible severe penalities.*

THE MEYERS CASE: FREEDOM FROM VAGUE RULES[16]

Fifteen-year-old Gregor Meyers, a student at Arcata High School in California, was suspended because he had long hair. Through his mother, acting as legal guardian, he brought suit against the school authorities for reinstatement.

Meyers had been suspended because the length of his hair violated a portion of the school's "dress policy." This policy, which

---

* It should be noted in this regard that state statutes often provide procedural rights in addition to those derived from constitutional principles.

every student received as part of a Student Handbook, read as follows:

Campus Clothes—Extremes of dress and personal appearance are not conducive to the well being of all. Simplicity, neatness, cleanliness, and good taste are the keynote for school dress. Excessive tightness in clothes as well as extremes in shirt tails and similarly, extremes in hair styles are not acceptable.

Girls shall wear skirts and blouses or sweaters or appropriate dresses. Girls (sic) clothes shall fit properly and be in current taste and style.

Boys shall wear conventional slacks or jeans properly adjusted. Shirts shall be buttoned to within one button of the collar. Shirt tails with a square cut or with a soft curve designed for outer wear and in good taste are acceptable wear.

Extremes in dress, in style, and in individual taste are to be avoided [italics added].[17]

The grooming rules were to be enforced by the principal or a person designated by him. In practice he delegated his authority to the vice-principal and the physical education staff, who screened the students and identified extremes in hair styles. The vice-principal testified that "he regarded 'extremes of hair styles' as meaning 'deviation from acceptable wear,' and that 'extremes' meant 'deviations' which were not acceptable to him." The vice-principal, as well as teachers, testified that "extremes of hair styling" became focal points for discussion and attention and tended to interfere with classroom learning. On the other hand, Meyers claimed that the regulation was too vague and indefinite and was, therefore, unconstitutional.

Questions to Consider

1. Do you think that a regulation prohibiting "extremes in hair styles" is too vague? Or do you think that it is sufficiently clear and that it can be understood by most people?
2. Can schools be administered if all policies and regulations must be highly specific?
3. Could you formulate a regulation concerning hair styles that would be clear and specific? Could you formulate such a rule regarding cleanliness, punctuality, or dress standards?

The opinion of the court

In its opinion the California court first recognized that both long hair and beards are entitled to protection as symbolic speech. For such protection, "adulthood is not a prerequisite: the state and its educational agencies must heed the constitutional rights of all persons, including school boys." However, it is also clear that school authorities may impose more limitations upon the rights of minors than upon those of adults. These limitations, however, must stand certain tests:

1. The regulation must rationally relate to an educational function.
2. The public benefits produced by the regulation must outweigh the impairment of the students' constitutional rights.
3. There must be no alternative "less subversive" of the students' rights.

Justice Rattigan for the California Supreme Court explained that the board policy against extreme hair styles failed to meet the requirements of the third test stated above. The regulation was too vague. Since the right to wear one's hair according to one's choice was considered by this court to be protected by the First and Fourteenth Amendments, "in this area, the standards of permissible statutory vagueness are strict and government may regulate 'only with narrow specificity.' "*

The student handbook was not describing facts in its prohibition of "extremes in hair styles." What was extreme was determined by the subjective appraisal of a single school official, the vice-principal. He alone could decide what was acceptable and what was a "deviation." "A 'law' violates due process 'if it is so vague and standardless that it leaves the public uncertain as to the conduct it prohibits or leaves judges or jurors free to decide, without any legally fixed standards, what is prohibited and what is not in each case.' " The "dress policy" in this instance was faulty because it was vague and without clear standards.

Could it be argued that the policy was not a law and therefore not subject to the same requirement? The court simply noted that whereas the "dress policy" is not a law in the same sense as a criminal law, its violation does bring on suspension from school.

---

* The court focused on criterion three without much attention to the first two. This does not necessarily imply the first two criteria were adequately met.

"The importance of an education to a child is substantial, and the state cannot condition its availability upon compliance with an unconstitutionally vague standard of conduct."

Thus the court struck down the "dress policy" of Arcata High School since the "words 'extremes of hair styles' conveyed no commonly understood meaning, and whether one such style at Arcata High School was 'extreme' was neither determinable nor predictable by anyone except the vice-principal."

A dissent

Although the majority of the court struck down the wording of "extremes of hair styles" as overly vague, Judge Christian disagreed. He argued that the day-to-day management of schools should be left to teachers and administrators as long as they acted reasonably. He noted the "almost infinite variety of disciplinary concerns which may arise in a public school: personal sanitation, dress, disorder in the passageways, disruptive speech or conduct in class, and use of bicycles or motor transport, to name a few." Pursuing the requirement of specificity to an absurd degree, he asked: "Must a school specify in a written regulation the minimum allowable frequency of baths before a teacher may require a student to be clean? What kind of specific regulation is required to enable teachers to restrain disruptive speech in classrooms or movement in passageways?" He would leave all such matters to the reasonable control of teachers acting informally and without the technicalities of specific regulations. "So long as the teacher acts reasonably, the Constitution does not require him to work in an atmosphere of litigious contest with any juvenile sea-lawyer who may appear in his class."[18] Although in this case Judge Christian's view was a minority opinion, it is a view that is accepted by many teachers, administrators, and parents.

THE SULLIVAN CASE: OVERBREADTH AND VAGUENESS[19]

"The school principal may make such rules and regulations that may be necessary in the administration of the school and in promoting its best interests. He may enforce obedience to any reasonable and lawful command." This was the only written regulation of the Houston, Texas, school board on which the principal of Sharpstown Junior/Senior High School based his expulsion of Mike Fischer and Dan Sullivan for publishing an underground newspaper. The principal considered the publication of "Pflashlyte" not "in the best interest of the school."

Plaintiffs Sullivan and Fischer alleged that the regulation under which they were expelled was unconstitutional under the "void-for-vagueness" doctrine. Two aspects of this doctrine have been developed by the Supreme Court. The first is overbreadth, and the second is vagueness. Under the first, we ask whether a regulation is too broad. "Could a reasonable application of its sanctions include conduct protected by the Constitution?" Secondly, is it too vague? A regulation "so vague that men of common intelligence must necessarily guess at its meaning and differ as to its application violates the first essential of due process."

The *Sullivan* court was convinced that in serious disciplinary matters, such as those that could result in expulsion or suspension, the fundamental elements of due process must apply. Essential to such due process is sufficient clarity and precision in rules to guide student conduct. In the words of the court:

School rules probably do not need to be as narrow as criminal statutes, but if school officials contemplate severe punishment they must do so on the basis of a rule which is drawn so as to reasonably inform the student what specific conduct is proscribed. Basic notions of justice and fair play require that no person shall be made to suffer for a breach unless standards of behavior have first been announced, for who is to decide what has been breached?[20]

Applying these principles to the situation at hand, the federal district court found the Houston regulation both vague and overbroad.

Little can be said of a standard so grossly overbroad as "in the best interests of the school." . . . It cannot be contended that it supplies objective standards by which a student may measure his behavior or by which an administrator may make a specific ruling in evaluation of behavior. . . . It patently "sweeps within its broad scope activities that are constitutionally protected free speech and assembly."[21]

In other words, the regulation was held void for two reasons: because it was too vague to inform students what they could or could not do and because it was so broad that many legitimate activities could fall under its prohibition. As a general rule, then, school policies, rules, and regulations that might bring on serious penalties must be fairly specific and sufficiently clear to inform students affected by them.

School Discipline

THE SIMS CASE: FREEDOM
FROM CORPORAL PUNISHMENT[22]

Zebediah Sims, a student in Independent School District 22 in the county of San Juan, New Mexico, allegedly took a tool from his crafts class in violation of school rules. His crafts teacher "inflicted three blows on Sim's posterior, with the principal of the school as a witness." He, as well as other students, had been spanked in school on various occasions.

The relevant policy of the school, under which the spanking was administered, was set forth in the Teachers' Handbook as follows:

The most advanced educational theory opposes corporal punishment in the school. By and large, the administration of our schools supports this theory. However, it must be recognized that situations arise which can be exceptions to the rule. When other means have repeatedly failed, it may be necessary for the school authorities to administer a "spanking" to some recalcitrant pupil. When this is necessary, the punishment shall be administered by the school principal or if administered by the teacher it should be witnessed by the principal or his delegated representative in his absence.[23]

Sims and his attorneys contended that the policy and the action pursuant to it were unconstitutional and that all corporal punishment should be enjoined by the courts because: (1) there is a violation of due process in not providing opportunity for a notice, hearing, and representation by counsel; (2) due process and equal protection are violated because corporal punishment is arbitrary and capricious and unrelated to educational purposes; (3) corporal punishment causes serious and lasting psychological damage, out of proportion to the offenses committed; (4) corporal punishment constitutes cruel and unusual punishment; and (5) the policy is vague and overbroad and therefore has a chilling effect on Sims and other students by discouraging them from expressing themselves freely.

Questions to Consider

1. Have you experienced or witnessed corporal punishment in the schools? Was it "cruel and unusual"?
2. What is your reaction to the policy quoted from the Teachers' Handbook? What are your reasons?
3. Do you think due process should be used before any school punishment is administered? How would "reinforcement theory" influence your response to this question?
4. Do you think the school policy is vague or overbroad? Does it deny equal protection?

The opinion of the court

Sims's lawyer put forth four arguments on behalf of his client, but the U.S. district court rejected all of them.

1. Is there a denial of due process in not providing a notice and hearing plus the right to be represented by counsel? The Supreme Court has repeatedly stated that due process is a somewhat elusive concept whose exact boundaries are undefinable. It varies from situation to situation according to the kind of problem involved and the complexity of relevant factors. As explained earlier, courts insist on the right to due process when severe sanctions, such as expulsion or long-term suspension, are involved. The *Sims* court, however, indicated that it "knows of no law which established the right of a school pupil to formal notice, hearing, or representation, before corporal punishment may be inflicted by school authorities." In fact the court maintained that some of the key purposes served by corporal punishment would be frustrated if formal notice, hearing, and representation were required. Learning theorists, although not necessarily recommending corporal punishment, tend to argue that the punishment should quickly follow whatever wrongdoing schools or parents are attempting to eliminate. The time required by notice and hearing in a formal due process sense would make such expedient handling of school discipline impossible. In light of the facts of this case, the court saw no violation of procedural due process in not according Sims a formal notice and hearing.

2. Is not corporal punishment inherently arbitrary and a denial of equal protection? The New Mexico court again was unimpressed by these contentions. Although arbitrary action does violate due process, Judge Eubanks indicated that in this case there was a legiti-

mate objective, and the means used were reasonably calculated to reach that objective. The so-called "ends-means" test was satisfied.

The ends-means test for arbitrary official action consists of three questions. First, is there a legitimate end or goal the authorities are trying to attain? Second, are the means selected to attain those ends useful or effective? And third, even if the means are useful to attain the ends, are there alternative means that would be less harmful to other protected interests? For example, expelling Sims from school or cutting off his hands for allegedly stealing the tools could be a means to punish him and deter others in the future. These means, however, are clearly extreme and would violate the third step of the ends-means test.

The court made it clear that it was expressing no opinion on the wisdom or educational soundness of corporal punishment. Those decisions are appropriately left to legislatures and educators. If legislators, boards, or administrators create policy and act within such policy, the courts will not scrutinize them for educational effectiveness or general desirability. They will examine them only for legitimacy in light of the specific provisions of our Constitution. The policy of Independent School District 22 was upheld against the due process attack.

3. Did the school policy violate equal protection? Sims and his attorneys claimed that corporal punishment forced "acceptance of an inferior class position upon plaintiffs" and others like him and constituted "an unreasonable and invidious discrimination" that was not related to any educational purpose. The Fourteenth Amendment provides that no state shall "deny to any person within its jurisdiction the equal protection of the laws;" but this clause guarantees against discrimination only if there is no rational basis for differentiating among people (or among students). If the policy and its application differentiate between students who obey regulations and those who disobey them, there is no denial of equal protection because such a distinction is reasonable. If the distinction is reasonable, legally it is not arbitrary. Therefore it does not violate the equal protection clause of the Fourteenth Amendment.

In discussing the relationship of corporal punishment to educational purposes, the court noted that teachers have customarily had discretionary power to punish students for violations of school rules. "Traditionally also this has included the power to impose corporal punishment commensurate with the gravity of the offense."

What if Sims had been treated differently from others who disobeyed established regulations? The court recognized that such "selective enforcement of the regulation" would have been a denial of equal protection of the law. In this case, however, there was no claim that Sims was treated differently from other students.

4. Is corporal punishment cruel and unusual? The court gave this allegation quick treatment. It noted that its use was common knowledge; it was practiced long before the adoption of the Fourteenth Amendment; and no case could be found in the law books declaring it unconstitutional. The judge then quoted from Justice Black's dissent in the *Tinker* case, where he said: "School discipline, like parental discipline, is an integral and important part of training our children to be good citizens—to be better citizens."

COMMENTS AND RELATED CASES

However conservative the opinion in the *Sims* case may seem, it accurately reflects the fact that no appellate court has yet found that corporal punishment inherently violates constitutional rights. In 1971, for example, a Texas court agreed with the *Sims* case.[24] Nevertheless lawsuits challenging the legitimacy of corporal punishment continue to be filed and are currently in the courts of several states.[25]

However, excessive punishment by teachers or school administrators is not protected. Even where corporal punishment is allowed by state law, students can sue for injuries received in the course of such punishment. An Illinois court, for example, acknowledged "the right of a teacher to inflict corporal punishment in the process of enforcing discipline"; but it emphasized that "he may not wantonly or maliciously inflict corporal punishment and may be guilty of battery if he does so."[26] In this case a teacher struck a 15-year-old boy several times while on duty to keep the crowd away from a fence at a football game.

In a similar case in Tennessee, a district court ruled that a teacher might be liable for damages if the student's injuries were proven to be serious or if the teacher's punitive action was motivated by racial prejudice. In the Tennessee case, it was alleged that the teacher jerked the chair out from under the student in a study hall, causing him injuries and humiliation in the presence of fellow students.[27]

If the state law and board policy allow corporal punishment, there is a presumption that the person who administered it acted reasonably. However, this presumption can be overcome by showing malice or excessive use of force. Whether or not the educator acted out of malice or used too much force is always a question of fact. Medical reports, photographs, statements made in anger, and injuries to the student are useful evidence in trying to prove malicious or excessive force. In such instances the person who abused his limited power to administer punishment may be liable to prosecution for assault and battery as well as for money damages.

THE RELEVANCE OF STATE AND LOCAL LAW

The *Sims* case established the proposition that, as a general principle, corporal punishment does not violate the *federal Constitution*. But most of the law related to school discipline is not federal law; it derives from the various state constitutions, laws, and local board regulations, with significant variations among the fifty states.*

In general the state laws specify the conditions under which serious punishment may be inflicted on public school students. Some states, like Massachusetts and New Jersey, forbid all physical punishment in their public schools. Others, like Montana or Florida, specify the conditions for its administration. Where states permit such punishment, local districts may still choose to ban it. Such prohibitions currently exist in many cities, including New York, Chicago, Washington, D.C., and Pittsburgh.

Expulsion, suspension, or corporal punishment are typically controlled by state statutes. However, if local school authorities are sufficiently innovative and invent a new punishment not yet described in state law, the penalty must not be arbitrary, wholly disproportionate to the offense, or clearly unreasonable. In 1918 Miss Valentine was to be denied her high school diploma for refusing to wear a cap and gown to graduation "by reason of the offensive odor emanating therefrom due to a recent fumigation through the use of formaldehyde by the city health authorities.[28] The Supreme Court of Iowa held that the punishment had "no reasonable relation to educational values" and therefore was not within the authority of the school. She could be denied the right to participate in the graduation ceremony but not her diploma. Her case illustrates the general rule that school discipline and punishment should be reasonable and related to educational purposes.

* One must check the laws of each state as well as the policies and regulations of each school district. Such information is usually available from the office of the local school superintendent, and it is often published in a variety of handbooks.

OTHER ASPECTS OF DISCIPLINE

School officials and boards have wide-ranging power to make and enforce rules and regulations related to the operation of schools. These powers are either expressly granted by state law or implied as necessary to carry out other educational responsibilities. Courts are reluctant to interfere with the daily operation of the schools and as long as disciplinary rules and procedures are reasonable and non-discriminatory, judges are not likely to curb the discretionary powers of school officials.

A clear statement of this principle was handed down by a district court in Texas in April 1973. Upholding the long-term suspension of a student for consuming vodka on school grounds, which violated known school rules, the opinion stated these generally accepted principles:

> *Among the things a student is supposed to learn at school . . . is a sense of discipline. Of course, rules cannot be made by authorities for the sake of making them but they should possess considerable leeway in promulgating regulations for the proper conduct of students. Courts should uphold them where there is any rational basis for the questioned rule. All that is necessary is a reasonable connection of the rule with the proper operation of the schools. By accepting an education at public expense pupils at the elementary or high school level subject themselves to considerable discretion on the part of school authorities as to the manner in which they deport themselves. Those who run public schools should be the judges in the business of running schools better. . . . Except in extreme cases the judgment of school officials should be final in applying a regulation to an individual case.*[29]

If rules, however, are unreasonable, or if there is evidence of excessive punishment, malice, or discriminatory enforcement, the courts are likely to help.

Punishment for conduct away from school

The law is not clear or uniform regarding discipline imposed by the school for conduct away from it. Early decisions tended to uphold the school officials, particularly if the student's conduct somehow related to the operation of the school. A Connecticut case in 1925, for example, noted: "The conduct of pupils outside of school hours and school property may be regulated by rules established by the school authorities if such conduct directly relates to and affects the management of the school and its efficiency."[30] Courts have reasoned this way under the *in loco parentis* doctrine. However, it is difficult to argue that doctrine when the parent and child are *both* suing the school over punishment administered for conduct while the child was away from school, namely at or near his home.

"Double jeopardy?"

If a student's conduct in or away from school gets him in trouble with the civil authorities, may the school also impose discipline for the same acts? Or is that double jeopardy?

The common-sense notion of double jeopardy is that people should not have to pay twice for the same wrongdoing or mistake. This is an oversimplification of a technical legal concept that was developed in criminal law. In brief, double jeopardy means that a person should not be tried in criminal court more than once for the identical offense.

One can, however, be held liable in both a criminal proceeding and a civil suit for the same behavior. For example, if you drive a car under the influence of alcohol and injure Ms. X, you can be sued by Ms. X for money damages, and the state may prosecute you for drunk driving in a separate action. You may not plead double jeopardy as a defense to the suit by Ms. X because you have already been convicted by the state. Similarly, the teacher who uses excessive force in disciplining a child might be liable for money damages for injures inflicted, and he also might be prosecuted for assault and battery in a criminal action.

THE HOWARD CASE[31]

In March 1969 Robert T. Howard, III, and Douglas Herman were arrested by the police and charged with the "criminal possession of a hypodermic instrument." The arrested high school students were reported to possess some heroin at the time of the arrest. A week later, New Rochelle High School, New York, suspended the two students. The superintendent relied on a board of education regulation requiring the suspension of a student "upon his indictment or arraignment in any court . . . for any criminal act of a nature injurious to other students or school personnel."

In this case, as in countless other lawsuits, the court avoided the constitutional issues and based its decision on state law.* The statute, Education Law Section 3214 (6) (a), provided that school authorities may suspend a minor from attending school in the following circumstances:

(1) *A minor who is insubordinate or disorderly;*

(2) *A minor whose physical or mental condition endangers the health, safety, or morals of himself or of other minors.*

Did the possession of hypodermic needles and heroin, away from the school, satisfy the conditions of (1) and (2) above? The court ruled in the *Howard* case that it did not. In the words of Judge Grady: "While the *use* of heroin by students off the high school premises bears a reasonable relation to, and may endanger the health, safety and morals of other students, the bare charges against petitioners of *possession* of heroin do not justify suspension on the grounds set forth in section 3214 (6)." Thus the court ruled that the school exceeded the powers conferred upon it by state law. Furthermore the court ordered the school to expunge the suspension from the school records.

In this case the students could not be disciplined by the school for alleged criminal behavior away from school. However, the court indicated that while the *mere possession* of heroin away from school could not be grounds for suspension, the *use* of it, even away from school, could be if it were shown to affect other students or the in-school behavior of the users. No double jeopardy issue is involved even though the same behavior would bring on punishment by the civil authorities as well as disciplinary action in the school.

The *Howard* case exemplifies how strictly some judges interpret state laws that grant powers to school officials. It is probable that there are judges in other courts who would have ruled against these students on these same facts. The point is that neither outcome would be vulnerable to the claim of double jeopardy.

An advanced view reflected in few judicial opinions is advocated by the American Civil Liberties Union, and it appears to be consistent with the *Howard* ruling.

When a student chooses to participate in out-of-school activities that result in police action, it is an infringement of his liberty for

* The judicial preference to avoid facing constitutional questions whenever the case can be decided on other grounds is almost universal in our courts.

the school to punish such activity, or to enter it on school records or report it to prospective employers or other agencies, unless authorized or requested by the student. A student who violates any law risks the legal penalties prescribed by civil authorities. He should not be placed in jeopardy at school for an offense which is not concerned with the educational institution.[32]

Notice that even the ACLU recommendation would permit school disciplinary action for out-of-school violations of law that have demonstrable consequences within the school.

Grades and discipline

Teachers have been known to lower a student's grade in a course as a disciplinary measure. Schools have also been known to withhold a diploma, prevent or postpone graduation, or even refuse to supply a transcript as punishment for the breaking of school rules. These practices seem to be quite unfair and unreasonable to many people; others urge their use and argue that they are legitimate means to discipline students, keep them learning, and prepare them for responsible citizenship. Where do the courts stand on these issues?

As a general rule, courts will not enter disputes over grades between students and their teachers. Educators have wide discretion in evaluating the quality of student work, and the courts will not supervise the exercise of this discretion. However, if a student claims that his grade was lowered for nonacademic reasons or can show that the teacher acted maliciously or arbitrarily, he will get help from the courts. However, the burden of proof is on the student to establish that the grade received was not related to the quality of the work. This is difficult to prove, and there are no cases reported from elementary or high schools challenging the assignment of grades. But there have been cases involving college students in Florida and Vermont that support the idea that improper conduct or discipline problems may not legally affect academic grades.

High schools and elementary schools today tend to give separate evaluations for academic achievement and for conduct, or "citizenship." Report cards reflect this separation, and some districts even formalize the separation by writing it into policy. In New York, for example, the following is operative:

Grades are estimates of academic achievement only. Pupils' behavior and attitude do not, in themselves, provide a legitimate basis for calculating grades. Evidences of excellence or deficiencies in char-

acter are to be recorded in other ways. . . . Continued absence or lateness should have an effect on the final grade only insofar as it affects actual achievement in the subject.[33]

One reason why it is important to separate academic from disciplinary matters is that courts tend to respect the educator's discretion in academic judgments; however, in alleged violations of school rules, they are more likely to require due process. Thus, by hiding a disciplinary punishment in a lowered grade, teachers can circumvent the constitutional requirement of due process.

Questions to Consider

1. If a grade reflects both achievement and effort, should not disruptive behavior lower the grade?
2. If citizenship training is a legitimate objective of schooling, is it not reasonable to withhold a diploma from students who defy authority and break rules?
3. What do you believe to be the proper relationship between grades, diplomas, graduation, and discipline problems? Why?

Diplomas and discipline

Can students be prevented from participating in graduation ceremonies or receiving a diploma because of some misconduct in school?

We noted previously that as early as 1921 the Supreme Court of Iowa ruled that Miss Valentine, a high school girl who successfully completed all academic requirements but refused to wear a formaldehyde-laden gown to graduation, had a right to receive her diploma. Denying her the diploma had "no reasonable relation to educational values" and therefore was not within the authority of the school. She could not be denied her diploma although she could be excluded from the graduation ceremony.

By contrast, a New York court in 1971 ruled that a student who supposedly threatened and struck the high school principal during a school disturbance could not be barred from graduation exercises.[34] Since the alleged misconduct occurred earlier, and since there was no evidence that the student's presence at the graduation exercises would be disruptive, the court said that excluding her would not be "a reasonable punishment meant to encourage the best educational results. . . . It would indeed be a distortion of an educational process in this period of youthful discontentment to snatch from a young woman at the point of educational fruition the savoring of her educational success." There are several rulings by the New York State commissioner of education upholding students' rights to participate in graduation ceremonies in cases where schools attempted to bar them for reasons of pregnancy or for "lack of good citizenship."[35] Other than these, there are no court rulings adjudicating such issues. A due process argument can always be made if the proposed official action is unreasonable in that it has no clear connection to a valid educational purpose.

Can the diploma be withheld as a disciplinary measure? The arguments would be similar to the ones proposed above. If a student has fulfilled all academic requirements, it does not seem reasonable to withhold from her the symbol of her accomplishment. Although there are no recent judicial decisions on this issue, a ruling of the chancellor of the New York City schools is instructive.

Students who violate rules of conduct are subject to disciplinary measures, but the manipulation of a diploma is not a proper or legitimate disciplinary tool in view of the inherent difficulty in defining "citizenship" and the clear danger and impropriety of labeling students as "good" or "bad" citizens. The school system should award the diploma on the basis of carefully defined educational criteria, and not deny or delay the diploma on other than educational grounds or as a means of discipline. In brief, the school is empowered to grant diplomas, not citizenship.[36]

It appears, then, that whereas ordinary grading practices and common disciplinary procedures are within the discretionary powers of educators, extraordinary discipline will be scrutinized by the courts. Excessive measures or those not reasonably related to educational purposes are likely to be struck down as going beyond the authority of schools or as violative of due process. There is a dearth of cases in this area, but it can be suggested with caution that whatever new law exists tends to recognize the expanding rights of students.

Unauthorized Searches

"A man's house is his castle" is a motto we inherited from the British. Our legal system has generally applied it to the protection of homes from unauthorized search by officials. Public authorities need either a person's consent or a valid court order (a search warrant) to legally search an individual's home, his car, the taxi he is using, the phone booth he temporarily occupies, or even a locker at a train station he is temporarily renting. Does such protection apply to the student's locker at school?

THE OVERTON CASE

At Mount Vernon High School, New York, police detectives showed a search warrant to the vice-principal and requested his assistance to search two students and their lockers. In Carlos Overton's locker they found four marijuana cigarettes.[37] It appeared, however, that the search warrant was defective; Overton therefore claimed that the entire search was illegal, invalidating the evidence found. The officials, on the other hand, claimed that the vice-principal consented to the search and that he had a right to do so. They contended that there was no unauthorized search, only one with consent and that therefore the evidence gained was properly used.

Questions to Consider

1. Who owns school lockers?
2. May school officials authorize outsiders to search student lockers?
3. Should authorities be allowed to search student lockers? Can you conceive of some situations in which they should be able to do so? Others in which they should not be able to do so?

The opinion of the court

Carlos Overton, through his lawyers, argued that the protection of the Fourth Amendment against unauthorized searches applies not only to dwellings but also to lockers and desks.* Furthermore, he argued that recent opinions of the Supreme Court have extended constitutional protections to students as well as to adults. Thus, since *he* did not consent to the search and since the search warrant was not valid, the search violated his Fourth Amendment rights.

The officials, on the other hand, argued that even if the search warrant was defective, the vice-principal could give consent to search the locker. The court ruled in favor of this position and against the claims of Carlos Overton.

According to Judge Keating, whereas lockers, desks, or cars are also protected from unauthorized searches, there are situations in

* The Fourth Amendment protects "the right of the people to be secure in their persons, houses, papers, and effects, against unreasonable searches and seizures."

which someone else is empowered to give consent on your behalf. In this instance the vice-principal gave consent, and the court held that he had the power to do so. "The power of Dr. Panitz to give consent to this search arises out of the distinct relationship between school authorities and students."

The school authorities have an obligation to maintain discipline over students. It is recognized that when large numbers of teenagers are gathered together, their inexperience and lack of mature judgment can create hazards for each other. Parents who surrender their children to this type of environment, in order that the children may continue developing both intellectually and socially, have a right to expect certain safeguards.

The judge went on to discuss the peculiar susceptibility of teenagers to the use of illegal drugs, which places a special obligation on school authorities to investigate charges of possession of narcotics and to take remedial action.

Furthermore, at Mount Vernon High School, as in most schools in the country, the locker combinations were known to the office as well as to the student. Each student had exclusive use of the locker vis-à-vis other students but not in relation to the school authorities. "In fact, the school issues regulations regarding what may and may not be kept in the lockers and presumably can spotcheck to insure compliance." The vice-principal occasionally inspected the lockers.

The New York court went so far as to say that the school had the affirmative duty to retain control over the lockers as part of its overall obligation to supervise students. Thus when the vice-principal learned of the detectives' suspicion, he had the power to consent to the search by the officials.

On appeal the New York Court of Appeals upheld the decision and specifically quoted this statement from Judge Keating:

Not only have the school authorities the right to inspect but this right becomes a duty when suspicion arises *that something of an illegal nature may be secreted there. When Dr. Panitz learned of the detectives' suspicion,* he was obligated to inspect the locker. *This interest, together with the nonexclusive nature of the locker, empowered him to consent to the search by the officers.*[38]

RELATED CASES

State v. *Stein* involved a search of the locker of a high school student who was suspected of having committed burglary, fraud, and

larceny.[39] The Supreme Court of Kansas agreed with the *Overton*
ruling previously discussed. After recognizing that the status of
school lockers "in the law is somewhat anomalous in that it is not
like a dwelling, a car, or even a private locker," the court upheld the
right of school officials to inspect them. In the words of the court:

*Although a student may have control of his school locker as
against fellow students, his possession is not exclusive against the
school and its officials. A school does not supply its students with
lockers for illicit use in harboring pilfered property or harmful sub-
stances. We deem it a proper function of school authorities to inspect the lockers under their control to prevent their use in illicit
ways or for illegal purposes. We believe this right of inspection is
inherent in the authority vested in school administrators and that
the same must be retained and exercised in the management of our
schools if their educational functions are to be maintained and the
welfare of the student bodies preserved.*[40]

The U.S. Supreme Court never has ruled directly on a school
locker search case. The lower court cases that have been reported
appear to be in agreement with the *Overton* decision.[41] Nevertheless
educational administrators themselves are increasingly sensitive to
the possibility that the growing recognition of students' constitutional
rights might in time protect lockers against unauthorized searches.
For example, a 1969 publication of the National Association of Secondary School Principals, entitled "The Reasonable Exercise of Authority," cautions principals against searching of a student's person,
desk, or locker "except under extreme circumstances, unless permission to do so has been freely given by the student, the student's
parent, and other competent witnesses are on hand."[42]

Rights Related to School Records

The educational reasons for keeping records of students' progress
were summarized by the National Education Association as follows:
"Records are kept to assist the school in offering appropriate educational experiences to the student. The interest of the student must
supersede all other purposes to which records might be put."

It would be difficult to argue with such a laudable statement. However, the gap between the ideal and the practice is often wide. What
is usually in a student's cumulative record (often referred to as a
"cum-folder")? Test scores, medical and psychiatric reports, guidance

conference summaries, and teachers' comments? Information about a student's health and his parents' education and occupation? Do they contain comments about students such as "a very well adjusted boy," "a troublemaker," "a Black militant," "a constructive worker," "disturbs class," "parents drink too much"?

Who has access to a "cum-folder"? Does the student or his parents? Can the local police or FBI see it? What about a prospective employer? Can derogatory information be removed from a folder? Does the Constitution have anything to say about school records?

THE VAN ALLEN CASE

A faculty member told Mr. Van Allen that his son, a New York public school student, needed psychological treatment and therapy. Mr. Van Allen went to a private physician, who secured a written report from the school guidance personnel. In the meantime, the father requested that the school make all of his son's records, not just the guidance report, available for his inspection. The superintendent of schools refused the request.

The conflict was resolved through court interpretation of the laws of New York. The state law required the records to be kept by the school and to be available for inspection by persons with an *interest* in it. If these were strictly *public* records, then anyone could inspect them. In the eyes of the law, however, school records have an unusual status. They are not public records in the ordinary sense; yet where state law requires them to be kept, the school officials must keep them. Where the state law indicated that a person with an *interest* in them has a right to the records, it would be difficult to argue that parents do not have the requisite "interest." In the words of the court: "It needs no further citation of authority to recognize the obvious interest which a parent has in the school records of his child. We are therefore constrained to hold as a matter of law that the parent is entitled to inspect the records."[43]

Student records and the right to privacy

The *Van Allen* case was decided under New York statutes and not on constitutional principles. In fact, as of now there are no reported decisions involving student records based on "right to privacy" or other constitutional grounds. Reported cases have been decided on the basis of state law or school district policy.

It is surprising to find how few states have specific laws in this area even though "virtually all school systems now maintain extensive school records containing, in addition to a pupil's attendance and achievement record, standardized test scores, personality data, information on family background and current status, health data, teacher and counselor observations, anecdotal records, and so on."[44] In the absence of state laws or clear school board regulations, most schools seem to deny students and their parents access to the records while tending to give such access to juvenile courts and CIA or FBI officials, even without subpeonas.[45]

Some states, such as Maine and Idaho, have laws that allow both parents and students to inspect school records, whereas others, such as Oregon, grant access only to parents. Still others, such as Massachusetts, have vague laws requiring school officials "upon request of any student or former student to furnish to him a written transcript of his record as a student."[46] The legal meaning of such a provision is not clear, for we cannot know just what is meant to be included in the term *record*. Does it include notations of academic achievement only, or does it include everything the cum-folder might contain? Furthermore does the guarantee of access to students and former students exclude access to others? In the absence of state laws or district policy, one may argue that the constitutional principle of right to privacy protects the records from everyone other than school officials, students, and parents; but as yet no cases have decided this issue.

Inaccuracies in the record

What can a student do if her school records contain inaccurate, false, or derogatory information? First, she must have access to the folder to know what it contains. It is quite probable that when a seriously damaging entry has been made, as for example, a reference to expulsion, suspension, or commission of a crime, and when court proceedings have cleared the student of the offense charged, the school records should also be cleared of such entries. Short of court action, some states, such as Washington and some cities, such as New York, by law permit students to challenge the accuracy of entries in their folders and, if they disagree with the school's version, to add their own version.[47]

Balancing competing interests

The area of school records reflects competing interests of different segments of society. Educators agree that, if competently handled, school records can be of substantial aid in the education of children and youth. Unfortunately there are too many examples of misuse of school records that work to the detriment of students. The careful use of such records for educational purposes is relatively new and the principle of confidentiality, or "privileged communication," which has been accepted in lawyer-client, physician-patient, priest-penitent relationships, has *not* gained acceptance in the educator-student setting. It is probable that educators will have to demonstrate much greater competence in the professional use of such records before the public and the law will extend the principles of confidentiality and privilege to them.*

The more probable resolution of the problems related to school records will come through carefully drafted state laws and district regulations. These might be the best ways to determine what goes into cum-folders, who has access to them, and under what conditions, as well as how entries are removed or modified.

SUMMARY AND CONCLUSIONS

In this chapter we have discussed cases directly related to procedural due process, as well as those indirectly related, such as school discipline, locker searches, and student records. According to our analysis of cases, substantial gains have been made by students in some of these areas of civil rights, but not in all.

Fair procedures

Courts tend to agree today that in serious disciplinary matters, that is, those that might result in expulsion or long-term suspension,

* For example, too many students' records contain such vague and uninstructive comments as "troublemaker," "Mary is a maladjusted child," "Eric is hostile and aggressive," "parents are uncooperative," or "Joel has trouble with math because he is unmotivated." Teachers might be helped by learning how to draw careful inferences and distinguish facts from opinions, conclusions, and generalizations. The instructional relevance and usefulness of such cum-folder entries must be constantly examined. The latest misuse of cum-folders is its nonuse, guided by the sophisticated cop-out: "I will not look at the record so that I will not have a 'set' or bias when I work with the student." It would be interesting to propose to well-trained physicians or lawyers that they not become acquainted with their clients' histories as the only way to maintain their objectivity!

students have a right to due process. The *Dixon* case is the leading authority for this, but even that case recognizes that a complete judicial hearing is seldom necessary. As a general rule, the more serious the alleged offense, the more thorough and careful the process must be. Where severe penalties might result, students have a right to adequate notice, to a hearing, to challenge the evidence, to cross-examine witnesses, and to be represented by their own lawyer.

Conversely, in minor matters, where no significant sanctions are likely to be imposed, some relatively simple procedures will be judged adequate and the presence of an attorney is inappropriate. However the *Lopez* case held that even students who were suspended for less than ten days are entitled to minimum procedural safeguards such as written notice and an informal hearing. The U.S. Supreme Court is now considering whether these safeguards should be required in all cases of suspension in the public schools.

As part of fair procedures, courts have held that school policies or rules must not be too vague or overly broad. A rule that is vague, such as one prohibiting "extremes in hair style," does not provide a clear standard or criterion for students. Therefore, the students cannot predict how the rule will be applied. Overly broad rules, on the other hand, are unconstitutional because they might prohibit conduct otherwise protected by the Constitution. For example, a school policy giving power to the principal to make all rules necessary to promote the "best interest of the school" is overly broad.

School discipline

A variety of issues have arisen in the broad area of school discipline. Courts have distinguished educational considerations related to school discipline from legal ones. They do not express opinions on the educational wisdom of corporal punishment and, as a general rule, find nothing unconstitutional about it. If such punishment were administered in a discriminatory manner (e.g., if teacher X only spanked tall boys or Black students), such practices would be unconstitutional. Generally state law controls the administration of corporal punishment. Its wisdom aside, as long as schools follow the law, a constitutional attack on corporal punishment is not likely to succeed. Excessive punishment, of course, is not protected by law and may even lead to civil suit for money damages or even to criminal prosecution for assault and battery.

Early cases tended to uphold the right of school officials to punish students for conduct away from school when such conduct had an adverse effect on the management of the school. Today there is no uniform agreement regarding this issue. It is probable that courts in the future will scrutinize more closely the claim that behavior away from school can impair the efficient administration of the school. If such misconduct is punished by the civil authorities and by school authorities, the claim of double jeopardy will not succeed.

Another aspect of discipline relates to the school practices of lowering academic grades, withholding diplomas, or preventing students from participating in graduation exercises as a result of misbehavior. Increasingly courts are protecting students, holding these practices to be arbitrary and unreasonable. School officials are asked to stay within the authority granted them by law and are encouraged to use their authority in a way that encourages the best educational results. However, they have a great deal of discretion in ordinary grading and disciplinary practices, and courts prefer to refrain from entering those areas, except in cases of clear abuse.

Locker searches

Schools have a duty to supervise their students, and this duty includes certain continuing authority over the use of lockers. When there are reasonable grounds for suspicion that something illegal has been secreted in the locker, some courts have even held that administrators have a duty to inspect it. They may cooperate with law enforcement officers and consent to the search of school lockers. Claims that such searches without a valid warrant are unconstitutional have so far been rejected by the courts.

School records

School records can help in educating students, but they can also be misused through the storage of inaccurate information and by being open to nonschool governmental agencies, institutions, and possible employers. In the past these records were often available to these outside agencies but not to the student and his family. In recent years significant changes have occured in this area, expanding the rights of students. The right to privacy is one claim under which some lawsuits have been brought; however, no reported case has been decided on this or any other constitutional ground. The changes that have come about have resulted from parental pressures, public criticism of school practices, and changes in state legislation. Carefully drafted state laws are probably more effective in dealing with problems related to school records than are challenges in the courts.[48]

NOTES

[1] *In re Gault*, 387 U.S. 1 (1967).

[2] *Ex parte Crouse*, 4 Whart. 9 (Sup. Ct. Pa. 1839); f.n. 21 in *In re Gault*, 387 U.S. 1, 17 (1966).

[3] *In re Gault* at 18.

[4] *Id.* at 20–21.

[5] *Tibbs et al.* v. *Board of Education of Township of Franklin*, 276 A.2d 165 (N.J. 1971), 284 A.2d 179 (N.J. 1971).

[6] *Id.* at 168.

[7] *Id.* at 170.

[8] 294 F.2d 150 (5th Cir. 1961).

[9] *Id.* at 159.

[10] Robert L. Ackerly, *The Reasonable Exercise of Authority*, Washington, D.C., National Association of Secondary School Principals, 1969, pp. 14–16.

[11] *Lopez* v. *Williams*, Civil Action 71–76 (U.S.D.C. S.D. Ohio September 17, 1973).

[12] On appeal, this case was renamed *Goss* v. *Lopez* and was accepted for review on February 19, 1974, 42 *Law Week* 3468 (1974).

[13] *Goldwyn* v. *Allen*, 281 N.Y.S.2d 899 (Sup. Ct. N.Y. 1967).

[14] *In re Gault*, 387 U.S. 1 (1967).

[15] *Madera* v. *Board of Education of City of New York*, 386 F.2d 778 (2nd Cir. 1967).

[16] *Meyers* v. *Arcata Union High School District*, 75 Cal.Rptr. 68 (1969).

[17] *Ibid.*

[18] *Id.* at 78.

[19] *Sullivan* v. *Houston Independent School District*, 307 F.Supp. 1328, 1345 (S.D. Tex. 1969). Some of the free press issues in a related Texas case are discussed in Chapter 3.

[20] *Id.* at 1344, 1345.

[21] *Id.* at 1345, 1346.

[22] *Sims* v. *Board of Education of Independent Sch. Dist. No. 22*, 329 F.Supp. 678 (D.N.M. 1971).

[23] *Id.* at 680.

[24] *Ware* v. *Estes*, 328 F.Supp. 657 (N.D. Tex. 1971).

[25] For example, in *Glaser* v. *Marietta*, 351 F.Supp. 555 (W.D. Pa. 1972), a federal court held that a school district could enforce its corporal punishment procedures, except as to those children whose parents had expressly requested school authorities not to use such discipline.

[26] *City of Macomb* v. *Gould*, 244 N.E.2d 634 (1969).

[27] *Patton* v. *Bennet*, 304 F.Supp. 297 (E.D. Tenn. 1969).

[28] *Valentine* v. *Independent School District*, 183 N.W. 434 (1921).

29 *Wingfield* v. *Fort Bend Independent School District*, (D.C., S.D., Texas, No. 72–H–232, April 23, 1973).

30 *O'Rourke* v. *Walker*, 102 Conn. 130 (1925).

31 *Howard* v. *Clark*, 299 N.Y.S.2d 65 (1969).

32 ACLU, *Academic Freedom in the Secondary Schools*, New York, 1968, p. 15.

33 Quoted in Alan H. Levine, *The Rights of Students*, Avon Books, 1973, p. 134.

34 *Ladson* v. *Board of Education, Union Free School District #9*, 323 N.Y.S.2d 545 (1971).

35 See *Matter of Murphy*, 11 Ed. Dept. Rep. 180 (1972); and *Matter of Wilson*, 11 Ed. Dept. Rep. 208 (1972).

36 *Matter of Carroll*, Decision of Chancellor (December 6, 1971).

37 *People* v. *Overton*, 229 N.E.2d 596 (N.Y. 1967).

38 *People* v. *Overton*, 249 N.E.2d 366 (N.Y. 1969).

39 456 P.2d 1 (Kan. 1969).

40 *Id.* at 3.

41 These cases often rely on *United States* v. *Jeffers*, 342 U.S. 48 (1951), as the authority for the principle that school officials have the power to search lockers without student permission or without warrant if "exceptional circumstances" exist that require immediate police action. The *Jeffers* case involved narcotics in a hotel room rented by adults, but the language used by the Supreme Court would certainly uphold the school administrator in situations where he had reason to believe that highly dangerous items were hidden in a student locker.

42 As quoted in *Student Rights and Responsibilities*, Washington, D.C., National School Public Relations Association, 1972, p. 24.

43 *Van Allen* v. *McCleary*, 211 N.Y.S.2d 501 (1961).

44 Russell Sage Foundation, *Guidelines for the Collection and Dissemination of Pupil Records*, Hartford: Connecticut Printers, 1969.

45 Russell Sage Foundation, *Guidelines for the Collection, Maintenance and Dissemination of Pupil Records*, a conference report, Hartford: Connecticut Printers, 1970.

46 Mass. Gen. Laws Ann. Ch. 71 34a (1969).

47 See the Russell Sage Foundation reports cited above for analysis and recommendations related to various aspects of school records.

48 Congress, as part of the Family Education Rights and Privacy Act of 1974, gave parents the right to inspect, challenge, and protect the school records of their children. This law will apply to all schools receiving federal funds.

10
Conclusions, trends, and frontier issues

The schools of the past have often been enclaves of totalitarianism. Just as the institutions were ruled by the near absolute authority of administrators and school boards, so the classrooms were ruled by teachers. It was somewhat over thirty years ago that Willard Waller, a noted sociologist, said that "The typical classroom is a dictatorship under constant threat of rebellion."

Times are changing. Although some schools and many classrooms still operate in an authoritarian mode, the past decade has brought some impressive changes in the civil rights of students. Some critics of our schools still refer to them as prisons and call for radical reform. A more objective view, however, recognizes the long-range gains, although the day-to-day changes sometimes are difficult to discern. As we have said elsewhere, concerning the civil rights of teachers, "Recognizing such gains should lead no one to smug satisfaction," for there is a continuing need "for vigilance and cooperative effort to protect gains made while striving for more complete attainment of all civil rights."[1]

As in other areas of social values, public attitudes toward the rights of students change slowly. Traditional arguments in favor of restricting students' rights still abound. They appear in judicial decisions as well as at meetings of local school boards.

As we read court opinions in cases involving the civil rights of students, we can observe our evolving culture. Disagreements are frequent in a culture in transition, and particularly so in a culture as diverse as ours. As we examine the disagreements in each case, we can identify the competing interests and observe the ways that courts resolve them. Thus we can understand where our court system stands on these important civil rights questions and possibly predict the course of future developments. In the following sections we will briefly present our conclusions, the trends we perceive, and identify some frontier issues.

Conclusions and Trends

FREEDOM OF SPEECH

Historically, the view that has predominated has been that children have a right to be cared for and that is all. Or as a professor said not too long ago: "To speak of the rights of students is a contradiction of terms." These traditional beliefs were reflected in the practice of punishing students when they made public statements that were disapproved by teachers or administrators.

Legal developments, which we believe reflect general cultural changes in attitudes toward the young, have dramatically expanded students' right to speak. As a general rule, students who are *away from school* have the same freedom to speak as anyone else. The *Tinker* case established that their right to speak *inside* the schools is also constitutionally protected. *Tinker*, it should be noted, applies only to public schools, for the Constitution usually does not apply to private schools unless they receive substantial support from governmental agencies.

The general principles established by *Tinker* hold that: (1) the First Amendment protects the free speech of students in public schools; (2) symbolic speech, such as the wearing of armbands, buttons, or other symbols, is protected as well as actual speech; (3) no right, not even the right to speak, is absolute, and this and other student rights may be limited under certain circumstances.

Under what conditions may school officials limit students' freedom of speech? If the speech, actual or symbolic, "materially disrupts classwork or involves substantial disorder or invasion of the rights of others," it is not protected by the First Amendment. Mere apprehension that a disturbance might result may not be sufficient, but courts have upheld restrictions in tense situations where there was evidence of student disorder and the facts showed reasonable grounds for "apprehension of disruption and violence." As in so many other areas dealing with constitutional rights, the general principle must always be applied to the unique facts of the situation in which students, teachers, and administrators find themselves.

Tinker was a landmark case in students' rights. Not only did it expand freedom of speech for students, but its general principles also have been applied to other civil rights areas.

FREEDOM OF THE PRESS

The weight of *Tinker* has also been felt in the area of freedom of the press for students. In years past, school administrators had broad discretion in censoring student publications or punishing students for distributing publications disapproved of by the administration. Recent legal developments have expanded students' rights and generally will allow restrictions only to prevent substantial or material interference with school activities or the rights of others. Proposed restrictions must be justified by the teachers or administrators, and it is not sufficient to claim that the publication would be controversial or unpopular.

The general rule does not grant an absolute right to students, nor is their freedom of press the same as that of adults. Since the primary educational activities of the school must proceed in an orderly atmosphere, reasonable restrictions on the distribution of student publications will be upheld by the courts. These include regulating the time, place, and manner of distribution. Some courts have even upheld regulations of off-campus distribution if near the school and likely to cause disruption.

Courts differ on a school's authority to require review prior to publication or distribution. Some courts have held such regulations to be unconstitutional "prior restraint," whereas others have upheld prior review under certain conditions. These conditions require clear standards, enough specificity to avoid vagueness and overbreadth, efficiency in administrative review, as well as a method and time specified for appeal of administrative decisions.

The materials students publish or distribute must not be obscene. The legal test of obscenity of student publications is that the work (1) "appeals to the prurient interest" of minors, (2) describes sexual conduct "in a patently offensive way," *and* (3) "lacks serious literary, artistic, political, or scientific value." The publication must be judged as a whole rather than by particular passages selected out of context, and the standards of the larger community must be considered rather than those of the narrower school community. Furthermore, school officials may not object to student language that is also found in materials in the school library.

Schools have substantial but not total control over a publication they sponsor. They can determine its goals, its level of financial support, its advertising policy, its criteria for selecting staff, and whether or not it should include student writing. Beyond such general rules, however, administrators' powers are restricted by constitutional principles. Thus they may not exclude advertising they dislike while accepting that which they approve; and they cannot punish editors who are critical of school or public officials.

Both the publication and distribution of controversial materials in the schools can "rock the boat" and make life very uncomfortable for some teachers and administrators. However, in balancing the competing interests involved, we agree with the judge who wrote that "the risk taken if a few abuse their First Amendment rights of free speech and press is outweighed by the far greater risk run by suppressing free speech and press among the young."

FREEDOM OF ASSOCIATION

Although freedom of association is not mentioned in the Constitution, courts have held the right to be implicit in the First Amendment freedoms of speech, assembly, and petition. As every dictator knows, dissent can often be prevented by controlling and restricting freedom of association. School issues related to this freedom involve four topics: (1) the right to join fraternities, sororities, and secret clubs; (2) the right to organize and use school facilities; (3) the right to protest and demonstrate; and (4) the right to invite speakers to school.

More than 20 states outlaw high school fraternities, sororities, and other organizations that select members in an undemocratic manner. Since every public school has among its goals the "preparation of democratic citizens," it is reasonable to argue that membership in such organizations, which fosters undemocratic attitudes, is inconsistent with those goals. Courts for over fifty years have upheld state laws barring membership in such societies. Clearly adults may organize and join organizations with restrictive membership practices. But courts have distinguished adolescents from adults on this issue, recognizing that the young are still in "their formative years." Furthermore the courts have deferred to the judgment of legislatures and school boards concerning the wisdom of allowing such membership.

Since no federal court has ruled on this issue since the *Tinker* decision, it is interesting to speculate how that decision would influence current judicial opinion on the right to join fraternities and sororities with restrictive membership practices. Perhaps the courts would bar such organizations only if they substantially interfered with the operation of the school. Or they might adopt the rule that school boards can regulate such organizations only inside the school, and attempts to regulate them outside the school would be unconstitutional. These are a few of the possible directions that courts might take in the post-*Tinker* era. Until such decisions are announced by courts, however, students should be aware of the risk in joining high school fraternities, sororities, or secret societies, particularly in states that prohibit them by statute.

The right to organize unrestricted student groups and use school facilities receives much greater constitutional protection. In fact, the burden of proof is on the schools to demonstrate why they should deny recognition to such an organization or withhold the right to use school facilities.

However, reasonable rules may be issued governing the use of school facilities, with particular reference to time, place, and manner in which the student groups should conduct their activities, and recognition may be denied to groups unwilling to subscribe to such reasonable rules. Furthermore, schools may deny the use of facilities to groups if there is reasonable basis to predict that such use will disrupt the functioning of the school.

Similarly protests and demonstrations receive protection under freedom of association, but here too reasonable rules governing them will be upheld by the courts. It would be unconstitutional for schools to ban demonstrations altogether, but workable rules that regulate "time, place, and manner" would be respected by the courts. Schools can prohibit such activities inside school buildings, particularly during school hours. Protests outside school buildings can be restricted to areas away from classroom buildings to protect the integrity of the teaching-learning process. Many schools have designated certain areas as "open forums" or "free speech areas," so that the demonstrations can occur without interfering with school activities.

In recent years many communities experienced conflicts concerning the appearance of controversial speakers in high schools and colleges. Such speakers ranged from Communists to Nazis; from "peaceniks" to members of the John Birch Society; from Black Panthers to women liberationists; from Hubert Humphrey to William

Shockley. Inviting controversial speakers to school sometimes presents a conflict between the First Amendment rights of students and the authority of school officials to regulate public speaking on school grounds.

It is generally held that schools may bar all outside speakers. However, schools are not likely to do this today since they recognize the educational value of bringing knowledgeable advocates of various causes onto the campus. Conflicts arise when administrators welcome some outside speakers but exclude others. In such situations, courts tend to rule that schools that allow some speakers on campus may not exclude others whose views they dislike. Administrators may require advance notice and approval for the outside speakers, but their approval can be withheld only if there is evidence that the proposed speech would constitute "a clear and present danger" to the orderly operation of the school. Reasonable appeals procedures must be available to review the administrator's adverse decision on a request for an outside speaker.

Thus we see again, in the area of freedom of association, an increasing recognition of the civil rights of students. Although the association right is not absolute, and although the conflict of interests must be considered in each situation, gains achieved by students in recent years are substantial.

Schools are more difficult to administer when students are vigorous in their exercise of civil rights and when they challenge the bounds of administrative authority. Yet an increasing number of educators recognize that such challenges may be the most effective vehicle to teach and learn about the meaning of our Bill of Rights.

FREEDOM OF RELIGION

Conflicts over the proper relationship of religion and public education are many and varied. In this book we do not address all these conflicts, only those directly related to the civil rights of students. We do not, for example, examine recent conflicts over "parochaid," "voucher plans," or "shared time." These issues are related to students, but they tend to focus on financial aspects of schooling and the competing interests of parents, churches, and the state. The issues of more immediate concern to students' rights relate to compulsory flag salute, Bible reading and prayers in the schools, and religious objections to schooling and ROTC training.

On the issue of flag salute, the Supreme Court first upheld the school requirement that students salute the flag but shortly thereafter reversed itself and supported the right of students not to partake in the ceremony if they had religious objections. Later decisions extended this right to students who did not necessarily belong to an organized religion but who, as a matter of conscience, would not salute the flag. In fact even school requirements that students who object to the flag salute must stand or leave the room have been declared unconstitutional. Since standing in such situations is "a gesture of respect and acceptance," refusal to stand is protected by the First Amendment. Exclusion of such students from the room would constitute punishing them for the exercise of their constitutional rights.

Prior to the 1960s Bible reading and prayers were common in public schools. In 1962 the Supreme Court declared that such practices violate the First Amendment and therefore are unconstitutional. It makes no difference whether students are compelled to participate or are excused from participation, such practices are unconstitutional in the public schools.*

In another important development, the Supreme Court ruled that Amish children cannot be compelled by the state to attend public high schools because the curriculum there would conflict with their religious way of life. Although this decision is viewed by some as a challenge to state-required high school attendance, others take a more conservative view of it. Since the Court emphasized the unique characteristics of the Amish, including their close-knit communal living for over three hundred years, the ruling is not likely to be applied to newer religious groups.

In a relatively recent development, a student who objected to ROTC participation as a matter of conscience or religion was protected by the courts. He was attending high school pursuant to state compulsory education laws. Earlier courts had upheld college-imposed ROTC in state institutions since college attendance is not compulsory. There is some question whether the compulsory-voluntary distinction would be supported today, since it could be argued that if one has a right to attend a state college or university, such attendance should not have an unconstitutional condition attached to it.**

* There are many communities where these practices have continued despite the Supreme Court's clear and repeated rulings. As long as no one challenges them, prayers and Bible reading continue. We can only speculate about the impact of such legal defiance on the attitudes of students and parents toward law in general.

** Although a state is under no obligation to make college-level education available, if it chooses to do so, its residents have a right to attend such institution on equal terms with other residents.

As we examine various court opinions related to freedom of religion, we conclude that courts have increasingly recognized the civil rights of students in this important area. Decisions related to freedom of religion tend to be highly controversial. It is a time-honored freedom in America and is viewed by the courts as one of the preferred rights under the Constitution. Consequently schools can restrict it only by showing that some compelling public interest must take precedence over the individual student's rights.

PERSONAL APPEARANCE

Personal appearance is not mentioned in the Constitution, yet adults are free to dress or groom themselves as they wish, subject only to laws aimed at public immorality.* The legal principles related to students are more complicated and are not uniform throughout the country. Historically schools had great discretion in regulating student dress and grooming, and no one thought of challenging such regulations on constitutional grounds. In recent years, however, both dress and grooming codes have been challenged and with mixed results.

Grooming

Since there are no Supreme Court rulings to give authoritative guidance to lower courts or to schools, we examined the opinions of U.S. circuit courts in the area of grooming. Eight out of eleven circuits have ruled on the right of students to wear their hair at the length they prefer. Four of these courts have upheld the students' rights, and four ruled in favor of school efforts to regulate hair length.

Hair cases represent conflicts of interest between male students, who, for reasons of esthetics, personal preference, individual expression, or peer pressure, choose to wear their hair long, and school officials, who want boys' hair to be relatively short. Many administrators (and some teachers and parents) seem to believe that long hair is likely to lead to discipline problems, to distract students from studying, and to constitute health or safety hazards.

Four circuit courts of appeals have upheld school efforts to create reasonable grooming regulations that forbade extremes in hair styles.

* We are quite aware of community pressures against the unorthodox. Various norms perpetuate the common taste, yet these norms change. In our discussions we refer to people's legal rights to freedom of personal appearance and not to informal pressures placed upon individuals by the folkways of various communities.

These decisions tend to reflect the reluctance of courts to interfere
in the management of schools. The courts do not want to take on
what they consider to be the many minor problems of school administration, nor do they consider the question of hair length to be a
fundamental issue that involves an important constitutional right.

In contrast, four other circuit courts of appeals have supported
the right of students to wear their hair as they wish. They have done
so by reference to various sections of the Constitution, including the
"liberty" guarantee of the due process and equal protection clauses
of the Fourteenth Amendment, the First Amendment right to freedom of expression, and the Ninth Amendment, which implies that
people have residual rights not specifically enumerated in the Constitution.

With appeals courts divided on the issue and with the Supreme
Court having refused to review any hair cases, how will the conflicting legal rulings be reconciled? It is probable that they will not
be. Students, parents, and school administrators can study the rulings in their particular judicial district and guide themselves accordingly. If the Supreme Court continues in its refusal to review school
grooming policies, the avenue to change will have to come through
political processes and through local efforts to create workable
grooming codes.*

Clothing

Do students have a right to wear the clothing of their choice? Most
courts hold there is no such constitutional right. School officials have
the authority to create reasonable dress codes, and courts do not
consider such regulations to be serious invasions of individual freedom. Even courts that strike down hair regulations hold that dress
codes only affect students during the school hours; after school they
can change clothes, which obviously is not possible with haircuts.

Whereas some courts have protected students' clothing preferences under the liberty guarantee of the Fourteenth Amendment, as
well as under the due process requirement that regulations must be
reasonable and related to educational goals, all courts uphold reasonable regulations related to the safety of students or aimed at
immodest clothing. The few cases related to clothing seem to in-

---

* This is not meant to dismiss the significance of legal efforts in the
recent past or possibly in the future. In many cases such efforts have
been quite fruitful.

dicate that our public schools are increasingly eliminating rigid dress codes and replacing them with more flexible approaches, often created cooperatively by students, parents, and school officials.* Thus, as with hair regulations, future changes in this area are likely to come through political processes rather than through litigation in the courts.

RACIAL AND ETHNIC SEGREGATION

No area of civil rights has been subject to more litigation during the past two decades than racial and ethnic segregation. Hundreds of cases have reached the appellate courts, and it is reasonable to predict that legal activity in this area will continue with vigor, although not at the same volume.

The bold outlines of the constitutional principles have been clarified by the Supreme Court. In its widely quoted *Brown* case, the Court ruled that racially segregated schools are unconstitutional if the segregation results from official action. Separate facilities for students of different racial or ethnic background "are inherently unequal" and therefore violate the equal protection clause of the Fourteenth Amendment. Later decisions reaffirmed this principle and urged schools to comply "with all deliberate speed."

Although some communities carried out the intentions of the Court, many cities and towns put up massive resistance. This resistance took various forms and resulted in the plethora of lawsuits aimed at implementing the *Brown* decision. Because each community has its unique circumstances, no single pattern of desegregation is applicable to all. Courts have respected a variety of local solutions as long as they represented good faith attempts to desegregate the schools. They struck down others, such as the "freedom-of-choice" plans, which were efforts to circumvent the *Brown* decision.

Attempts to create a more reasonable "racial balance" in the schools need not result in mathematical exactness in racial compositions of student populations. Mathematical ratios may be used as starting points in formulating remedies but not as fixed quota requirements. Furthermore one-race schools are not necessarily unconstitutional. School districts that have them will be closely examined by the courts, but the overall desegregation plans of such districts will be considered and not single schools in isolation. Busing may be used as a legitimate means to integrate schools; so can the technique

* See Appendix E for examples of dress and grooming codes.

of "pairing" schools or altering attendance zones. One decision, indicating the pragmatism of our courts, stated that the only desegregation plan that is legal is one that works.

The principles of school desegregation apply to Northern communities as well as to Southern ones; to Asian-Americans, Chicanos, and Indians as well as to black and white students. School officials must guard not only against the *creation* of segregated schools but also against their *perpetuation* when past practices created them or when population shifts within a community tended to create them.

It is probable that the idea of *de facto* segregation will be challenged in the years ahead, and school boards may face the duty of changing attendance zones as population compositions of areas shift. Since education is a state function and since states merely delegate responsibility over education to local communities, the exact nature of statewide responsibility for desegregation will continue to be at issue. Cases in Denver and Detroit have already questioned whether schools should be desegregated on an all-inclusive metropolitan area basis or within the confines of a single city. This is a particularly important and difficult question, since central cities tend to have much higher percentages of minority families than do nearby suburbs. However, the size of a metropolis leads many policy-makers to believe that the creation of a metropolitan area school desegregation plan would be economically too burdensome as well as educationally unsound. These issues and other related ones will be with us in the years ahead as the country continues its attempt to implement the *Brown* decision, which declared racial segregation in public schools unconstitutional.

SEX DISCRIMINATION

The Fourteenth Amendment has been the weapon used in recent years to attack various school policies and practices as being sexist. Two lines of attack have been used: (1) the claim that certain policies violate the equal protection clause of the Fourteenth Amendment and (2) the claim that these policies are arbitrary and unreasonable and thus do not meet due process requirements.

Most schools and school athletic leagues separate boys and girls in competitive sports. Furthermore schools tend to offer more encouragement to athletic competition among boys than to that among girls. Various cases have challenged such practices, claiming them to be discriminatory and thus in violation of the equal protection clause. Courts tend to agree with such contentions and have ruled that in noncontact sports, if there are no teams for girls, they may compete for positions on boys' teams. If there are teams for both, courts uphold school policies separating boys and girls for athletic competition since there are "reasonable grounds" for such separation. Although advocates of the women's liberation movement reject all such policies, most educators, women as well as men, believe that girls would suffer if all athletic competition were sexually mixed. Physical education specialists tend to recommend separation of girls and boys for most competitive sports, and courts uphold such policies when schools provide teams for both sexes.

Other discriminatory practices in the curriculum are rapidly disappearing. Courses in various shops, cooking, sewing, or shorthand used to be sexually segregated, but most schools have recently opened them to both boys and girls. We realize, however, that although legal barriers may have disappeared, informal discrimination persists in many schools. The law is of little help against such discriminatory practices, and they will be overcome only through the slow process of reeducating people, as well as through local political action.

Sex discrimination in admission to public schools has been rare below the college level. When it has occurred, as for example, when different scores on standardized tests for girls and boys have been used as the basis for admission to public academic high schools, the courts have struck it down. Discriminatory admission policies of public colleges and universities have suffered the same fate. They are unconstitutional since they violate the equal protection clause of the Fourteenth Amendment.

Court rulings have not been uniform concerning school policies related to married students, pregnant students, or students who are parents. Most schools continue to discourage early marriages and teenage pregnancies. To achieve these goals, schools frequently use policies excluding married and/or pregnant students from school activities, particularly from extracurricular activities such as athletics, drama, or student government.

Courts have ruled that students have a right to continue schooling if they marry and/or if they become pregnant. Such decisions are based on state laws that specify the age limits for compulsory attendance. Some courts have also ruled that marriage is an insufficient reason to exclude students from participation in extracurricular activities. Others, however, have upheld such school restrictions and ruled that they are reasonable means to discourage early marriages.

The differences in legal decisions seem to be related to the way judges view the importance of extracurricular activities. Traditional schools believe that extracurricular activities are of less importance than the academic program. Courts that accept this view tend to rule that the denial of participation in such activities is a reasonable means to discourage early marriages and pregnancies. A more modern view in education recognizes the increasing significance of extracurricular activities, and the judges who accept this view are more likely to consider it unreasonable for schools to exclude married or pregnant students from the full benefits of schooling. These decisions expanding the rights of such students reflect the current trend of judicial opinion. This is not to say that courts and communities are inclined to encourage early marriages or pregnancies. Rather, they will use other means to discourage them and will also realize that continued schooling is at least as important to students who reject adult advice in these matters as to students who accept it.

DUE PROCESS

Historically teachers and administrators have had the power to decide when a student misbehaved, to determine the punishment, and to administer it. Questions of due process were seldom raised; and, under the principle of *in loco parentis*, schools wielded significant power over students. In the chapter on due process we considered the gains made by students in securing fair procedures.

Today courts generally hold that students have a right to due process before serious punishment, such as expulsion or long-term suspension, can be imposed. The more serious the alleged offense, the more careful the process must be. Conversely, for minor offenses relatively simple procedures will suffice. This balance has been reached by courts in their efforts to be fair to students and, at the same time, to make it possible for schools to function efficiently. In situations involving possibly serious infractions, due process requires adequate notice, a hearing, the right to one's own lawyer, and the opportunity to challenge evidence and cross-examine witnesses. There is no rigid formula for what constitutes fair procedures; therefore the courts will consider the circumstances of each case with the foregoing principles as guiding criteria.

Procedures are not fair if the rules alleged to have been violated are too vague. Some specificity is required for students to be able to understand what the rules mean and to guide themselves accordingly.

Furthermore rules that are too broad are also unconstitutional because they might prohibit otherwise legitimate conduct and give administrators too much power.

Various cases have challenged the constitutionality of corporal punishment of students. As a general rule, such challenges have failed, unless unequal or discriminatory administration of punishment was proved. In the absence of such discrimination, however, it is necessary to examine relevant state legislation. Most states, for example, have laws governing corporal punishment that schools must obey. Excessive punishment is not protected by law and may result in a criminal suit for assault and battery as well as a civil suit for money damages.

Practices of lowering academic grades or withholding diplomas as punishment for misbehavior are increasingly struck down by courts as arbitrary and unreasonable. Schools have great discretion in disciplining as well as grading students, but courts will scrutinize these actions in cases of alleged abuse.

In recent years several cases have arisen over unauthorized searches of school lockers. Since schools have the duty of supervising their students, courts have usually held that lockers could be searched if there were reasonable grounds to suspect that something illegal was hidden. "Right of privacy" attacks against such unauthorized searches have been rejected by the courts.

In the area of school records, however, students have gained ground during the past decade. Recent developments have tended to open these records to the scrutiny of students and their parents, while making them unavailable to outside agencies without student consent. These changes resulted from parental pressures, public criticism, and shifts in state laws rather than attacks on the constitutionality of school practices.

DISTINGUISHING EDUCATIONAL FROM LEGAL MATTERS

Although this book has focused on legal problems, most conflicts involving students, parents, and school officials are not appropriate matters for the courts. School boards, not courts, are the competent bodies to determine most educational policies. Boards are responsible for the planning, construction, and operation of schools; for policies and procedures related to students, teachers, and administrators; for budget allocations and similar matters. Within each of these areas disagreements arise, and the board has discretion to resolve the disputes. Generally, courts do not interfere with this discretionary power even when school board decisions seem unwise. The courts will intervene only if someone brings a lawsuit and if the action of the board violates state law or the Constitution.

Since this book has focused on legal disputes involving the schools, some examples of educational conflicts in which the courts will not intervene might be useful.

School District A and B are next to one another. District A uses letter-grade report cards in its elementary schools, whereas District B reports to parents only in conferences. A group of students and parents in District A complain about the report cards and demand that the grading practice stop.

School Districts X and Y are in the same state. District X offers a variety of foreign languages in its schools; but District Y offers only one. Students and parents in District Y complain that this is unequal treatment.

Newville School District is converting its old "egg-crate" schools into "open-structure" buildings in which all classes will be team taught. A group of teachers brings suit to prevent this change because they have succeeded for many years in self-contained classrooms and believe the new approach will have dangerous consequences.

In each of these cases, judges will respect the discretion of the school board and will not substitute their judgment. When they defer to a school board's discretion in matters such as these, the courts neither approve nor disapprove the particular decision. In acknowledging the right of schools to regulate student clothing, courts are not recommending those regulations any more than their protection of the right to distribute underground papers indicates their approval of such activity.

As has been indicated in this book, educational decisions can be subject to legal challenge if they violate statutory or constitutional rights. For example, if a student is transferred to another school for racially motivated reasons or if student expression is restricted because officials disagree with its content, then civil rights concerns intrude into educational decisions, and courts will consider such matters.

Frontier Issues

The preceding chapters have examined student rights topics about which there has been substantial litigation. In this section we consider questions about which there are few if any judicial decisions. These are the frontier issues—issues that will provoke educational and legal debate during the coming years.

TESTING AND THE RIGHT TO PRIVACY

Schools administer various tests to their students. Among these are psychological tests used to analyze students' emotional health, self-concepts, and even their potential for future drug use. Although society may have a legitimate interest in the development of emotionally healthy citizens and in preventing drug abuse, the students' right to privacy must not be ignored. We believe that one frontier issue for the 1970s will be the conflict between an individual's right to privacy and the social interests pursued through psychological testing. This conflict might be heightened with the advent of "humanistic education" in our schools, with its attendant techniques that probe the "private" lives of students. At least one such case has already ruled in favor of the right of privacy. In 1972 a federal judge in Pennsylvania enjoined the use of psychological questionnaires since, "as the program now stands, the individual loses more than society can gain in its fight against drugs."[2] Psychological tests are likely to be carefully scrutinized in the years to come, and it is probable that only those that are clear and specific will be allowed; even then, informed consent by parents and students will generally be required.

GROUPING AND TRACKING

Grouping for instruction is a double-edged sword; it can be used to benefit students, but it can also work to their detriment. When students are grouped on the basis of inadequate or discriminatory criteria, or when they are rigidly kept in groups for long periods of time without reexamining their placement ("tracking"), these procedures may be held unconstitutional.

Several cases have successfully challenged certain grouping and tracking practices. A Washington, D.C., court ruled unconstitutional a tracking system that had the effect of segregating students along racial and economic lines.[3] A Pennsylvania court required that due process be followed "whenever any mentally retarded or allegedly mentally retarded child . . . is recommended for a change in educational status by a school district."[4] And a California court prohibited the use of standardized IQ tests to determine placement of students into classes for the retarded.[5]

An obvious instance of misuse of standardized tests for educational placement is the use of tests in English with non-English-speaking students. Such practices have been successfully challenged in Arizona, California, and Texas. These practices are so clearly unfair that they are generally settled out of court once the suit has been filed.[6]

While some lawsuits related to grouping have already been adjudicated, it is probable that the procedure will come under increasing legal attacks during the next decade. Grouping is widespread, yet the tests used to place students into groups are so inadequate that they are vulnerable to claims that they violate the due process and equal protection clauses of the Fourteenth Amendment.*

ECONOMIC INEQUALITY

Due to our tradition of local control and our historic practice of financing schools primarily with local real property taxes, we came to have both "Rich Schools and Poor Schools" within the same state.[7] In recent years various scholars, legislators, and parents began to question whether the quality of schooling, measured in money terms, should be a function of local wealth. "Interdistrict resource inequality" came under increasing attack. Critics argued that since education was a state responsibility there must be statewide "fiscal neutrality" in financing the schools. And in 1971 an important California decision declared that school financing denies the equal protection of the laws if "it makes the quality of a child's education depend upon the resources of his school district and ultimately upon the pocketbook of his parents."[8]

In part as a reaction to the California ruling, several states established special commissions to study new ways to finance schools. Lawsuits were filed in at least 38 states, and the Supreme Court ruled on the question of "fiscal neutrality" in the *Rodriquez* case in 1973.[9] In *Rodriquez* the court concluded that current school financing practices do not violate the equal protection clause of the U.S. Constitution since education is not a "fundamental" interest whose unequal provision would require "strict judicial scrutiny."

As a result of *Rodriquez*, challenges to inequalities in school finance will have to be based on state constitutions, or new legislative efforts will have to be mounted. Since most state constitutions con-

---

* Grouping for instruction is justifiable as long as groups remain flexible and regrouping occurs often.

tain an equal protection clause or provide for a "thorough and efficient" or "uniform" system of schooling, it is likely that legal attacks on inequalities in school finance will rely on these provisions. Such an attack succeeded in New Jersey[10] and is being pursued in several other states. While legal efforts continue, educators must also face the difficult challenge of demonstrating the relationships between the quality of education (i.e., the results of schooling) and the level of financial support. Since studies exploring such relationships are not conclusive, they do not yet provide a solid basis for legal arguments.

SCHOOL ACCOUNTABILITY

If students must attend school for approximately twelve years, do they not have a right to expect reasonable returns for their investment of time and energy? If a student "passes" from grade to grade but graduates from high school with academic skills that are substantially below the average of his peers, can the school be held accountable? Is the school district liable in money damages to such a student? Although no authoritative court decisions answer these questions, they have been asked in at least one case in San Francisco. The next decade may develop alternative ways of holding schools accountable to students, parents, and taxpayers, but it seems doubtful that courts will require schools to pay damages to students who did not succeed in their programs.

THE USE OF DRUGS TO CONTROL STUDENTS

The use of drugs to control the behavior of students is fairly widespread. In recent years, newspapers and popular magazines as well as professional journals have carried articles about this controversial practice. If students are compelled to attend school, by what right do schools administer drugs to them to control their behavior? If some children are "hyperactive," cannot schools adjust programs to fit their needs rather than drug them into conforming with existing school programs? Since children cannot consent to drug use, who can properly give such consent? If the use of drugs might have long-range consequences on the students' lives, should parents be able to consent to such use? Since the highest proportion of drug use to control student behavior occurs among minority groups, does this practice constitute racial discrimination? These are some of the difficult questions posed by this issue.

THE RIGHT TO CHOOSE:
ACADEMIC FREEDOM FOR STUDENTS

In recent years an increasing number of people have argued that high school students should have the right to determine the goals, methods, and content of their education. They believe that students should be able to decide what courses they should take, what books should be used, what kinds of people should teach them, and how they should be evaluated. This, of course, is in sharp conflict with the traditional view that school boards should establish academic policy and resolve all disputes between conflicting educational alternatives.[11] On the other hand, many school boards are currently increasing the range of curricular choice for students, and some are granting student representatives the right to participate in formulating academic policy. In addition, alternative public schools and alternative learning programs within schools are a recent development that could greatly increase student choice.

If teachers are entitled to academic freedom, shouldn't students have a parallel right? Shouldn't they able to participate in making the academic decisions that will affect their lives? Should schools be required to provide courses that are requested by a significant number of students? Should students have a right to evaluate their teachers? Should students have an equal voice with educators in choosing the books and materials they must use? These are some of the questions we can expect to hear more frequently during the coming years.

THE RIGHT NOT TO GO TO SCHOOL

An increasing number of minority groups see the compulsory education laws as the process by which the dominant majority is training all the children of the community to accept the values, goals, and methods of the American "establishment." They feel that any public school system that reflects the views of a politically selected school board will be in conflict with the beliefs and life style they wish to instill in their children. Therefore these ethnic, religious, racial, and social minorities believe that their children should have the right not to go to school, and many of their children agree. Such groups range from Christian fundamentalist sects to members of certain counter-culture communities. Although these individuals usually recognize the need to "educate" their children, they reject specific state laws concerning teacher qualifications, school building codes, or curricular requirements.

If the Amish do not have to send their children to schools that endanger their religious community, shouldn't other parents have the right not to send their children to schools that would similarly threaten their values and beliefs? Since Justice Douglas suggested that the views of the Amish children should be considered in determining whether or not they should go to school, shouldn't the views of all children above the age of 12 or 14 be considered in making such decisions? And if there is a dispute between parents and children, shouldn't mature students have a right to have their views considered and respected? Although the Supreme Court limited its ruling in the *Yoder* case to members of established religious communities, this decision, which allowed one minority group to escape the compulsory attendance laws, can be expected to encourage others to seek similar rulings in the coming years.

These appear to be some of the major frontier issues of the decade, but we can expect many others also to emerge out of the diversity and conflict of our rapidly changing society.

A FINAL NOTE

In 1969 a Texas court upheld the right of students to distribute their underground newspapers. In the paper the editors explained the importance of understanding and working for student rights:

We cannot sit back and relax just because of a few Amendments and Court rulings. Establishments are reluctant to change and are apt to ignore the essence of the justice that they themselves teach. To protect our rights we must understand them fully and we must be willing to work to preserve them. If we give up and knuckle under to injustice . . . what will happen later in life when we have to face abominations considerably more unbearable than the ones we face here in school. . . . IT'S OUR CHOICE!"[12]

Is the expansion and protection of student rights still a choice in the 1970s? As we enter a judicial era that is dominated by a conservative Supreme Court, many are concerned that the Court is not continuing to expand the rights of students as it did in the 1960s. However, we do not share this concern because we do not believe that the judicial expansion of student rights is today's major issue. The most urgent problem now is to help teachers, administrators, and parents as well as students become more aware of the rights students already have and to protect these rights in our public schools. This we believe should be the task of the next decade. And this work has only begun.

NOTES

[1] Louis Fischer and David Schimmel, *The Civil Rights of Teachers,* New York, Harper & Row, 1973, p. 146.

[2] The *Merriken* case was decided by the U.S. District Court for the Eastern District of Pennsylvania (1972, unreported.)

[3] *Hobson* v. *Hansen,* 269 F.Supp. 401 (D.D.C. 1967).

[4] *Pennsylania Association for Retarded Children* v. *Commonwealth of Pennsylvania,* 334 F.Supp. 1257 (E.D. Pa. 1971).

[5] *Larry P.* v. *Riles,* 343 F.Supp. 1306 (N.D. Cal. 1972).

[6] See, for example, *Guadalupe Organization, Inc.* v. *Tempe Elementary School District,* Civ. No. 71–435 Phx (D. Ariz. Jan. 24, 1972).

[7] This became the title of one of the first books raising the issue of inequality of schooling based on local wealth. See Arthur E. Wise, *Rich Schools, Poor Schools,* Chicago, University of Chicago Press, 1968.

[8] *Serrano* v. *Priest,* 96 Cal.Rptr. 601, 487 P.2d 1241 (1971).

[9] *San Antonio Independent School District* v. *Rodriguez,* 411 U.S. 1 (1973).

[10] *Robinson* v. *Cahill,* 62 N.J. 473, 303 A.2d 273 (1973).

[11] When a New York school board removed a controversial book from the library shelves, a group of students, parents, and teachers claimed that the action violated their constitutional rights. Since this case dealt with the library of a public school, the court pointed out that some authorized person or group had to decide what books would be selected. Judge Mulligan predicted that no matter what choice was made, some person or group could dissent. Therefore the court ruled that "shouts of book burning" and "violation of academic freedom" did not elevate this dispute concerning curricular choice into a constitutional issue. If it did, the courts could be asked to resolve all school controversies. *President Council, Dist. 25* v. *Community School Board, No. 25,* 457 F.2d 289 (2nd Cir. 1972).

[12] *Sullivan* v. *Houston Independent School District,* 307 F.Supp. 1328, 1350 (1969).

Appendix A
Constitutional amendments most relevant to the rights of students

AMENDMENT I

Congress shall make no law respecting an establishment of religion, or prohibiting the free exercise thereof; or abridging the freedom of speech, or of the press; or the right of the people peaceably to assemble, and to petition the Government for a redress of grievances.

AMENDMENT IV

The right of the people to be secure in their persons, houses, papers, and effects, against unreasonable searches and seizures, shall not be violated, and no Warrants shall issue, but upon probable cause, supported by Oath or affirmation, and particularly describing the place to be searched, and the persons or things to be seized.

AMENDMENT V

No person shall be held to answer for a capital, or otherwise infamous crime, unless on a presentment or indictment of a Grand Jury, except in cases arising in the land or naval forces, or in the Militia, when in actual service in time of War or public danger; nor shall any person be subject for the same offense to be twice put in jeopardy of life or limb; nor shall be compelled in any criminal case to be a witness against himself, nor be deprived of life, liberty, or property, without due process of law; nor shall private property be taken for public use, without just compensation.

AMENDMENT IX

The enumeration in the Constitution, of certain rights, shall not be construed to deny or disparage others retained by the people.

AMENDMENT X

The powers not delegated to the United States by the Constitution, nor prohibited by it to the States, are reserved to the States respectively, or to the people.

AMENDMENT XIV

Section 1   All persons born or naturalized in the United States, and subject to the jurisdiction thereof, are citizens of the United States and of the State wherein they reside. No State shall make or enforce any law which shall abridge the privileges or immunities of citizens of the United States; nor shall any State deprive any person of life, liberty, or property, without due process of law; nor deny to any person within its jurisdiction the equal protection of the laws.

PROPOSED EQUAL RIGHTS AMENDMENT

Equality of rights under the law shall not be denied or abridged by the United States or by any state on account of sex.

Appendix B
How the
system works[1]

In this section we examine questions laymen often ask about our legal system. Among others, we consider why local school officials are governed by the federal Constitution; how the federal and state judicial systems are organized; and how to find the law. There are other matters that lawyers must know in order to understand how the system works. These, however, are too technical for inclusion in this volume.[2]

EDUCATION AS A STATE FUNCTION

One must understand the relationship between the schools and their respective states to realize that when a school official acts it is a state action within the meaning of constitutional law. When the school board of a town in Massachusetts prescribes that each school day begin with a prayer, it is a state action that violates the "separation of church and state" doctrine. When a school psychologist in California, using a standarized test written in English, determines that Chicano children are mentally retarded and therefore must be placed in separate classes, he is acting as a state official and is violating the equal protection and due process clauses of the Fourteenth Amendment. And when teachers or principals systematically treat some children differently from others because of the color of their skin or their national origin, such actions are state actions for civil rights purposes. Similarly when teachers frisk students' briefcases and lockers, or when a counselor systematically "guides" black and brown students into vocational classes, these are also state actions.

Another important principle of constitutional law is that the basic liberties of our Bill of Rights apply to state actions through the Fourteenth Amendment. This was a controversial development at one point in American history. However, today it is widely accepted by scholars and certainly by the courts that the adoption of the Fourteenth Amendment made "national citizenship primary and state citizenship derivative therefrom."[3] Consistent with this principle, for example, is the pronouncement of the Supreme Court that "the fundamental concept of liberty embodied in the Fourteenth Amendment embraces the liberties guaranteed by the First Amendment."[4] Thus, although the words of the first ten amendments restrained only the federal government, after the Fourteenth Amendment was adopted in 1868, it became possible to apply some of these restraints to the states as well. This was accomplished by the Court's interpretation that the Fourteenth Amendment incorporated the basic protections of the First Amendment and specifically applied them to all state actions. In practice this means that all the civil rights protections of the First Amendment apply to the actions of all public school officials just as much as those of the Fourteenth Amendment.

THE CONSTITUTION AND SCHOOLING

Our federal Constitution is strangely silent on schooling. Scholars have speculated through the years about the reasons for this omission and tend to agree that were the Constitution to be reframed today, education would occupy a prominent place in it.[5]

By implication the federal government could move into the field of public education under several provisions of the Constitution. Prominent among these is Article I, Section 8: "The Congress shall have power to lay and collect taxes, duties, imports and excises, to pay the debts and provide for the common defense and general welfare of the United States." The welfare clause has been used without difficulty or distortion to imply congressional power to legislate in school matters.[6]

Although it is arguable that under the implied powers embodied in the Constitution our federal government could have developed a system of schools, as a matter of fact it did not do so. Instead, another provision of the Constitution has been relied on to establish the principle that education is primarily a state function. The Tenth Amendment, ratified in 1791, stipulates that "the powers not delegated to the United States by the Constitution, nor prohibited by it to the States, are reserved to the States respectively, or to the people." Consistent with this principle, every state constitution makes provision for a system of state-supported schools. These provisions vary from state to state; some are quite general, whereas others are more specific and include such matters as the minimum length of the school year and the age range between which schooling must be freely provided.[7]

The courts have accepted the general principle that power over the schools is among those reserved to the states. In the words of Supreme Court Justice Jackson:

A Federal Court may interfere with local school authorities only when they invade either a personal liberty or a property right protected by the Federal Constitution. . . .

We must have some flexibility to meet local conditions, some chance to progress by trial and error.

Justice Jackson further warned that adoption by the Court of "an unchanging standard for countless school boards . . . is to allow zeal for our own ideas of what is good in public instruction to induce us to accept the role of a superior board of education for every school district in the Nation."[8]

It is clear, then, that education is primarily a state function to be carried out pursuant to the constitutions, legislative enactments, and administrative agencies of the several states. All of these, of course, are subject to the principles of the federal Constitution as interpreted by the Supreme Court of the United States. That Court itself has spoken to this matter as follows:

The Fourteenth Amendment, as now applied to the states, protects the citizen against the State itself and all of its creatures—Boards of Education are not excepted. These have, of course, important delicate and highly discretionary functions, but none that they may not perform within the limits of the Bill of Rights. That they are educating the young for citizenship is reason for scrupulous protection of Constitutional freedoms of the individual, if we are not to strangle the

*free mind at its source and teach youth to discount important prin-
ciples of our Government as mere platitudes.*[9]

State responsibility has often been forgotten in our historical emphasis on local control of schools. It is true that states may delegate
certain powers over schooling to regions within the states such as
counties, cities, towns, or other political subdivisions. However, the
basic authority remains with the states. Thus local school boards,
superintendents, principals, and teachers perform state functions when
they act in their professional capacities.

THE STRUCTURE OF THE SYSTEM

Perhaps a more accurate heading for this section would be "The
Structure of the Systems," for in the United States we have a system
of federal courts and 50 systems of state courts. For our purposes,
general descriptions of the federal system and the state systems will
suffice.

The federal courts

The Supreme Court was specifically created by the Constitution
(Article III, Section 2), but the other federal courts were established
by Congress. Congress also has the power to alter the federal court
system, creating new courts and abolishing existing ones to meet the
needs of our changing culture. Currently, except for some special
courts like the Court of Claims, Court of Customs and Patent Appeals, and Tax Court, we have a hierarchic system of three levels.
The first level, the trial court, is the U.S. district court. Each state has
at least one district court, and some more populous states have as
many as four. Cases from these courts, as a general rule, are review-
able by the U.S court of appeals, of which there are eleven, including
one in the District of Columbia. (See map, p. 292.) The top level, of
course, is the Supreme Court of the United States. This three-level
hierarchy is depicted in the chart on p. 293.

Except for the Supreme Court, whose jurisdiction is specified in
the Constitution (Article III, Section 2, Clause 1), Congress determines which cases shall be tried where,* the route each type of case

* This is where disagreements arose between Congress and President
Nixon during the spring of 1972, when the President proposed to limit the
jurisdiction of the courts (eliminate court power) over desegregation cases.

will follow, and the relationship between the courts and the many administrative agencies of the government.

The state courts

Since state courts are created by state constitutions and legislative bodies, they vary considerably in titles, authority, and procedures. Nevertheless there are commonalities among them that make a general description and schematic presentation possible.

The court systems of the states are organized on four levels. At the lowest level are the small claims, traffic, and police courts, justices of the peace, and magistrates' courts. Cases heard at this level usually cannot be appealed to higher courts. At the next higher level we find probate, municipal, and superior courts, as well as special trial courts such as juvenile courts. From this level appeal is possible to the next, the intermediate appellate courts, variously named in the different states. At the zenith of the state court hierarchy is the state supreme court; in Massachusetts, the Supreme Judicial Court; in Kentucky, the Court of Appeals; in Connecticut, the Supreme Court of Errors. The chart on p. 293 depicts the general pattern of state court hierarchies.

The appellate courts within a state also have power to review the decisions of state administrative agencies. Since states vary in their provisions for appeal from both courts and administrative agencies, it is necessary to know the laws of the particular state involved. One final but significant point must be noted in this brief sketch of our legal structures. Although it may appear that the state and federal systems are completely parallel, it must be remembered that the Supreme Court of the United States has final authority on all questions of federal law. Consequently, cases litigated in the state courts that involve questions related to the U.S. Constitution or to federal laws may be appealed from the state supreme courts to the highest court of the land.

A NOTE ON APPEALS

Trial courts, both state and federal, determine (1) what the facts are in a particular controversy and (2) what legal principles should be applied. Appeals courts do not retry the case; they usually accept the facts as determined by the trial court unless it is clear that the evidence for such facts was inadequate. Thus appeals courts hear arguments by counsel for each side and resolve conflicts about the proper legal principles to be applied to the particular case.

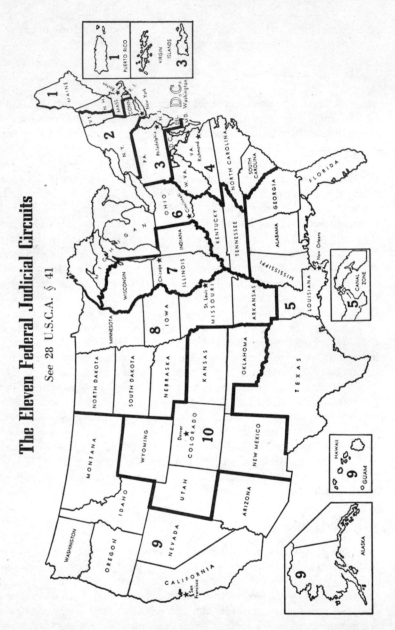

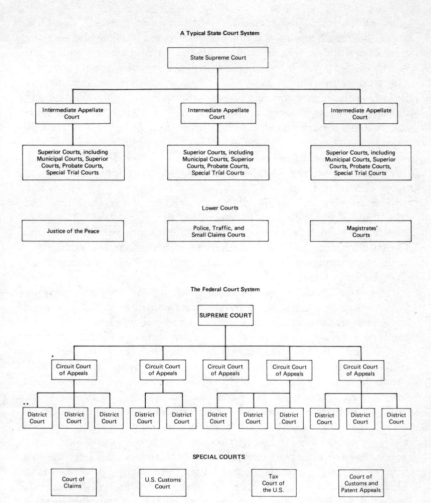

A Typical State Court System

The Federal Court System

SPECIAL COURTS

*There are currently 11 Circuit Courts of Appeals including one in the District of Columbia. Several judges
 may serve on any of these courts, on District Courts as well as other courts.
**There are currently 89 District Courts, including one in the District of Columbia.

A school, for example, might want to suspend or expel John Doe, a student, for disrupting the educational process by allegedly entering classrooms and offices to hand out an "underground" paper and recruit students to demonstrate against the school's grading system. The trial court must decide what the facts were, whether or not John Doe performed the acts alleged against him. When, where, and under what circumstances did these occur? To whom and under what circumstances did he hand out the papers, and were his acts actually disruptive. After the facts are established, the appropriate legal principles are applied to them. Where is the law found? In legislation, other cases, and the state and national constitutions that govern these particular facts.

The state courts handle all matters arising under state law, but they must also handle claims arising out of federal law.* The latter is required by Article IV of the Constitution which provides that the Constitution and the "Laws of the United States" and "Treaties . . . shall be the supreme Law of the Land" and that "Judges in any State shall be bound thereby."

The state appeals court hierarchy will be the final authority on laws created by that state or by the state constitution unless federal questions are also involved. In other words, the federal courts and the U.S. Supreme Court are not superior to state courts in all matters, only in those that involve federal laws, treaties, the Constitution, or conflicts among state laws. This is one reason why we cannot talk about the court system of the United States, but must recognize that there are 51 systems—50 state and one federal.

As our chart of the federal judicial circuits indicates, each circuit except that of the District of Columbia includes several states and a large number of federal district courts. The circuit courts of appeals, however, have no power over states courts and do not hear appeals from them; their decisions are not binding precedents for state courts. Their rulings are authoritative only for the federal district courts within their circuits. This is exemplified by the different holdings in various circuits on school regulation of students' hair length. Thus a case tried initially in a state court is appealed to higher state courts and not to federal courts, whereas a case tried in a federal district court is appealed to higher federal courts and never to higher state courts.

* For example, if a suspended student editor claims that her suspension violated the state education laws and her rights under the First Amendment, the state court where she filed suit must consider the applicable state laws as well as the relevant constitutional principles.

At the pinnacle of the court systems stands the Supreme Court of the United States. As indicated before, in all cases that involve federal law, this court is the final authority. The Court, however, has great discretion over which cases it will review. It cannot possibly handle all the appeals addressed to it plus the cases it must take as specified in the Constitution (Article III, Section 2, Clause 1) and in federal law. It hears relatively few cases and each year renders about 120 full opinions. Approximately two-thirds of these are in civil cases, the rest criminal.[10]

Review by the Supreme Court is usually sought under a "petition for *certiorari*." The petitioner, through this document, tries to convince the Court that the issues involved are of national significance and therefore warrant attention by the Court. Of the approximately 3000 petitions for *certiorari* submitted annually to the Court, only a small percentage are granted.[11]

CONGESTION AND DELAY

"Justice delayed is justice denied" is a popular saying that reflects an old concern. "Delay, of course, is no newcomer to the law. It was condemned in the Magna Carta, criticized by Shakespeare, and immortalized by Dickens in 'Bleak House.' About a century ago, a legislative committee in Massachusetts was pondering again the famous statement in the Magna Carta: to no one will we sell, to no one will we deny or delay right or justice."[12]

The congestion and delay in the administration of justice in U.S. courts, however, is unprecedented in its seriousness.* Thoughtful scholars, lawyers, and judges are raising alarming questions about the very survival of the "rule of law" under present conditions. In fact Chief Justice Burger of the Supreme Court considers the streamlining of judicial administration among his highest priorities. Such an effort must involve the courts and the various legislatures; it may require constitutional amendments; and it will certainly necessitate attitudinal changes on the part of lawyers and the public.[13]

WHERE TO FIND THE LAW

With many different governmental units creating law and with various courts adjudicating cases, the task of "finding the law" can be very complicated. A little knowledge in this instance may indeed be

---

* In some cities it takes a year or more for a criminal case to reach trial and a civil suit might take four to five years before the trial stage.

dangerous, for when one is faced with a real problem a thorough search of the law library is necessary. Short of a good course in legal research or its equivalent in experience, one cannot master the tools of legal research. Consequently it is wise to seek counsel from legal aid, legal services, or a private lawyer. The following explanations are merely introductory and should enable the reader to understand references we have used and to look up cases we have cited.

Decisions of appellate courts, state and federal, are published both as official reports and by private publishing houses. The decisions of the Supreme Court of the United States, for example, are published officially as the *United States Reports* (cited "U.S.") by the U.S. Government Printing Office and in the *Supreme Court Reporter* (cited "S.Ct.") by the West Publishing Company, the best-known private publishing firm in this field. These decisions are also published by Lawyers Cooperative Publishing Company, as the *United States Supreme Court Reports* or *Lawyers Edition* (cited "L.Ed."). Thus the same case may be followed by three separate citations—for example *Brown* v. *Board of Education of Topeka*, 349 U.S. 294, 75 S.Ct. 753, 99 L.Ed. 1083 (1955). This means that the *Brown* case can be found in volume 349 of the *United States Reports* at page 294, in volume 75 of the *Supreme Court Reporter* at page 753, or in volume 99 of the *Lawyers Edition* at page 1083, and that the decision was handed down in 1955.

The National Reporter System of the West Publishing Company includes both federal and state courts in a comprehensive regional reporting system. It is advisable that anyone interested in doing legal research become acquainted with these reporters and practice using them. Librarians specifically trained in the search for legal materials can be found in most libraries that have such holdings, and they can be quite helpful.

The cases adjudicated by the appellate courts of the various states are reported by the National Reporter System in nine regional units as follows:

Title	States Included	Cited
The Pacific Reporter	Montana, Wyoming, Idaho, Kansas, Colorado, Oklahoma, New Mexico, Utah, Arizona, Nevada, Washington, Oregon, California, Alaska, and Hawaii	"P." or "P. 2d"
The South Western Reporter	Kentucky, Tennessee, Missouri, Arkansas, and Texas	"S.W." or "S.W. 2d"

The North Western Reporter	Michigan, Wisconsin, Iowa, Minnesota, North Dakota, South Dakota, and Nebraska	"N.W." or "N.W. 2d"
The Southern Reporter	Florida, Alabama, Mississippi, and Louisiana	"So." or "So. 2d"
The South Eastern Reporter	Virginia, West Virginia, North Carolina, South Carolina, and Georgia	"S.E." or "S.E. 2d"
The Atlantic Reporter	Maine, New Hampshire, Vermont, Connecticut, New Jersey, Pennsylvania, Maryland, and Delaware	"A." or "A. 2d"
The North Eastern Reporter	Massachusetts, Rhode Island, New York, Ohio, Indiana, and Illinois	"N.E." or "N.E. 2d"
The New York Supplement	New York	"N.Y. Supp."
The California Reporter	California	"Cal. Rptr."

The reader will notice that all of the states are included in regional reporters and that various states such as New York and California have separate series in addition. Where there are state reports, a case is reported by its official state citation, followed by the regional reporter citation together with the year of the decision—for example, *Morse* v. *San Diego High*, 34 Cal. App. 134, 166 P. 839 (1917).

Notice that as the regional reporters climb to high numbers owing to the many volumes of cases reported, the publisher begins a second series. For example, in the *Pacific Reporter* series, "P.2d" is a continuation of "P.," as in *School District* v. *Bruck*, 255 Ore. 496, 358 P.2d 283 (1960).

A further important tool in legal research is the American Digest System, an index of cases to the National Reporter System. A publication of the West Publishing Company, it consists of the Century Digest, spanning cases from 1658 to 1896, the Decennials for cases in each ten-year period from 1897 to 1956, and the General Digest, third series, covering cases since 1957.

For the beginner or for anyone interested in an overview of a particular topic, a variety of legal encyclopedias are available. Among these perhaps the best known are *Corpus Juris Secundum* (cited as

"C.J.S.") and *American Jurisprudence* (cited as "Am. Jr."). Note, however, that although the materials cited should suffice to introduce educators to the highly organized mysteries of legal research, the sources of law as well as the research tools necessary to find them are more extensive than indicated here.[14]

Warning

The brief descriptions and explanations we have provided should lead no one to believe that he can now act as his own legal counselor. In fact, even among trained lawyers there is a widely accepted saying: "He who is his own lawyer has a fool for a client." It might be of interest to the reader to know that when Clarence Darrow, one of the country's great criminal lawyers, was accused of tampering with a jury, he hired a lawyer to defend him.

Our goal is to sensitize students and educators to the range of civil rights problems that permeate the public schools. We want to inform them of overall principles as well as some problem areas and unanswered questions. However, anyone who suspects that he is involved in a civil rights violation should discuss his situation with a lawyer. In addition, advice and help is often available from the American Civil Liberties Union (ACLU), a nonpartisan organization long active on behalf of the civil rights of all Americans. Since the enforcement of one's constitutional rights is often an expensive, prolonged, and technical process, it is highly recommended that an aggrieved individual seek help and support of interested organizations.

NOTES

[1] This appendix draws heavily on Appendix 1 in Louis Fischer and David Schimmel, *The Civil Rights of Teachers*, New York, Harper & Row, 1973.

[2] For a brief but excellent analysis comparing the American and British legal systems, see Delmar Karlen, *Judicial Administration*, The American Experience, Dobbs Ferry, N.Y., Oceana Publications, 1970.

[3] Edward S. Corwin, *The Constitution and What It Means Today*, New York, Atheneum, 1963, p. 248.

[4] *Cantwell* v. *Connecticut*, 310 U.S. 296 (1940).

[5] See, for example, Ellwood P. Cubberley, *Public Education in the United States*, Boston, Houghton Mifflin, 1934, pp. 84–85. See also Corwin, *op. cit.*

[6] In fact, as many as fourteen different parts of the Constitution have influenced educational development in the United States. *Federal Relations*

to *Education*, Part, II: Basic Facts, Report of the National Advisory Committee on Education, Washington, D.C., National Advisory Committee on Education, 1931, pp. 4–9.

[7] See Cubberley, *op. cit.*, and Edward C. Bolmeier, *The School in the Legal Structure*, Cincinnatti, W. H. Anderson, 1968, pp. 65–77.

[8] *McCollum* v. *Board of Education*, 33 U.S. 203 (1948).

[9] *West Virginia State Board of Education* v. *Barnette*, 319 U.S. 624 (1943).

[10] The annual November issue of the *Harvard Law Review* is one of the sources of analysis of the work of the Court and a statistical summary of the disposition of its cases.

[11] See *Harvard Law Review*, annual November issue.

[12] Karlen, *op. cit.*, p. 60.

[13] For a hard-hitting analysis, see Karlen, *op. cit.*, Chapter 3.

[14] A useful little volume we recommend is Arthur A. Rezny and Madeline Kinter Remlein, *A Schoolman in the Law Library*, Danville, Ill., Interstate Printers and Publishers, 1962.

Appendix C
Leading cases

347 U.S. 483

BROWN ET AL.

v.

BOARD OF EDUCATION OF TOPEKA, SHAWNEE COUNTY, KAN., ET AL.

BRIGGS ET AL. *v.* **ELLIOTT** ET AL.

DAVIS ET AL.

v.

COUNTY SCHOOL BOARD OF PRINCE EDWARD COUNTY, VA., ET AL.

GEBHART ET AL. *v.* **BELTON** ET AL.

Nos. 1, 2, 4, 10.

Reargued Dec. 7, 8, 9, 1953.—Decided May 17, 1954.

[Summary]

Class actions originating in the four states of Kansas, South Carolina, Virginia, and Delaware, by which minor Negro plaintiffs sought to obtain admission to public schools on a nonsegregated basis. On direct appeals by plaintiffs from adverse decisions in the United States District Courts, District of Kansas, 98 F.Supp. 797,

Eastern District of South Carolina, 103 F.Supp. 920, and Eastern District of Virginia, 103 F.Supp. 337, and on grant of certiorari after decision favorable to plaintiffs in the Supreme Court of Delaware, 91 A.2d 137, the United States Supreme Court, Mr. Chief Justice Warren, held that segregation of children in public schools solely on the basis of race, even though the physical facilities and other tangible factors may be equal, deprives the children of the minority group of equal educational opportunities, in contravention of the Equal Protection Clause of the Fourteenth Amendment.

Cases ordered restored to docket for further argument regarding formulation of decrees.

No. 1:

Mr. Robert L. Carter, New York City, for appellants Brown and others.

Mr. Paul E. Wilson, Topeka, Kan., for appellees Board of Education of Topeka and others.

Nos. 2, 4:

Messrs. Spottswood Robinson III, Thurgood Marshall, New York City, for appellants Briggs and Davis and others.

Messrs. John W. Davis, T. Justin Moore, J. Lindsay Almond, Jr., Richmond, Va., for appellees Elliott and County School Board of Prince Edward County and others.

Asst. Atty. Gen. J. Lee Rankin for United States amicus curiae by special leave of Court.

No. 10:

Mr. H. Albert Young, Wilmington, Del., for petitioners Gebhart at al.

Mr. Jack Greenberg, Thurgood Marshall, New York City, for respondents Belton et al.

Mr. Chief Justice WARREN delivered the opinion of the Court.

These cases come to us from the States of Kansas, South Carolina, Virginia, and Delaware. They are premised on different facts and different local conditions, but a common legal question justifies their consideration together in this consolidated opinion.[1]

In each of the cases, minors of the Negro race, through their legal representatives, seek the aid of the courts in obtaining admission to the public schools of their community on a nonsegregated basis. In each instance, they have been denied admission to schools attended by white children under laws requiring or permitting segregation according to race. This segregation was alleged to deprive the plaintiffs of the equal protection of the laws under the Fourteenth Amendment. In each of the cases other than the Delaware case, a three-judge federal district court denied relief to the plaintiffs on the so-called "separate but equal" doctrine announced by this Court in Plessy v. Ferguson, 163 U.S. 537, 16 S.Ct. 1138, 41 L.Ed. 256. Under that doctrine, equality of treatment is accorded when the races are provided substantially equal facilities, even though these facilities be separate. In the Delaware case, the Supreme Court of Delaware adhered to that doctrine, but ordered that the plaintiffs be admitted to the white schools because of their superiority to the Negro schools.

The plaintiffs contend that segregated public schools are not "equal" and cannot be made "equal," and that hence they are deprived of the equal protection of the laws. Because of the obvious importance of the question presented, the Court took jurisdiction.[2] Argument was heard in the 1952 Term, and reargument was heard this Term on certain questions propounded by the Court.[3]

Reargument was largely devoted to the circumstances surrounding the adoption of the Fourteenth Amendment in 1868. It covered exhaustively consideration of the Amendment in Congress, ratification by the states, then existing practices in racial segregation, and the views of proponents and opponents of the Amendment. This discussion and our own investigation convince us that, although these sources cast some light. it is not enough to resolve the problem with which we are faced. At best, they are inconclusive. The most avid proponents of the post-War Amendments undoubtedly intended them to remove all legal distinctions among "all persons born or naturalized in the United States." Their opponents, just as certainly, were antagonistic to both the letter and the spirit of the Amendments and wished them to have the most limited effect. What others in Congress and the state legislatures had in mind cannot be determined with any degree of certainty.

An additional reason for the inconclusive nature of the Amendment's history, with respect to segregated schools, is the status of public education at that time.[4] In the South, the movement toward free common schools, supported by general taxation, had not yet taken hold. Education of white children was largely in the hands of private groups. Education of Negroes was almost nonexistent, and practically all of the race were illiterate. In fact, any education of

Negroes was forbidden by law in some states. Today, in contrast, many Negroes have achieved outstanding success in the arts and sciences as well as in the business and professional world. It is true that public school education at the time of the Amendment had advanced further in the North, but the effect of the Amendment on Northern States was generally ignored in the congressional debates. Even in the North, the conditions of public education did not approximate those existing today. The curriculum was usually rudimentary; ungraded schools were common in rural areas; the school term was but three months a year in many states; and compulsory school attendance was virtually unknown. As a consequence, it is not surprising that there should be so little in the history of the Fourteenth Amendment relating to its intended effect on public education.

In the first cases in this Court construing the Fourteenth Amendment, decided shortly after its adoption, the Court interpreted it as proscribing all state-imposed discriminations against the Negro race.[5] The doctrine of "separate but equal" did not make its appearance in this Court until 1896 in the case of Plessy v. Ferguson, supra, involving not education but transportation.[6] American courts have since labored with the doctrine for over half a century. In this Court, there have been six cases involving the "separate but equal" doctrine in the field of public education.[7] In Cumming v. Board of Education of Richmond County, 175 U.S. 528, 20 S.Ct. 197, 44 L.Ed. 262, and Gong Lum v. Rice, 275 U.S. 78, 48 S.Ct. 91, 72 L.Ed. 172, the validity of the doctrine itself was not challenged.[8] In more recent cases, all on the graduate school level, inequality was found in that specific benefits enjoyed by white students were denied to Negro students of the same educational qualifications. State of Missouri ex rel. Gaines v. Canada, 305 U.S. 337, 59 S.Ct 232, 83 L.Ed. 208; Sipuel v. Board of Regents of University of Oklahoma, 332 U.S. 631, 68 S.Ct. 299, 92 L.Ed. 247; Sweatt v. Painter, 339 U.S. 629, 70 S.Ct. 848, 94 L.Ed. 1114; McLaurin v. Oklahoma State Regents, 339 U.S. 637, 70 S.Ct. 851, 94 L.Ed. 1149. In none of these cases was it necessary to reexamine the doctrine to grant relief to the Negro plaintiff. And in Sweatt v. Painter, supra, the Court expressly reserved decision on the question whether Plessy v. Ferguson should be held inapplicable to public education.

In the instant cases, that question is directly presented. Here, unlike Sweatt v. Painter, there are findings below that the Negro and white schools involved have been equalized, or are being equalized, with respect to buildings, curricula, qualifications and salaries of teachers, and other "tangible" factors.[9] Our decision, therefore, cannot turn on merely a comparison of these tangible factors in the Negro and white schools involved in each of the cases. We must look instead to the effect of segregation itself on public education.

[1] In approaching this problem, we cannot turn the clock back to 1868 when the Amendment was adopted, or even to 1896 when Plessy v. Ferguson was written. We must consider public education in the light of its full development and its present place in American life throughout the Nation. Only in this way can it be determined if segregation in public schools deprives these plaintiffs of the equal protection of the laws.

[2] Today, education is perhaps the most important function of state and local governments. Compulsory school attendance laws and the great expenditures for education both demonstrate our recognition of the importance of education to our democratic society. It is required in the performance of our most basic public responsibilities, even service in the armed forces. It is the very foundation of good citizenship. Today it is a principal instrument in awakening the child to cultural values, in preparing him for later professional training, and in helping him to adjust normally to his environment. In these days, it is doubtful that any child may reasonably be expected to succeed in life if he is denied the opportunity of an education. Such an opportunity, where the state has undertaken to provide it, is a right which must be made available to all on equal terms.

[3] We come then to the question presented: Does segregation of children in public schools solely on the basis of race, even though the physical facilities and other "tangible" factors may be equal, deprive the children of the minority group of equal educational opportunities? We believe that it does.

In Sweatt v. Painter, supra, [339 U.S. 629, 70 S.Ct. 850], in finding that a segregated law school for Negroes could not provide them equal educational opportunities, this Court relied in large part on "those qualities which are incapable of objective measurement but which make for greatness in a law school." In McLaurin v. Oklahoma State Regents, supra, [339 U.S. 637, 70 S.Ct. 853], the Court, in requiring that a Negro admitted to a white graduate school be treated like all other students, again resorted to intangible considerations: "* * * his ability to study, to engage in discussions and exchange views with other students, and, in general, to learn his profession." Such considerations apply with added force to children in grade and high schools. To separate them from others of similar age and qualifications solely because of their race generates a feeling of inferiority as to their status in the community that may affect their hearts and

minds in a way unlikely ever to be undone. The effect of this separation on their educational opportunities was well stated by a finding
in the Kansas case by a court which nevertheless felt compelled to
rule against the Negro plaintiffs:

> Segregation of white and colored children in public schools has a
> detrimental effect upon the colored children. The impact is greater
> when it has the sanction of the law; for the policy of separating the
> races is usually interpreted as denoting the inferiority of the negro
> group. A sense of inferiority affects the motivation of a child to learn.
> Segregation with the sanction of law, therefore, has a tendency to
> [retard] the educational and mental development of Negro children
> and to deprive them of some of the benefits they would receive in
> a racial[ly] integrated school system.[10]

Whatever may have been the extent of psychological knowledge at
the time of Plessy v. Ferguson, this finding is amply supported by
modern authority.[11] Any language in Plessy v. Ferguson contrary to
this finding is rejected.

[4] We conclude that in the field of public education the doctrine
of "separate but equal" has no place. Separate educational facilities
are inherently unequal. Therefore, we hold that the plaintiffs and
others similarly situated for whom the actions have been brought
are, by reason of the segregation complained of, deprived of the
equal protection of the laws guaranteed by the Fourteenth Amendment. This disposition makes unnecessary any discussion whether
such segregation also violates the Due Process Clause of the Fourteenth Amendment.[12]

[5] Because these are class actions, because of the wide applicabil-
ity of this decision, and because of the great variety of local conditions, the formulation of decrees in these cases presents problems of
considerable complexity. On reargument, the consideration of appropriate relief was necessarily subordinated to the primary question
—the constitutionality of segregation in public education. We have
now announced that such segregation is a denial of the equal protection of the laws. In order that we may have the full assistance of the
parties in formulating decrees, the cases will be restored to the docket,
and the parties are requested to present further argument on Questions 4 and 5 previously propounded by the Court for the reargument
this Term.[13] The Attorney General of the United States is again invited to participate. The Attorneys General of the states requiring or
permitting segregation in public education will also be permitted to

appear as *amici curiae* upon request to do so by September 15, 1954, and submission of briefs by October 1, 1954.[14]

It is so ordered.

NOTES

[1] In the Kansas case, Brown v. Board of Education, the plaintiffs are Negro children of elementary school age residing in Topeka. They brought this action in the United States District Court for the District of Kansas to enjoin enforcement of a Kansas statute which permits, but does not require, cities of more than 15,000 population to maintain separate school facilities for Negro and white students. Kan.Gen.Stat.1949, § 72–1724. Pursuant to that authority, the Topeka Board of Education elected to establish segregated elementary schools. Other public schools in the community, however, are operated on a nonsegregated basis. The three-judge District Court, convened under 28 U.S.C. §§ 2281 and 2284, 28 U.S.C.A. §§ 2281, 2284, found that segregation in public education has a detrimental effect upon Negro children, but denied relief on the ground that the Negro and white schools were substantially equal with respect to buildings, transportation, curricula, and educational qualifications of teachers. 98 F.Supp. 797. The case is here on direct appeal under 28 U.S.C. § 1253, 28 U.S.C.A. § 1253.

In the South Carolina case, Briggs v. Elliott, the plaintiffs are Negro children of both elementary and high school age residing in Clarendon County. They brought this action in the United States District Court for the Eastern District of South Carolina to enjoin enforcement of provisions in the state constitution and statutory code which require the segregation of Negros and whites in public schools. S.C.Const. Art. XI, § 7; S.C. Code 1942, § 5377. The three-judge District Court, convened under 28 U.S.C. §§ 2281 and 2284, 28 U.S.C.A. §§ 2281, 2284, denied the requested relief. The court found that the Negro schools were inferior to the white schools and ordered the defendants to begin immediately to equalize the facilities. But the court sustained the validity of the contested provisions and denied the plaintiffs admission to the white schools during the equalization program. 98 F.Supp. 529. This Court vacated the District Court's judgment and remanded the case for the purpose of obtaining the court's views on a report filed by the defendants concerning the progress made in the equalization program. 342 U.S. 350, 72 S.Ct. 327, 96 L.Ed. 392. On remand, the District Court found that substantial equality had been achieved except for buildings and that the defendants were proceeding to rectify this inequality as well. 103 F.Supp. 920. The case is again here on direct appeal under 28 U.S.C. § 1253, 28 U.S.C.A. § 1253.

In the Virginia case, Davis v. County School Board, the plaintiffs are Negro children of high school age residing in Prince Edward County. They brought this action in the United States District Court for the Eastern District of Virginia to enjoin enforcement of provisions in the state constitution and statutory code which require the segregation of Negroes and whites in public schools. Va.Const. § 140; Va.Code 1950, § 22–221. The three-judge District Court, convened under 28 U.S.C. §§ 2281 and 2284, 28 U.S.C.A. §§ 2281, 2284, denied the requested relief. The court found the Negro school inferior in physical plant, curricula, and transportation, and ordered the defendants forthwith to provide substantially equal curricula and transportation and to "proceed with all reasonable diligence and dispatch to remove" the inequality in physical plant. But, as in the South Carolina case, the court sustained the validity of the contested provisions and denied the plaintiffs admission to the white schools during the equalization program. 103 F.Supp. 337. The case is here on direct appeal under 28 U.S.C. § 1253, 28 U.S.C. A. § 1253.

In the Delaware case, Gebhart v. Belton, the plaintiffs are Negro children of both elementary and high school age residing in New Castle County. They brought this action in the Delaware Court of Chancery to enjoin enforcement of provisions in the state constitution and statutory code which require the segregation of Negroes and whites in public schools. Del.Const. Art. X, § 2; Del.Rev.Code, 1935, § 2631, 14 Del.C. § 141. The Chancellor gave judgment for the plaintiffs and ordered their immediate admission to schools previously attended only by white children, on the ground that the Negro schools were inferior with respect to teacher training, pupil-teacher ratio, extracurricular activities, physical plant, and time and distance involved in travel. Del.Ch., 87 A.2d 862. The Chancellor also found that segregation itself results in an inferior education for Negro children (see note 10, *infra*), but did not rest his decision on that ground. 87 A.2d at page 865. The Chancellor's decree was affirmed by the Supreme Court of Delaware, which intimated, however, that the defendants might be able to obtain a modification of the decree after equalization of the Negro and white schools had been accomplished. 91 A.2d 137, 152. The defendants, contending only that the Delaware courts had erred in ordering the immediate admission of the Negro plaintiffs to the white schools, applied to this Court for certiorari. The writ was granted, 344 U.S. 891, 73 S.Ct. 213, 97 L.Ed. 689. The plaintiffs, who were successful below, did not submit a cross-petition.

[2] 344 U.S. 1, 73 S.Ct. 1, 97 L.ED. 3, Id., 344 U.S. 141, 73 S.Ct. 124, 97 L.Ed. 152, Gebhart v. Belton, 344 U.S. 891, 73 S.Ct. 213, 97 L.Ed. 689.

[3] 345 U.S. 972, 73 S.Ct. 1118, 97 L.Ed. 1388. The Attorney General of the United States participated both Terms as *amicus curiae*.

[4] For a general study of the development of public education prior to the Amendment, see Butts and Cremin, A History of Education in American Culture (1953), Pts. I, II; Cubberley, Public Education in the United States (1934 ed.), cc. II–XII. School practices current at the time of the adoption of the Fourteenth Amendment are described in Butts and Cremin, supra, at 269–275; Cubberley, supra, at 288–339, 408–431; Knight, Public Education in the South (1922), cc. VIII, IX. See also H. Ex. Doc. No. 315, 41st Cong., 2d Sess. (1871). Although the demand for free public schools followed substantially the same pattern in both the North and the South, the development in the South did not begin to gain momentum until about

1850, some twenty years after that in the North. The reasons for the somewhat slower development in the South (e. g., the rural character of the South and the different regional attitudes toward state assistance) are well explained in Cubberley, supra, at 408–423. In the country as a whole, but particularly in the South, the War virtually stopped all progress in public education. Id., at 427–428. The low status of Negro education in all sections of the country, both before and immediately after the War, is described in Beale, A History of Freedom of Teaching in American Schools (1941), 112–132, 175–195. Compulsory school attendance laws were not generally adopted until after the ratification of the Fourteenth Amendment, and it was not until 1918 that such laws were in force in all the states. Cubberley, supra, at 563–565.

[5] In re Slaughter-House Cases, 1873, 16 Wall. 36, 67–72, 21 L.Ed. 394; Strauder v. West Virginia, 1880, 100 U.S. 303, 307–308, 25 L.Ed. 664.

It ordains that no State shall deprive any person of life, liberty, or property, without due process of law, or deny to any person within its jurisdiction the equal protection of the laws. What is this but declaring that the law in the States shall be the same for the black as for the white; that all persons, whether colored or white, shall stand equal before the laws of the States, and, in regard to the colored race, for whose protection the amendment was primarily designed, that no discrimination shall be made against them by law because of their color? The words of the amendment, it is true, are prohibitory, but they contain a necessary implication of a positive immunity, or right, most valuable to the colored race,—the right to exemption from unfriendly legislation against them distinctively as colored,—exemption from legal discriminations, implying inferiority in civil society, lessening the security of their enjoyment of the rights which others enjoy, and discriminations which are steps towards reducing them to the condition of a subject race.

See also State of Virginia v. Rives, 1879, 100 U.S. 313, 318, 25 L.Ed. 667; Ex parte Virginia, 1879, 100 U.S. 339, 344–345, 25 L.Ed. 676.

[6] The doctrine apparently originated in Roberts v. City of Boston, 1850, 5 Cush. 198, 59 Mass. 198, 206, upholding school segregation against attack as being violative of a state constitutional guarantee of equality. Segregation in Boston public schools was eliminated in 1855. Mass. Acts 1855, c. 256. But elsewhere in the North segregation in public education has persisted in some communities until recent years. It is apparent that such segregation has long been a nationwide problem, not merely one of sectional concern.

[7] See also Berea College v. Kentucky, 1908, 211 U.S. 45, 29 S.Ct. 33, 53 L.Ed. 81.

[8] In the Cumming case, Negro taxpayers sought an injunction requiring the defendant school board to discontinue the operation of a high school for white children until the board resumed operation of a high school for Negro children. Similarly, in the Gong Lum case, the plaintiff, a child of Chinese descent, contended only that state authorities had misapplied the doctrine by classifying him with Negro children and requiring him to attend a Negro school.

[9] In the Kansas case, the court below found substantial equality as to

all such factors. 98 F.Supp. 797, 798. In the South Carolina case, the court below found that the defendants were proceeding "promptly and in good faith to comply with the court's decree." 103 F.Supp. 920, 921. In the Virginia case, the court below noted that the equalization program was already "afoot and progressing," 193 F.Supp. 337, 341; since then, we have been advised, in the Virginia Attorney General's brief on reargument, that the program has now been completed. In the Delaware case, the court below similarly noted that the state's equalization program was well under way. 91 A.2d 137, 139.

10 A similar finding was made in the Delaware case: "I conclude from the testimony that in our Delaware society, State-imposed segregation in education itself results in the Negro children, as a class, receiving educaional opportunities which are substantially inferior to those available to white children otherwise similarly situated." 87 A.2d 862, 865.

11 K. B. Clark, Effect of Prejudice and Discrimination on Personality Development (Midcentury White House Conference on Children and Youth, 1950); Witmer and Kotinsky, Personality in the Making (1952), c. VI; Deutscher and Chein, The Psychological Effects of Enforced Segregation: A Survey of Social Science Opinion, 26 J. Psychol. 259 (1948); Chein, What are the Psychological Effects of Segregation Under Conditions of Equal Facilities?, 3 Int. J. Opinion and Attitute Res. 229 (1949); Brameld, Educational Costs, in Discrimination and National Welfare (MacIver, ed., 1949, 44–48; Frazier, The Negro in the United States (1949), 674–681. And see generally Myrdal, An American Dilemma (1944).

12 See Bolling v. Sharpe, 347 U.S. 497, 74 S.Ct. 693, concerning the Due Process Clause of the Fifth Amendment.

13 "4. Assuming it is decided that segregation in public schools violates the Fourteenth Amendment

"(a) would a decree necessarily follow providing that, within the limits set by normal geographic school districting, Negro children should forthwith be admitted to schools of their choice, or

"(b) may this Court, in the exercise of its equity powers, permit an effective gradual adjustment to be brought about from existing segregated systems to a system not based on color distinctions?

"5. On the assumption on which questions 4(a) and (b) are based, and assuming further that this Court will exercise its equity powers to the end described in question 4(b),

"(a) should this Court formulate detailed decrees in these cases;

"(b) if so, what specific issues should the decrees reach;

"(c) should this Court appoint a special master to hear evidence with a view to recommending specific terms for such decrees;

"(d) should this Court remand to the courts of first instance with directions to frame decrees in these cases, and if so what general directions should the decrees of this Court include and what procedures should the courts of first instance follow in arriving at the specific terms of more detailed decrees?"

14 See Rule 42, Revised Rules of this Court, effective July 1, 1954, 28 U.S.C.A.

393 U.S. 503
JOHN F. TINKER *and* MARY BETH TINKER,
Minors, etc., ET AL., Petitioners,

v.

DES MOINES INDEPENDENT COMMUNITY SCHOOL DISTRICT
ET AL.

No. 21.

Argued Nov. 12, 1968—Decided Feb. 24, 1969.

[Summary]

Action against school district, its board of directors and certain administrative officials and teachers to recover nominal damages and obtain an injunction against enforcement of a regulation promulgated by principals of schools prohibiting wearing of black armbands by students while on school facilities. The United States District Court for the Southern District of Iowa, Central Division, 258 F.Supp. 971, dismissed complaint and plaintiffs appealed. The Court of Appeals for the Eighth Circuit, 383 F.2d 988, considered the case en banc and affirmed without opinion when it was equally divided and certiorari was granted. The United States Supreme Court, Mr. Justice Fortas, held that, in absence of demonstration of any facts which might reasonably have led school authorities to forecast substantial disruption of, or material interference with, school activities or any showing that disturbances or disorders on school premises in fact occurred when students wore black armbands on their sleeves to exhibit their disapproval of Vietnam hostilities, regulation prohibiting wearing armbands to schools and providing for suspension of any student refusing to remove such was an unconstitutional denial of students' right of expression of opinion.

Reversed and remanded.

Mr. Justice Black and Mr. Justice Harlan dissented.

Dan Johnston, Des Moines, Iowa, for petitioners.

Allan A. Herrick, Des Moines, Iowa, for respondents.

Mr. Justice FORTAS delivered the opinion of the Court.

Petitioner John F. Tinker, 15 years old, and petitioner Christopher Eckhardt, 16 years old, attended high schools in Des Moines, Iowa. Petitioner Mary Beth Tinker, John's sister, was a 13-year-old student in junior high school.

In December 1965, a group of adults and students in Des Moines held a meeting at the Eckhardt home. The group determined to publicize their objections to the hostilities in Vietnam and their support for a truce by wearing black armbands during the holiday season and by fasting on December 16 and New Year's Eve. Petitioners and their parents had previously engaged in similar activities, and they decided to participate in the program.

The principals of the Des Moines schools became aware of the plan to wear armbands. On December 14, 1965, they met and adopted a policy that any student wearing an armband to school would be asked to remove it, and if he refused he would be suspended until he returned without the armband. Petitioners were aware of the regulation that the school authorities adopted.

On December 16, Mary Beth and Christopher wore black armbands to their schools. John Tinker wore his armband the next day. They were all sent home and suspended from school until they would come back without their armbands. They did not return to school until after the planned period for wearing armbands had expired—that is, until after New Year's Day.

This complaint was filed in the United States District Court by petitioners, through their fathers, under § 1983 of Title 42 of the United States Code. It prayed for an injunction restraining the respondent school officials and the respondent members of the board of directors of the school district from disciplining the petitioners, and it sought nominal damages. After an evidentiary hearing the District Court dismissed the complaint. It upheld the constitutionality of the school authorities' action on the ground that it was reasonable in order to prevent disturbance of school discipline. 258 F.Supp. 971 (1966). The court referred to but expressly declined to follow the Fifth Circuit's holding in a similar case that the wearing of symbols like armbands cannot be prohibited unless it "materially and substantially interfere[s] with the requirements of appropriate discipline in the operation of the school." Burnside v. Byars, 363 F.2d 744, 749 (1966).[1]

On appeal, the Court of Appeals for the Eighth Circuit considered the case *en banc*. The court was equally divided, and the District Court's decision was accordingly affirmed, without opinion. 383 F.2d 988 (1967). We granted certiorari. 390 U.S. 942, 88 S.Ct. 1050, 19 L.Ed.2d 1130 (1968).

I.

The District Court recognized that the wearing of an armband for the purpose of expressing certain views is the type of symbolic act that is within the Free Speech Clause of the First Amendment. See West Virginia State Board of Education v. Barnette, 319 U.S. 624, 63 S.Ct. 1178, 87 L.Ed. 1628 (1943); Stromberg v. California, 283 U.S. 359, 51 S.Ct. 532, 75 L.Ed. 1117 (1931). Cf. Thornhill v. Alabama, 310 U.S. 88, 60 S.Ct. 736, 84 L.Ed. 1093 (1940); Edwards v. South Carolina, 372 U.S. 229, 83 S.Ct. 680, 9 L.Ed.2d 697 (1963); Brown v. Louisiana, 383 U.S. 131, 86 S.Ct. 719, 15 L.Ed.2d 637 (1966). As we shall discuss, the wearing of armbands in the circumstances of this case was entirely divorced from actually or potentially disruptive conduct by those participating in it. It was closely akin to "pure speech" which, we have repeatedly held, is entitled to comprehensive protection under the First Amendment. Cf. Cox v. Louisiana, 379 U.S. 536, 555, 85 S.Ct. 453, 464, 13 L.Ed.2d 471 (1965); Adderley v. Florida, 385 U.S. 39, 87 S.Ct. 242, 17 L.Ed.2d 149 (1966).

First Amendment rights, applied in light of the special characteristics of the school environment, are available to teachers and students. It can hardly be argued that either students or teachers shed their constitutional rights to freedom of speech or expression at the schoolhouse gate. This has been the unmistakable holding of this Court for almost 50 years. In Meyer v. Nebraska, 262 U.S. 390, 43 S.Ct. 625, 67 L.Ed. 1042 (1923), and Bartels v. Iowa, 262 U.S. 404, 43 S.Ct. 628, 67 L.Ed. 1047 (1923), this Court, in opinions by Mr. Justice McReynolds, held that the Due Process Clause of the Fourteenth Amendment prevents States from forbidding the teaching of a foreign language to young students. Statutes to this effect, the Court held, unconstitutionally interfere with the liberty of teacher, student, and parent.[2] See also Pierce v. Society of Sisters, etc., 268 U.S. 510, 45 S.Ct. 571, 69 L.Ed. 1070 (1925); West Virginia State Board of Education v. Barnette, 319 U.S. 624, 63 S.Ct. 1178, 87 L.Ed. 1628 (1943); Illinois ex rel. McCollum v. Board of Education of School Dist. No. 71, 333 U.S. 203, 68 S.Ct. 461, 92 L.Ed. 649 (1948);

Wieman v. Updegraff, 344 U.S. 183, 195, 73 S.Ct. 215, 220, 97 L.Ed.
216 (1952) (concurring opinion); Sweezy v. New Hampshire, 354
U.S. 234, 77 S.Ct. 1203, 1 L.Ed.2d 1311 (1957); Shelton v. Tucker,
364 U.S. 479, 487, 81 S.Ct. 247, 251, 5 L.Ed.2d 231 (1960); Engel v.
Vitale, 370 U.S. 421, 82 S.Ct. 1261, 8 L.Ed. 601 (1962); Keyishian
v. Board of Regents, 385 U.S. 589, 603, 87 S.Ct. 675, 683, 17 L.Ed.2d
629 (1967); Epperson v. Arkansas, 393 U.S. 97, 89 S.Ct. 266, 21
L.Ed.2d 228 (1968).

In West Virginia State Board of Education v. Barnette, supra,
this Court held that under the First Amendment, the student in
public school may not be compelled to salute the flag. Speaking
through Mr. Justice Jackson, the Court said:

*The Fourteenth Amendment, as now applied to the States, protects
the citizen against the State itself and all of its creatures—Boards of
Education not excepted. These have, of course, important, delicate,
and highly discretionary functions, but none that they may not
perform within the limits of the Bill of Rights. That they are educating the young for citizenship is reason for scrupulous protection of
Constitutional freedoms of the individual, if we are not to strangle
the free mind at its source and teach youth to discount important
principles of our government as mere platitudes. 319 U.S., at 637, 63
S.Ct. at 1185.*

On the other hand, the Court has repeatedly emphasized the need for
affirming the comprehensive authority of the States and of school
officials, consistent with fundamental constitutional safeguards, to
prescribe and control conduct in the schools. See Epperson v. Arkansas, supra, 393 U.S. at 104, 89 S.Ct. at 270; Meyer v. Nebraska,
supra, 262 U.S. at 402, 43 S.Ct. at 627. Our problem lies in the area
where students in the exercise of First Amendment rights collide
with the rules of the school authorities.

II.

The problem posed by the present case does not relate to regulation
of the length of skirts or the type of clothing, to hair style, or deportment. Cf. Ferrell v. Dallas Independent School District, 392 F.2d 697
(C.A. 5th Cir. 1968); Pugsley v. Sellmeyer, 158 Ark. 247, 250 S.W.
538, 30 A.L.R. 1212 (1923). It does not concern aggressive, disruptive
action or even group demonstrations. Our problem involves direct,
primary First Amendment rights akin to "pure speech."

The school officials banned and sought to punish petitioners for a silent, passive expression of opinion, unaccompanied by any disorder or disturbance on the part of petitioners. There is here no evidence whatever of petitioners' interference, actual or nascent, with the schools' work or of collision with the rights of other students to be secure and to be let alone. Accordingly, this case does not concern speech or action that intrudes upon the work of the schools or the rights of other students.

Only a few of the 18,000 students in the school system wore the black armbands. Only five students were suspended for wearing them. There is no indication that the work of the schools or any class was disrupted. Outside the classrooms, a few students made hostile remarks to the children wearing armbands, but there were no threats or acts of violence on school premises.

The District Court concluded that the action of the school authorities was reasonable because it was based upon their fear of a disturbance from the wearing of the armbands. But, in our system, undifferentiated fear or apprehension of disturbance is not enough to overcome the right to freedom of expression. Any departure from absolute regimentation may cause trouble. Any variation from the majority's opinion may inspire fear. Any word spoken, in class, in the lunchroom, or on the campus, that deviates from the views of another person may start an argument or cause a disturbance. But our Constitution says we must take this risk, Terminiello v. Chicago, 337 U.S. 1, 69 S.Ct. 894, 93 L.Ed. 1131 (1949); and our history says that it is this sort of hazardous freedom—this kind of openness—that is the basis of our national strength and of the independence and vigor of Americans who grow up and live in this relatively permissive, often disputatious, society.

In order for the State in the person of school officials to justify prohibition of a particular expression of opinion, it must be able to show that its action was caused by something more than a mere desire to avoid the discomfort and unpleasantness that always accompany an unpopular viewpoint. Certainly where there is no finding and no showing that engaging in the forbidden conduct would "materially and substantially interfere with the requirements of appropriate discipline in the operation of the school," the prohibition cannot be sustained. Burnside v. Byars, supra, 363 F.2d at 749.

In the present case, the District Court made no such finding, and our independent examination of the record fails to yield evidence that the school authorities had reason to anticipate that the wearing of the armbands would substantially interfere with the work of the school or impinge upon the rights of other students. Even an official memorandum prepared after the suspension that listed the reasons for the ban on wearing the armbands made no reference to the anticipation of such disruption.[3]

On the contrary, the action of the school authorities appears to have been based upon an urgent wish to avoid the controversy which might result from the expression, even by the silent symbol of armbands, of opposition to this Nation's part in the conflagration in Vietnam.[4] It is revealing, in this respect, that the meeting at which the school principals decided to issue the contested regulation was called in response to a student's statement to the journalism teacher in one of the schools that he wanted to write an article on Vietnam and have it published in the school paper. (The student was dissuaded.[5])

It is also relevant that the school authorities did not purport to prohibit the wearing of all symbols of political or controversial significance. The record shows that students in some of the schools wore buttons relating to national political campaigns, and some even wore the Iron Cross, traditionally a symbol of Nazism. The order prohibiting the wearing of armbands did not extend to these. Instead, a particular symbol—black armbands worn to exhibit opposition to this Nation's involvement in Vietnam—was singled out for prohibition. Clearly, the prohibition of expression of one particular opinion, at least without evidence that it is necessary to avoid material and substantial interference with schoolwork or discipline, is not constitutionally permissible.

In our system, state-operated schools may not be enclaves of totalitarianism. School officials do not possess absolute authority over their students. Students in school as well as out of school are "persons" under our Constitution. They are possessed of fundamental rights which the State must respect, just as they themselves must respect their obligations to the State. In our system, students may not be regarded as closed-circuit recipients of only that which the State chooses to communicate. They may not be confined to the expression of those sentiments that are officially approved. In the absence of a specific showing of constitutionally valid reasons to regulate their speech, students are entitled to freedom of expression of their views. As Judge Gewin, speaking for the Fifth Circuit, said, school officials cannot suppress "expressions of feelings with which they do not wish to contend." Burnside v. Byars, supra, 363 F.2d at 749.

In Meyer v. Nebraska, supra, 262 U.S. at 402, 43 S.Ct. at 627, Mr. Justice McReynolds expressed this Nation's repudiation of the principle that a State might so conduct its schools as to "foster a homogeneous people." He said:

In order to submerge the individual and develop ideal citizens, Sparta assembled the males at seven into barracks and intrusted their subsequent education and training to official guardians. Although such measures have been deliberately approved by men of great genius, their ideas touching the relation between individual and State were wholly different from those upon which our institutions rest; and it hardly will be affirmed that any Legislature could impose such restrictions upon the people of a state without doing violence to both letter and spirit of the Constitution.

This principle has been repeated by this Court on numerous occasions during the intervening years. In Keyishian v. Board of Regents, 385 U.S. 589, 603, 87 S.Ct. 675, 683, 17 L.Ed.2d 629, Mr. Justice Brennan, speaking for the Court, said:

"The vigilant protection of constitutional freedoms is nowhere more vital than in the community of American schools." Shelton v. Tucker, [364 U.S. 479], at 487 (81 S.Ct. 247, 5 L.Ed.2d 231). The classroom is peculiarly the "marketplace of ideas." The Nation's future depends upon leaders trained through wide exposure to that robust exchange of ideas which discovers truth 'out of a multitude of tongues, [rather] than through any kind of authoritative selection."

The principle of these cases is not confined to the supervised and ordained discussion which takes place in the classroom. The principal use to which the schools are dedicated is to accommodate students during prescribed hours for the purpose of certain types of activities. Among those activities is personal intercommunication among the students.[6] This is not only an inevitable part of the process of attending school; it is also an important part of the educational process. A student's rights, therefore, do not embrace merely the classroom hours. When he is in the cafeteria, or on the playing field, or on the campus during the authorized hours, he may express his opinions, even on controversial subjects like the conflict in Vietnam, if he does so without "materially and substantially interfer[ing] with the requirements of appropriate discipline in the operation of the school" and without colliding with the rights of others. Burnside v. Byars, supra, 363 F.2d at 749. But conduct by the student, in class or out of it, which for any reason—whether it stems from time, place, or type of behavior—materially disrupts classwork or involves substantial disorder or invasion of the rights of others is, of course, not immunized by the constitutional guarantee of freedom of speech. Cf. Blackwell v. Issaquena County Board of Education, 363 F.2d 749 (C.A. 5th Cir. 1966).

Under our Constitution, free speech is not a right that is given only to be so circumscribed that it exists in principle but not in fact. Freedom of expression would not truly exist if the right could be exercised only in an area that a benevolent government has provided as a safe haven for crackpots. The Constitution says that Congress (and the States) may not abridge the right to free speech. This provision means what it says. We properly read it to permit reasonable regulation of speech-connected activities in carefully restricted circumstances. But we do not confine the permissible exercise of First Amendment rights to a telephone booth or the four corners of a pamphlet, or to supervised and ordained discussion in a school classroom.

If a regulation were adopted by school officials forbidding discussion of the Vietnam conflict, or the expression by any student of opposition to it anywhere on school property except as part of a prescribed classroom exercise, it would be obvious that the regulation would violate the constitutional rights of students, at least if it could not be justified by a showing that the students' activities would materially and substantially disrupt the work and discipline of the school. Cf. Hammond v. South Carolina State College, 272 F.Supp. 947 (D.C.S.C.1967) (orderly protest meeting on state college campus); Dickey v. Alabama State Board of Education, 273 F.Supp. 613 (D.C.M.D.Ala.1967) (expulsion of student editor of college newspaper). In the circumstances of the present case, the prohibition of the silent, passive "witness of the armbands," as one of the children called it, is no less offensive to the constitution's guarantees.

As we have discussed, the record does not demonstrate any facts which might reasonably have led school authorities to forecast substantial disruption of or material interference with school activities, and no disturbances or disorders on the school premises in fact occurred. These petitioners merely went about their ordained rounds in school. Their deviation consisted only in wearing on their sleeve a band of black cloth, not more than two inches wide. They wore it to exhibit their disapproval of the Vietnam hostilities and their advocacy of a truce, to make their views known, and, by their example, to influence others to adopt them. They neither interrupted school activities nor sought to intrude in the school affairs or the lives of others. They caused discussion outside of the classrooms, but no interference with work and no disorder. In the circumstances, our Constitution does not permit officials of the State to deny their form of expression.

We express no opinion as to the form of relief which should be granted, this being a matter for the lower courts to determine. We reverse and remand for further proceedings consistent with this opinion.

Reversed and remanded.

Mr. Justice STEWART, concurring.

Although I agree with much of what is said in the Court's opinion, and with its judgment in this case, I cannot share the Court's uncritical assumption that, school discipline aside, the First Amendment rights of children are co-extensive with those of adults. Indeed, I had thought the Court decided otherwise just last Term in Ginsburg v. New York, 390 U.S. 629, 88 S.Ct. 1274, 20 L.Ed.2d 195. I continue to hold the view I expressed in that case: "[A] State may permissibly determine that, at least in some precisely delineated areas, a child— like someone in a captive audience—is not possessed of that full capacity for individual choice which is the presupposition of First Amendment guarantees." Id., at 649–650, 88 S.Ct. at 1285–1286 (concurring in result). Cf. Prince v. Massachusetts, 321 U.S. 158, 64 S.Ct. 438, 88 L.Ed. 645.

Mr. Justice WHITE, concurring.

While I join the Court's opinion, I deem it appropriate to note, first, that the Court continues to recognize a distinction between communicating by words and communicating by acts or conduct which sufficiently impinges on some valid state interest; and second, that I do not subscribe to everything the Court of Appeals said about free speech in its opinion in Burnside v. Byars, 363 F.2d 744, 748 (C.A. 5th Cir. 1966), a case relied upon by the Court in the matter now before us.

Mr. Justice BLACK, dissenting.

The Court's holding in this case ushers in what I deem to be an entirely new era in which the power to control pupils by the elected

"officials of state supported public schools *   * *" in the United
States is in ultimate effect transferred to the Supreme Court.[1] The
Court brought this particular case here on a petition for certiorari
urging that the First and Fourteenth Amendments protect the right
of school pupils to express their political views all the way "from
kindergarten through high school." Here the constitutional right to
"political expression" asserted was a right to wear black armbands
during school hours and at classes in order to demonstrate to the
other students that the petitioners were mourning because of the
death of United States soldiers in Vietnam and to protest that war
which they were against. Ordered to refrain from wearing the armbands in school by the elected school officials and the teachers vested
with state authority to do so, apparently only seven out of the school
system's 18,000 pupils deliberately refused to obey the order. One
defying pupil was Paul Tinker, 8 years old, who was in the second
grade; another, Hope Tinker, was 11 years old and in the fifth grade;
a third member of the Tinker family was 13, in the eighth grade;
and a fourth member of the same family was John Tinker, 15 years
old, an 11th grade high school pupil. Their father, a Methodist
minister without a church, is paid a salary by the American Friends
Service Committee. Another student who defied the school order and
insisted on wearing an armband in school was Christopher Eckhardt,
an 11th grade pupil and a petitioner in this case. His mother is an
official in the Women's International League for Peace and Freedom.

As I read the Court's opinion it relies upon the following grounds
for holding unconstitutional the judgment of the Des Moines school
officials and the two courts below. First, the Court concludes that the
wearing of armbands is "symbolic speech" which is "akin to 'pure
speech'" and therefore protected by the First and Fourteenth Amendments. Secondly, the Court decides that the public schools are an
appropriate place to exercise "symbolic speech" as long as normal
school functions are not "unreasonably" disrupted. Finally, the Court
arrogates to itself, rather than to the State's elected officials charged
with running the schools, the decision as to which school disciplinary
regulations are "reasonable."

Assuming that the Court is correct in holding that the conduct of
wearing armbands for the purpose of conveying political ideas is
protected by the First Amendment, cf., e.g., Giboney v. Empire
Storage & Ice Co., 336 U.S. 490, 69 S.Ct. 684, 93 L.Ed. 834 (1949),
the crucial remaining questions are whether students and teachers
may use the schools at their whim as a platform for the exercise of

free speech—"symbolic" or "pure"—and whether the courts will allocate to themselves the function of deciding how the pupils' school day will be spent. While I have always believed that under the First and Fourteenth Amendments neither the State nor the Federal Government has any authority to regulate or censor the content of speech, I have never believed that any person has a right to give speeches or engage in demonstrations where he pleases and when he pleases. This Court has already rejected such a notion. In Cox v. Louisiana, 379 U.S. 536, 554, 85 S.Ct. 453, 464, 13 L.Ed.2d 471 (1965), for example, the Court clearly stated that the rights of free speech and assembly "do not mean that everyone with opinions or beliefs to express may address a group at any public place and at any time."

While the record does not show that any of these armband students shouted, used profane language, or were violent in any manner, detailed testimony by some of them shows their armbands caused comments, warnings by other students, the poking of fun at them, and a warning by an older football player that other, nonprotesting students had better let them alone. There is also evidence that a teacher of mathematics had his lesson period practically "wrecked" chiefly by disputes with Mary Beth Tinker, who wore her armband for her "demonstration." Even a casual reading of the record shows that this armband did divert students' minds from their regular lessons, and that talk, comments, etc., made John Tinker "self-conscious" in attending school with his armband. While the absence of obscene remarks or boisterous and loud disorder perhaps justifies the Court's statement that the few armband students did not actually "disrupt" the classwork, I think the record overwhelmingly shows that the armbands did exactly what the elected school officials and principals foresaw they would, that is, took the students' minds off their classwork and diverted them to thoughts about the highly emotional subject of the Vietnam war. And I repeat that if the time has come when pupils of state-supported schools, kindergartens, grammar schools, or high schools, can defy and flout orders of school officials to keep their minds on their own schoolwork, it is the beginning of a new revolutionary era of permissiveness in this country fostered by the judiciary. The next logical step, it appears to me, would be to hold unconstitutional laws that bar pupils under 21 or 18 from voting, or from being elected members of the boards of education.[2]

The United States District Court refused to hold that the state school order violated the First and Fourteenth Amendments. 258 F.Supp. 971. Holding that the protest was akin to speech, which is

protected by the First and Fourteenth Amendments, that court held
that the school order was "reasonable" and hence constitutional.
There was at one time a line of cases holding "reasonableness" as the
court saw it to be the test of a "due process" violation. Two cases
upon which the Court today heavily relies for striking down this
school order used this test of reasonableness, Meyer v. Nebraska, 262
U.S. 390, 43 S.Ct. 625, 67 L.Ed. 1042 (1923), and Bartels v. Iowa,
262 U.S. 404, S.Ct. 628, 67 L.Ed. 1047 (1923). The opinions in both
cases were written by Mr. Justice McReynolds; Mr. Justice Holmes,
who opposed this reasonableness test, dissented from the holdings as
did Mr. Justice Sutherland. This constitutional test of reasonableness
prevailed in this Court for a season. It was this test that brought on
President Franklin Roosevelt's well-known Court fight. His proposed
legislation did not pass, but the fight left the "reasonableness" constitutional test dead on the battlefield, so much so that this Court in
Ferguson v. Skrupa, 372 U.S. 726, 729, 730, 83 S.Ct. 1028, 1030–1031,
10 L.Ed.2d 93, after a thorough review of the old cases, was able to
conclude in 1963:

> "There was a time when the Due Process Clause was used by this
> Court to strike down laws which were thought unreasonable, that
> is, unwise or incompatible with some particular economic or social
> philosophy.
>
> * * *
>
> "The doctrine that prevailed in Lochner [Lochner v. New York,
> 198 U.S. 45, 25 S.Ct. 539, 49 L.Ed. 937], Coppage [Coppage v. Kan-
> sas, 236 U.S. 1, 35 S.Ct. 240, 59 L.Ed. 441], Adkins [Adkins v.
> Children's Hospital, 261 U.S. 525, 43 S.Ct. 394, 67 L.Ed. 785], Burns
> [Jay Burns Baking Co. v. Bryan, 264 U.S. 504, 44 S.Ct. 412, 68 L.Ed.
> 813], and like cases—that due process authorizes courts to hold laws
> unconstitutional when they believe the legislature has acted unwisely
> —has long since been discarded."

The Ferguson case totally repudiated the old reasonableness-due
process test, the doctrine that judges have the power to hold laws
unconstitutional upon the belief of judges that they "shock the conscience" or that they are "unreasonable," "arbitrary," "irrational,"
"contrary to fundamental 'decency,'" or some other flexible term
without precise boundaries. I have many times expressed my opposition to that concept on the ground that it gives judges power to
strike down any law they do not like. If the majority of the Court
today, by agreeing to the opinion of my Brother FORTAS, is

resurrecting that old reasonableness-due process test, I think the constitutional change should be plainly, unequivocally, and forthrightly stated for the benefit of the bench and bar. It will be a sad day for the country, I believe, when the present-day Court returns to the McReynolds due process concept. Other cases cited by the Court do not, as implied, follow the McReynolds reasonableness doctrine. West Virginia State Board of Education v. Barnette, 319 U.S. 624, 63 S.Ct. 1178, 1179, 87 L.Ed. 1628, clearly rejecting the "reasonableness" test, held that the Fourteenth Amendment made the First applicable to the States, and that the two forbade a State to *compel* little schoolchildren to salute the United States flag when they had religious scruples against doing so.[3] Neither Thornhill v. Alabama, 310 U.S. 88, 60 S.Ct. 736, 84 L.Ed. 1093; Stromberg v. California, 283 U.S. 359, 51 S.Ct. 532, 75 L.Ed. 1117; Edwards v. South Carolina, 372 U.S. 229, 83 S.Ct. 680, 9 L.Ed.2d 697; nor Brown v. Louisiana, 383 U.S. 131, 86 S.Ct. 719, 15 L.Ed.2d 637, related to schoolchildren at all, and none of these cases embraced Mr. Justice McReynolds' reasonableness test; and *Thornhill, Ewards,* and *Brown* relied on the vagueness of state statutes under scrutiny to hold them unconstitutional. Cox v. Louisiana, 379 U.S. 536, 555, 85 S.Ct. 453, 464, 13 L.Ed2d 471, and Adderley v. Florida, 385 U.S. 39, 87 S.Ct. 242, 17 L.Ed2d 149, cited by the Court as a "compare," indicating, I suppose, that these two cases are no longer the law, were not rested to the slightest extent on the *Meyer* and *Bartels* "reasonableness-due process-McReynolds" constitutional test.

I deny, therefore, that it has been the "unmistakable holding of this Court for almost 50 years" that "students" and "teachers" take with them into the "schoolhouse gate" constitutional rights to "freedom of speech or expression." Even *Meyer* did not hold that. It makes no reference to "symbolic speech" at all; what it did was to strike down as "unreasonble" and therefore unconstitutional a Nebraska law barring the teaching of the German language before the children reached the eighth grade. One can well agree with Mr. Justice Holmes and Mr. Justice Sutherland, as I do, that such a law was no more unreasonble than it would be to bar the teaching of Latin and Greek to pupils who have not reached the eighth grade. In fact, I think the majority's reason for invalidating the Nebraska law was that it did not like it or in legal jargon that it "shocked the Court's conscience," "offended its sense of justice," or was "contrary to fundamental concepts of the English-speaking world," as the Court has sometimes said. See, e. g. Rochin v. California, 342 U.S. 165, 72

S.Ct. 205, 96 L.Ed. 183, and Irvine v. California, 347 U.S. 128, 74 S.Ct 381, 98 L.Ed. 561. The truth is that a teacher of kindergarten, grammar school, or high school pupils no more carries into a school with him a complete right to freedom of speech and expression than an anti-Catholic or anti-Semite carries with him a complete freedom of speech and religion into a Catholic church or Jewish synagogue. Nor does a person carry with him into the United States Senate or House, or into the Supreme Court, or any other court, a complete constitutional right to go into those places contrary to their rules and speak his mind on any subject he pleases. It is a myth to say that any person has a constitutional right to say what he pleases, where he pleases, and when he pleases. Our Court has decided precisely the opposite. See, e. g., Cox v. Louisiana, 379 U.S. 536, 555, 85 S.Ct. 453, 464, 13 L.Ed.2d 471; Adderley v. Florida, 385 U.S. 39, 87 S.Ct. 242, 17 L.Ed. 149.

In my view, teachers in state-controlled public schools are hired to teach there. Although Mr. Justice McReynolds may have intimated to the contrary in Meyer v. Nebraska, supra, certainly a teacher is not paid to go into school and teach subjects the State does not hire him to teach as a part of its selected curriculum. Nor are public school students sent to the schools at public expense to broadcast political or any other views to educate and inform the public. The original idea of schools, which I do not believe is yet abandoned as worthless or out of date, was that children had not yet reached the point of experience and wisdom which enabled them to teach all of their elders. It may be that the Nation has outworn the old-fashioned slogan that "children are to be seen not heard," but one may, I hope, be permitted to harbor the thought that taxpayers send children to school on the premise that at their age they need to learn, not teach. The true principles on this whole subject were in my judgment spoken by Mr. Justice McKenna for the Court in Waugh v. Mississippi University in 237 U.S. 589, 596–597, 35 S.Ct. 720, 723, 59 L.Ed. 1131. The State had there passed a law barring students from peaceably assembling in Greek letter fraternities and providing that students who joined them could be expelled from school. This law would appear on the surface to run afoul of the First Amendment's freedom of assembly clause. The law was attacked as violative of due process and of the privileges and immunities clause and as a deprivation of property and of liberty, under the Fourteenth Amendment. It was argued that the fraternity made its members more moral, taught discipline, and inspired its members to study harder and to obey better the rules of discipline and order. This Court rejected all the "fervid" pleas of the fraternities' advocates and decided unanimously against these Fourteenth Amendment arguments. The Court in its next to the last paragraph made this statement which has complete relevance for us today:

It is said that the fraternity to which complainant belongs is a moral and of itself a disciplinary force. This need not be denied. But whether such membership makes against discipline was for the State of Mississippi to determine. It is to be remembered that the University was established by the state and is under the control of the state, and the enactment of the statute may have been induced by the opinion that membership in the prohibited societies divided the attention of the students and distracted from that singleness of purpose which the State desired to exist in its public educational institutions. *It is not for us to entertain conjectures in opposition to the views of the state and annul its regulations upon disputable considerations of their wisdom or necessity. (Emphasis supplied.)*

It was on the foregoing argument that this Court sustained the power of Mississippi to curtail the First Amendment's right of peaceable assembly. And the same reasons are equally applicable to curtailing in the States' public schools the right to complete freedom of expression. Iowa's public schools, like Mississippi's university, are operated to give students an opportunity to learn, not to talk politics by actual speech, or by "symbolic" speech. And, as I have pointed out before, the record amply shows that public protest in the school classes against the Vietnam war "distracted from that singleness of purpose which the state [here Iowa] desired to exist in its public educational institutions." Here the Court should accord Iowa educational institutions the same right to determine for themselves to what extent free expression should be allowed in its schools as it accorded Mississippi with reference to freedom of assembly. But even if the record were silent as to protests against the Vietnam war distracting students from their assigned class work, members of this Court, like all other citizens, know, without being told, that the disputes over the wisdom of the Vietnam war have disrupted and divided this country as few other issues ever have. Of course students, like other people, cannot concentrate on lesser issues when black armbands are being ostentatiously displayed in their presence to call attention to the wounded and dead of the war, some of the wounded and dead being their friends and neighbors. It was, of course, to distract the attention of other students that some students insisted up to the very point of their own suspension from school that they were determined to sit in school with their symbolic armbands.

Change has been said to be truly the law of life but sometimes the old and the tried and true are worth holding. The schools of this Nation have undoubtedly contributed to giving us tranquility and to making us a more law-abiding people. Uncontrolled and uncontrollable liberty is an enemy to domestic peace. We cannot close our eyes to the fact that some of the country's greatest problems are crimes committeed by the youth, too many of school age. School discipline, like parental discipline, is an integral and important part of training our children to be good citizens—to be better citizens. Here a very small number of students have crisply and summarily refused to obey a school order designed to give pupils who want to learn the opportunity to do so. One does not need to be a prophet or the son of a prophet to know that after the Court's holding today some students in Iowa schools and indeed in all schools will be ready, able, and willing to defy their teachers on practically all orders. This is the more unfortunate for the schools since groups of students all over the land are already running loose, conducting break-ins, sit-ins, lie-ins, and smash-ins. Many of these student groups, as is all too familiar to all who read the newspapers and watch the television news programs, have already engaged in rioting, property seizures, and destruction. They have picketed schools to force students not to cross their picket lines and have too often violently attacked earnest but frightened students who wanted an education that the pickets did not want them to get. Students engaged in such activities are apparently confident that they know far more about how to operate public school systems than do their parents, teachers, and elected school officials. It is no answer to say that the particular students here have not yet reached such high points in their demands to attend classes in order to exercise their political pressures. Turned loose with lawsuits for damages and injunctions against their teachers as they are here, it is nothing but wishful thinking to imagine that young, immature students will not soon believe it is their right to control the schools rather than the right of the States that collect the taxes to hire the teachers for the benefit of the pupils. This case, therefore, wholly without constitutional reasons in my judgment, subjects all the public schools in the country to the whims and caprices of their loudest-mouthed, but maybe not their brightest, students. I, for one, am not fully persuaded that school pupils are wise enough, even with this Court's expert help

from Washington, to run the 23,390 public school systems[4] in our
50 States. I wish, therefore, wholly to disclaim any purpose on my
part to hold that the Federal Constitution compels the teachers, parents, and elected school officials to surrender control of the American
public school system to public school students. I dissent.

Mr. Justice HARLAN, dissenting.

I certainly agree that state public school authorities in the discharge of their responsibilities are not wholly exempt from the requirements of the Fourteenth Amendment respecting the freedoms of
expression and association. At the same time I am reluctant to believe
that there is any disagreement between the majority and myself on
the proposition that school officials should be accorded the widest
authority in maintaining discipline and good order in their institutions. To translate that proposition into a workable constitutional
rule, I would, in cases like this, cast upon those complaining the
burden of showing that a particular school measure was motivated
by other than legitimate school concerns—for example, a desire to
prohibit the expression of an unpopular point of view, while permitting expression of the dominant opinion.

Finding nothing in this record which impugns the good faith of
respondents in promulgating the armband regulation, I would affirm
the judgment below.

NOTES

[1] In *Burnside*, the Fifth Circuit ordered that high school authorities be
enjoined from enforcing a regulation forbidding students to wear "freedom
buttons." It is instructive that in Blackwell v. Issaquena County Board
of Education, 363 F.2d 749 (1966), the same panel on the same day reached
the opposite result on different facts. It declined to enjoin enforcement
of such a regulation in another high school where the students wearing
freedom buttons harassed students who did not wear them and created
much disturbance.

[2] Hamilton v. Regents of University of California, 293 U.S. 245, 55
S.Ct. 197, 79 L.Ed. 343 (1934), is sometimes cited for the broad proposition that the State may attach conditions to attendance at a state university that require individuals to violate their religious convictions. The case
involved dismissal of members of a religious denomination from a land
grant college for refusal to participate in military training. Narrowly
viewed, the case turns upon the Court's conclusion that merely requiring
a student to participate in school training in military "science" could not

conflict with his constitutionally protected freedom of conscience. The decision cannot be taken as establishing that the State may impose and enforce any conditions that it chooses upon attendance at public institutions of learning, however violative they may be of fundamental constitutional guarantees. See, e. g., West Virginia State Board of Education v. Barnette, 319 U.S. 624, 63 S.Ct. 1178, 87 L.Ed. 1628 (1943); Dixon v. Alabama State Board of Education, 294 F.2d 150 (C.A. 5th Cir. 1961); Knight v. State Board of Education, 200 F.Supp. 174 (D.C.M.D.Tenn.1961); Dickey v. Alabama State Board of Education, 273 F.Supp. 613 (D.C.M.D. Ala. 1967). See also Note, Unconstitutional Conditions, 73 Harv.L.Rev. 1595 (1960); Note, Academic Freedom, 81 Harv.L.Rev. 1045 (1968).

[3] The only suggestions of fear of disorder in the report are these:

A former student of one of our high schools was killed in Viet Nam. Some of his friends are still in school and it was felt that if any kind of a demonstration existed, it might evolve into something which would be difficult to control.

Students at one of the high schools were heard to say they would wear arm bands of other colors if the black bands prevailed.

Moreover, the testimony of school authorities at trial indicates that it was not fear of disruption that motivated the regulation prohibiting the armbands; the regulation was directed against "the principle of the demonstration" itself. School authorities simply felt that "the schools are no place for demonstrations," and if the students "didn't like the way our elected officials were handling things, it should be handled with the ballot box and not in the halls of our public schools."

[4] The District Court found that the school authorities, in prohibiting black armbands, were influenced by the fact that "[t]he Viet Nam war and the involvement of the United States therein has been the subject of a major controversy for some time. When the arm band regulation involved herein was promulgated, debate over the Viet Nam war had become vehement in many localities. A protest march against the war had been recently held in Washington, D.C. A wave of draft card burning incidents protesting the war had swept the country. At that time two highly publicized draft card burning cases were pending in this Court. Both individuals supporting the war and those opposing it were quite vocal in expressing their views." 258 F.Supp., at 972–973.

[5] After the principals' meeting, the director of secondary education and the principal of the high school informed the student that the principals were opposed to publication of his article. They reported that "we felt that it was a very friendly conversation, although we did not feel that we had convinced the student that our decision was a just one."

[6] In Hammond v. South Carolina State College, 272 F.Supp. 947 (D.C. S.C. 1967), District Judge Hemphill had before him a case involving a meeting on campus of 300 students to express their views on school practices. He pointed out that a school is not like a hospital or a jail enclosure. Cf. Cox v. Louisiana, 379 U.S. 536, 85 S.Ct. 453, 13 L.Ed.2d 471 (1965); Adderley v. Florida, 385 U.S. 39, 87 S.Ct. 242, 17 L.Ed.2d 149 (1966). It is a public place, and its dedication to specific uses does not

imply that the constitutional rights of persons entitled to be there are to be gauged as if the premises were purely private property. Cf. Edwards v. South Carolina, 372 U.S. 229, 83 S.Ct. 680, 9 L.Ed.2d 697 (1963); Brown v. Louisiana, 383 U.S. 131, 86 S.Ct. 719, 15 L.Ed.2d 637 (1966).

[Notes from Justice Black's Dissent]

[1] The petition for certiorari here presented this single question:

"Whether the First and Fourteenth Amendments permit officials of state supported public schools to prohibit students from wearing symbols of political views within school premises where the symbols are not disruptive of school discipline or decorum."

[2] The following Associated Press article appeared in the Washington Evening Star, January 11, 1969, p. A–2, col. 1: "BELLINGHAM, Mass. (AP)—Todd R. Hennessy, 16, has filed nominating papers to run for town park commissioner in the March election.

"'I can see nothing illegal in the youth's seeking the elective office,' said Lee Ambler, the town counsel. 'But I can't overlook the possibility that if he is elected any legal contract entered into by the park commissioner would be void because he is a juvenile.'

"Todd is a junior in Mount St. Charles Academy, where he has a top scholastic record."

[3] In Cantwell v. Connecticut, 310 U.S. 296, 303–304, 60 S.Ct. 900, 903, 84 L.Ed. 1213 (1940), this Court said:

The First Amendment declares that Congress shall make no law respecting an establishment of religion or prohibiting the free exercise thereof. The Fourteenth Amendment has rendered the legislatures of the states as incompetent as Congress to enact such laws. The constitutional inhibition of legislation on the subject of religion has a double aspect. On the one hand, it forestalls compulsion by law of the acceptance of any creed or the practice of any form of worship. Freedom of conscience and freedom to adhere to such religious organization or form of worship as the individual may choose cannot be restricted by law. On the other hand, it safeguards the free exercise of the chosen form of religion. Thus the Amendment embraces two concepts—freedom to believe and freedom to act. The first is absolute but, in the nature of things, the second cannot be. Conduct remains subject to regulation for the protection of society.

[4] Statistical Abstract of the United States (1968), Table No. 578, p. 406.

Appendix D
Suggestions
for classroom use[1]

The people who read this book, as well as the teachers who use it, vary considerably. They come to it with different backgrounds, with different purposes, and with variations in their previous knowledge of civil rights and constitutional law. Consequently the suggestions that follow may be useful to some readers and not to others. They are probably most applicable to classroom situations where students have little knowledge of civil rights law or legal principles.

1. Interview or invite to class a local attorney acquainted with both trial and appeal procedures. Prepare questions that will elicit information about:
   a. Court costs and legal fees; how much are they and who pays them?
   b. How long do cases take from initial disagreement to final resolution? Why do they take so long?
   c. What is the structure of the court system of your state? Which courts have jurisdiction over what kinds of problems?
   d. How are judges selected in your state? How are they removed?
   e. May students sue for themselves or must their parents sue on their behalf?
   f. Other items of interest to your class.

2. Interview officials of the local NEA, AFT, and ACLU chapters to find out what assistance a student might expect in protecting his civil rights.

3. Using volunteers from the class, role play selected cases. In each of these civil rights cases as well as in conflicts that never reach the courts, there are important ideas and powerful feelings represented on both sides of an issue. Through role playing the alternative positions become explicit, and their logic as well as emotional appeal can be more clearly examined.

4. With the help of student volunteers, role play the controversies briefly described in Chapter 1. Create all the supporting roles you deem necessary for full presentation of the conflicting interests.

5. Construct a questionnaire based on cases and controversies presented in this book and administer it to local groups of students, teachers, administrators, and parents. Analyze their responses to see if there are any systematic differences among these groups in their views of the civil rights of students.

6. Administer the questionnaire constructed for no. 5 above to civic and social groups like the League of Women Voters, the American Legion, the Young Republicans or Young Democrats, the Chamber of Commerce, and others. Hypothesize the probable outcomes and test your hypotheses.

7. Look up the reports based on the Purdue Opinion Polls (POP) (H. H. Remmers and R. D. Franklin, "Sweet Land of Liberty," **Phi Delta Kappan,** October 1962, pp. 22–27) and see whether the answers to your questionnaire support the findings or challenge them.

8. Administer POP no. 30 before and after studying the civil rights of students. Are there significant differences in the responses? The poll may be obtained from earlier reports or from the Measurement and Research Center, Purdue University.

9. Search your local papers and those of a contrasting rural or urban area for news items related to school controversies. Keep a scrapbook for the period of your school term, and analyze the accounts to see how many controversies involved civil rights and which civil rights seem to be most problematic in your area.

10. Have members of the class look up the constitution of their particular state to see whether it has civil rights provisions similar to those of the federal Constitution.

11. It has come to our attention that the expression "civil rights" has leftist connotations, whereas "constitutional rights" has a rightist flavor. Do you find this to be the case? Do people in your

area react differently to the same questions if they refer to "constitutional rights of students" rather than to "civil rights of students"?

12. Have members of the class make a wall chart or transparencies showing the structure of the local and state court systems together with the kinds of cases each court handles.

13. Check the calendars of nearby courts and have students sit in on some of the cases.

14. Have students look through recent Supreme Court reports and share their findings on recent civil rights cases.

15. If there are law schools in your area, third-year law students could be an excellent resource in helping the class or individual students in understanding and discussing technical legal questions. It would also be a good experience for the law students to explain constitutional and procedural matters to students.

16. In this book we do not explain the law of contracts or torts, yet these areas are of interest and relevance to students. Law students could be of great assistance in describing basic principles and illustrating them with examples.

17. The following quotations might be of interest to consider and discuss:

   a. While a great many people "believe" in the Bill of Rights as a somewhat familiar, friendly fiction, they really do not believe in the principles set forth within it. And this becomes all the more true when, as you will find often happens, the Bill of Rights is attacked—or some provision of it is attacked—in the name of some presumably great virtue. Attacks on the rights of individuals by those in power, those in control of the government, always come in the name of some great virtue [Justice William J. Brennan, "Progress and the Bill of Rights," speech delivered at The Third Independence Day Dinner at the Earl Warren Institute of The University of Judaism, Los Angeles, June 30, 1966, pp. 12–13].

   b. Because of this policy, public officials cannot be constitutionally vested with powers to select the ideas people can think about, censor the public views they can express, or choose the persons or groups people can associate with. Public officials with such powers are not public servants; they are public masters [Justice Hugo Black, in *Adler* v. *Board of Education*, 342 U.S. 485, 497 (1952)].

   c. "Respect for law," my late revered colleague Mr. Justice Frankfurter warned, "cannot be turned off and on as though it were a hot faucet." Those who flout the law when the law displeases them only undermine the system they need to save them [Justice William J. Brennan, "Progress and the Bill of Rights," p. 15].

d. Freedom is an unstable compound. Because one man's liberty can be another man's constraint, because conditions of life in our dynamic society continue to change and because freedom at large is grand but elusive in the particular, the task of formulation is never ending. . . . We must bear in mind that our Bill of Rights was written in another age for another society. This heritage with its noble concepts of liberty and freedom has to be re-defined and re-defended by every generation [Willard H. Pedrick, 49 Cornell L.Q. 581, 608 (1964)].

e. What our Constitution says, what our legislatures do, and what our courts write are vitally important. But the reality of freedom in our daily lives is shown by the attitudes and policies of people toward each other in the very block or township where we live. There we will find the real measure of a living Bill of Rights [Justice William J. Brennan, "Progress and the Bill of Rights," p. 11].

f. Many long years ago a great philosopher in Athens, Solon, was asked how justice could be attained in his land. Said Solon, "Justice can be attained in a society only when those who are not injured feel as indignant as those who are" [Justice Mosk of the California Supreme Court].

g. When many of our courts are so careful in the protection of those charged with crimes that they will not permit the use of evidence illegally obtained, our sense of justice should be outraged by denial to students of the normal safeguards. It is shocking that the officials of a state educational institution, which can function properly only if our freedoms are preserved, should not understand the elementary principles of fair play. It is equally shocking to find that a court supports them in denying a student the protection given to a pickpocket. [Warren Seavey, "Due Process," 70 Harvard Law Review 1406].

h. *Differences in Due Process Between High Schools and Colleges.* It is apparent that providing public school students with hearing prior to suspension would result in a disruption of the educational process which cannot be permitted.

In reaching this conclusion we have attempted to balance the rights of public school students with the demands imposed upon the educators by the community at large. Public school children suspended for misconduct are not criminals. The legal processes due them are less exacting than that due one who is accused under a criminal statute.

There are significant factual distinctions between a college suspension and a public school suspension. For example, in a college or university, teachers and students are rarely in class for more than a few hours a day, whereas in the public school system teachers and students are in class throughout the day. While public school teachers and administrators would be called upon to miss class if a prior hearing is held, the same is not usually true in colleges and universities. The disruption of the educational process that occurs as a result of a prior hearing therefore is less likely to occur in the college than it is in the public school.

Additionally, the consequences of a public school suspension are considerably less serious than those which follow from a university suspension. In fact, School Board Policy-Regulation 5114 provides, in cases of ten-day and thirty-day suspensions, that there shall be no evidence of the suspension posted on the pupil's permanent record. However, suspension or expulsion from a college or university may seriously affect a student's opportunity to obtain a graduate or postgraduate degree, or otherwise achieve professional status [Excerpts from *Banks* v. *Board of Public Instruction of Dade County*, 314 F.Supp., 285, 292–293 (1970)].

i. *Hairy Issue*. The hair issue seems to invite judges to metaphoric expression and social commentary. Here are two interesting examples:

"Putting the question in a rhetorical sense, what is the nature of the right threatened by the hair code? Before this unnamed right is labeled and in an effort to comb this problem into a neater part, it should be observed that the Constitution does not stop at the public school doors like a puppy waiting for his master, but instead it follows the student through the corridors, into the classroom, and onto the athletic fields" [*Dunham* v. *Pulsifer*, 312 F.Supp. 411, 417 (1970)].

Commenting on society and human nature, Judge Wyzanski wrote:

"Whether hairstyles be regarded as evidence of conformity or individuality, they are one of the most visible examples of personality. This is what every woman has always known. And so have many men without the aid of an anthropologist, behavioral scientist, psychiatrist, or practitioner of any of the fine arts or black arts" [*Richards* v. *Thurston*, 304 F.Supp. 449, 451 (1969)].

18. The following excerpts from various newspapers present recent civil rights controversies related to education. What rights are involved? How would you resolve them after reading this book?

a. *Urbana, Ohio.* Sharon Boldman, 17, an unwed mother, has been ruled off the Homecoming Queen ballot at Urbana (Ohio) High School by a school principal who told her "only virgins can run for homecoming queen." She had been nominated by her classmates. Sharon's parents have filed suit in US District Court asking that the election be voided [*Boston Globe*, October 1, 1973].

b. *Colorado.* A Boulder youth was arrested for wearing a portion of the American flag sewn to the seat of his blue jeans. He was charged with violating a state statute in that he unlawfully "mutilated, defaced and defiled the flag of the United States of America with intent to cast contempt thereupon." The defense claimed that the act was symbolic speech, therefore protected by the First Amendment [*Massachusetts Daily Collegian*, October 3, 1973].

c. *New Brunswick, N.J.* Rutgers University forfeited a home basketball game to the University of Pittsburgh last night when a protest by about 100 black Rutgers students stopped the game.

The students sat down in the middle of the gymnasium about three minutes before halftime, apparently protesting the university's treatment of blacks. Rutgers was losing the game when play was halted.

The campus patrol was called in to break up the protest when the students did not heed a plea to end the protest [*Worcester Telegram Gazette*, December 5, 1973].

d. *Clifton, Ariz.* A teenage girl whose parents said they were too poor to buy her a new dress was sent home in tears from her eighth grade graduation ceremony because her clothing did not conform with school rules.

School principal Billy C. McDowell said Wednesday that he had no alternative but to send the girl home because students "had been given their instructions long before the graduation."

"I felt a girl who did not abide by the required dress should not participate."

The parents of 13-year-old Eleanor Stacy said their daughter was ordered to leave her classmates May 30. They said she was told she could not march in the graduation ceremony of Clifton Elementary School because her yellow-flowered dress had not been approved by school officials beforehand.

"Sure it hurt her feelings," McDowell said. "But we wanted it to be a formal affair and not have many different kinds of dresses. Long before graduation, I sent three other girls to change their dresses, and I felt the only alternative was not to allow her to participate."

The girl's father, Ed Stacy, said neither he or his wife remembered seeing a notice on what kind of dress should be worn.

"We're kind of poor right now," said Stacy, a carpenter. "Our finances have been a little tight. We couldn't afford to buy a dress."

Instead, he said, the girl's aunt made a dress.

Stacy said his car had broken down and Eleanor had left early for the graduation ceremonies with friends. He said he and his wife waited for relatives to arrive and then drove to the school.

"The headlights of the car caught this girl walking along the highway," he said. "It was Eleanor. We couldn't believe it. She was crying her eyes out."

Stacy said he took the matter before the school board June 4 but "they treated it as a joke, more than anything else. As far as I'm concerned, it's beyond the joke stage."

Stacy said he plans to bring the matter up again at the board's July meeting.

William Blair, board president, said school officials decided a month before the graduation that the girls should wear plain pastel dresses.

"Yes, I saw the Stacy girl's dress, and it wasn't a wrong dress. It just had pastel flowers on it," Blair said.

"But we had 66 graduates, and we couldn't have everybody different. She was defying authority."

Clifton is a small mining community of about 2000 in eastern Arizona [*Boston Globe,* June 22, 1973].

e. *Topeka, Kan.* Almost 20 years since the Supreme Court ruled that school segregation was unconstitutional there still is no

clear legal consensus on what constitutes genuine desegregation, and thousands of classrooms throughout the country are
still not integrated.

It was in Topeka, two decades ago, that 10-year-old Linda
Brown (now 30-year-old Mrs. Linda Smith) was turned away
from an all-white school because her skin was black. Although
a midwestern city, Topeka then had a southern-style law that
separated black and white elementary school pupils.

The new suit, a class action filed by an activist lawyer in
the name of another 10-year-old black girl, Evelyn Rene Johnson, contends that Topeka is still "systematically" discriminating against Negro students by relegating hundreds of them to
dilapidated, poorly equipped and inadequately staffed schools
that continue to be predominently black in a city whose population of 130,000 is more than 90 per cent white.

. . . implementation of the 1954 decision, along with a 1971
decision permitting massive busing, has been so thorough in
the rural South, that Dixie's country schools are now the most
desegregated in the U.S. In Mississippi, once the ultimate segregationist stronghold, blacks and whites study, eat and play
together with increasing ease in almost every little rural school.

At least a dozen cities outside the South have recently been
found guilty of discriminating against black students through
such acts as gerrymandering attendance zones, assigning Negro
teachers to predominantly black schools and spending more
money on white students than on black students.

In one case earlier this year regarding the Denver school
system, the Supreme Court held such low-key segregation unconstitutional and ordered the system integrated. Some legal
experts consider the Denver ruling the non-Southern equivalent
of Brown versus Board of Education [New York Times, October 28, 1973].

f. *Hampton, N.H.* Forty-five parents in this area have called for
the elimination of an English course at the regional high school
here because the course "teaches the occult" and is "dangerous
for our youth."

Mrs. Blanche Bragg of Seabrook led the protest against the
course, called "Mystery and the Supernatural in Literature."

The course has been offered at Winnacunnet High School,
a regional school serving four towns, for the past three years.
This year more than 100 students are enrolled in the elective

course, which is taught in five sections because of its popularity.

Supt. Richard Hamilton said yesterday he is investigating the course and will make a full report to the school board Nov. 19.

Last week the five-man school board was taken by surprise when Mrs. Bragg presented a petition of 45 signatures calling for the removal of the course from the curriculum.

She said yesterday the course outline shows that the students study reincarnation, ESP, witchcraft, seances, and mystical experiences.

"I feel that this course is teaching a religion," she said. "I am a Born-Again Christian, and I feel that this course work is of the devil."

"It is unconstitutional to have God in the schools, and so I object to the schools teaching this religion."

She said that since the petition was given to the school board she has received "more than 100 calls" from local citizens supporting her views.

Hamilton said he does not believe that the course "teaches religion. The course teaches reading skills."

He said the course, offered only to juniors and seniors, includes a broad range of literary works, covering "ghosts, goblins and private eyes—the reality of these creatures as they appear in various stories" and books.

Winnacunnet students are circulating their own petition seeking to keep the course in the curriculum [*Boston Globe,* October 25, 1973].

g. *Baltimore, Md.* All of the school's students are pregnant.

Teen-age pregnancy, in fact, is a prerequisite to enroll at Edgar Allan Poe High School.

"Being pregnant is a traumatic experience for many girls, and they need to be away from their peers to regroup their forces," explains Poe's principal, Vivian Washington.

The 520 pregnant teen-agers enrolled at the 7-year-old public school are keeping up with students in other high schools and preparing for jobs and motherhood.

"The girls have strong feelings about themselves, that maybe they're not good persons," says Mrs. Washington, but "we say 'All right, . . . what are you going to do about the future?'"

" 'You're going to be a parent, responsible for another life.
But first you must be responsible for yourself.' "

Enrollment required. While at Poe, the girls also must be enrolled in health clinics and social-service programs. Nutrition-
ists and doctors pay regular calls to supplement the care.

The curriculum is designed to ease the teenagers' return to
their former high schools or find jobs after delivery. They may
transfer to their former schools six weeks after a post-delivery
medical checkup.

Poe alumnae who do not return to finish high school get
help finding work from job placement coordinator Jean Bowman, who says she helped 187 girls get jobs last year.

The dropout rate is low, according to teachers, because
attendance is not compulsory. "It's much more satisfying because they want to be here," says business-education teacher
Ruth Wilmore, one of 22 faculty members.

Crisis center. Mrs. Washington describes Poe as a kind of a
crisis center where pregnant teen-agers can count on support
from their classmates and teachers in an informal atmosphere.

Along with a brisk student turnover, one of the toughest
problems is "Puncturing the unreality" that accompanies many
expectant mothers to Poe, says Lois White, a job placement
staffer.

When they arrive, most students do not grasp what is
required in having, and caring for, a baby, Mrs. White adds.

"What is needed," says Mrs. Washington, "is to bring home
what being the head of a family means—the responsibility as
well as the sex and pregnancy" [*Christian Science Monitor*
February 6, 1973].

h. *Gay Liberation.* U.S. District Court Judge Hugh Bownes ruled
in favor of the Gay Student Organization in a suit brought
against the University of New Hampshire and Gov. Meldrim
Thomson.

Bownes ruled that the university must treat the group of
homosexual students like any other campus organization, and
he enjoined the university trustees from prohibiting on-campus
social functions of the "gays."

The decision was based on the First and Fourteenth amendments to the U.S. Constitution.

According to Judge Bownes, the university has the right to
restrict the "gays" if they incite violence or commit crimes,

but the university presented no evidence that anything illegal had been done.

The New Hampshire Civil Liberties Union brought the federal suit last fall after the trustees barred "the gays" from holding on-campus social functions [based on a news report from Concord, New Hampshire, January 17, 1974].

i. *Due Process?* In Grafton, Massachusetts, a high school junior was suspended for distributing literature on school grounds entitled "Crimes Against Chastity." The literature, distributed without authority from the school, condemned the state's sex laws. Among the subtitles in the brochure are "Unnatural?" "Rape (statutory)," "Adultery," and "Blasphemy" etc. The student's request for a formal hearing was refused by the Grafton School Committee. The chairman said that state law does not require a hearing on a student's suspension. [based on a news report in the *Worcester Telegram*, January 22, 1974].

j. *Sexism.* A proposed new law in Massachusetts, Chapter 622, would outlaw sex discrimination in the public schools. Massachusetts would be the first state to enact such a law, aimed at ending discrimination in curriculum, budgets for athletic activities, occupational programs, and textbooks [based on a news item in the *Worcester Telegram*, January 17, 1974].

k. *Locker Search.* Following reports of drug use at Rutland High School, Vermont, the police searched students' lockers. Some drugs were allegedly found. Students were angry about the search and parents complained about embarrassment caused to their children. "Police were reported to have read a student's 'love letter' aloud during the search" [based on a news item in the *Boston Globe*, January 13, 1974].

l. *The Equal Rights Amendment (ERA).* "Equality of rights under the law shall not be denied or abridged by the United States or by any state on account of sex." These twenty-four words constitute the proposed Twenty-sixth Amendment, adopted by Congress in 1972. As of February 1974, 33 states have ratified it, five short of passage. Whether the proposed Amendment ever becomes law is still an open question, for some states that have already approved it seem to be ready to reconsider their action.

Currently there are various debates in progress over the need for the ERA. In recent years, the Supreme Court struck down statutes and policies that were sexist. It overruled school policies that arbitrarily specified pregnancy leaves for teachers. It also struck down laws that gave preference to men over women as executors of estates and which provided for more military benefits to servicemen than for servicewomen.

In addition to court decisions, it is often argued that legislation enacted in the past decade has made the ERA superfluous. Title VII of the 1964 Civil Rights Act forbids unions or employers from discriminating on the basis of sex; the Equal Pay Act of 1963 includes similar prohibitions; and the 1972 Education Amendments outlaw sexual discrimination by schools and colleges.

With these developments in mind, does it still make sense to pursue passage for the Amendment? David Kirp, professor of law at the University of California, Berkeley, answers yes, in an editorial, a portion of which follows:

> The amendment merits adoption. Its passage will dramatically foreshorten the process of reviewing and discarding laws and practices which, as the Supreme Court has observed, put women not on a pedestal, but in a cage. . . .

> More important, however, is the symbolic significance of the amendment. If passed it will both mark and confirm a change in the social consensus, formally recognizing a new and altogether more fitting attitude toward the role of women in this country.

> The equal rights amendment is no panacea. It will not wipe out discrimination but will make discrimination harder to practice. It will not uproot deeply-held chauvinistic attitudes, but it may prompt searching reconsideration of those attitudes and their effects. It will not liberate women, but it will provide women with yet another means toward their liberation. The vague and intangible nature of those factors should not detract from their overriding significance [Christian Science Monitor, October 12, 1973].

m. *Student Files Now Opened to Parents.* School records, long held highly confidential by school officials, can now be opened to parents, guardians, and students over 18.

The legislation, recently was signed by Gov. Francis W. Sargent.

The bill was filed by Rep. Lois G. Pines (D.-Newton) and Leonard Bird and Sarah Noll, students at Newton North High School.

Mrs. Pines said the policy will help protect Massachusetts school children from "potential irrevocable harm incurred as a result of inadequate attention on the part of teachers to students' school records."

One of the strongest advocates of the legislation was educational consultant and author John Holt. He argued that "for the schools to compile, as they do, secret dossiers on students, often full of what could be fairly called malicious gossip, diagnoses and labels to be circulated later to other schools, employers and any government snooper who asks to see them, is educationally unnecessary and a gross and dangerous violation of the civil liberties of the student."

"The whole notion of such dossiers is repugnant in a free and democratic society," he said.

Holt disputed the right of schools to keep or distribute the records.

Mrs. Pines interpreted the student record issue as related to the freedom of the press. She said: "This parental request for information is related to a general right-to-know interest which has found expression in certain areas of the law, especially as manifested in the First Amendment of the U.S. Constitution." [Muriel L. Cohen, *Boston Globe*, October 18, 1973].

n. Finally, consider the following item, which calls for the application of age-old principles to a very different and complex contemporary problem.

Deprogramming. How far may parents go in regulating the religious lives of their children? National attention is focusing on this erupting religious liberty problem as a result of the "deprogramming" activities of Californian Ted Patrick.

Hundreds, perhaps thousands, of young people—some minors, some not—have departed from the religious traditions and affiliations of their parents to join such odd little sects as the Children of God or the New Testament Missionary Fellowship. Many distressed parents have turned to Ted Patrick for help. Patrick, who believes that these sects "spiritually seduce" and "brainwash" young people, assists parents in abducting and "deprogramming" their children who have gone off to join these sects. Deprogramming itself is evidently a process quite akin to brainwashing. Patrick claims to have conducted 139 successful deprogrammings and to have inspired or been involved in about 700 more.

One attempted abduction in New York, of a youth a few weeks shy of his twenty-first birthday, resulted in Patrick's trial on charges of unlawful imprisonment. He was acquitted by a jury, however, evidently because they felt the forceful action by Patrick and the parents he was aiding was justified. Elated by the verdict, Patrick apparently intends to continue deprogramming.

One can understand the feelings of parents whose children have gone off to join some "objectionable" sect, particularly when the sects encourage members to sever their family ties. One can also note, however, that young people may be attracted to odd sects when their families and their churches are not perceived as providing help in the face of today's tensions and uncertainities.

But deprogramming poses serious religious and personal liberty problems.

Even if parents view certain sects as "subversive" or "dangerous," do they have the right to use force to try to free their children from their influence? At what age may children freely choose to change religious affiliation? At 14? At 18? At 21? If parents may use force to seize and deprogram their children, may a Protestant family do so to a son who has converted to Catholicism, or may a Catholic family do so to a daughter who has joined a Protestant church or converted to Judaism? Indeed, how far may parents go in the religious training of their young to insure that they do not "depart from the ways of their fathers"?

The central church-state issue, of course, is whether or not civil authorities will permit abductions, kidnappings, and forcible detentions by relatives of young persons who have changed their religious affiliations.

The Supreme Court did not clarify the matter when it ruled in 1972 that Amish parents may restrict their children's education.

There are certainly more questions than answers with regard to this problem. But there are bedrock constitutional principles which can help guide us.

All persons and religious groups have the right to express their views and to seek converts. Every person has the right to

the free exercise of religion, which includes the right to change
or discontinue religious affiliation [*Church & State, 26*, no. 9
(October 1973) pp. 4, 5].

NOTES

[1] Portions of this appendix are reproduced from a section of the same
title in Louis Fischer and David Schimmel, *The Civil Rights of Teachers*,
New York, Harper & Row, 1973.

Appendix E
Sample dress
and grooming codes

1. **P**ittsfield, *New Hampshire* The following dress code was adopted by the Pittsfield School Board. Its dungaree prohibition was contested in the *Bannister* case discussed in Chapter 6.

DRESS CODE
1970-71

BOYS

1. Hair cannot be over the eyes, ears or over the collar. Sideburns are allowed provided they are not below the earlobe.
2. Shirts must be tucked in unless they are square cut in which case they can be left out. T-shirts, sweatshirts will not be allowed as outside garments. Jersey shirts without lettering or pictures will be allowed.
3. Dungarees will not be allowed.
4. Cleats will not be added to shoes. Socks must be worn at all times. Sandals are not allowed.
5. No neck jewelry.
6. Outer clothing will remain in the locker unless specific permission is given by the office.
7. No bell bottoms will be allowed.

GIRLS

1. No dungarees, slacks or shorts will be worn during the school day.
2. Blouses will be tucked in unless designed with a straight edge.
3. Skirts must be a reasonable length and in lady like appearance.
4. Culottes may be worn.
5. Makeup may be worn with discretion. No hairclips, curlers, or kerchiefs may be worn.
6. Sandals are not allowed.
7. Maxi and midi skirts will be allowed.

GENERAL

1. Ankle high footwear may be worn.
2. No bleached clothing will be worn.

> *Bannister* v. *Paradis*, 316 F.Supp. 185, 189 (1970).

2. *Greendale's Dress Code: A Nonrestrictive Approach.* Following is the dress code used by the Greendale (Wis.) Public Schools:

The responsibility for the appearance of the students of Greendale High School rests with the parents and the students themselves.

They have the right to determine such student's dress providing that such attire is not destructive to school property, complies with the health code of the State of Wisconsin and does not interfere with the educational process.

This right may not be restricted, even by a dress code arrived at by a majority vote of students.

> *Student Rights and Responsibilities*, Washington, D.C., National School Public Relations Association, 1972, pp. 62–64.

3. *A Small High School's Dress Code: A Restrictive Approach.* The following dress code was adopted by a small Massachusetts high school in September 1971 (the school wished to remain anonymous):

DRESS CODE FOR BOYS: Modesty and good grooming in dress and personal wear shall be observed at all times.

Shirts: All shirts shall be worn inside the trousers, unless they are made to be worn outside the trousers. Turtle neck and crew neck shirts are acceptable. Tank tops and underwear type T-shirts are not acceptable.

Trousers: Blue jean-type dungarees are not acceptable. Any bleached, faded, worn, fringed or torn pants are not acceptable. Shorts and bermudas are not acceptable.

Belts: Belts should be worn on trousers designed for belts.

Sweatshirts: Sweatshirts are not acceptable at any time in the school building proper.

Sweaters: Shirts must be worn with a "U" or "V" neck sweater.

Footwear: Any type footwear determined to be destructive to the floor is prohibited. Sandals are acceptable. Rubber beach thongs are not acceptable.

Haircuts: We strongly recommend to parents that they use discretion in determining the style and length of their son's or daughter's hair. Good grooming, cleanliness and safety are considered imperative. Sideburns must not be grown beyond the outer corner of the eye widthwise and the corner of the mouth lengthwise. Beards and moustaches are not allowed.

DRESS CODE FOR GIRLS: Modesty and good grooming in dress and personal wear shall be observed at all times.

Skirts: Length should be in good taste according to the standards of contemporary style. No blue jean-type dungarees are acceptable. Slacks that are bleached, frayed, fringed or faded are not acceptable. Culottes and hot pants are acceptable, providing they are covered, skirted, paneled in front and back, and are part of an ensemble. Shorts of any type are not acceptable.

Blouses: Only overblouses may be worn outside skirts and slacks, all others may be worn inside. Appropriate undergarments must be worn. Styles should be appropriate for school wear, no extremes such as "off the shoulder," low back or front should be worn. Sweatshirts and underwear-type T-shirts are not acceptable. Tank tops are also not acceptable.

Sweaters: All sweaters must fit properly.

Footwear: Beach thongs are not acceptable. Sandals and clogs are acceptable. Boots are acceptable as long as they are not destructive to the floor. Students are encouraged not to wear whole or half cleats on the heels or toes of their shoes.

Makeup: The purpose of makeup is to enhance natural beauty and should be used in good taste.

The combined Dress Code Committee of High School X strongly

recommends that the students be made well aware of the proper dress and of the discipline to be administered to violators.

Also, the combined Dress Code Committee recommends that a copy of this dress code be sent home with every final report card, to aid in purchasing clothes for next fall.

[*Student Rights and Responsibilities*, pp. 62–64.]

4. *Escondido's Dress Code: A Moderate Approach.* Following is the dress code used by the Escondido (Calif.) Union High School District:

All students must wear clothing which is clean and safe. Clothing should promote the health and welfare of the wearer. Student dress, personal appearance and conduct are required to be of such character as not to disrupt nor distract from the instructional procedure of the school nor tend to diminish the disciplinary control of the teacher. Clothing which bears inappropriate words or pictures is prohibited. Footwear must be worn at all times.

Girls are to abide by the following standards:

1. Dresses are not required to be of any specific length but must conform to good taste. Proper undergarments are to be worn at all times and not to be exposed when girls are walking, standing, kneeling or sitting.
2. Transparent or open stitched blouses may be worn with a full slip.
3. Girls' slacks or long pants may be worn. They must be of the type specifically designed for girls (12 inches maximum flare). Jeans, jean fabrics, lounging pants and slinkies are not permitted.
4. The wearing of culottes is permitted. Bermudas may be worn on specific occasions as approved by the school principal.

Boys are to abide by the following standards:

1. Hair must be neat and clean and must be off the collar at all times and combed in such a manner that it will not cause undue attention. No head bands, bobbi pins or other objects to support hair will be allowed.
2. Sideburns may extend to the bottom of the ears.
3. Beards and mustaches are not permitted.
4. Socks shall be worn with all shoes other than sandals.
5. Bermudas may be worn on specific occasions as approved by the school principal.

[*Student Rights and Responsibilities*, pp. 62–64.]

Appendix F
Selected bibliography

BUSS, WILLIAM G. "Procedural Due Process for School Discipline: Probing the Constitutional Outline," 119 U. Pa. L. Rev. 547 (1971).

Code of Student Rights and Responsibilities, National Education Association, 1201 16th St. N.W., Washington, D.C.

GADDY, DALE *Rights and Freedoms of Public School Students: Directions from the 1960's*. Published by and available from National Organization on Legal Problems of Education, 825 Western Avenue, Topeka, Kansas 66606 (1971).

Guidelines for Student Rights and Responsibilities, New York State Department of Education, Albany, New York 12224 (1972).

KIRP, DAVID L., and MARK G. YUDOF. *Educational Policy and the Law*, Berkeley, California, McCutchan Publishing Corp., 1974.

LEVINE, ALAN H. *The Rights of Students*, New York, Avon Books, 1973.

NUSSBAUM, MICHAEL *Student Legal Rights*, New York, Harper & Row, 1970.

REUTTER, E. EDMUND *Legal Aspects of Control of Student Activities by Public School Authorities*, Topeka, Kansas, National Organization on Legal Problems of Education (1970).

SANDMAN, PETER M. *Students and the Law*, New York, Collier Books, 1971.

Student Rights and Responsibilities: Courts Force Schools to Change, National School Public Relations Association, 1201 16th St. N.W., Washington, D.C. (1972).

Students Rights Handbook, New York Civil Liberties Union, 84 Fifth Avenue, New York 10011 (1971).

Your Rights as a Student, Massachusetts Law Reform Institute, 2 Park Square, Boston, Massachusetts 02116 (1971).